Bodies like Bright Stars

Bodies like BRIGHT STARS

Saints and Relics in Orthodox Russia

ROBERT H. GREENE

NORTHERN ILLINOIS UNIVERSITY PRESS

DeKalb

© 2010 by Northern Illinois University Press

Published by the Northern Illinois University Press, DeKalb, Illinois 60115

Manufactured in the United States using postconsumer-recycled, acid-free paper.

All Rights Reserved

Design by Julia Fauci

Library of Congress Cataloging-in-Publication Data

Greene, Robert H., 1975–

Bodies like bright stars : saints and relics in Orthodox Russia / Robert H. Greene

    p.   cm.

Includes bibliographical references (p.   ) and index.

ISBN 978-0-87580-409-5 (clothbound : alk. paper)

1. Relics—Russia—History—19th century. 2. Christian saints—Cult—Russia—History—19th century. 3. Russia—Religious life and customs. 4. Relics—Soviety Union—History. 5. Christian saints—Cult—Soviet Union—History. 6. Soviet Union—Religious life and customs. 7.Russkaia pravoslavnaia tserkov'—History. I. Title.

BX577.G74 2009

235'.2088281947—dc22

2009032478

For Phyllis, Kelly, and Joseph

Contents

List of Figures   ix

Acknowledgments   xi

Introduction   3

1—In the Eye of the Beholder—
   The Russian Orthodox Church and the Problem of Incorruptibility   17

2—Going to See the Saints—*Miracles, Shrines, and Relics*   39

3—Making Saints—*Canonization and Community*   73

4—The Revolution and the Saints   103

5—Toppling the Saints from Their Thrones—
   The Bolshevik Exhumation of Holy Relics   122

6—Relics in Red Russia—*Orthodox Responses to the Exhumation Campaign*   160

Epilogue and Conclusion—*The Passing of the Saints?*   196

Notes   213

Selected Bibliography   269

Index   293

List of Figures

1—Saint Dimitrii Rostovskii   30

2—The shrine of Saint Simeon, Verkhoturskii monastery, 1910   49

3—The relics of Saint Dimitrii Rostovskii open for veneration   50

4—View of Kashin from the bridge of the Dmitrovskii monastery, 1910   81

5—At the shrine of Saint Anna Kashinskaia, 1910   85

6—The courtyard of the Troitskaia Lavra stuffed with bags of money   108

7—The exhumation commission at the Blagoveshchenskii monastery   128

8—Children and soldiers at the Blagoveshchenskii monastery   129

9—Exhumation of Saint Makarii Zhabynskii, in Tula Province, on 16 March 1919   131

10—Caricatures of the exhumed saints Tikhon Zadonskii, Prince Konstantin, and Sergii Radonezhskii   133

11—The Incorruptibles. God addressing the assembly of saints   134

12—P. A. Krasikov   139

13—Clergy uncover the relics of Saint Tikhon Zadonskii, Voronezh Province, 28 January 1919   143

14—The mummified relics of Bishop Saint Nikita Novgorodskii   147

15—The relics of Archbishop Saint Ioann Novgorodskii   165

16—Children file past the relics of Saint Gavriil the Martyr   169

Acknowledgments

It is fitting, perhaps, that a book on saints should begin with a litany of names. This project began as a dissertation at the University of Michigan, where I was fortunate to work with Val Kivelson and Bill Rosenberg. Both gave generously of their time and wisdom, and I could not have asked for a better pair of advisers. Many of the ideas developed in this book began as conversations with Val Kivelson and Tom Tentler, and I'm grateful to both for their warmth, kindness, and scholarly example. Thanks also to my undergraduate teachers at the University of Rochester, especially Gerald Bond, John Givens, Richard Kaeuper, Anna Maslennikova, William McGrath, Kathleen Parthé, and the late Brenda Meehan.

My friends and fellow graduate students in Ann Arbor were a welcome source of intellectual energy, discontented cynicism, and convivial distraction. I'm thankful, especially, to Gene Avrutin, E. M. W. Besté, Chris Birkel, Chris Borhani, Michael Chiang, Laura Culbertson, Annie Fisher, Justin Fox, Rob Haug, David Hughes, Vadim Jigoulov, Joon-Sung Park, Joel Pitkin, Orlando Quiroz, Paul Spence, Lareena Thepveera, and Sarah Womack. Gene Avrutin, Gabriel Coleman, Masha Iakovleva, Olga Ismagilova, Lynette Ray, and Mike Villa made my research trips to Moscow and St. Petersburg particularly memorable and productive. Thanks also to my Muscovite landlords, a pair of intrepid entrepreneurs and devout *bezbozhniki*, who found the idea of a young American researching Russian Orthodox relics impossibly amusing.

Jane Burbank, Gregory Freeze, David Goldfrank, Nadia Kizenko, Eve Levin, Olga Maiorova, Brian Porter, Roy Robson, Jennifer Spock, Mark Steinberg, Isolde Thyrêt, Bill Wagner, and Christine Worobec have all offered helpful comments and criticism on various incarnations of this manuscript at conferences and workshops; any errors or lapses in the finished product, of course, are mine alone. I appreciate the written feedback offered by members of the faculty reading group at the University of Montana, especially Richard Drake, Linda Frey, Paul Lauren, Ken Lockridge, Mike Mayer, and Fred Skinner; I am especially grateful to Kyle Volk and Jeff Wiltse for their invaluable insights. Thanks to Lily Scott and Glenn Kneebone for their assistance with the illustrations for this volume, to Diane Rapp for her logistical expertise, and to my editor, Amy Farranto, for gently shepherding this project through to completion.

I owe an enormous debt to Jeffrey Burds, who has been a patron saint and mentor for the past fifteen years. This book would not have been written had Jeff not taken me under his wing many years ago and taught me by example what it means to be a historian. I thank my family, especially my aunt, Joanne Saas, for their unflagging support and confidence. Finally, I thank Elyse Dvorsak, as ever, for her love and patience, and everything else. My parents and brother are no longer here to read this book. I dedicate this work in their memory, with love and gratitude.

Funding for this project was provided by the Woodrow Wilson Foundation, the Foreign Language and Area Studies Fellowship Program of the U.S. Department of Education, the Horace H. Rackham School of Graduate Studies, and the Center for Russian and East European Studies at the University of Michigan. I am grateful to these institutions for their support. Parts of Chapter Three were published as "Making Saints: Canonization and Community in Late Imperial Russia," in *The Carl Beck Papers in Russian and East European Studies*, no. 1801 (2006). I thank the Center for Russian and East European Studies at the University of Pittsburgh for permission to republish portions of this article.

All translations are my own unless otherwise indicated. Transliteration follows a modified Library of Congress style, retaining the idiosyncrasies of prerevolutionary Russian orthography. The names of certain figures in the text have been rendered in forms more familiar to English-language readers (thus Zinoviev, not Zinov'ev; Gorky, not Gor'kii; and Nicholas the Wonder-Worker, not Nikolai Chudotvorets).

Bodies like Bright Stars

Introduction

Shortly after arriving in Moscow in 1838, the celebrated German travel writer Johann Kohl attended religious services at the Cathedral of the Archangel inside the Kremlin. Kohl marveled that this ancient church, with its "diminutive windows" and its walls still blackened by the great fires of 1812, could boast so many reliquaries and sacred rarities, including the blood of John the Baptist. After his Protestant eyes had adjusted to "all the glitter of [the cathedral's] gold and its shrines," Kohl soon discovered that for the Russian Orthodox faithful who filled the church that day, the main attraction was not the blood of Christ's cousin but a tiny coffin containing the miracle-working relics of the martyred boy saint Dmitrii Ivanovich, son of Tsar Ivan IV and last prince of the Riurikid dynasty:

> [T]he mummy of a boy of five or six years of age, magnificently clad, is exposed on festivals in an open coffin. Every part is veiled but the forehead, which is kissed by his adorers. Above the coffin, the portrait of the little canonized prince is attached to a pillar set in a raised frame of the finest gold. . . . A whole body must necessarily take precedence of a few drops of blood. Hence, a few drops of the veritable blood of John the Baptist, after he was beheaded, are little regarded, although set in gold, with diamond rays like the centre of a star. One would think that the blood of John the Baptist was immeasurably dearer to Christendom than that of this royal child; but in Russia the *Christian* religion is every where overshadowed by the *Russian*. The pictures of Paul, Peter and the other apostles, are seldom found, either in the churches or private houses; whereas, St. Vladimirs, Demetriuses, Nicholases, and Gregorys meet us hourly.[1]

Further surprises were in store for Kohl at the neighboring Cathedral of the Annunciation, a "little church . . . rich in relics of all the saints in the calendar":

> They lie in different little divisions in glass cases; a bone for every day in the year, but the cases are no longer covered with glass. The priests said that this glass caused too great an expense to the convent, none having yet been found

that united the necessary transparency with sufficient strength; the throng of kissers was always so great on holidays, that the glass was broken every time, that they might bring their warm lips into contact with the sacred bones.[2]

To a man of Kohl's self-described "cool Lutheran temperament" (theologically and culturally predisposed to look askance at relic veneration and other material trappings of saintly cults), the deep devotion that Russian Orthodox believers displayed for their saints was baffling.[3] The sober German could not understand why the Russian faithful should lavish kisses on cases of bones or favor the dubious body of an obscure Muscovite princeling over the blood of a great New Testament prophet. Unable to discern the internal meaning behind what he saw as "outward practices," Kohl fell back on the comfortable and well-worn assumption that Russian Orthodox believers, with their focus on the material dimension of sanctity and their seemingly endless array of saintly bodies and bones, were somehow less refined and less theologically astute than their counterparts in Western Europe. Kohl was wrong.[4]

In the nineteenth and early twentieth centuries, the most important people on the religious landscape of Orthodox Russia were already dead. More specifically, they were the holy dead, men and women recognized as saints (*sviatye*) by the Orthodox Church and regarded as intimate friends and helpers by tens of millions of Russian believers.[5] Churches consecrated in their memory and shrines housing their holy relics (*moshchi*) dotted the cities, towns, and villages of the Russian empire, from the multi-ethnic and multi-confessional western borderlands to the distant stretches of the Siberian taiga, from the foothills of the Caucasus Mountains all the way to the icy shores of the Arctic Sea. A nineteenth-century "census" of the holy dead found the relics of some 455 saints on Russian soil, not including those belonging to men or women not officially canonized by the Orthodox Church or those whose causes for canonization were still under consideration.[6] Given the absence of Purgatory from Orthodox theology, the Russian faithful, unlike their Catholic counterparts, did not require the assistance of the saints to expedite the progress of their dearly departed to paradise.[7] Rather, they relied on the saints exclusively to work miracles—even the most mundane—here on earth.

This book examines lay and clerical devotion to the cult of the saints as a way of understanding what Russian Orthodoxy meant to believers in the late nineteenth and early twentieth centuries. In *The Varieties of Religious Experience*, William James famously posited that "the gods we stand by are the gods we need and can use."[8] James's supposition is eminently applicable to the Russian Orthodox scenario, where the saints—"the friends of God"—were needed, used, and consequently treasured by Orthodox believers for centuries. The belief that praying to the saints and making pilgrimages to their relics *mattered*, the belief that the holy dead yielded practical and tangible results for those who appealed to them with true faith, made the cult of the saints one of the most enduring aspects of the lived Russian Orthodox experience. Examining the ways in which the Orthodox faithful actively and routinely sought heavenly solutions to earthly problems compels us, then, to recast the traditional scholarly stereotypes associated with Orthodoxy as it was practiced in Russia at the end of the imperial period and during the first decade of Soviet power. I argue that, rather than a passive, submissive, otherworldly faith focused on the glories of the world to come while ignoring the travails of this life, Russian Orthodoxy was, in fact, an active—indeed, proactive—religion whose consoling power lay in the promise of divine intervention to rectify terrestrial misfortunes and provide solace in this life. Seen in this light, the bone-kissing, self-prostration, and devotional acrobatics that so troubled Johann Kohl take on a great deal more meaning and real importance.

By the time that Orthodox Christianity arrived in Rus', the Byzantine empire had already weathered the storms of the iconoclast controversy and reasserted devotion to the icons and relics of the saints as a fundamental point of Orthodox doctrine.[9] The *Primary Chronicle* tells how Prince Vladimir brought the relics of Pope Saint Clement and Saint Phoebus from Kherson to Kiev in 988, when he ordered that the people of Rus' be baptized en masse in the Dnepr' River. As they had in the late antique and early medieval West, relics helped cement the new Christian faith in Russia.[10] In the six centuries that followed, as the Orthodox faith spread beyond the monastery walls and into the towns and villages of the Russian lands, hundreds of native-born holy men and women supplanted these early imported saints, swelling the Russian liturgical calendar with feast days and filling new churches and monasteries with their holy relics.[11] Saints were at the center of Russian Orthodox naming practices, and by the late seventeenth century most Russians routinely took the names of Christian saints at baptism.[12] Throughout the eighteenth and nineteenth centuries, the lives of the saints and tales of the miracles they wrought were among the most eagerly read and best-selling titles in print, and from princely palace to peasant hut it was the rare Orthodox dwelling that did not boast at least a few modest icons or lithograph prints of those saints particularly dear to the household.[13]

Saints played a fundamental role in the spiritual lives of millions of Orthodox believers. On the basis of conciliar precedent and canonical tradition, the Russian Church held that saints were deserving of special merit both by virtue of their holy lives and by the miracles they had wrought either in life or after death. For most believers, however, whose spiritual concerns were more pragmatic than those of learned theologians and prelates, the latter quality took far greater precedence. Saints were saints, first and foremost, because they worked miracles.[14] Not coincidentally, perhaps, the most popular Russian saints who attracted the most worshipers to their shrines were the ones who worked the most miracles. In times of need and hardship, the Orthodox faithful turned to their saints for medical help and legal recourse, employment opportunities and economic amelioration. By the turn of the twentieth century, as many as one million Orthodox pilgrims traveled every year by steamship, railroad, carriage, and foot to worship and seek miracles at the monasteries and churches where the relics of their heavenly patrons lay; countless more frequented the shrines of miracle-workers closer to home, in their own towns, districts, and provinces.[15] As the thousands of recorded miracle stories and pilgrim narratives attest, Orthodox men and women brought with them to these shrines their sorrows and griefs, anxieties and expectations, hopes and fears.

This book is based on three methodological principles—first, the recognition of the notion that religious practice is *meaningful*; second, the corollary principle that religious practices and rituals are imbedded in theological knowledge; and third, the acknowledgment that religion is a dynamic and developing process. These principles, in turn, give rise to the main questions that underlie this present work. If the Russian Orthodox faithful expressed their religious convictions in ritual practice, then what do the devotional practices associated with the cult of the saints tell us about the way in which Russian believers on earth understood their relationship with the saints in heaven? To put the question a different way, why did long-dead saints matter to the living faithful? Furthermore, if these devotional practices were deeply informed by theology, then how does a study of the cult of the saints allow us to challenge the long-dominant paradigm positing the Russian lay faithful as semiliterate ritualists barely conversant with even the most rudimentary doctrines of the faith? Finally, given that the form and content of religious practices can and do change over time, how did the devotional practices associated with the cult of the saints evolve from the mid-nineteenth century to the end of the first decade of Soviet power? How did believers adapt their religious practices vis-à-vis the saints to address new concerns brought on by the anxieties of political, social, and economic modernization? To the extent that Orthodoxy was able to remain relevant for believers amid such tremendous and often tumultuous change, particularly after the Bolshevik Revolution of 1917, I argue that it was largely the adaptability and flexibility of the cult of the saints that allowed it to do so.

THE CULT OF THE SAINTS IN THEORY AND PRACTICE

For many generations and until quite recently, the scholarly literature on Russian Orthodoxy dealt almost exclusively with two major themes. Secular-minded historians in the West concentrated their energies on the study of Russian Church-state relations, from the Church's apogee of influence under the imperial autocracy to its trials and tribulations at the hands of the Bolshevik regime.[16] Meanwhile, Soviet scholars produced a well-researched—but ideologically driven—body of literature that indicted the prerevolutionary Orthodox Church for its role in enslaving the minds of unliberated workers and peasants and for fighting tooth and nail against socialist construction after 1917.[17] Although these studies have contributed to our understanding of the development of the Orthodox Church as an institution, they have told us little of Russian Orthodoxy as a dynamic system of belief or how this faith shaped—and was shaped by—the lives of the people who practiced it.

As Gregory Freeze has remarked, "the greatest lacuna in the historiography pertains to *Orthodoxy* itself: historians have yet to refocus from ecclesiastical to religious history—that is, the religious culture and its practice."[18] In examining devotion to the cult of the saints as a central aspect of the Russian Orthodox religious experience in the late imperial and early Soviet periods, this present book is part of a more recent trend of writing the history of Orthodoxy with the religion left in; that is to say, a trend that places attention less on the institutional apparatus of the Russian Orthodox Church and more on the practices and faith of the ordinary people—the lay believers and parish priests, men and women—who made up its ranks.[19] Influenced by historians of medieval and early modern Western Christianity, this new approach argues for a more inclusive interpretive framework that stresses the dialogic, interactive process between those who make doctrine and those who live it.[20] Such an approach, of course, does not mean ignoring the role of the Church as an institution or the influence of religious elites in safeguarding the integrity of official doctrines and practices. Rather, it insists on a more comprehensive picture that treats religion not just as a set of prescriptive norms superimposed onto the lives of the faithful but as a continuing process whereby doctrine and dogma are acted out in everyday life.

In Pierre Delooz's formulation, a saint is a "constructed figure," whose "sanctity depends on the opinion of others. . . . One is never a saint except *for other people*."[21] The Russian Orthodox cult of the saints, like all saintly cults, was the result of an ongoing process of negotiation, interaction, and compromise between "elite" and "popular" cultures, between "high" and "low" traditions. On the one hand, the cult of the saints was officially sanctioned, theologically grounded, and zealously promoted by religious elites. At the same time, however, the cult was continually molded and adapted by believers to serve their own religious needs. What did the cult of the saints mean to the Orthodox men and women who made pilgrimages to their graves, kissed their relics, and prayed to them for help in their everyday lives? Similarly, how and to what degree did the Church's official teachings on sanctity and sainthood inflect believers' practices and attitudes toward the saints?

As Peter Burke reminds us, saints are not born but made.[22] In the Russian tradition, the process of making saints was an evolving one that unfolded over the course of several centuries. Unlike the Roman Catholic Church, where papal authority over the canonization of saints was asserted as early as the first half of the thirteenth century, the Russian Orthodox Church, in Eve Levin's words, "had no standardized procedures for canonization before the eighteenth century."[23] Following the institutional reforms of the Church under Peter the Great, the religious establishment sought greater centralized supervision over the cult of the saints, with the Holy Synod acting, in essence, as the official authority in all matters pertaining to the cult—canonizing new holy men and women, curtailing the cults of spurious saints, and supervising the laity's devotional practices as needed.[24] This mission was spelled out in the Petrine *Spiritual Regulation* of 1721, which entrusted the Holy Synod with the responsibility of purging from its rolls any spurious saints with "doubtful" relics and shoddy vitae—the former on the grounds that they were mere "frivolity," the latter because "they lack content and are deserving of ridicule."[25] In accordance with these directives, agents of the imperial police and the Holy Synod attempted to curb the veneration of false saints throughout the seventeenth, eighteenth, and nineteenth centuries.[26]

Russian Church officials sought to ensure not only that believers prayed to the right saints but that they did so for the right reasons. As part of their efforts to improve the spiritual condition of the Orthodox laity, Church hierarchs began in earnest in the nineteenth century to place greater emphasis on the saints as divine agents, willing and able to assist in the salvation of the faithful. In countless sermons, books, and pamphlets, Orthodox believers were reminded repeatedly that saints were not just miracle-workers but exemplars of piety to be emulated. By the same token, religious writers and academics asserted that the shrines and relics of the saints were more than automatic miracle-dispensers—they were great reservoirs of spiritual strength from whence the faithful could draw the resolve to spur them on to a more pure and Christian life.

If bishops and prelates sought to reorient popular piety to engage more seriously with the concerns of salvation, lay believers and parish priests preferred to pray to tried-and-true saints with a proven track record of granting miracles and cures in times of need. Theologians and religious elites valued the saints as shining beacons to lead the faithful to eternal life, while ordinary believers prized the saints for their assistance in matters more immediately relevant to this world. Yet, although there were differences of degree between the way in which an Orthodox bishop and an ordinary believer understood the saints and called upon them for aid, I would argue that these differences should not be overstated as overly divisive or divergent.[27] It is important to stress that Church hierarchs, parish clergy, and the lay faithful alike believed firmly, often unquestioningly, in saints, relics, and miracles and saw the workings of the world from within the same religiously inflected mental framework.[28] Indeed, while the Russian Church was concerned throughout the late imperial period with raising the spiritual knowledge of the laity, it was also conscious, as Gregory Freeze has observed, that it needed "to bring [believers] into the Church rather than to drive them away."[29] Fearful of losing its flock to the predations of sectarians, socialists, and secularists, the Church in the last decades of the old regime grew more tolerant of "popular" religious practices surrounding the saints—so long as these devotions were centered around saints that the Church deemed acceptable, not false bodies canonized by acclamation of the laity.[30] In order to counter the criticism of sectarians who charged that the saints were unnecessary impediments to "true" Christian worship, the late imperial Church made concessions to the religious practices of the laity, endorsing an understanding of sainthood that encompassed both the spiritual and material dimensions of sanctity while celebrating the salvational and miraculous powers of the holy dead.

In Orthodox Russia, "sainthood" was a word with a history and a theology behind it. Nevertheless, the concept was defined broadly enough that there was ample room to accommodate a variety of opinions and outlooks. Understood as both paragons of moral virtue whose lives could be read as roadmaps to heaven and as miracle-workers with the power to produce positive changes in this world, the saints, in essence, could be all things to all believers. Similarly, when we speak of devotion to the saints, we are dealing with a set of practices whose basic precepts and parameters were established by scriptural and conciliar tradition and reinforced by the teachings of the Orthodox Church, but which were still pliable and flexible enough to accommodate improvisation by lay believers. As Laura Engelstein has suggested, such an argument obliges us to imagine Russian Orthodoxy not in oppositional terms of Church versus laity but as a "spectrum . . . broad enough to embrace a range of styles."[31]

INDIVIDUALS AND COMMUNITIES

To be Russian Orthodox at the turn of the last century meant, at least in theory, that one was never alone. Believers were not only part of the visible Church on earth but were inextricably linked to the eternal Church in heaven. At baptism, it was believed, the Holy Spirit assigned each christened child a special guardian angel whose mission, as one nineteenth-century Orthodox writer put it, was to "exhort us in faith and piety, preserve our souls and bodies, act as our champions throughout the course of our earthly life, pray to God for us, stand with us at the end of our earthly life, and lead our souls to eternity."[32] So, too, were the saints always present to watch over the faithful and pass their prayers on to God in heaven. Orthodox theologians spoke of the saints assembled in concert before the throne of God as "the link between the Heavenly Church and the Earthly Church," whose constant concern for the souls of the faithful made them powerful intercessors between man and God.[33] A parish priest in Ekaterinburg diocese described this cosmology in a popular text published at the turn of the twentieth century:

> Christ's Church is divided into [a church] visible and invisible. All of us, Orthodox Christians, belong to the church visible; to the invisible [belong] the deceased saints in heaven, the Angels, and the Lord Himself. The living on earth and the deceased saints possess between them a close relationship. When they pray to God, true Christians living on earth are, at the same time, calling upon the saints living in heaven for help. Nearer to God and taking pleasure in the heavenly bliss, the saints do not forget us who live here on earth; they love us, they hear our prayers, and they petition on our behalf before God.[34]

Judging from extant miracle stories, devotional literature, and spiritual memoirs, Orthodox believers interpreted this unity as a source of comfort and solace, forging intimate and highly personalized relationships with their saintly protectors. While imperial-era Church newspapers and religious journals often published wondrous tales of the saints appearing in dreams and visions to the errant faithful and wayward sectarians, exhorting them to turn away from a life of sin and return to the embrace of the Church, the writings of Orthodox lay believers described a more affable sort of understanding with their saints. When saints appeared to the slumbering faithful in the miracle stories authored by ordinary believers, it was not to threaten their souls with perdition but to offer friendly medical advice or genial moral instruction, with the saint often suggesting that the believer visit his shrine to pray for a miraculous cure at the site of his holy relics.[35]

Such miracle stories suggest that where one prayed to the saints was as important as how one prayed to the saints. Russian Orthodox believers placed an enormous emphasis on the physicality and tangibility of their saints, an emphasis that exceeded the spiritual and salvational dimensions of sanctity. In a tradition going back to the first centuries of the Christian Church, Russian Orthodox believers privileged the kissing of relics and the touching of saintly shrines as the most immediate and efficacious way to access the power of the divine.[36] As Johann Kohl witnessed firsthand, Orthodox worshipers regarded the saint's tomb, the shrine containing his or her holy relics, as a particularly potent site for channeling the saint's miraculous powers. Although the saint's soul was in heaven, the body remained physically present on earth, and it was through the corporeal remains of the saint, whether entire bodies or mere fragments thereof, that miracles were most commonly performed.[37] While miracles could be performed through silent prayer, most saintly miracles and healings recorded in the late imperial period were said to be the result of the believer coming into contact with either the saint's holy relics or "proxy relics"—objects that had been suffused with healing power through their proximity to saintly bodies, such as oil from the lanterns above a saint's shrine, cotton wool that had been laid inside or atop the saint's tomb or pressed against a saint's relics, holy water and icons blessed at the saint's shrine, or even articles of saintly apparel.[38]

The Greek Orthodox adage that "no one burns incense for a saint who doesn't work miracles" can be read on two complementary levels.[39] On the one hand it suggests, quite accurately, that Orthodox believers preferred to petition those saints whose reputations for miraculous generosity were well-known. On the other, it demonstrates how Orthodox men and women understood and expressed their relationships with their saintly protectors in reciprocal terms. In her study of nineteenth-century customary practice, the Russian ethnographer M. M. Gromyko has shown how important the concept of reciprocity was to the cult of the saints. While Russian believers expected their saints to work miracles for them, they acknowledged at the same time that there were certain duties incumbent upon themselves to give thanks for miracles rendered.[40] Giving thanks to the saints could take many forms—lighting a candle before the saint's icon at home or in church, going on pilgrimage to venerate the saint's holy relics, making offerings of money or gifts in-kind to the church or monastery where the miracle-worker's relics were housed, or paying for priests to sing prayers of thanksgiving (*molebny*) at the saint's grave. The thousands of miracle stories authored by lay faithful and clerics across the empire are the best evidence for how Russian Orthodox believers understood their ongoing relationship with their saintly protectors as both intimate and personal but, simultaneously, bound up with requirements and obligations that, while not onerous, had to be met in order to ensure the continued favor of the saints.

Church figures and religious writers encouraged such gestures of thanksgiving, particularly the offering of molebny, as ways for the faithful to give proper expression to their piety. As one Orthodox journal from the 1880s described it, deeds done in fulfillment of a pledge to the saints (*po obetu*) "were not only judicious and pleasing to God, but also conducive to the salvation of the soul . . . and the moral success of a Christian."[41] Most believers, however, seem to have required little prompting in such matters. When Church writers and religious authors told their audiences that saints grant miracles to believers "in measure with their faith," most lay readers or listeners would have nodded knowingly, albeit with one slight caveat.[42] In the minds of most believers, faith alone in the power of the saints was insufficient; if one wanted the saints to intervene and produce positive changes, one had also to take active steps to *show* one's faith—whether going on pilgrimage, kissing the saint's holy relics, or offering a piece of handiwork to adorn the saint's shrine. In other words, it was not so much that the saints would only help those who first helped themselves; the saints tended, largely, to help those who also helped the saints.

Invaluable to individuals, the shrines of the saints were also important to local Orthodox communities more broadly. As Peter Brown has argued for the late antique and early medieval West, the graves of saints were sites around which Christian communities came together and cohered.[43] The locally specific liturgical calendars that appeared in Rus' from the late thirteenth century show how communities understood local saints not as universal sources of inspiration and intercession for all Christians but primarily as specific champions of the town or region and its people.[44] In modern Russia, too, villages, cities, districts, even entire provinces continued to regard their local saints as the special patrons of the community. On a local saint's feast day, communities would stage grand religious processions (*krestnye khody*) in which the saint's relics and shrine would be borne aloft along the city streets and throughout the neighboring villages and townships, thus marking the boundaries of the sacred community under the saint's protection.[45] Because many monasteries and churches would open the lids of the saints' shrines on feast days, such festivals were highly anticipated by miracle-seekers who treasured the rare opportunity to kiss the bodies of the saints unimpeded by protective glass casings. In prerevolutionary Russia, where doctors and hospitals were in short supply, the avenues of legal action often impeded by bureaucratic channels, and the economic climate oppressive for all but a privileged few, individuals and communities viewed the saints and their relics as providers of social services offering assistance to members of the Orthodox community in all spheres of everyday life. The governor of Chernigov, for example, received petitioners every morning from half past eight to half past nine, whereas the shrine of Saint Feodosii Chernigovskii was accessible to Orthodox believers round the clock.[46]

With some five hundred saintly bodies and bundles of bones scattered across churches and monasteries in the Russian empire, Orthodox believers possessed a vast array of saintly intercessors whom they could choose to call upon for help. There is ample evidence, however, to suggest that, like the early modern Parisians described by Moshe Sluhovsky, Russian believers tended to prefer the patronage of local saints, whose "living presence within the city" made them "familiar neighbour[s] rather than . . . remote figure[s]."[47] Similar to the Catholic shrines of north-central Spain described by William Christian, the shrines and reliquaries of the Russian Orthodox saints were "located images" that attracted primarily the patronage of a specific community bounded both by geography and by a particular affinity for the miraculous benefits accessible at the grave of the saint.[48] Miracle stories, devotional tracts, and spiritual pamphlets published during the religious resurgence of the late nineteenth century reveal the degree to which believers saw their religious, geographical, and political communities as overlapping and mutually constitutive. As one author explained, on the eve of the city's one-thousandth anniversary in 1906, life in the provincial town of Chernigov in eastern Ukraine would be unthinkable without its local patron and tireless miracle-worker, Saint Feodosii. With enormous civic pride and without a shade of irony, the same author assured readers that the single most important event to take place in the Chernigov region over the last half century was Feodosii's canonization in 1896.[49]

As Patrick Geary has argued for the medieval West, "the symbolic value of a new or rediscovered relic was . . . a reflection of the values assigned by the society that honored it."[50] Archival documents and local newspapers provide illuminating glimpses of how communities across the Russian empire honored their prized relics—preparing for the anniversaries and feast days of local saints, feverishly petitioning the emperor and the Holy Synod for the official recognition of a local holy man or woman, and staging grand ceremonies and festivals to commemorate long-awaited canonizations of local saints. To be sure, the attention lavished on local saints was far from selfless. The canonization of a new saint, the solemn opening of his relics for public veneration (*otkrytie*), was an event certain to bring hundreds of thousands of pilgrims (and rubles) pouring in from all corners of the empire. But from a theological point of view, the discovery or recovery of holy relics in a particular locality was interpreted always as incontrovertible proof of God's favor for the city, village, or district, a sign of God's unconditional love for His children and His desire to provide the Russian Orthodox faithful with a means to channel His grace through prayer to the saints. In addition, the presence of holy relics placed a community, no matter how small, on par with other holy sites throughout the Russian empire and the Orthodox world at large, thus serving to create a sort of religious geography that put the community on an equal footing with other localities possessed of similar spiritual treasures.

Saints in Modern Russia

Chronologically, this book treats the period from 1861 to 1929, from the era of the Great Reforms through the beginning of the First Five Year Plan, deliberately straddling the critical year of 1917 in order to trace the changes and continuities in religious practice across the dividing line of the Russian Revolution. The question of religion's role and relevance in the modern age is thus foregrounded in my work. During the last half century of Romanov rule, the Russian empire experienced not only unprecedented economic development, social mobility, and political liberalization (however halting this latter may have been) but also a religious resurgence expressed, in part, by the dramatic upsurge in the number of saints canonized by the Orthodox Church—nearly a dozen in the final two decades of the empire, compared with only four in the preceding two centuries.[51] Thanks to the great advances made in communication and transportation networks in these same years, religion for the first time became a mass phenomenon. By the 1890s railroads and riverboat steamships were bringing crowds of worshipers to distant shrines and monasteries that had once been all but unreachable to any but the most devoted pilgrim; many believers now even dispatched prayer requests and pledged their votive gifts to the saints by telegram.[52] Far from sweeping away the sacred in its wake, as the more secular-minded had hoped, technology and transportation made locally venerated shrines and relics even more accessible to believers across the Russian empire.

As the forms and means of religious expression evolved during this period, so also did the content and character of devotion. My reading of the miracles stories and eyewitness accounts collected and published in diocesan newspapers and bulletins in the prerevolutionary period shows that the faithful not only continued to make traditional prayers and petitions for the well-being and health of themselves and their loved ones but also appealed to their tried-and-true saintly intercessors for assistance with the new problems and needs engendered by the processes of modernization—such problems as unemployment, economic insecurity, and political instability. The improvisational ease with which the faithful adapted a centuries-old set of ritual practices to meet the exigencies of everyday life at the turn of the twentieth century reveals the degree to which Russian Orthodoxy was able to incorporate innovation into practice and remain culturally relevant in an age of supposed "secularization."[53] Thus, if the cult of the saints was bound with strong ties to the past, it was by no means fettered by it. Far from being an anachronistic and increasingly archaic set of practices and traditions, the cult of the saints proved flexible enough not only to withstand but also to accompany and ease the economic, social, and political anxieties produced by Russia's transition to modernity in the late imperial period.

Chapter One begins with the Orthodox Church's mission in the nineteenth century to improve the spiritual condition of its flock. The great religious publishing boom of the latter half of the nineteenth century witnessed a concerted effort by Russian Orthodox clerics to remind their readers that the saints served a purpose even greater than providing healing cures and miracles—the saints were models of piety whose holy lives were to be imitated by all believers who sought eternal life. Thus, from the middle of the nineteenth century to the very end of the old regime, the Russian Orthodox Church tried to reorient the way in which lay believers understood their relationship with the saints in heaven. Without diminishing the great miracle-working powers wielded by the saints, the Church attempted to introduce on an equal footing the notion that the saints existed not solely to heal toothaches and bring relief to drought-stricken fields but also to help guide the faithful on the road to salvation by serving as their "elder brethren in the faith." Evidence suggests, however, that such prescriptive norms had little practical effect on the ways in which believers understood their relationship with the saints. Though not discounting the saints' ability to minister to their souls, most believers continued to place greater importance on the saints' talent for healing bodies and solving earthly problems.

In the next two chapters the focus shifts from official prescriptions and norms to a study of the cult of the saints as it was practiced on the ground. Chapter Two deals primarily with individual Orthodox men and women, examining pilgrim narratives and miracle stories concerning the emerging cults of Saint Feodosii Chernigovskii and Patriarch Saint Germogen as a way to study the personalized, reciprocal interaction between believers and their saints in the late nineteenth and early twentieth centuries. Using the cults of Saint Anna Kashinskaia and Saint Sofronii Irkutskii as localized case studies, Chapter Three charts the efforts of Orthodox communities at opposite ends of the empire seeking official canonization for their locally venerated saints at the turn of the twentieth century. Evidence from provincial newspapers and petitions to the Holy Synod suggests that believers regarded it their personal responsibility to secure formal recognition for local miracle-workers from whose miraculous intervention they and their families had benefited for generations. Such grassroots campaigns (which often took decades to bear fruit) testify to the sense of obligation that believers felt toward saints who had helped them and their families over the course of many years.

The final three chapters bring us to the Bolshevik Revolution and the first decade of Soviet rule in Russia. The cult of the saints had proved its ability to remain culturally relevant amid the turmoil of the prerevolutionary decades but was regarded as a superstitious anachronism by the new regime, which settled on saints and relics as first targets in the confrontational antireligious campaigns launched after 1917. In a series of orchestrated demonstrations staged from 1918 through 1924, specially appointed "exhumation committees" uncovered the relics of over seventy Orthodox saints on Soviet soil in order to reveal to the faithful that the bodies of the saints were not preserved in a state of divinely ordained incorruptibility but were, in fact, mere matter subject to the ravages of time and nature—exposing figuratively and literally the decay and rot of the Orthodox religion and its obsolescence in an age of science and progress.

The polemical writings that appeared in the Soviet central and provincial press during the relic campaign harped consistently on the discrepancies between the sweet-smelling bones and uncorrupted bodies attributed to the saints and the all-too-human remains uncovered in shrines and reliquaries. The campaign's architects, though, failed to take into consideration that none but theologians and academics worried about such theological and etymological niceties as the "true" meaning of the word "*moshchi*," and even these experts could never arrive at a true consensus among themselves. The average Orthodox believer in the city or the countryside subscribed to a more instrumentalist (and tautological) definition—relics were relics because they worked miracles. And so, while many believers were shocked and appalled by the decayed or desiccated remains discovered in the shrines of their beloved saints, most were able to overlook these lurid revelations and continue in their devotions, so long as the relics—regardless of their condition—remained accessible to the faithful in the churches and monasteries where they had resided and performed miracles for decades, if not centuries, before.

In his sociological study of Soviet secularization, Paul Froese emphasizes that the new regime, once in power, could shut off religious supply, but it could not eliminate religious demand.[54] For all their efforts to dismantle and subsequently reconstitute political, social, and economic life, the Bolsheviks proved unable or unwilling to recognize how deeply the cult of the saints permeated so many aspects and avenues of Orthodox believers' everyday lives. What the Bolsheviks saw as a cringing, slavish adherence to pre-Christian vestiges incommensurate with modernity was, in fact, a source of solace for individuals and a vibrant and powerful unifying force for communities. The consoling presence of a miracle-working saint in one's own backyard not only linked Orthodox men and women to the traditions of generations past but provided recourse and comfort in times of uncertainty. The new regime's failure to separate the faithful from their faith speaks to the central role of the cult of the saints in Orthodox practice, the limitations of early Soviet antireligious policy, and the persistence of prerevolutionary religious traditions in the world's first socialist state.

1

In the Eye of the Beholder

THE RUSSIAN ORTHODOX CHURCH AND THE PROBLEM OF INCORRUPTIBILITY

> "Let it not be forgotten that time lays waste to bronze and marble, but the relics of the saints remain uncorrupted; time does not act on them."[1]
>
> —*CHERNIGOVSKIIA EPARKHIAL'NYIA IZVESTIIA*, 1896

> "[O]f all these signs, of all these miracles on which our faith is founded, the incorruptibility of holy relics is the clearest and most indisputable validation of its truth.... The incorruptibility of holy relics is a miracle that lasts forever and is evident to all."[2]
>
> —ANONYMOUS TREATISE ON HOLY RELICS, 1902

In the spring of 1919, Bishop Aleksandr of Vologda submitted a tactfully worded letter of protest to the chairman of the Vologda Province executive committee (ispolkom) concerning the recent exhumation and public display of the body of Saint Feodosii Totemskii by local Bolshevik officials. Describing the exhumation as a "profound desecration of the deceased" and objecting to Feodosii's "extraordinarily blasphemous" status as a curiosity piece under glass, the bishop asked that the saint be returned to his shrine "with due dignity," lest his continued exposure "elicit great unrest among the Orthodox population."[3] In a response subsequently published in the Vologda newspaper, *Krasnyi sever* (Red north), chairman M. K. Vetoshkin absolved his deputies in Tot'ma of any alleged improprieties and refuted the bishop's charges of sacrilege. It was irrelevant and misleading to speak of Bolshevik blasphemy or profanation, the chairman argued, because the corrupted state of Saint Feodosii's body—"bones covered with dried patches [of skin] . . . a brittle, crumbling mass that turns to dust at the touch of a finger"—meant that the object in question was not a true holy relic: "The exhumation confirmed that the remains of the venerable Feodosii in no way constitute uncorrupted relics as the church billed them, but are, rather, the ordinary, mortal remains of a human body. . . . Do these really look like uncorrupted relics?"[4]

Undaunted, Bishop Aleksandr fired back with a lengthy and detailed letter in which he declared his intent "to outline the Church's true opinion on holy relics" and prove that Feodosii's body was, in fact, a holy relic.[5] The early Christians, he argued, understood relics to mean bones or bodily fragments, not entire bodies (which, for understandable reasons, were few and far between in the first centuries of martyrdom and persecution). It was this definition of the word "relics" (*moshchi*), Aleksandr argued, that had been bequeathed to the Russian Church from the Greek and Slavonic tradition and that still held force over the centuries to the present day. Invoking the authority of patristic texts, sacred history, and old Russian chronicles, the bishop insisted that "our Orthodox Church has never looked upon the relics of God's saints as unconditionally and absolutely intact, incorruptible bodies. . . . [B]y 'relics' the Church means, in general, the remains of saints, whether in the form of bodies more or less entire (that is, bones with flesh), or in the form of bones alone."[6] Further, Aleksandr criticized those who held to the error that relics were necessarily and exclusively complete bodies intact and free of any traces of corruption. Such people, he suggested, are "possessed of a zeal for God beyond the bounds of reason. . . . One-sided and incorrect, the opinion of these people brings much harm to the church."[7]

Not surprisingly, Vetoshkin managed to fire the final salvo in this pamphlet war. The commissar dismissed Aleksandr's arguments entirely, drawing attention to the fact that the bishop's definition of holy relics, based on etymological evidence and conciliar doctrine, was far removed from the understanding possessed by the vast majority of the Orthodox faithful:

> Even if you, a man well-read in church books, think that relics are only the remains of a body, principally bones, can you really hold the position, then, that all peasants, think the same, [peasants] who have not read Professor Golubinskii, or the *Sinaksarist* of Nicodemus, or the *Novyi Limonar*, [peasants] who do not know what Zinovii Otenskii or Zakharii Kopystenskii once said about this? . . . The majority of the faithful (that is, primarily the peasantry) understand relics as uncorrupted bodies, not as the remains of bones. No one would have believed in bones, no matter how many of them there were. You

cannot persuade some naïve peasant woman to worship bones and expect a "miracle" from them. No one calls bones relics. It is in vain that you turn to philology for help. Bones are bones, why call them "relics" when everyone is accustomed to calling them bones? Ask any believer . . . whether plain bones packed up in a pile of cotton wool and sprinkled with sawdust are called "relics." He will tell you no. All believers will tell you this.[8]

What began as a diocesan protest against revolutionary intrusion into the religious life of the faithful quickly spiraled into a public debate on the very meaning of a contested term, with bishop and commissar both claiming to represent the "true" definition of holy relics. That such a debate could even have been waged in the pages of the Bolshevik press is surprising enough. Even more curious, perhaps, is the commissar's insistence that holy relics need always be preserved inviolate and uncorrupted to warrant the appellation of moshchi. According to the Bolshevik calculus, anything less than an entire body could not be classified as genuine moshchi. Bolsheviks like Vetoshkin claimed that they were speaking on behalf of the common folk (narod), arguing that no matter how carefully bishops and other religious elites might phrase their definitions, ordinary believers understood moshchi only in the sense of uncorrupted bodies. Coming out of an intellectual tradition that held the religious knowledge of the Orthodox laity in great disdain, most Bolsheviks assumed that theological nuances such as the definition of holy relics were beyond the grasp of lay believers, whom they imagined as barely literate, semi-pagan, and entirely unfamiliar with even the most rudimentary tenets of the Orthodox faith. That the laity clung so stubbornly to the idea of bodily incorruptibility was assumed a priori and, of course, blamed on the deceptions of the clergy. Indeed, in what would become a recurring motif in early Soviet antireligious propaganda, agitators and publicists frequently trotted out the argument that the Orthodox Church had spun unscrupulous tales of incorruptible bodies in an effort to enrich its own coffers at the expense of the workers and peasants. According to the Bolsheviks, the imperial Church had always privileged bodily incorruptibility above all other entries on a saint's résumé and had taught for centuries that a complete body was the sine qua non for a genuine holy relic. It was only when relic exhumation had uncovered holy bodies in various stages of decay and decomposition and caught the conniving clergy red-handed that the "princes of the Church" (so the argument went) were obliged to backpedal and modify their definition of moshchi to include bones, ashes, bodily fragments, and other eminently corruptible elements.[9]

Vetoshkin and his comrades, however, were better skilled in dialectics than in doctrine. Despite the commissar's claims to the contrary, the

Russian Orthodox Church's definition of holy relics had, in fact, remained more or less consistent over the centuries. Gail Lenhoff, for instance, has demonstrated that while the Kievan Christians displayed "a decided preference for the whole rather than the part" in their saintly bodies, this view shifted over the Muscovite period.[10] From at least the mid-seventeenth century onward, the Russian Orthodox Church articulated the position that relics referred not solely to bodies preserved in their entirety but simply to the remains of dead saints and, vice versa, emphasized that an uncorrupted body was not, in and of itself, incontrovertible proof of the deceased's sanctity. The 1666–1667 Church Sobor, for example, warned believers to "dare not . . . honor newly found uncorrupted bodies without trustworthy verification (*svidetel'stvo*) and conciliar command: for there are many whole and uncorrupted bodies that are not so from holiness, but who have died excommunicated by episcopal or priestly cures, or are whole and undestroyed because of their violation of divine rules and laws."[11] Genuine uncorrupted moshchi were, of course, regarded as a wondrous miracle, and their discovery was hailed in priestly sermons and devotional texts as a show of God's unceasing love for the Russian people. But saintly remains did not need to possess *netlenie* (incorruptibility) in order to be classified as moshchi; holy relics were holy relics because they had the power to work miracles, whether or not they were uncorrupted. Conversely, in the absence of miracles, it was a matter of great difficulty to determine whether relics were really relics. A nineteenth-century source based on the archives of the Chernigov diocesan consistory notes that the relics of Feodosii Chernigovskii were first discovered in the Borisoglebskii Cathedral in 1781, some eighty years after the bishop's death, but that no great significance was placed on their discovery because no one had ever heard of a miracle emanating from them. The clergy adopted a wait-and-see attitude, which paid off handsomely in the mid-nineteenth century, by which time Feodosii had acquired the reputation of being the preeminent miracle-worker in the diocese.[12]

Although bodily incorruptibility was never a necessary precondition for relics to be regarded as relics, nor for a holy man to be hailed a saint, Orthodox writers began in the latter half of the nineteenth century to place greater emphasis on the phenomenon of bodily integrity. When Orthodox authors wrote about physical incorruptibility in the late imperial period, and they did so with great frequency, it was with the seemingly contradictory goal of directing the laity's focus *away* from holy bodies as objects of this world and toward the spiritual and salvational lessons that believers needed to tease out from the miraculous and uncorrupted presence of a long-dead saint. As we shall see below, the Church's emphasis on relics in the late imperial period was part of a larger trend toward catechizing the faithful, improving the quality of the laity's religious knowledge, and ensuring that ordinary believers possessed a proper understanding of and reverence toward the sacred. To achieve this last goal, Church authorities attempted to draw clear boundaries between which relics were genuine and worthy of adoration and which were not.

Beginning in the mid-nineteenth century, with the help of new educational institutions like the diocesan press and an expanded network of parish schools, the Church began to use the uncorrupted state of God's holy saints both as a prism through which fundamental truths of the faith could be reflected to enlighten the faithful and, increasingly, as a metaphor to establish Orthodoxy's claim as the one true Church of Christ over and against sectarians, Old Believers, and radical nonbelievers.[13] Only Orthodoxy, its champions claimed, could boast such a cache of wondrously preserved bodies, whose physical integrity and purity gave believers a glimpse of the resurrection to come on the Day of Judgment. In the texts they produced during this period, Orthodox authors and intellectuals sought to refine and elevate popular understandings of uncorrupted relics and the devotional practices associated with them, asserting that holy relics were more than all-access miracle dispensers from which the faithful could improve the material conditions of their daily lives. They were also models that all Christians needed to emulate in order to attain eternal life.

"A MIRACLE THAT LASTS FOREVER AND IS EVIDENT TO ALL"
DEFINITIONS AND DESCRIPTIONS OF BODILY INCORRUPTIBILITY

In the nineteenth and early twentieth centuries, all Orthodox authors who tackled the subject of relics unanimously acknowledged that bodily incorruptibility was a great and awesome miracle authored by God Himself.[14] Following patristic tradition, Russian Orthodox theologians read the preservation of a saint's body after death as a special favor granted by God, for reasons known only to Him, in recognition of the deceased's exemplary life.[15] As the late-nineteenth-century Orthodox writer P. M. Vlastov observed, for a saint to be spared from corruption meant that he had been set aside for all time and for all to see as one of God's elect, one of the chosen few whose upright lives had earned them a reprieve from the common fate that awaited all men and women through the sin of Adam and Eve. Thus, incorruptibility was nothing less than a visible sign of God's power to bend even the inexorable laws of nature to which everything in the world had been subject since the fall in Eden—"Dust thou art, and to dust shalt thou return" (Genesis 3:19).[16]

In the same breath, however, Church writers were quick to point out that, while God had bestowed this gift on many of His saints, not every holy body was so blessed. "Though not unprecedented," it was, indeed, as one author claimed, a "rare phenomenon" for a saint's body to be preserved entire and inviolate.[17] To receive "the crown of incorruptibility" was more the exception than the rule.[18] As such, holy relics did not need to take the shape of complete bodies to be defined as moshchi. Arguably the most learned, and certainly the lengthiest, exposition of this argument was E. E. Golubinskii's *Istoriia kanonizatsii sviatykh v Russkoi tserkvi* (History of the canonization of saints in the Russian Church). In this influential work Golubinskii, a professor of Church history at the Moscow Theological Academy, laid out a detailed philological and historical analysis of the word "moshchi," arguing that the word itself originally referred not to entire bodies but to bones or fragments of bodies, and that it should by no means be understood in an exclusive or restrictive sense.[19] So thorough was his treatment of the topic that most subsequent Orthodox writers seem to have regarded the definitional question as settled once and for all, seeing fit to simply repeat the venerable Golubinskii's description verbatim, sprinkled alongside citations from the usual patristic suspects: John Chrysostom, Basil the Great, Gregory the Theologian, and the like.[20]

Similarly, priests and religious writers taught their parishioners and readers (or reminded those who needed refreshing) that if bodily incorruptibility was not a mandatory criterion for a relic to be designated "holy," neither was it required for a saint to be canonized. A saint was a saint not by virtue of his body but because of verified evidence of miracle-working, either in life or after death, coupled with an exemplary résumé of piety and an irreproachably holy life. As one author described it, "the physical integrity [*tselost'*] of relics is a supplementary and unnecessary sign [of sanctity]."[21] To believe otherwise, as Bishop Aleksandr chided the unconvinced commissar, was "one-sided and incorrect."[22] According to the popular religious writer Evgenii Poselianin, it was little more than "spiritual ignorance" to assume that an uncorrupted body was the touchstone of sainthood. When a clerical commission discovered on the eve of Saint Serafim Sarovskii's 1903 canonization that the relics of the soon-to-be-saint had not been preserved uncorrupted, Poselianin was quick to dismiss both the disappointment of some Orthodox and the unconcealed laughter of radicals and nonbelievers. Uncorrupted or not, he maintained, Serafim was undoubtedly a saint: "The Lord alone knows His ways. And He alone knows why after having glorified the elder Serafim with inexhaustible miracle-working powers, He did not see fit for his relics to be discovered intact."[23]

Because incorruptibility was a mystery beyond the pale of human reckoning, most writers were content with attributing the causality of the phenomenon to the ineffable workings of the Holy Spirit and declaring the matter closed. In a religious textbook authorized by the Ministry of Education for use in girls' secondary schools, students were taught simply that the presence of divine grace was what made relics holy: "[H]oly relics are called holy because the Holy Spirit . . . lived in them and lives in them still."[24] An Orthodox missionary and pamphleteer in Kherson diocese explained that saints' bodies remained uncorrupted because in life they had been filled with the Holy Spirit, which dwelled "not only in their souls but also in their bodies, and did not deprive them of Its grace even after their death."[25] As one priest put it, the uncorrupted bodies of the saints, "the former dwelling places of earthly angels," were truly "temples of the Holy Spirit."[26]

The question of why the Holy Spirit chose to grant incorruptibility to some of its "temples" and not to others was not a matter that was up for debate. Such "perplexing questions," one authority explained, were not for humans to ponder.[27] Brooding on the hows and whys of incorruptibility brought with it the danger of sliding down the slippery slope of materialism and rationality. Late imperial Orthodox polemicists repeatedly challenged the arguments of secular intellectuals and skeptics who attributed bodily incorruptibility to the work of artificial embalming or natural climate conditions.[28] Others sought to use science in support of their arguments. Some clerics argued that the recent discovery of mammoth remains frozen in the Siberian tundra made the incorruptibility of the saints appear all the more marvelous; experience showed that a mammoth, preserved entire for thousands of years, would begin to decay soon after it was thawed, but the uncorrupted bodies of the saints, impervious to climate, were a miracle that stood outside of time.[29] In short, the "vain sophistries of modern-day materialists" could never hope to explain a mystery so profound as incorruptibility.[30] As one priest tersely noted, true Christians would do better to simply acknowledge the preservation of holy bodies as an awesome display of God's power and not trouble themselves with unnecessary speculation: "To apprehend the miraculous, an inquisitive mind is not needed, but rather, simple and humble faith."[31]

Although Orthodox thinkers attempted to package the question of incorruptibility within a framework of definitional clarity, lingering questions and unresolved inconsistencies remained. How uncorrupted did a body have to be before it could be considered incorruptible? Could a holy relic be partially uncorrupted? Did a small patch of decay on a saint's extremities disqualify his or her relics from incorruptible status? Detractors of Saint Anna Kashinskaia, for example, claimed that blackened spots on her cheek and heel disproved her incorruptibility, while others dismissed these as minor flaws, given that the rest of her body was pure and pristine.[32] At a public lecture on holy relics delivered in Chernigov, a speaker argued that the miracle-workers of Kazan, Saints Gurii and Varsonofii, could be spoken of as uncorrupted even though the former was famously lacking an upper lip and the latter was without any flesh or skin on his legs. They were still *netlennye moshchi*, the lecturer maintained, because "the bones are not broken down" (*kosti ne razrusheny*).[33]

Since there were no clear guidelines on these seemingly fundamental questions, and because Church sources were themselves inconsistent, never deigning to discuss such mundane matters as to what constituted a threshold or rule of thumb for determining incorruptibility, the result was that *netlenie* was a concept often difficult to pin down, despite the Church's repeated emphasis that it was a miracle "evident to all."[34] The lingering hint of a sweet-smelling fragrance—the so-called odor of sanctity—had been generally regarded as a telltale sign of incorruptibility since the earliest centuries of the Christian Church. But not all sweet smells came from uncorrupted bodies, nor did all incorruptible saints exude the odor of sanctity.[35] Serafim Sarovskii's body, for example, was undeniably corrupted, and yet when his relics were sprinkled with holy water during his canonization ceremonies in 1903, eyewitnesses reported a "fragrant odor clearly perceptible to everyone . . . smelling of carnations and fresh white honey."[36] The sweet smell associated with the relics of the Siberian cleric Sofronii Irkutskii, for example, was apparently seasonal. An episcopal commission that examined Sofronii's shrine in 1910 reported an unmistakable smell of fragrant myrrh emanating from his uncorrupted body, but at other times visitors detected nothing. One husband and wife who visited the shrine in the late nineteenth century were disappointed to smell only "dampness, mold and mustiness."[37] Certain uncorrupted bodies, such as that of Prince Saint Gleb in Vladimir Province, were said to retain a "softness and pliability" in their limbs, while other relics were stiff and rigid.[38] Some uncorrupted bodies dripped myrrh or holy oil (*miro*) that was highly prized for its curative powers. Yet the collection of saintly skulls deep in the caverns of the Kiev Monastery of the Caves also leaked sweet-smelling oils, and no one could hope to win an argument that a bare skull alone could be classified as an uncorrupted relic.[39] To paraphrase a twentieth-century American jurist, the definitional boundaries of incorruptibility were difficult to define, but the Church claimed to know an uncorrupted body when it saw it.

"WE MUST STRIVE TO IMITATE THEIR FAITH"
CHURCH TEXTS AND THE SPIRITUAL DIMENSION OF SANCTITY

If incorruptibility was often in the eye of the beholder, the Russian Orthodox Church had far more concrete notions when it came to the question of what an uncorrupted body *meant*.[40] As one Orthodox priest noted in 1897, Christian believers should pay close attention to uncorrupted relics not just because they worked miracles but because they were instructive tools given to the faithful by God to teach them the most fundamental tenets of the true Orthodox faith; as such, uncorrupted bodies possessed both "doctrinal and moral significance."[41] Such arguments began to appear with greater frequency in the latter half of the nineteenth century, as Church writers and intellectuals increasingly used the physicality of uncorrupted relics as points of entry into talking about higher spiritual truths and more elevated matters. The uncorrupted bodies of the saints, Orthodox publicists maintained, could do more than mend bodies and cure disease; they could heal souls, treat sicknesses of the spirit, and most important, lead the faithful on the path to heaven.

The discursive shift whereby incorruptible bodies became avenues for accessing incorporeal truths was part of a larger movement within the nineteenth-century Church aimed at raising the level and quality of religious knowledge among the laity and standardizing belief and practice across all regions of the empire. To this end, the Church sought to catechize the faithful and replace their superstitious beliefs with what Gregory Freeze has called "cognitive Orthodoxy," a theologically grounded understanding of the articles of faith and tenets of Orthodoxy that would provide lay believers with the doctrinal tools they needed to attain salvation.[42] Holy relics in general, and uncorrupted bodies in particular, became lynchpins in the Church's "civilizing mission," as religious elites and Orthodox authors sought to redirect the laity's enthusiasm for the saints to a higher and more spiritually pristine plane. While late imperial literature on saints and holy relics continued to speak of their miraculous powers and the material benefits of health and healing cures that the faithful could receive through the intercession of their "elder brethren" in heaven, greater emphasis was increasingly placed on the spiritual and salvational dimensions of the cult of the saints.

Those saints whom the Church acknowledged to be preserved in a state of divinely ordained incorruptibility were reinvented and repackaged in the late nineteenth century, not just as miracle-workers but first and foremost as paragons of virtue, "little beacons of Christianity," to be emulated and followed by the faithful.[43] To this end, sermons and devotional literature enjoined believers to live according to the model of the saints, that "they [may] provide us an example for imitation and guidance in our wandering path to the heavenly fatherland."[44] One way was for the faithful to imitate those saints whose walks of life and backgrounds most closely resembled their own:

> If thou art a prince or a grandee, follow the example of Saint Aleksandr Nevskii; if thou art a rich merchant, follow in the footsteps of Saint Filaret the Merciful or Aleksii the Man of God; if thou art a monk, follow the example of the saintly hermits; if thou art a peasant tiller of the land, live like Saint Artemii, Saint Ioann the Holy Fool, and Saint Aleksandr Svirskii. On earth, they were peasants, they busied themselves with the same labors in the field as thee, yet nothing hindered them from achieving the Kingdom of God. Follow their example if thou wouldst be together with them [in heaven].[45]

Lest believers grow frustrated and disheartened at the apparent impossibility of living like a saint, they were frequently reminded in the popular devotional literature not to despair, for the saints, too, had sinned and stumbled in life, and yet they had mended their ways, improved their souls, and earned a place in heaven as well as uncorrupted relics on earth. As one priest explained to his readers, the saints "breathed the same air as we":

> Many of the Saints were great sinners who then became great righteous folk. From being a great sinner, the Venerable Mariia of Egypt became one of the earliest apostles. From being a fierce persecutor of God's Church, the Apostle Saint Paul became the most zealous apostle. The Apostle Saint Peter denied the Savior at the very moment of His passion, but his sincere repentance once again elevated him to the dignity of the Most Gloried and Lauded Highest-Ranking Apostle. Among the Saints there are other sinners who were worthy of sanctity by virtue of their pure-hearted repentance, pious life, and sincere abjurement of their sins. Never despair of your salvation."[46]

To be sure, imitation of the holy dead was difficult in these troubled times of "blasphemy and irreligion," but it was far from impossible. Orthodox authors assured their readers that they could achieve this goal without renouncing the world and entering the monastery.[47] As one author explained, being like the saints did not mean copying the "outward actions of the saints, but rather their *spirit*—their firmness of faith, their passionate love for God, their obedience to the will of God, their meekness and endurance, their zeal for salvation, or, as the Apostle succinctly says: [we] *must imitate their faith* (Hebrews 13:7)."[48]

As Jeffrey Brooks has demonstrated in his study of reading habits in late imperial Russia, the lives of the saints (*zhitiia*) were wildly popular among readers and listeners of all ages.[49] While they were often skeptical of lay believers delving headfirst and unsupervised into Holy Scripture, Church leaders encouraged the practice of reading saints' lives and even sought to increase the already high exposure that the zhitiia enjoyed. In several dioceses in the 1880s, reform-minded officials recommended that parish priests reintroduce the "ancient and commendable custom" of supplementing the morning liturgy with a reading from the lives of the saints. As one supporter of the project noted, the lives of the saints have much to teach the faithful about "doctrine and rules of morality" and by their "living and concrete examples" may even be of more benefit to the laity than a traditional sermon, which, "no matter how lively, lucid, and comprehensible it may, all the same, not be entirely free from . . . abstractness and dogmatism." "The service will not be lengthened much by these [extra] five to ten minutes, but the benefit will be obvious. The Church and her divine services are indeed a school for faith and morality."⁵⁰ Literate parishioners were enjoined to borrow copies of the saints' lives from the church library and familiarize themselves in their free time with these texts, praised by one of the most prominent religious journals as "the best reading" for an Orthodox Russian.⁵¹ In the southern diocese of Don and Novocherkassk, funds from the consistory's coffers went to purchase copies of the lives of the saints in Russian and Church Slavonic, so that parish churches could set up lending libraries for their parishioners' use.⁵² Although a saint's zhitie was seldom lengthy, condensed versions of the lives were published, often with a helpful paragraph at the end of each, summarizing the valuable lessons that believers needed to learn from the saint in question. In 1895, for example, the religious journal *Kormchii* (The helmsman) ran a yearlong series entitled "Lessons from the Lives of the Saints," in which readers were given succinct and easy-to-read instruction on such various moral and religious topics as the preservation of chastity, the importance of visiting the sick, the need to believe in miracles, how to live in Christian harmony with one's spouse, how to avoid both gossip and flattery, and the significance of confession and communion for an Orthodox Christian.⁵³

The Church stressed that the truths contained within the lives of the saints were timeless and could be applied with as much benefit now as when the saints themselves had walked the earth. Just as the saints' uncorrupted relics remained vivid and vibrant many centuries after their deaths, so too were the lessons that could be learned from their lives. An 1895 book entitled *Besedy iz zhizni sviatykh* (Conversations from the lives of the saints) was intended as a handbook to guide parish priests in preparing for informal discussion groups with their parishioners. The book encouraged priests to remind their flock that the life of each saint had a particular moral lesson to impart to the faithful and, moreover, that this lesson had relevance for modern times. For example, the lives of the uncorrupted Prince Saint David of Murom and his wife, Saint Evfrosiniia, taught Christian couples how to lead an "honorable and pious life."⁵⁴ Young boys and girls could learn from the studious youth of Saint Tikhon Zadonskii, while the exemplary life of Prince Saint Feodor Iaroslavovich of Novgorod showed older believers how to prepare for death with a pure heart and faith in the life to come.⁵⁵ And even though one did not need to perch atop a stone pillar for forty-seven years like Saint Simeon the Stylite, all Orthodox Christians could learn from his devotion, rigor, and self-discipline.⁵⁶

By the end of the nineteenth century, it was impossible to open up a religious journal, a devotional pamphlet, or a diocesan newspaper without being exhorted to live like the saints whose uncorrupted relics the Church revered. For those believers who had little time for books, the lesson was preached every week from the pulpit, as well. Thus, as Church authors sought to deepen the laity's knowledge of and familiarity with the most basic precepts of the Orthodox faith, the saints were increasingly cast in roles that showcased their God-given abilities to guide the faithful along the path of a Christian life and to lead them to salvation.

OUT OF THE MOUTHS OF SAINTS
CAUTIONARY TALES, PEDAGOGUE SAINTS, AND THE PERILS OF MOCKERY

Religious writers and pamphleteers also used incorruptibility as a pedagogical tool to teach the laity the duties and responsibilities expected of them as Orthodox Christians. Didactic Church texts placed great emphasis on the expectation that Christians must first lead pious lives before the saints could pass their prayers on to God. In an 1877 treatise on Christian names, one author reminded his readers that the saints were powerless to help those who did not live truly Christian lives: "The Lord does not accept the Saints' petitions and prayers on our behalf if our life is not in accordance with the spirit of the Saints' earthly life, which was a living embodiment of God's commandments."[57] As the Tver diocesan newspaper reminded its readers, the fault lay not in their stars but in themselves that their prayers sometimes went unanswered: "Therefore it is obvious that if it seems to us that God is not answering our prayers, then the cause of this must lie not in Him, but in the character of our prayers and in us ourselves."[58] Bowing before shrines and kissing relics was not enough. One had to live and act like a Christian if one expected to receive help from God and His saints.

Fortunately for the faithful, the saints were always present to lend a helpful, if not always friendly, hand. A common subgenre of miracle stories that appeared in the diocesan press and in devotional anthologies at the end of the imperial period cast the uncorrupted saint in the role of moral instructor, counselor, and giver of good advice.[59] Judging from published accounts, one of the busiest holy pedagogues was the indefatigable Saint Feodosii Chernigovskii who, when he was not rescuing Old Believers from the errors of schism or serving as an auspicious sign of God's favor for the new emperor, Nicholas II, was showing up in believers' bedrooms in the middle of the night to berate the slumbering faithful for disregarding the Lenten fast, neglecting to make confession, or otherwise failing to live up to the duties and responsibilities required of an Orthodox Christian.[60] In these tales the saint functions primarily as a mouthpiece for the Church's official norms and standards of Christian behavior, teaching the faithful what they must do so that their prayers will be answered. Usually laconic in his admonitions, Feodosii could be more forthcoming at times, as in this sound advice to a possessed man whose demons had turned him into a notorious blasphemer: "Go to church, pray, and thou shalt be cured; ask the priests to pronounce the prayers of exorcism over thee at every service for an entire week, so that little by little thine health may be restored to thee. Think not upon thy suffering during the fits, despair not, but be strong of faith, ask for help, offer prayers before [the icon of] the Dormition of the Most Blessed Virgin Mother of God, and afterwards make confession and receive the Holy Sacraments."[61] On another occasion, Feodosii tried to teach a woman the proper way to position her hands when praying, advising her to fold the right hand over the left for best results. "Art thou not ashamed that thou dost not even know how to ask for a blessing?" he inquired of the woman, with some exasperation.[62] During Lent, when a sick woman "in great suffering" prayed to Feodosii for relief, the saint appeared to her in a dream and rebuked her for not keeping the fast: "Thou hast not fasted—this is not good, thou art not worthy to eat of the *Paskha* [the cake eaten by Orthodox believers on Easter Sunday after forty days of the Lenten fast]. Try to take communion on Holy Saturday." The archpriest of the cathedral where Feodosii's relics lay included this story in a Sunday sermon on the eve of Lent, urging his parishioners to heed the saint's words as "instructions edifying for us all. . . . This is the standard for all of us Christians—to fulfill piously our Christian duty during the coming Lenten season, to make confession and receive Holy Communion whilst we are free of sins, so as to be able to worship unburdened the holy Resurrection of Christ."[63]

Similar stories attempted to instill in the faithful a proper respect for the uncorrupted bodies of the saints. As one religious writer observed, "The least carelessness or slight toward [holy relics] is an affront, a slight, and offense against Divine grace . . . [and] a serious sin against the Holy Spirit. This carelessness is in no way excusable, insofar as Divine grace reveals itself [in holy relics] manifestly and openly."[64] According to canon law, the official punishment for such acts of sacrilege was anathema for a period of no less than fifteen years.[65] To make matters worse, the offender also ran the risk of incurring "righteous wrath" from heaven, which had the potential to be a far more exacting penalty. Cautionary tales from the late imperial period recounted in lurid detail the "true" stories of horrible punishments inflicted by the saints on those who sneered at holy relics or who simply entertained doubts as to the reality of bodily incorruptibility. The recipients of saintly wrath in these stories are generally Lutherans, Catholics, Old Believers, and lapsed Orthodox. In the majority of cases (provided they survived their lesson), the experience is said to have convinced them that saints and holy relics were indeed genuine and to have effected either their conversion to Orthodoxy or, in the case of Orthodox backsliders, helped foster a newfound appreciation for the faith.

One such tale, for example, published in the 1890s, told of an Old Believer who mocked a picture of the uncorrupted Saint Dimitrii Rostovskii (see Figure 1). When the image was shown him in the house of an Orthodox acquaintance, the Old Believer laughed: "Who's this with his hand

FIGURE 1—Saint Dimitrii Rostovskii. Library of Congress, Prints & Photographs Division, Prokudin-Gorskii Collection, LC-DIG-prok-10127 DLC.

raised up and his fingers spread out? What, does he want to hit somebody?" His Orthodox friend urged him to take back his words, but in vain. The Old Believer fell ill and died within a week. The story's title, "The Punishment of a Schismatic by the Prelate Dimitrii Rostovskii," leaves no doubts as to who was responsible for the Old Believer's unhappy end.[66]

Even worse than laughing at the picture of a saint in a book was laughing at a saint in the flesh. In a story reported to have taken place at the beginning of the nineteenth century, a Roman Catholic schoolteacher in Kursk Province, a man "infected with non-belief," insulted the relics of the local miracle-worker, the Prelate Ioasaf Belgorodskii, during a tour of the city cathedral. He claimed that the bishop's body was not really uncorrupted and that conniving clergymen had gathered together some bones and covered them with shrouds and lacquer to give the impression that a real body lay inside the coffin. That same night, Ioasaf appeared to the schoolteacher in a dream, glaring down at him with an "awful visage," and reminded the nonbeliever that incorruptibility was a great gift from God. The terrified man tried to take his leave of Ioasaf, but the prelate seized hold of his arm and said, "Stay, thou shalt not leave me, I will make thee believe." The schoolteacher woke up the next morning screaming and "sobbing loudly." He rushed to the cathedral and informed the bishop of Kursk that he desired to convert to the Orthodox faith at once.[67] Another sarcastic resident of Kursk, a Lutheran watchmaker, was fond of mocking the Orthodox obsession with saints and often "spoke out sharply" against the Prelate Ioasaf. One day, after being subjected to a particularly offensive stream of abuse, Ioasaf himself, dressed in his full episcopal regalia, appeared before the Lutheran's astonished eyes and rebuked him for his disrespect: "Thou dost not know me, and yet thou doth revile me. I, Ioasaf, want to bring thee to thy senses. And lest thou thinkest that what transpires before thee is but a dream, let this be in memory for thee." And with that, the sainted bishop struck the Lutheran's hands and arms with his crozier, leaving behind bruises that lingered so long the frightened man decided to convert to Orthodoxy.[68]

One of the most striking of these cautionary tales is a firsthand account written by an anonymous seminary graduate and published as an oversized broadsheet on the eve of the First World War. The author explains that he had often been plagued by doubts but that the beauty of the Orthodox service and the singing of the choir had always managed to dispel any nagging reservations. But one day, during a visit to Moscow, an "insane notion" led the young man to make a very foolish error:

> [A]s I was standing in the Uspenskii Cathedral the prayers didn't come into my head and terrible doubts began to grip my soul. I was standing beside the shrine where the relics of God's Saint, the Prelate Filipp, lie in peace, when suddenly an insane notion grabbed hold of me—to see whether uncorrupted relics really lay beneath the shroud.
>
> This sinful thought stuck in my head like a nail and despite all my efforts I could not get rid of it. Finally I decided to see whether or not I could go through with it. Early one morning, before the first ringing of the bells for

morning services, I left the house and set out along the quiet streets toward the cathedral. My heart was pounding and the blood was rushing to my head; I realized that I was about to do something foolish but, obviously, the demon-tempter whispered to me: "Go!" and so I went. I boldly entered the half-lighted church and suppressing my fear I headed straight for the shrine of the Prelate Filipp. The flickering lights of the oil lanterns before the images of the saint cast strange and mysterious shadows on the icons. I tried not to look at them, and walking up to the Prelate's shrine I pulled back the first shroud with my presumptuous hands, then the second [shroud], and then my heart froze with terror and the breath caught in my throat. The Prelate raised up his head, looked at me sternly and majestically, and said something to me.

I collapsed at the foot of the shrine and I remember nothing of what happened next. I came to my senses again only after a long and serious illness. The Prelate saw fit to punish me for my presumptuous thoughts. By the time I had finally recovered to the point that I could leave my bed, I was unrecognizable. My hair had turned completely gray and my whole face was lined with deep wrinkles. Since then, I have become a different man, a new man, as if I were completely reborn; my heart is filled with passionate and boundless faith in the wisdom of He Who is a Mystery, Who commanded us not to seek out with our own frail minds that which must be founded on faith alone.[69]

After his harrowing experience, the young man entered the monastery, where "now I am peacefully living out the remainder of my days." He closes by urging his readers to "let not the slightest doubt creep in to your souls!" lest they too be haunted by "the stern and majestic gaze of the Prelate, profaned by my presumptuous hand," an image, he adds, that "has never left my memory."[70]

The publication and dissemination of such stories represent an attempt by the Orthodox Church to co-opt the very real popularity of the saints and turn them toward pedagogical purposes designed to improve the moral character of the faithful. Tales of saintly retribution and moral exhortation taught the laity the importance of gravity, respect, and reverence toward the sacred—a project that Peter Brown has described as "learning an etiquette toward the supernatural."[71] At the same time, such cautionary tales also reinforced the notion that to revere and venerate saints and holy relics was an important part of what it meant to be Orthodox and reaffirmed the article of faith, disputed by sectarian critics and nonbelievers, that unexplainable miraculous things can and do happen at the graves of the uncorrupted holy dead. In these stories, those who transgress the bounds of Orthodoxy are either set apart and branded as outsiders (like the bruised Lutheran) or else suffer the ultimate exclusion: death. To return to the Orthodox fold, penitent doubters had first to accept the power of the relics and beg forgiveness of the saints they had offended. For pious-minded readers, these stories, in their very repetitiveness, could also serve as a comforting reminder that they themselves were a very small part of a very long tradition. In one tale concerning a young woman who eventually overcomes her doubts about the incorruptibility of relics, a priest remarks: "The entire Orthodox Church has believed thus for whole centuries, millions of Orthodox people have believed this and believe this still."[72] Indeed, as these stories show, to do otherwise was not only foolish but even hazardous, both to body and soul.

"COME AND SEE"

RELICS, SECTARIANS, AND RUSSIAN ORTHODOX CLAIMS TO EXCLUSIVE TRUTH

In 1911 the editors of the Orthodox journal *Dukhovnaia beseda* (Spiritual conversation) urged their clerical subscribers to mark the feast of the translation of the relics of Saint Nicholas the Wonder-Worker by treating parishioners to a special sermon on the meaning of holy relics and bodily incorruptibility. To assist the clergy in their efforts, a helpful index was provided of relevant biblical passages that could be used as clerical crib notes in preparing a sermon justifying the cult of relics.[73] Heading the list of scriptural citations was a reference to 1 Corinthians, in which the apostle Paul reminds the Christian faithful that all the "dead shall be raised incorruptible" when the trumpet sounds on Judgment Day:

> For that which is corruptible must clothe itself with incorruptibility, and that which is mortal must clothe itself with immortality. And when this which is corruptible clothes itself with incorruptibility, and this which is mortal clothes itself with immortality, then the word that is written shall come about: Death is swallowed up in victory. Where, O death, is your victory? Where, O death, is your sting? (1 Corinthians 15:53–55).

Those priests who followed the editorial board's recommendations and duly delivered a sermon on Corinthians that day were sending an important message to their parishioners—the state of divinely ordained incorruptibility in which God had kept His saints for entire centuries prefigured the bodily resurrection that awaits all mankind on the Last Day. This was the greatest truth that uncorrupted relics could impart to the Orthodox faithful.[74] Theologian S. D. Bulgakov praised incorruptibility as "an especially great mercy of the Almighty, All-Knowing, and All-Merciful God," one that gives the living faithful "an image of the wholeness [*polnota*] of our future bodily resurrection."[75] To mark the occasion of the canonization of Saint Feodosii

Chernigovskii in September 1896, a priest in Chernigov reminded his readers that holy relics, "by their very silence, are the most eloquent preachers of the truth and life-giving nature of our holy Orthodox faith.... In their incorruptibility they bear visible witness that one day all of those who died in Christ will rise again uncorrupted and that we shall be changed in the blinking of an eye at the last trumpet, when the dead, having heard the blast of the Son of God, shall rise, clad already in new flesh which shall be uncorrupted and of the spirit."[76] The incorruptible bodies of the saints that dotted Orthodox churches and monasteries across the empire provided, then, a sneak preview of what was in store for all men and women when Christ came again to judge the living and the dead and thus served as proof of the timeless truths of the Orthodox faith against the claims of rival denominations.[77]

In the writings of Church publicists and in priestly sermons, then, incorruptibility became "one of the distinguishing characteristics of Orthodoxy," and a metaphor for Orthodoxy's status as the one true Christian Church.[78] As one writer for *Kormchii* explained, God used the example of incorruptibility not only "to convince us of the resurrection of our own bodies" but also "to show the truth of the Orthodox faith we profess."[79] The hearts of the faithful could be assured of this truth every day, a Siberian monk explained, simply by gazing upon the uncorrupted bodies of saints like Innokentii Irkutskii: "The Spirit of God lives now in Christ's Church, as the Lord promised, and our faith is confirmed in this by God's glorious saint who lies in peace uncorrupted and adorned with heavenly glory."[80] Of all rival claimants to exclusive Christian revelation, only Russian Orthodoxy possessed so many incorruptible repositories of the Holy Spirit, and Orthodoxy alone gave its sons and daughters a glimpse in life of the uncorrupted flesh that awaited them all in the world to come. The special love that God possessed for His Orthodox Church was made manifest by the uncorrupted bodies of His saints:

> Why in Christianity, and namely in the Orthodox Church, do some saints remain uncorrupted but not in any other [religion]? Why has the western [Roman Catholic] Church, unlike the Eastern Church, grown scarce in holy relics, even though it numbers several of its most recent members among the ranks of its saints?... Because it cannot be that the Lord God possesses goodwill toward those who profess a faith not pleasing to Him, toward members of a non-Orthodox church. It cannot be that He, the righteous judge, could pour forth His blessings on those who perform works not pleasing to Him and at the same time deprive His mercy to those who fulfill His will. The incorruptibility of holy relics, which smells so fragrant in our churches, has always been and will always be a true sign and proof of the truth of our faith and the right worship of our Church.[81]

Taking this author's arguments one step further, the Lord's "goodwill" for the Orthodox people continued to make itself abundantly clear in the modern age because uncorrupted relics—something of an endangered species in the Catholic West by century's end—continued to appear in Russia with remarkable frequency. As Peter Brown has observed for the early Christian West, "the discovery of a relic . . . made plain, at a particular time and place, the immensity of God's mercy" for a particular region and people.[82] It was interpreted by Orthodox commentators as no accident, then, that God had given the Russian people the uncorrupted body of Saint Feodosii Chernigovskii precisely at the moment when the new emperor, Nicholas II, succeeded his father to the Romanov throne. A popular Orthodox periodical, for example, saw the glorification of Feodosii's relics as proof that "a new era is beginning in our country—a soothing of minds, a cooling of passions, a return to national ideals. For now God's Saint comes down to us with a message of peace, love, and hope . . . here at the beginning of the reign of our beloved Monarch, coinciding with His holy coronation. The Lord hath laid open for Him a great treasure, this new source of blessings and miracles! And by the prayers of Christ's Prelate, may the Lord's grace rest on His crowned head!"[83] In his sermon during the liturgy at Feodosii's canonization ceremony, the metropolitan of Kiev also called attention to "this wondrous glorification of God's saint" as "important and instructive for our age of disbelief, of blind concern for the interests and pleasures of the flesh," and as proof that "the Lord has not held his wrath against us forever for our sins and lawlessness."[84] On the eve of the First World War, an article in *Dukhovnaia beseda* offered the reassuring conclusion that new saints were a gift from God. The Lord had caused the uncorrupted body of Pitirim Tambovskii to be discovered precisely at this opportune moment so that its promise of a life to come might rescue His children from the wickedness of a modern age marked, especially after the tumultuous Revolution of 1905, by "an impoverishment of faith, the transgression of God's commandments, an obliviousness and disregard toward the Church's statutes and dictates, [and] hostility and hatred among Orthodox Christians."[85] Incorruptibility could be used not only to justify the primacy of the Orthodox Church over all others but to make political pronouncements on the strength of the Russian state and God's love for its people.[86]

If Orthodoxy was the one true Church of Christ, it necessarily followed that all others were imposters, or as one Siberian cleric indelicately phrased it, "false, man-made, and perilous to the soul."[87] The very fact that the Orthodox Church could boast so many uncorrupted bodies while the Baptists were unable to scrape together even a single relic from among their flock was interpreted tautologically by this same priest as indisputable evidence that Christ favored the native Russian Church over its rival German upstarts. After all, he observed, "the Lord has not chosen a single one from among them [the Baptists] whose memory is to live on from generation to generation, and whose bones are to be preserved after death, for according to the word of God: *the Lord keepeth all the bones of the righteous and not a single one of them shall be broken.*"[88] "Was there ever, at any time or place, such a similar, miraculous phenomenon of incorruptibility [found] among persons who did not profess the Christian faith?" the editors of *Dukhovnaia beseda* mused. "Never and nowhere—not among the Jews, not among the Mohammedans, not among the pagans."[89]

In the last decades of the empire, the central publishing houses and diocesan presses printed hundreds of articles and pamphlets celebrating the miracle of incorruptibility as the surest and most obvious way to pick holes in the circular arguments of sectarian opponents.[90] After the edict on religious toleration of 1905 made the perceived threat of sectarian incursion much more acute, such treatises became more and more common.[91] Popular examples of this polemical subgenre included scripted dialogues and how-to manuals, intended for the use of Orthodox missionaries and concerned believers who suddenly found themselves in discussion with a wily heretic. Readers of the *Pravoslavno-missionerskii listok* (The Orthodox missionary leaflet), for example, were provided with numerous citations to scriptural passages that justified the veneration of the saints, on the grounds that such information "may be used in conversations with sectarians," who rejected the cult of the saints as idolatry.[92] It was expected that Orthodox readers, armed with a hefty list of biblical references under their belt, would be able to beat sectarians at their own game of scriptural exegesis, or at least make a valiant effort by citing chapter and verse in support of the cult of the saints.

Among the verses commonly mentioned in these handbooks was "Come and see" (John 1:39). As one member of the Kiev Society for the Dissemination of Religious-Moral Enlightenment told his readers, Old Believers and other non-Orthodox believers were like Doubting Thomas of the gospels; they needed to see and touch the truth for themselves before they could accept it.[93] Orthodox writers challenged naysayers, then, to let the evidence of their eyes and senses dispel whatever preconceived prejudices they may have: "[A]nd to any doubter or nonbeliever it must always be said: *Come and see*; place thy finger here, feel this body by nature perishable like the bodies of others, but here preserved uncorrupted by Divine strength, and sayest thou still that [Orthodox] Christianity, in which this miracle is everywhere wrought, comes not from God?"[94]

Indeed, so staggering were these truths that it was said only the most intransigent heretics and backsliders could resist rushing to embrace Orthodoxy once they "came and saw" the miracle of incorruptibility with their own eyes. The diocesan press and popular pamphlets delighted in recounting wondrous tales in which uncorrupted relics figured as the agents of miraculous conversion. Once again, featuring prominently in such stories is the indomitable Feodosii Chernigovskii, resident miracle-worker for the empire's multi-confessional western borderlands.[95] The sight of his perfectly preserved body was said to have convinced Jews to accept Christ as their savior, brought Baptists to convert, and led Old Believers to return en masse to the Orthodox fold.[96] A miracle story published in the Chernigov diocesan press in 1897 told of how Old Believer peasants from Vladimir Province and Old Believer Cossacks from the Don and Kuban regions had embraced the Orthodox faith after gazing on (and touching) the uncorrupted body of Saint Feodosii:

> Not only the Prelate's hands, but the fingers and thumbs, as well—all were whole and intact, as if the Prelate had been dead not for two hundred years but for two or three days; and the non-believers touched the legs, too, of God's Saint. . . . The schismatics' hearts were touched by the presence of grace. Not a single one of them could suppress their emotions and tears of penitence and joy; all of them touched the holy relics with great reverence, which earlier they would not do. . . . "O Saint of God, now I believe, forgive me my unbelief!" They kissed the relics and for a long time they could not be torn from the saint's coffin, fixing their gaze upon it.[97]

Orthodox writers also deployed the metaphor of bodily totality to mirror the harmonious relation between the two bodies of the Christian Church—the church terrestrial on earth and the church triumphant in heaven. As one Orthodox writer explained, the living faithful and the saints in heaven were complementary parts of the same greater whole: "As in an ordinary body, the members, being in such close connection, look after one another, and if 'one suffers, then all members suffer with it; and if one member is glorified, then all members rejoice with it' (1 Corinthians 12:26); so too must there be the same close relationship in the spiritual body between the members of the church terrestrial and the church [in heaven]."[98] By rejecting the saints and their holy bodies, sectarians denied the unity between the world seen and the world unseen, much to the detriment of their souls. It was a sin of arrogance and false pride to presume that one could attain paradise without the aid of the saints: "Falsely thinking themselves saints, sectarians like the Baptists have deprived themselves of true saints—the friends of the Lord, to whom God Himself gives glory and through whose prayers we are much heartened on the path to life everlasting."[99] Even worse, those who spurned the saints were insulting God Himself: "[The saints] are but small in comparison with Christ, but whosoever disparages God's little ones disparages the majesty of God, and whosoever gives reverence to them, gives reverence to God, who is Wondrous in His Saints."[100] Thus, at the end of the old regime, Russian Orthodox writers and publicists staked their claims to the title of Christ's one true church in part, at least, on the uncorrupted bodies of their holy dead. Like God Himself, the Orthodox Church was "Wondrous in Its Saints."

In the last decades of the old regime, uncorrupted bodies occupied center stage in the Russian Orthodox Church's sweeping project to improve the religious knowledge of the faithful, as Church authors and elites began increasingly to use holy relics as a way of redirecting the laity's religious gaze toward higher and more pristine spiritual truths. This entailed a recoding of what holy relics, especially uncorrupted ones, meant in the Orthodox tradition. While the miracle-working powers of holy bodies continued to be celebrated by the Church as self-evident signs of the hand of God working in the world, devotional literature, priestly sermons, and theological treatises increasingly held up holy relics as vessels of grace and mercy; roadmaps that the pious Christian should study as he traveled on the path to heaven; and visible, tangible evidence of Orthodoxy's right to claim for itself the status of Christ's true church and sole repository of revealed truth. Cautionary tales of saintly punishment warned of the dangers that befell doubters and mockers, while stories of miraculous conversion stressed the point that even deluded sectarians and schismatics could see and feel the truth of Orthodoxy as embodied in its rich cache of holy relics.

At the same time, however, the power of holy relics to produce miracles that would redound to the earthly benefit of the faithful was somewhat downplayed in favor of a theology that stressed the salvational aspects of sainthood. The greatest miracle to be obtained from the saints and their relics was not bodily healing or a wondrous cure but eternal life and the kingdom of heaven. When a believer knelt before a saintly shrine to kiss an uncorrupted body, his thoughts should be focused not so much on what the saint could do for him on earth but, rather, how he must live his life so that he might one day join the saint in heaven. As the author of a treatise on uncorrupted relics in the northern diocese of Vologda remarked of his saintly subjects, "Not to know them is not to know what's best for you and to suffer of thirst in the presence of a flowing fountain."[101] Yet while Church authors attempted to situate the saints and their relics in the context of a larger, universal narrative of grace and salvation, we shall see in the following chapter that the overwhelming majority of the lay faithful, indifferent to theological fineries, continued to understand the holy dead in terms of the more immediate milieu of the localized, the personalized, and the efficacious.

2

Going to See the Saints

MIRACLES, SHRINES, AND RELICS

> "The tangibility, so to speak, of the relics makes a very powerful impression on those who pray to them and touch them. Everything is up front and straight-forward here, and there is no room for flights of fancy. See and believe . . ."[1]
>
> —A VISITOR TO THE SHRINE OF FEODOSII CHERNIGOVSKII, C. 1900

> "They [the saints] are not separated from us either in spirit or in body. Through [the presence of] their remains, they clearly indicate their nearness to us, their readiness to pray for us earthly wanderers and to help us in all our needs. The power of the saints to petition on our behalf is nowhere so manifest and striking as at the site of their holy relics."[2]
>
> —ANONYMOUS TREATISE ON RELICS, 1902

At the turn of the twentieth century, K. I. Fomenko, an Orthodox archpriest and member of the Kiev Religious-Enlightenment Society, set out on pilgrimage to venerate the miraculous relics of Saint Nicholas the Wonder-Worker, housed in an eleventh-century basilica in the Italian town of Bari, nestled on the Adriatic coast. In his memoirs Fomenko reluctantly concluded that the experience had left much to be desired. There were two routes for Russian pilgrims to reach Italy—a "country strange to us in faith and nationality"—and each was fraught with peril. Passage by sea was speedier, but more dangerous, while the overland route through eastern and central Europe was marked by "obstacles almost insurmountable" for the average pilgrim traversing lands "unfriendly to us, where our currency is not in use, where they do not know our Russian language, where they look even upon our dress with laughter." For those travelers who survived the journey unscathed, "a joyless greeting" awaited them in Italy, where "cunning folk" sought to separate the Russian pilgrims from the few possessions they carried with them, and unscrupulous innkeepers and provisioners gouged them with high prices. "Where is the stranger to find shelter?" Fomenko wondered. "There is no Orthodox cloister here, with the customary lodging house for pilgrims. This is a Roman Catholic country. Our pilgrims take cramped little rooms from the locals, nearby the church. . . . And these little rooms don't come cheap!"[3]

The basilica, too, was terra incognita for an Orthodox pilgrim. When Fomenko asked where he might find Saint Nicholas's oil-exuding holy relics, he was told that the saint's body lay not in a grand canopied shrine in a side chapel or adjacent to the altar, as was commonly the case in Orthodox Russia, but in an underground crypt marked off by an iron railing. A Catholic cleric led the visiting pilgrim down the steps and hovered behind him while he paid his respects to Saint Nicholas. Yet even this, the culmination of his long pilgrimage, was unsatisfying:

> Having taken a certain fee from [the pilgrim], they let him touch his head to the altar and only sneak a quick peek at the chrism-producing grave of the great Prelate of the Church Universal. So you see, brothers, the ritual for venerating holy relics in the Catholic West is not the same as our ritual for honoring the remains of God's saints. There are no great throngs of our pilgrims at the . . . grave of the Prelate. . . . Why? [The Russian pilgrim] does not receive the sort of edification desired.[4]

Utterly disenchanted with the experience, Fomenko sniffed that Orthodox pilgrims would do well to spare themselves the trouble and expense of the arduous journey to Italy and pray to Saint Nicholas in their own churches and homes in their own land: "The Prelate Nicholas is a great Miracle-Worker. And one needn't think that only in Bari does he receive our prayers."[5]

It was more than the hardships of travel and the discomfort of poor lodgings that spoiled Fomenko's long-awaited trip to Bari. Pilgrimage, in the Russian tradition, was understood as a "deed of the spirit" (*podvig*), and Orthodox pilgrims expected to endure privations and self-sacrifices, just as the saints themselves had done in life.[6] What particularly troubled Fomenko was that he did not receive the "edification desired" at Saint

Nicholas's shrine. He could not touch and kiss the saint's body, nor could he linger long in prayer and ask the saint to intercede on behalf of himself and his loved ones. Although he did not say for certain in his memoirs, we can assume also that Fomenko was not permitted to capture some of the famed miracle-working oil that seeped from Nicholas's tomb, nor could he place articles of the saint's miraculous vestments on an ailing body part, both practices that sympathetic Orthodox clerics back home freely allowed. The overall experience was far more mediated and less intimate than an Orthodox worshipper, accustomed to the devotional practices surrounding holy relics in Russia, would have expected. In short, Saint Nicholas's relics were a disappointment. The physicality and intimacy that Russian believers sought at the shrines of their saints were missing at Bari.

This chapter examines the question of how Russian Orthodox men and women forged relationships with the saints in heaven by interacting with their relics on earth. As we saw in the preceding chapter, the Orthodox Church at the end of the old regime expended much ink and effort in attempting to improve and, indeed, reconfigure the way in which believers imagined their relationship with the holy dead, urging the laity to elevate their gaze from terrestrial concerns to questions of spiritual salvation. Yet the enormous amount of existing evidence from pilgrim narratives and miracle stories strongly suggests that most lay believers were more interested in the material benefits that could be obtained from the miraculous bodies and bones of the saints. Orthodox believers—men and women, priests and parishioners, peasants and townspeople—relied on the saints to work miracles in this world.

In order to secure these rewards, believers cultivated elaborate friendships with their saints, which lasted for many years and often spanned generations. The relationship between believer and saint was not, however, a one-way street. These friendships were predicated on the principle of reciprocity—the believer owed certain obligations to the saint who, in turn, responded to the performance of these duties by granting the favors asked.[7] Believers frequented the graves of their saintly friends, touched and kissed their holy relics, accompanied them in procession on feast days, placed candles before their shrines, offered prayers for the repose of their souls, pledged monetary donations and votive gifts to outfit their shrines and beautify their graves, and publicized instances of miracle-working in order that the saint might receive full glory and credit for his pains. Believers' miracle stories and tales about their saints demonstrate a deep, located sense of place, underscoring the notion that where one prayed to the saints was often as important as how one prayed to the saints.[8] As we shall see below, these practices were centered around the site of the saint's shrine, his resting place on earth, and required personal, physical contact with his bodily remains for the encounter to be, in Fomenko's phrase, an "edifying" experience.

Miracle stories and pilgrim narratives from the end of the imperial era allow us to see how these notions of proximity, tangibility, and reciprocal obligation were put into practice by Orthodox believers of all estates. Although they too subscribe to a certain formulaic composition, these sources provide a different perspective from the prescriptive texts we dealt with in the previous chapter, a perspective that allows the voices of ordinary believers to be heard. Tales of Orthodox individuals seeking solace at the shrines of the saints offer a very different portrait of religious devotion, a devotion more rooted in the material benefits that could be obtained by cultivating friendships with saintly patrons and fulfilling the obligations that these relationships required. As case studies, I will examine the cults of Saint Feodosii Chernigovskii and Patriarch Saint Germogen, both of whom in the last decades of the empire underwent a posthumous makeover—from respected and revered prelates to popular miracle-workers—as wondrous events at their shrines began to be reported with ever greater frequency. My focus here is not on the saints themselves, in their historical or hagiographical contexts, but on how Russian Orthodox believers imagined their relationships with the holy dead and how their religious values and practices were imbedded in the stories they told.[9]

PUBLICIZING SANCTITY

Pilgrimage was big business at the end of the imperial era, and localities across the empire competed for the patronage of Orthodox worshipers. Eager to attract pilgrims and tourists, provincial printing presses published city guidebooks and manuals with detailed information on which miracle-working saints resided in the city limits or in nearby monasteries, the addresses at which they might be found, and the special feast days associated with their memories.[10] A guidebook published in 1880 to acquaint visitors with the spiritual treasures in the town of Vladimir boasted of four uncorrupted bodies (the princely saints Gleb, Georgii, and Andrei, and the martyr Avraamii) and more than 110 relic fragments within the city limits.[11] An 1887 study published in the Iaroslavl diocesan newspaper concluded that no less than ninety-three saints had resided in the diocese at one time or another, and a great number of them could still be found there, either in toto or in the form of relic fragments.[12] A decade later, local historians of Tver determined that the province was studded with shrines and reliquaries of saints, many of whom were "as yet unknown to the scholarly world," but "kept in holy memory by the narod."[13] An 1896 guidebook published for out-of-town guests attending the canonization of Feodosii Chernigovskii was obliged to admit that the town had little to offer visitors other than the miracle-working relics of the new saint. If Chernigov seemed small and shabby, and if its architecture "could not compare with that of other provincial cities," tourists should remember that over the course of its thousand-year history, the town had been besieged and sacked twenty-nine times, had endured four "devastating fires," and had suffered five waves of epidemic disease. Nevertheless, the author cheerfully promised pilgrims they would "find much that is precious to their religious feelings here in our God-preserved city of Chernigov" and assured readers that their "pilgrimage will not be in vain."[14]

Not only civic pride but economic self-interest motivated the promotion of religious tourism. Saints and relics meant big money, especially for small towns and monasteries otherwise off the beaten path. In the 1860s, for instance, the miracle-working relics of Mitrofan Voronezhskii brought 40,000 pilgrims a year to a town of only 36,000.[15] Within five years of Mitrofan's canonization in 1832, the coffers of the Mitrofanskii monastery where his relics were housed had swelled from 16,784 rubles to 296,555.[16] Monasteries that could boast miracle-working relics stood to make much more money than those that could not. In 1898, for example, the Spasskii monastery in Murom, Vladimir Province, which had no relics, brought in 2,726 rubles and 20 kopecks from prayer requests and donations. That same year, its cross-town rival, the Blagoveshchenskii monastery, home to the miracle-working relics of Prince Saint Konstantin and his sons, brought in prayer requests and pilgrim offerings totaling 6,330 rubles and 68 kopecks.[17]

The influx of pilgrims and rubles served also as a boost to local economies. A nineteenth-century source noted that pilgrimage "formed a significant branch of industry in Voronezh. An entire street has been created for pilgrims, with inns and whole rows of trading stalls that traffic exclusively in those objects demanded by pilgrims."[18] A pocket guidebook published by the diocese of Vladimir gently prodded pilgrims into parting with their rubles by reminding them that spiritual souvenirs were available for sale at the cathedral bookshop, two religious supply stores downtown, two photography studios, and any number of icon stalls and workshops with convenient locations across the city: "Without a doubt, every pilgrim to Vladimir will desire to acquire for himself an image of the Miracle-Working Saints of Vladimir, as well as crosses, books of prayers to the saints, altar bread [*prosfora*], holy oil, and so forth."[19] Similar publicity machines operated across the empire. The journal *Russkii palomnik* (The Russian pilgrim), which began publishing in 1885, kept its audience abreast of miracles being performed in all corners of Orthodox Russia, with tantalizing photographs of the saintly shrines where healing cures could be obtained.[20] Editors culled particularly impressive tales from the pages of the diocesan press and reprinted them in miracle anthologies or as separate pamphlets.[21] By the eve of the First World War, the popular series of *Troitskie listky* (Trinity leaflets), published at the Troitskaia Lavra in Sergiev Posad, had more than 1,300 titles, numbering 5,300 pages. Chock-full of edifying examples drawn from the lives of the saints and vivid stories of miracles wrought by their relics, the pamphlets were distributed free of charge to pilgrims visiting the Lavra. The pamphlets were wildly popular, and because so many readers had "expressed a desire to have the complete series of all published titles," back issues were available for purchase and delivery.[22]

Faced with such an embarrassment of spiritual riches, how did Orthodox worshipers decide which shrines to venerate? As Roy Robson has shown for Solovki, by the middle of the nineteenth century technological innovation made religious travel cheaper, quicker, and safer. Steamships and railroads allowed more Orthodox pilgrims than ever before to venture as far as the White Sea, the Holy Land, or even, in Fomenko's case, to Bari.[23] Yet the proliferation of sacred sites all across European Russia meant that pilgrims seldom had to venture so far in search of a saintly shrine. Although long-distance pilgrimage was easier than ever, evidence suggests that most Orthodox believers chose to keep their devotional practices local. A. N. Kurtsev estimates that by the beginning of the twentieth century as many as 800,000 rural worshipers in the Central Black Earth region set off every year on so-called close pilgrimage (*blizhnee bogomol'e*), that is, to destinations within the borders of their home provinces, whereas only 200,000 ventured farther.[24] Thus, four times as many worshipers interacted with their saints on a local level and practiced their devotion from within a discrete geographic space. Although new opportunities for transportation made the Russian empire increasingly smaller and easy to traverse, Orthodox believers in need of a miracle seldom had to look farther than their own backyards.

Yet even within a particular province or diocese, some shrines were more popular destinations than others. What were believers looking for in a saintly shrine, and how did they choose which shrines to visit? As religious consumers, Orthodox believers valued miracles first and foremost in their saints, and while all saints had the ability to work miracles, those who displayed a greater propensity to do so saw the popularity of their cults soar. Good publicity could make or break a saintly shrine. Chris Chulos has shown that the shrine of Saint Tikhon Zadonskii soon "overshadowed" that of Mitrofan Voronezhskii as a pilgrimage destination point after 1861, in large part because the miracles of the junior saint, Tikhon, received far more attention in the Voronezh press.[25] By the spring of 1895, Feodosii and his fellow countryman Prince Saint Mikhail enjoyed such prominent status as miracle-workers that the pair had become the poster boys for the *Chernigov-*

skiia eparkhial'nyia izvestiia (Chernigov diocesan news), with their images replacing those of Jesus Christ himself, who had graced the masthead of the paper for five years straight. Yet as Feodosii's rising status eclipsed that of the senior saint, Mikhail, images of the latter quietly disappeared from the front page of the Chernigov diocesan newspaper.[26] In 1896, the year of his canonization, Feodosii's portrait replaced that of Chernigov governor Evgenii Konstantinovich Andreevskii on the frontispiece of the annual provincial almanac; the two-hundred-year-old bishop was arguably the most important man in the province that year.[27]

As Ronald Finucane has observed, for the medieval West, "Nothing succeeded like success in the miracle world."[28] Indeed, throughout the imperial period, the most frequented shrines were those whose saintly occupants were believed to be particularly generous in granting favors to the faithful. Word of mouth and print culture both played a large role in publicizing miraculous healings and in influencing the choices of believers searching for a saintly patron. Patriarch Germogen, the seventeenth-century Orthodox cleric famed for his defiance of the Poles during the Time of Troubles, is an excellent case in point. For most of the nineteenth and early twentieth century, religious and historical texts represented Germogen as a national hero with a reputation for a pious life, but with no miracles to his credit. A patriotic homage to the patriarch published at the turn of the nineteenth century celebrates Germogen as a martyr of sorts, but not as a miracle-worker. The patriarch was a "true patriot," whose grave "serves as a monument to an esteemed elder who sacrificed everything, even his own life, for the salvation of his fatherland, for the salvation of Russia." Throughout the text, the author describes the body of this "steadfast, unshakeable bulwark of the Fatherland" not as moshchi, which worked miracles, but as *prakh* and *ostanki* (remains), which did not.[29]

When healing cures began to be reported at his shrine in 1910, however, word of mouth soon transformed Germogen from a remote historical figure into a much-sought-after saint with contemporary relevance for Orthodox believers.[30] The miracle stories reported by grateful believers describe how the patriarch's growing reputation influenced them to seek out his particular assistance. "When word spread throughout Moscow that many sick people were being cured at the grave of the Most Holy Patriarch," relatives of Elena Alekseevna Zhelubalina, a townswoman from Moscow Province who had suffered from leg problems for more than two months, brought her to Germogen's shrine; after praying before the miracle-worker's holy relics, Zhelubalina was able to walk home from the cathedral "without any help."[31] Aleksandr Dmitrevich Novikov, a worker at the Morozov factory outside Moscow, informed the archpriest of the Uspenskii Cathedral that he and his family had been the beneficiaries of a wondrous cure, thanks to the intercession of the new miracle-worker:

[Novikov] declared that his daughter Antoniia, two years old, was dying from pneumonia and was suffering terribly as a result. The father, *having heard that many people are receiving cures at the tomb of the Most Holy Patriarch Germogen*, went to Moscow before the Day of the Holy Trinity and offered a requiem service [*panikhida*] at the coffin of the Most Holy Patriarch Germogen, praying fervently for the Saint to either heal his daughter or take her, and thereby cease her sufferings. Having returned from Moscow, he discovered, to his great astonishment, that his daughter was all better and at the present time, in the father's words, she is a perfectly healthy and bouncing little baby.[32]

Another Moscow townswoman named Kraiushkina found relief from the head pains that had troubled her for more than a decade after she followed the advice of others and anointed her head with lantern oil at Germogen's shrine. For "the next day and the days that followed" Kraiushkina was a constant fixture at the cathedral, telling anyone who would listen "of her cure from such long suffering" and doing her part to spread news of the patriarch's powers.[33] By the eve of Germogen's canonization in 1913, word of mouth had created such a reputation for the saint's newfound status as a miracle-worker that sources describe the interior of the Uspenskii Cathedral as packed with a "continuous line" of worshipers, "a multitude of people, day after day."[34]

As Nadieszda Kizenko's study of the "living saint," Father John of Kronstadt, demonstrates, print culture also played a major role in publicizing saintly cults and in keeping a growing Russian reading public abreast of the latest miracles being performed by the saints.[35] This trend grew particularly pronounced from the mid-nineteenth century onward, with the great increase in the number and circulation of religious and secular publications.[36] The earliest miracle stories that appeared in the 1860s, in the first years of the diocesan press, were terse and spared few words. Typical is this account from 1861 of a young boy from Iaroslavl Province healed through the intercession of Saint Sil'vestr Obnorskii: "The head of Petr, the two-year-old son of priest Sergii Al'ferov, Liubimskii district, Nikol'skoe village, was twisted to the right side, and he was crippled in his entire body. Brought by his parents to the Venerable Sil'vestr, he felt relief and, after returning home, he recovered entirely."[37]

By the latter half of the century, the diocesan press had moved away from publishing brief third-person accounts of miraculous healings, opting instead to print more elaborate and detailed tales told in the recipient's own words. These stories not only helped fuel a popular demand for miracles but also influenced the religious choices that believers made. Many miracle-story writers tell of how they were inspired to seek a particular saint's aid by reading accounts of others who had benefited from the saint's intercession. Thus, the wife of an infantry captain stationed outside Warsaw credited the "various news stories concerning . . . the miracles manifested repeatedly at the shrine of God's Saint" with influencing her decision to take her injured son, blinded in the left eye by a playmate's arrow, to seek help from Saint Feodosii Chernigovskii.[38] Reading a popular book of miracles attributed to Feodosii also inspired a village psalmist in Chernigov Province to turn to the prelate for help in healing his six-month-old daughter.[39] "Having learned from the newspapers about cures at the tomb of the Patriarch Germogen," the Moscow resident and former Riazan peasant Sergii Alekseev visited the prelate's shrine in August 1911 to seek relief from the chronic stomach pains that had plagued him for twenty-five years. Germogen healed the man instantly "and at the present time," the cathedral's archpriest reported, Alekseev "is completely healthy."[40]

At the end of the nineteenth century, the new medium of mass-published miracle stories combined with the traditional method of word of mouth to spread and, more important, create a saint's reputation for miracle-working. Armed with information as to which saints were most likely to be forthcoming with their miraculous assistance, Orthodox believers made their own "wager on the strong," choosing to cultivate relationships with those saints with proven track records of miracle-working and whose devotees reaped the benefits of their friendship.

CHANNELING THE POWER OF HEAVEN

ORTHODOX PRACTICES AT SAINTLY SHRINES

In an 1891 article in praise of home prayer, the Orthodox journal *Kormchii* reminded readers that the saints in heaven could heed the requests of the faithful on earth because their "spiritual hearing is perfect": "From them not the single beating of a heart escapes, not a single thought, not a single word, intention, or desire, because the Holy Spirit in Which the Saints reside and through Which they see and hear us is All-Perfect and All-Powerful, it sees and hears everything because it is Omnipresent."[41] Although the saints could see and hear the faithful no matter where they were, patterns of devotional practice suggest that believers felt the saints' senses were sharpest at the shrines where their holy relics resided. The saint's shrine—the site where heaven and earth met, in Peter Brown's famous phrasing—was the most immediate portal for accessing his or her intercessory powers, and it was to these holy graves that believers came in search of miracles.

What did believers see when they came to venerate the saints? Saintly shrines were always housed in churches, cathedrals, or monasteries, that is to say, within a consecrated, sacred space.[42] The saints thus "lived" in the house of God, with their bodies laid inside massive silver or gold shrines of intricate craftsmanship and design, many of which were already several hundred years old by the end of the nineteenth century. In churches that possessed only a portion of a holy body, relic fragments were generally housed inside a chest (*kovcheg*) made of cypress wood or precious metals, or else mounted behind glass in an icon setting or altar cross.[43] Befitting the status of its sainted occupant, the shrine stood in a prominent place of honor inside the church, either against one of the interior walls, to the side of the altar, or in a side chapel, generally beneath an ornate gilded canopy from which lighted icon lanterns (*lampady*) were suspended. On the walls above and to the side of the shrine were hung icons and images depicting scenes from the lives of the saint and from notable miracles performed. Floor-mounted candleholders and offertory boxes stood close at hand for the benefit of donors. In cathedrals and parish churches, an attending cleric or church watchman (*storozha*) stood nearby the shrine to monitor the flow of worshipers and take requests for prayers; in monastery churches or chapels, the position of shrine attendant (*grobovoi monakh*) was usually held by one of the senior monks. Many shrines, like that of Saint Simeon Verkhoturskii (see Figure 2), were surrounded by a low iron railing and set atop a raised dais, which required believers to mount a small set of steps in order to reach the saint's body. Miracle stories describe how crippled worshipers and those suffering from paralysis or arthritis would have to be carried up the steps, either by an attendant cleric or, more commonly, by family or friends.[44]

At most shrines, the lid was propped open and held in place with a fastening rod so that believers could see and touch the relics; the interior surface of the lid generally featured a full-length image of the saint within (see Figure 3). Wrapped in shrouds and cotton wadding and covered in layers of brocaded silk vestments, saints lay swaddled in their shrine "as if just recently laid to rest," with only a small part of their actual bodies exposed.[45] A visitor to Feodosii Chernigovskii's shrine at the turn of the twentieth century reported that the saint was fitted in clerical vestments that reached from his neck down to his slippers. Feodosii's face and head, topped off by a bishop's mitre, were shrouded in cloths and silk wrappings and rested on a velvet pillow. The saint's right hand lay on his breast, wrapped in a cloth and ready to receive the kisses and caresses of worshipers. A Chernigov cleric noted approvingly that "thousands of worshipers flock every day . . . to kiss with tenderness and faith that hand which bestows blessings."[46] Indeed, pilgrim narratives reveal that the saint's hand had been kissed and touched so many times that the cloth wrapping had worn thin and the fingers beneath were clearly visible.[47]

In addition to the sight of the saint's relics, the tactile sensation of touching the body, and the smell of the incense, the sensory experience at the shrine was rounded out by the sounds that worshipers made as they called

FIGURE 2—The shrine of Saint Simeon, Verkhoturskii monastery, 1910. Library of Congress, Prints & Photographs Division, Prokudin-Gorskii Collection, LC-DIG-prok-02104 DLC.

out to their saints. Sources seldom fail to mention the weeping, moaning, and groaning that echoed in the cathedrals and churches where holy relics were housed, particularly during the opening of a saint's shrine for public veneration following his canonization. One eyewitness described the scene at the shrine of Feodosii Chernigovskii in 1896 as "a heart-rending picture . . . of human afflictions and illnesses":

> Day and night the air resounded with the vulgar shrieks of women possessed, the senseless words of those who had lost the power of reason, the prayerful shouts of the deaf, the pitiful moans of the crippled, the loud wailing of

50 ~ Bodies like Bright Stars

FIGURE 3—The relics of Saint Dimitrii Rostovskii open for veneration. Spaso-Iakovlevskii monastery outside of Rostov, 1911. Library of Congress, Prints & Photographs Division, Prokudin-Gorskii Collection, LC-DIG-prok-11379 DLC.

the inconsolable children, fathers, wives, and mothers of those hundreds of sufferers who now placed their hopes in the issuance of grace-given healing power from the all-curing relics of God's newly discovered Saint. "Feodosii, Prelate of Christ, heal, heal! Father Feodosii, teach, enlighten!! O, Feodosii, Feodosii, raise me (or him) up from the sick bed, Feodosii—give me back my son or daughter or father or mother!" The suffering and their companions cried out, shedding hot tears, wringing their hands, beating their breasts, shaking their heads.[48]

The same sort of emotional abandon that Church figures and religious authors deplored in the veneration of unsanctioned saintly cults was praised in the worship of "real" saints whose devotion was approved by the Church. Testimonials from visitors to saintly shrines give some sense of how emotional and awe-inspiring it was for believers to see and touch the saints' holy bodies. A woman who had been healed of leg pains while praying at the shrines of the princely saints of Murom described the experience in a letter to her parish priest:

> I felt reinvigorated. I felt light, free, and clear. Suddenly I realized that this was a miracle. . . . Tears poured from my eyes. On account of my emotions and the tears, I couldn't even sing, though I wanted to. I forgot everything around me. . . . By this time the moleben had ended. Lord! what were these feelings? Even now I weep as I write this. How miraculous it was at that moment! How I would desire to experience this often, to be in such a state! When I stepped up to the relics for the second time, I was possessed at that moment with some sort of special love for everyone. I had never experienced anything like it. I had never felt so good. I firmly believe . . . that I had experienced the happiest moments of my entire life. May God grant everyone [the opportunity] to experience this, and may it remain forever in the memory of each who has.[49]

A visitor from Kharkov who traveled to Chernigov in 1896 for the canonization ceremonies of Saint Feodosii later called to mind how "striking and vivid" it was to see and kiss the holy relics for the first time: "The Prelate's coffin was open and he himself reclined inside with his incorruptible body, as if he were ready to leap up to the aid of those calling out to him for help."[50] D. D. Ivanchenko's recollections of worshiping at the holy relics of Saint Serafim Sarovskii in 1903 describe the experience as initially unnerving but ultimately cathartic and spiritually soothing:

> Upon taking my first steps into the church, I was filled with fear. I remembered that an important moment in my life had now come to pass, a moment in which I had to gather together my mind and all my thoughts for passionate, ardent prayer. Having purchased a candle, I stepped up to the shrine of the venerable Serafim and knelt before him with great piety. My heart poured out everything that it had wanted to say for so long. I believed that here before me was a great benefactor, one who was able, through his intercession before God, to save me from the sorrows and sicknesses that had so long oppressed [me]. . . . [Everything] became light and joyous.[51]

Once they were at the shrines, Orthodox believers could deploy a wide array of techniques to tease a miracle out of the saints. The most reliable of these involved some degree of physical contact, such as kissing or touching the saint's shrine or body. In Orthodox Russia, as in the Catholic West, the saint's miracle-working power was believed to radiate outward from his body, encompassing everything that came into contact with it. Items that touched the saint's body—so-called "proxy relics"—were said to have absorbed this power and could themselves work miracles.[52] Friends and family members often brought shirts, blouses, or other articles of clothing to drape atop saintly shrines while they prayed for the recovery of their loved ones. These garments would then be retrieved and placed on the sick person in hopes of a miraculous cure. Nikanor Prokof'evich Goriachev, a peasant from Kolomenskii district, Moscow Province, suffered from an inflammation of the skin that defied medical treatment and left him in "unendurable pain." In the spring of 1911, shortly before Easter, Goriachev despaired of any further doctors' visits and had a set of "clean linen" sent to the Uspenskii Cathedral to be placed atop the shrine of Patriarch Germogen. The now miraculous linen, combined with days of prayer "so passionate that I can't even describe it," led to the peasant's full recovery.[53] Saintly power could be transmitted even to the most unusual objects. In 1910, Aleksandra Lipatova, a teenaged girl, delirious and near death after a recent bout of diphtheria, was cured instantly after eating a roll and a small piece of altar bread, baked goods made miraculous after her aunt had touched them to the shrine of Metropolitan Iosif the Murdered of Astrakhan.[54]

The saint's holy presence extended also to the oil that fueled the icon lanterns that hung above saintly shrines. Whereas the Orthodox sacrament of the anointing of the sick could be administered only by a priest and under certain prescribed conditions, lay believers could perform their own rites of healing with lantern oil quite freely, applying it to themselves or to loved ones as needed.[55] Much prized for its curative powers, lantern oil could be applied on the skin to ease arthritis, headaches, or swelling and even rubbed on the gums or swallowed in case of toothache or internal pains. Believers would often approach the shrine during services and pour out a cup of oil from the lanterns, either to take home or to administer on the spot.[56] Tucked away in pantries or medicine chests and applied with a dose of prayer, a vial of holy oil from a saintly shrine became an indispensable home remedy in an Orthodox household. A miracle story submitted in 1911 by Ol'ga Petrovna Nagatinka, a townswoman living in the Arbat district of Moscow, describes how an opportune application of oil taken from the shrine of Saint Germogen saved her from an untimely, and unshriven, death:

> It was on the Monday of Holy Week when the Lord honored me with a wondrous miracle through the prayers of God's Saint, the Most Holy Patriarch Germogen. My son, a student at the Moscow Military School No. 3, came to visit me on the day before Palm Sunday. I boiled some sturgeon for his visit. He

and I ate the fish on Sunday and I saved the broth. After my son left, I didn't prepare anything for myself. I just had some kasha and water, and so I think, well, no sense letting good things go to waste, so I decided to have a little kasha with the leftover fish broth. I had just finished drinking the kasha out of a little bowl, a bit too quickly, and I don't remember how but a big pointed fish scale from the sturgeon's back got stuck in my throat and completely blocked my windpipe and not even water could dislodge it. Barely able to breathe and all by myself in the apartment, I could only cry out: "Heavenly queen! Don't let me die without confessing!" Then I remembered the oil from the lantern of the Most Holy Patriarch Germogen, which I had gotten not long ago for eye and leg troubles and which had always helped. With prayers to God's Saint, I rubbed my throat with the oil and I felt completely better at once: the fish scale went down without even scratching my throat and [disappeared] completely without a trace. Glory to God's wondrous Saint! God is Wondrous in His saints![57]

One late imperial devotional tract reminded believers that "miracles are wrought not only from the relics of the saints, but also from objects that belonged to them in life."[58] The Orthodox faithful appear to have taken this particular point of dogma to heart. In 1873, for example, a nun at the Kamenskii convent outside Chernigov reported that she had been cured of her illnesses after drinking from a bowl that had once belonged to Saint Feodosii Chernigovskii.[59] Indeed, so comfortable were believers in the presence of their saints that they thought nothing of borrowing articles of their clothing or items from their coffins. Sofronii Irkutskii's miracle-working slipper, for example, was loaned out on more than one occasion by the cathedral clergy; in 1899, one woman reported that she was healed of an unspecified "illness of the breast" after applying Sofronii's slipper to her chest.[60] The monks who attended the shrine of Saint Sergii Radonezhskii would routinely parcel out pieces of cotton wool from the pillow beneath Sergii's head. One visitor to the monastery told of how he dipped the woolen souvenir in lantern oil and wore it in his right ear. Combined with prayers to Saint Sergii, the oily earpiece restored the man's hearing completely.[61] Visitors to Tikhon Zadonskii's shrine could don the sainted bishop's mitre, which was believed to possess miracle-working powers.[62] The hair-shirt (*vlasianitsa*) worn by Metropolitan Iosif the Murdered during his ascetic devotionals was said to have healed an Astrakhan townsman of an unspecified illness after the sick man slipped it over his head "with faith."[63] The metropolitan's *srachitsa* (a long undershirt worn beneath clerical vestments) was also believed to possess certain curative properties for those who wore it.[64] A more onerous burden was taken up by visitors to the Uspenskii convent in Vladimir, who would drape themselves in a pair of heavy iron chains that the Martyr Avraamii had worn to mortify his flesh while in prayer. A pilgrim guidebook informed the curious that "sick people who come to the Miracle-Worker's shrine with passionate prayers for a cure place these fetters upon themselves, and thus they stand before the relics for the course of the entire [liturgy]."[65]

For believers who could not be brought to the saint's shrine, proxy relics served also as a way for the saint's healing presence to be brought to them. Feodosii Chernigovskii's miracle-working gloves and sandals, for example, were available for home delivery within the city limits for the benefit of those too ill to travel to the cathedral themselves.[66] The clergy of the Chernigov cathedral did a brisk business in mailing out vials of holy oil from the dozens of lanterns at Saint Feodosii's shrine (for a nominal charge, of course) while priests visiting the city could bring back oil for their parishioners.[67] Because they made the saint's presence portable, proxy relics also allowed believers to maintain their relationships with the saints even across great distances. Ivan Vasil'evich Bretman, a craftsman working in a porcelain manufactory in Riga, some five hundred miles removed from the curative relics of Saint Feodosii Chernigovskii, wrote that he could still rely on the saint's miraculous intercession because he kept an icon of Feodosii in his home. In a letter published in the Chernigov diocesan press, Bretman described how scouring his teeth and gums with the corner edge of a wooden icon of the saint had instantly cured him of a painful toothache. Once, when a visitor to the house was unable to take tea because of a throbbing tooth, he encouraged her to follow his example, with the same miraculous results. Nor was the icon's healing abilities limited only to dental complaints. When their young son injured his knee, Bretman's wife placed Feodosii's image on the boy's leg, said a short prayer, "and the pain passed."[68]

By borrowing clothes from holy wardrobes, placing items atop a saint's shrine, or taking holy oil and cotton wool home with them, believers could make the miracle-working power of their saints both portable and possessible. In 1895, for example, Mikhail Petrov, a Chernigov storeowner who suffered from dizzy spells and blurry vision, came to the cathedral to try on Feodosii's hat. He felt instant relief and asked whether he could take the hat home for a few days, to which the priests freely agreed. Petrov later reported that "I wore the hat for three days and the pain in my head disappeared completely and did not return."[69] The image of a provincial shopkeeper conducting his daily business for three whole days while wearing the episcopal mitre of a saint who had been dead for two hundred years is, admittedly, a curious one. Yet the frequency with which such requests were made—and granted—speaks to the intimacy and friendship that believers felt for their saints. Surely Feodosii would not begrudge the faithful the use of his hat, when it was widely known to possess such wondrous powers. Such stories demonstrate also that, while believers treated saintly graves with great reverence, their practices at the shrine reflect an informal ease and comfortable familiarity with their saints. That such customary practices were tolerated, and even encouraged, by the clergy and widely publicized in diocesan newspapers and Church-sponsored miracle anthologies reminds us that lay believers and clerics inhabited the same fundamental religious terrain, one that accepted, and indeed sought out, instances of miraculous heavenly intervention in the everyday lives of Orthodox Russians.

"The Chief Doctor of Them All"
SAINTS, MIRACLES, AND HEALINGS

Many miracle stories from the late imperial period show how the faithful could interact with their saints even while sleeping, through dreams and visions. As one popular Orthodox publication explained, dreams could be divided into three general categories: "ordinary dreams from nature," which had no spiritual meaning and were therefore of little theological interest; dreams that came "from evil angels or the devil," filled with nighttime temptations to be rejected steadfastly; and dreams sent by God, "good angels," and the saints, which the faithful needed to take to heart as a message from heaven.[70] As we saw in Chapter One, Church sources often published cautionary tales in which the saints appeared in the dreams of the faithful to affirm the articles of the faith or to rebuke an errant slumberer for failing to show proper reverence for holy relics. In the miracle stories that believers told themselves, however, the saints came not to discipline and punish but to offer healing, solace, and words of encouragement.

Feodosii Chernigovskii, who appeared frequently in Church-authored cautionary tales as a voice of reason urging people to confess their sins and keep the fasts, had a gentler side, which emerged in the stories that believers themselves submitted to their parish priests. In 1851, for example, Feodosii consoled a gentrywoman who had cried herself to sleep worrying about her sick husband. "Do not weep," he told her, "I shall pray to God and thy husband will be healthy."[71] A peasant woman living outside of Moscow told the archpriest of the Uspenskii Cathedral how Patriarch Germogen had appeared before her in her sleep to thank her for coming to pray at his shrine and to promise her relief from the epileptic seizures that had plagued her for nearly five years: "Sleep peacefully, my child, I shall take thine illness upon myself."[72] In these stories the saints still give advice and instruction to believers, but in a kinder, gentler tone; the saints address the faithful with the intimate and personal "thou" (*ty*), as if they are speaking to friends and relations. There is also a practical worldly dimension to their counsel that is lacking in the Church-authored tales discussed in Chapter One. The stories told by believers themselves depict the saints more often teaching their human charges how to cope with the myriad problems encountered in this world than instructing them how to prepare their souls for the next.

Chief among these earthly concerns was the problem of sickness. In a miracle story from the archives of the Chernigov cathedral church, the wife of a civil servant reported how her teenaged daughter had suffered from an acute case of anemia during Easter week of 1889. The "best doctors" in the province—"not even Sikorskii"—could do nothing to help the girl and the case was pronounced hopeless.[73] Distraught but undaunted, the girl's mother went out into the woods near the Troitskii monastery to gather medicinal herbs, where she saw "an old monk clad in a radiant cassock and cap." When the monk asked what she was doing in the forest, the woman explained that her daughter lay dying and that medical experts were powerless to help. "I want to try folk cures," she explained, showing him the herbs she had collected in her basket. The monk shook his head: "But thou hast forgotten the chief doctor of them all. Go to Saint Feodosii, request that a moleben be served, and ask that some piece of the Prelate's vestments be laid upon [the sick girl]." The woman was about to speak, but the monk vanished before she could ask his name. Realizing that this radiant figure could have been no ordinary monk but, rather, Saint Feodosii himself, the woman rushed home to take her daughter to the cathedral, where they followed the saint's instructions to the letter and the girl was instantly cured.[74]

As in the medieval and early modern eras, the vast majority of miracles reported at the end of the imperial period involve wondrous cures and the restoration of health. This particular story crystallizes many themes common to Orthodox tales of miraculous healings: the recipient's initial despair of a cure; the consultation of medical experts, combined with their inability to either properly diagnose or treat the disorder; friendly advice proffered by a saint or the recommendation of a loved one or priest to seek out saintly assistance; and finally, a cure received in loco at the saint's shrine.

As Christine Worobec has observed, "the thaumaturgical arsenal of saints' cults was still powerful in an age when medical science had limited if increasing impact."[75] Historians of medicine in imperial Russia have noted that, while the number of doctors and medical professionals rose steadily between the period of the Great Reforms and the Revolutions of 1917, personnel were still spread too thin, especially in the rural localities. While urban centers like Moscow and provinces with proactive zemstvo organizations such as Kursk were relatively well supplied with physicians, in the countryside trained doctors were few and far between. V. A. Kovrigina has estimated that by 1910 the average ratio in Russia was one doctor per every 28,000 people.[76] In terms of treatment, these numbers translated into 756 people per hospital bed and nearly 22,000 women per maternity bed.[77] As Samuel C. Ramer has observed, the dearth of doctors meant that many Russians, particularly in rural localities, were obliged to rely on the skills of a physician's attendant (*fel'dsher*), who generally had only the most rudimentary formal education, if any, in the medical sciences.[78]

Despite these dismal statistics, miracle stories demonstrate that Orthodox Russians did, in fact, consult their physicians whenever possible. Thomas A. Kselman's observation that French Catholics at the end of the nineteenth century turned to miracles as "a supplement to professional medicine," not as a replacement, holds true for the Russian Orthodox case as well.[79] Scientific medicine and recourse to the saints were not seen in oppositional terms in late imperial Russia, nor were Orthodox believers expected to choose between these two routes and hope for the best. To the contrary, religious literature from the end of the nineteenth century taught that Orthodox Christians should make every possible use of prayer to preserve and repair their health—but always in conjunction with medical science and treatment. As a correspondent for *Kormchii* explained, medical fatalism was nothing less than a sin: "It stands to reason that the health of us all is in God's hands, but for our own part we must do everything to preserve it. . . . [It is] an affront to God to say: 'God's will be done!' or 'I won't take care of myself or be treated, let God save me!'"[80] While religious writers never entirely abandoned the position that illness could be the physical manifestation of spiritual disease or a punishment from God for a sinful life, Orthodox literature at the end of the nineteenth century reflects a growing awareness and concern regarding the natural causes of sickness and that the proper method to deal with this problem involved a complementary measure of both science and prayer.[81]

The authors of miracle stories frequently mention that they had consulted numerous physicians and medical experts before turning to the saints, but all to no avail. A merchant in Cherepovets, blind in one eye, sought medical treatment in Moscow, Kharkov, and Iaroslavl without any success; his vision was only restored after a deacon anointed him with holy oil at the shrine of Saint Feodosii Chernigovskii and pressed the prelate's hand to his sightless eye.[82] Although Saint Germogen had acquired a reputation for miracle-working only in the three years immediately prior to his 1913 canonization, the patriarch was credited with numerous healing cures that defied the expectations of qualified doctors. A townswoman from Liublino, southeast of Moscow, notified the clergy of the Uspenskii Cathedral that holy oil from the shrine of Saint Germogen rubbed on the neck of her six-year-old son had reduced a large tumor that doctors had said would require surgery to remove.[83] In 1912 doctors diagnosed Anna Martinovna Gaug with an "inflammation of the heart and a dilation of the aorta." After the woman suffered a series of heart attacks in the course of two weeks, experts at the Tsanderovskaia clinic in Moscow "pronounced hers a hopeless case. . . . The sick woman's nails had already turned blue, her breathing had almost entirely ceased, and the death rattle had already begun." The doctors had given up on the woman and sent for a priest to administer last rites, when Saint Germogen appeared to her in her sleep, blessed her three times, and told her that she would be saved from her illness if she prayed to him. Gaug "felt much better" after this vision, to the astonishment of the medical experts who "admitted that only a miracle could have saved her."[84] In December of that same year, Major-General Ivan Savostin informed the archpriest of the Uspenskii Cathedral that Saint Germogen had succeeded where "well-known specialists" had failed:

> At the end of July of this year, I fell ill with a severe inflammation of the nerves in my left arm, and then the pain spread into my right arm. I was afflicted day and night with acute and unbearable pain, and my situation became desperate. I turned to six doctors for medical help, well-known specialists among them, but nothing helped. Thereupon the doctors told me that similar illnesses drag on for years, and they prescribed electro-therapy as the only means [for relief], in order to prevent the paralysis of my arms. For more than four months I lost all hope of recovery.
>
> Having tried all medical means, I decided to turn for help to the great prayerful intercessor, the Most Holy Patriarch Germogen. Having offered a panikhida to the Prelate, I began to anoint my sore arms with oil from the lanterns of this great saint and to bind them with cotton wool that had been placed beforehand in his coffin. After that, my health began to improve rapidly with each day, and after a week I was almost completely healthy.
>
> Thus, this cure, so rapid, was performed through the prayers of the great saint, Patriarch Germogen.[85]

What is particularly significant about these stories is not that the saint healed the believers who came to them for a cure (these are, after all, miracle stories), but that so many believers describe seeking medical attention before turning to the saints.[86] Ronald Finucane, in his analysis of medieval English miracle stories, refers to this trope as the "hierarchy of resort"—believers would first exhaust all medical options at their disposal and then, when the ailment appeared irremediable, turn to the saint for a miracle.[87] One of the very earliest miracle stories attributed to Saint Feodosii, dated 1861, tells of Anna Dmitrievna Stefanovskaia, the fourteen-year-old daughter of a Chernigov sacristan, who suffered from incurable pains in her back that prevented her from walking; the girl could not lie on her back without sharp shooting pains. Her father took her to six doctors in Chernigov and to another half dozen outside the city, but the physicians were baffled. Each doctor, the miracle story notes with some smugness, arrived at a different diagnosis, ranging from a pinched nerve to St. Vitus' Dance. In the end, Anna's father brought her to the cathedral, where they offered a panikhida at the grave of "the sainted doctor," Saint Feodosii himself, who cured the girl at once and with great ease.[88] Irina Afanas'evna Smirnova, the wife of a village priest from Kaluga Province, reported that she had been healed of chronic heart problems and recurring bouts of gastrointestinal disorders through the miraculous intercession of Saint Feodosii Chernigovskii. "For confirmation that I am telling the absolute truth," Smirnova included a written affidavit from the zemstvo doctor who had treated her "regularly" during her sickness, attesting to the fact that she had been diagnosed with the ailments she described.[89]

From the historian's perspective, the readiness of Orthodox believers to consult trained doctors first and the saints second reveals a pragmatism that is often overlooked or denied in discussions of Orthodox religiosity and devotional practice. By including such details in their miracle stories, Orthodox believers established their own medical histories and lent an aura of legitimacy and credence to the stories they told. The testimony of doctors confirmed that the illness was indeed genuine, that the cure was indeed miraculous, and that the entire event could not be explained away as the over-excited imagination of a zealous believer predisposed to see a miracle where there was none. As we shall see in Chapter Three, diocesan canonization commissions were looking for precisely these kinds of details when they studied stacks of miracle stories in order to assess whether a holy candidate's credentials qualified him for sainthood.

At the same time, however, by recounting the tangled web of dead ends and erroneous diagnoses that had led believers to forgo their physicians and seek the help of the saints, Orthodox miracle stories highlighted the inherent limitations of medical science. This theme is expressed most vividly in a miracle story concerning a certain Mariia Popova, an Irkutsk townswoman who suffered from a painful abscess in her leg. In 1913 Popova told her parish priest that a monk "so kind and gentle" had appeared before her in her sleep. Using the formal address of "you" (*vy*), Popova asked the monk his name, to which he replied familiarly and with some wonderment: "How is it that thou dost not know me? I live in the cathedral and thou hast been before me." The monk spoke to her with such "love and compassion" that she poured out her soul to him and launched into a litany of her medical ailments. The monk listened thoughtfully and then told the woman to avoid the hospital, recommending instead a course of spiritual treatment for her pain: "If thou goest [to the hospital], thou shalt die there; better to serve a panikhida to Sofronii, take some oil from the lantern [above his shrine], anoint thyself with it and thou shalt be well." Popova explained that all of her acquaintances, including her landlady, had told her to follow the doctors' instructions and have the recommended operation performed. The monk repeated his warning, kissed her, and vanished. When the woman woke up, she realized that the monk in her dream was none other than the Blessed Sofronii Irkutskii, whom she recognized from his icons in the cathedral. She did as the saint had told her, forsaking the hospital for the cathedral, and soon after experienced a full recovery from her pain.[90]

This particular story is an extreme example. Indeed, it is the only miracle story that I have encountered where a saint speaks out against medical treatment. Nevertheless, this story accents a theme that underscores nearly all tales of saintly healing, namely, the fallibility of medical science and the limits to its knowledge and utility. No miracle story ever ends with a physician's triumph; rather, doctors are left shrugging their shoulders or throwing up their hands, powerless to explain a cure that science said was impossible. By contrast, the saints' power is represented as limitless and infinitely more efficacious. By showing the saints as willing and able to step in where medical science had failed, tales of miraculous healings affirmed the article of faith, adhered to by believers at all levels of the Orthodox community, that the bodies of the holy dead were possessed of healing powers that defied rational explanation. Thus, while Orthodox writers and religious texts at the end of the nineteenth century urged the faithful to take all measures for the preservation of their health, miracle stories themselves undercut the effectiveness of these arguments. In the end, the holy oil of Saint Germogen or the healing hand of Saint Feodosii would always trump the ointments and operations prescribed by earthly doctors.

"Answers to Modern-Day Questions"
MIRACLES AT THE TURN OF THE TWENTIETH CENTURY

For Orthodox elites, as for ordinary believers, the powers of the saints knew no bounds. Evidence from devotional literature shows that Orthodox believers saw their saints not as specialists but as general practitioners, who were qualified to treat any number of diseases and sicknesses. The résumé of the tireless Feodosii Chernigovskii, for example, included cures from epileptic seizures and convulsions, toothaches, deafness, rheumatism, fever, migraines, blurry vision, blindness, paralysis, difficulty walking, open wounds and bedsores, heart palpitations, strokes, and even cancer. "Whom do we *not* find among the cured?" one pamphlet asked in wonderment.[91] Indeed, Orthodox believers attributed to their saints a great range of abilities in ameliorating all aspects of the human condition. In addition to healing bodies, Saint Feodosii was credited with having converted schismatics to Orthodoxy, helped villagers raise funds to build a new wooden church, cast out demons from the possessed, and rescued an elderly priest and his family from robbers who tried to break down the door to their house.[92] Saintly doctors moonlighted also as financial consultants, employment agents, firefighters, and legal counselors.[93]

The introduction to a published collection of the miracle stories attributed to Saint Germogen notes that in addition to the usual requests surrounding sickness and health, Orthodox worshipers also came to the patriarch's shrine "seeking help and answers to modern-day questions."[94] Evidence from miracle stories offers some insight into the sort of contemporary problems that believers brought with them when they went to worship at saintly shrines. Nadieszda Kizenko's study of saints' cults in late imperial Petersburg, for example, has shown that a great number of miracles attributed to Blessed Kseniia and Father John of Kronstadt from the 1880s onward hinge around the problem of securing employment and establishing financial security. As Kizenko notes, the dating of these miracle stories is significant. The opportunities and prospects that opened up after the mid-nineteenth century, in the wake of Emancipation, the Great Reforms, and the onset of industrialization, brought with them also enormous social dislocations, economic hardships, and new strains and stresses on families and individuals.[95]

Miracle stories from this period show that believers of all estates turned to the saints for assistance in coping with these new trials and tribulations. In his study of Marian devotion in modern-day Haiti, Terry Rey argues, after Bourdieu, that socioeconomic realities give shape to the content of religious practices and that different classes invest different meanings in the sacred. The Haitian poor, for example, read the Virgin Mary as a mediatrix for social justice, whereas upper-class Haitian Catholics pray to Mary in order to capitalize on "the personally lucrative potential of their piety."[96] It is difficult to discern such distinctions in the Russian Orthodox cult of the saints. Miracle stories from peasants, townspeople, parish priests, and gentry nobles may differ in language or style or in the specifics of the miracle received, but the basic contours are the same across class lines and socioeconomic boundaries. Orthodox believers from all estates and backgrounds, rich and poor, elite or otherwise, sought out the miraculous intercession of the saints in order to effect positive changes in their everyday lives. Christine Worobec's quantitative data on the social origins of miracle recipients at the end of the old regime supports the contention that "miracle tales . . . visions, and practices involving holy objects were egalitarian with regard to social grouping and status."[97]

It is not surprising that many of the "modern-day questions" to which believers sought answers center around the problem of money, or lack thereof. While older miracle stories sometimes featured the saints advising believers where they could look to recover a misplaced pocketbook or a cache of coins, these later stories show how believers used the saints to navigate their way through the complicated institutional frameworks established during the Great Reforms. In a story published in the Chernigov diocesan press, for example, a provincial nobleman named Ivan Ivanovich Iunitskii described how Saint Feodosii had miraculously intervened to prevent his hereditary estate from being sold by the mortgage holders.[98] In December 1884 or 1885 (Iunitskii claimed he could not remember the exact year), the nobleman had received final notice from a Petersburg bank that his property would be put up for sale for nonpayment. Through a series of bureaucratic mishaps, Iunitskii learned of this event only forty-eight hours in advance, leaving him no time to send a telegram to the capital and request an extension. With his estate deep in arrears and no ready cash of his own, he turned to his friends and acquaintances for help, but "I received the exact same answer from everyone: that they had no money." In desperation, he stopped short in the middle of the street "and offered an impassioned prayer—perhaps the only one in my entire life— asking for the Prelate Feodosii's intercession." Shortly after concluding his prayer, Iunitskii met an acquaintance in town who insisted on loaning him the money to pay the mortgage. "How can what happened to me not be ascribed to a miracle of the Prelate Feodosii? I turned to my friends and kinsmen and they rebuffed me; but a strange face, barely an acquaintance of mine, offered me help without any prompting on my part. . . . All that I have written is the holy truth, and if there is anything written here that is not, then may God help me nevermore."[99]

In the fall of 1896, Liubov' Ivanovna Brezhneva, a peasant woman from Kursk Province, dictated a miracle story to her parish priest describing how Feodosii had intervened in the judicial system to decide a pending case in her favor and "protect [her] from injustice":

> I was very grieved about an inheritance that my brother, Semen Brezhnev, had seized from me through the courts. I was threatened with the danger of being cast out of my parents' home and having to seek shelter among strangers because the claim case, which had dragged on for eleven years, was decided in favor of my brother. I filed appeals to protect against this imminent danger, and in my grief I began to turn more often with prayers to God's Saint Feodosii— the opening of [his] relics [for public veneration] had been announced in our parish church—and I began with tears to ask for His help and to protect me from injustice. On 3 September, I was in the Sumskii district court and learned there with joy that the case had been overturned in my favor. Everyone who knew about my suit was astounded by such an unexpected reversal of the case. All the way home I did not stop giving thanks to the Prelate Feodosii . . . and I will continue to give thanks to the Prelate Feodosii for His blessings, which have given me life.[100]

Feodosii was also said to have helped a Russian woman who left her home in Helsinki for unspecified reasons to start a new life in Chernigov. In an 1896 letter to her bishop, the woman, Andreeva, told how the saint had rescued her from the brink of starvation and found her temporary employment. In return, she wrote, "I feel that I must report the miraculous help rendered me by the Prelate Feodosii":

> It happened like this. I was in dire need, so dire that it was hard for me to imagine that anyone could endure such want. Having spent my last bit of money to come here [to Chernigov], I was several days without a kopeck to my name. I was literally starving for several days. There was no money to pay for a room. The cold weather had set in and I had nothing to keep me warm. I wandered around all day in the frost, hungry and dejected in spirit, and with only a summer coat, even though it was 2 November. Finally I went to the cathedral. I prayed. I went to kiss [Feodosii's relics].... And then, at the very moment I was kissing [them], I called out from the very depths of my soul, "Prelate Saint Feodosii, help me!! Help me in my cruel need!" I suddenly felt as if a great weight had been lifted from me; my soul grew calm, joyous, and I came to the clear realization that help would come, just as if someone had said to me, "Relax, I will help you." That is how it felt, and I was already fully certain that sooner or later help could come, and indeed it did. Today the chair of the provincial zemstvo administration sent word to tell me that I would be employed by the administration as of 4 November.
>
> In order to judge the nature of the circumstances here, one needs to know just how difficult it is to get such employment, especially for someone not from these parts, without any connections or recommendations. Several days before, when I had submitted an application, [the zemstvo chairman] plainly said that he could not fulfill my request. So it's understandable, then, how I was just staggered by this help, and even though this help is only temporary, since the position is temporary, all the worst has passed. Who but the Prelate instilled in [the chairman] the desire to help me![101]

The tale of the miraculous mortgage and Feodosii's further interventions into the problems of everyday life show believers turning the expertise of familiar saints to new ends. There was no established tradition in Russian Orthodoxy, for example, of saints being able to secure loans, win legal cases, find jobs, or keep impressionable children from falling in with the wrong crowd at school, and yet stories from the late imperial period depict Feodosii, Germogen, and other adroit miracle-workers doing just that.[102] These stories suggest that believers were so confident in the powers of their saints, so sure their abilities were limitless, that they felt free to improvise and push the boundaries of the cult.[103] As one priest marveled in a 1911 brochure, the faithful who came to venerate the relics of Feodosii Chernigovskii brought with them a seemingly limitless array of requests and appeals: "The Orthodox residents of Chernigov consider it their bound duty to seek the blessing of the Prelate Feodosii in all circumstances of family and social life, in all enterprises and undertakings."[104]

Although these stories attribute new skills to the saints, there is an inherent similarity between the traditional miracles of bodily healing and the modern-day miracles of law courts and land banks. In all cases, the emphasis is on the practical, the worldly, and the immediate; believers' goals are focused on the here and now, not the hereafter. These tales bear out Kizenko's observation that "the qualities people valued in the saints from the late imperial period reflect their temporal concerns in life."[105] The improvisational ease with which the faithful adapted the saints to meet the exigencies of everyday life at the turn of the twentieth century reveals the degree to which Russian Orthodoxy was able to incorporate innovation into practice and remain culturally relevant in an era of uncertainty.

THANKING THE SAINT
PROMISES, PRESENTS, AND THE CONCEPT OF OBET

Believers deployed a variety of techniques and strategies, such as kissing holy relics and touching saintly shrines, to increase the likelihood of obtaining miracles from saints who had reputations for generosity. But the relationship between believer and saint did not end when the miracle was granted or the cure received. The etiquette of interaction that believers practiced with their saints was based on notions of reciprocity that required Orthodox believers to repay the favors bestowed on them by making gestures of thanks to the holy dead who had helped them. To this end, believers in search of heavenly intercession made pledges or vows to their saintly protectors, promising to provide some sort of service to the saints in exchange for the performance of the miracle desired. The content of this pledge (*obet*) could take many forms, including the presentation of votive gifts to adorn the saint's shrine, monetary donations for the offering of prayer services and funerary masses at the saint's grave, and (as we shall see further in Chapter Three) pledges to publicize instances of miracle-working for the glory of the saint's reputation. Whatever its content, obet was understood by believers as a personal debt owed to the saints in acknowledgment of their service to the living.

Gestures made in fulfillment of a pledge (*po obetu*) could be undertaken either as preemptive measures to succor the favor of a particular saint, or as follow-ups in recognition of miracles already granted.[106] The evidence from late imperial miracle stories suggests that the most common form of obet entailed making a pledge to travel to the saint's shrine and worship at his holy relics. Notification of these pledges was often made via post or, increasingly, through the new medium of the telegraph. A rich store of such documents comes from Chernigov, where the clergy of the city cathedral handled a voluminous correspondence of letters and requests concerning their resident holy man. In 1896, Mariia Semenovna Golovocheskaia, a priest's wife from Starodubskii district, Chernigov Province, wrote to the cathedral thanking Saint Feodosii for healing her young son and infant daughter. She explained that she had first promised to visit the saint's relics in 1892, when Feodosii cured her son, but "I could not fulfill [this pledge] on account of family circumstances, being a mother of young children and a housewife." In the interim, to tide the saint over, she asked the psalmist of the village church, who was traveling to Chernigov, to place two candles before Feodosii's shrine. She dutifully informed the cathedral clergy, however, that on 19 July 1896 she finally made good on her promise and "arrived at the holy relics of the Prelate Feodosii . . . in accordance with a pledge made long ago."[107] In a letter received in 1898 a married couple in distant Arkhangel'sk notified the clergy that they would soon be making the long journey to Chernigov, in fulfillment of a pledge they had made to venerate Feodosii's relics if the saint healed the wife of her "acute tuberculosis." The couple had hedged their bets on the sacred, also offering molebny to the Mother of God in hopes of a cure and sending a telegram to Father John of Kronstadt requesting his prayers. Feodosii, however, was the saint who had delivered the miracle, and therefore it was to him that the couple owed their gratitude.[108]

A visit to a saintly shrine that coincided with the holy man's canonization and the ceremonial opening of his relics was believed to be a particularly efficacious and impressive gesture of obet. One woman walked more than a hundred miles on foot to attend the canonization ceremonies of Saint Feodosii and thank him in person for having granted her a healing cure.[109] Liubov' Brezhneva, whose legal woes, as we saw above, had been resolved through Feodosii's intercession in the courtroom, repaid the favor by traveling to Chernigov with her sister to witness the canonization ceremonies. As Brezhneva recalled, Feodosii himself had suggested the idea, appearing to her in a dream and "instruct[ing] me to get up quickly and go to Chernigov for the opening of His sainted relics." Unfortunately, Brezhneva and her sister did not go quickly enough. The pair arrived in Chernigov and worshiped at the saint's relics but missed the ceremonies by just a few days. The saint appeared to Brezhneva again in a dream, this time kneeling as if in prayer, with his arms reaching up to heaven and the Holy Spirit hovering above him. Brezhneva assigned great importance to the vision and interpreted it as a sign that Feodosii appreciated her efforts, forgave her tardiness, and considered the favor repaid.[110]

Debts to the saints could also be settled by offering votive gifts in a show of thanks for miracles rendered. The Russian tradition of presenting gifts to the saints dates back to Kievan Rus' and Muscovy. Princes and tsars would routinely donate extravagant gold and silver shrines to house the relics of the saints, gestures that demonstrated both their piety and royal power, while Muscovite princesses and noble women "expressed their zeal for God's saints through their handiwork," producing brocaded vestments and silk shrouds to cover the saints' bodies.[111] Although the royal practice seems to have fallen into some abeyance by the middle of the nineteenth century, the tradition was vigorously revived under the emperors Alexander III and Nicholas II, who self-consciously patterned their holy gift-giving on the Muscovite autocrats whom they sought to emulate.[112]

In the modern period, however, the practice of giving grand gifts extended beyond donors of noble lineage to include the new commercial and industrial aristocracy. At the end of the nineteenth century, factory owners, entrepreneurs, and industrialists were vying to outdo each other in lavishing expensive gifts on the saints. In 1896, for example, the philanthropist and sugar magnate N. A. Tereshchenko demonstrated both his piety and wealth by donating a new gilded shrine for the relics of the recently canonized Feodosii Chernigovskii. Produced by one of the finest Moscow workshops, the massive shrine weighed nearly four hundred pounds and cost upward of twenty-five thousand rubles.[113] Wealthy patrons in Chernigov marked the occasion by donating twenty silver icon lanterns, commissioned from the finest silversmiths in Moscow and Tula, and "many expensive shrouds" to adorn Feodosii's relics.[114] While widowed princesses, dowager empresses, and nuns continued the feminine tradition of handiwork, society women and ladies of leisure also asserted their elite status by producing ornate gifts to adorn saintly shrines. In 1896, for example, the governor's wife and other "gentleladies of Chernigov" wove an intricately patterned purple rug, more than eighteen feet long, to place beneath the saint's new silver shrine. A public announcement in the Chernigov provincial newspaper ensured that the donors' pains (and names) would not go unnoticed.[115]

Such occasional gifts were deliberately lavish and intended by their donors to say as much about their great wealth as about their great piety. The more modest votive gifts that were brought to saintly shrines every day tell us more about the personal friendships between ordinary believers and their saints. Such gifts were generally made po obetu and were usually of a value proportionate to the donor's means. Although in some cases these votive gifts were presented anonymously, the inventory of gifts donated to the shrine of Saint Anna Kashinskaia to commemorate her canonization in 1909 includes samples of handmade linen cloth—offerings "from the labors of the righteous"—to adorn the saint's shrine, and several altar cloths with woven inscriptions bearing the names of the donors: "For the health of Fedor and Mariia" or "For the health of Pavel, Aleksandra, and Agrippina." It was important for believers that the saints knew where their presents came from; more than two-thirds of the 130 gifts presented at the canonization ceremonies included the donors' names.[116] A description of Saint Feodosii

Chernigovskii's shrine written some six months before his canonization paints a similar picture of small offerings and heartfelt gifts: "The worshipers of God's saint . . . bring incense, olive [branches], and small pieces of yellow wax; velvet and silken gloves adorned with rich embroidery to place on the prelate's hands; sandals for his feet; shrouds and palls stitched with gold, silver, and silk; pillows for behind his head; and other offerings, both material and monetary, dropping the latter in the offertory box which stands beside the grave."[117] In a sermon delivered on the two-hundredth anniversary of Feodosii's death, the archpriest of the cathedral drew his audience's attention to the "great number of trinkets" that stood nearby at the saint's shrine. The cleric described these gifts, brought to the shrine as a show of thanks for heavenly help, as "silent but eloquent witnesses of the miracles performed through the prelate's intercession."[118]

Another common way for believers to fulfill their obligations to a particular saint was to pledge monetary donations that could be used either for the upkeep and maintenance of the shrine or to pay for clerics to perform prayer services at the saint's grave. In a letter to the archpriest of the Chernigov cathedral, dated November 1890, a villager from Izmail'skii district, Bessarabia Province, announced that he was sending money to Saint Feodosii's shrine both as a show of thanks for the generosity that Feodosii had shown him over the years and to ensure the saint's continued favor:

> Father prior! Enclosing two rubles herein, I most humbly ask you, upon receipt, not to forget to serve a panikhida and moleben to the Prelate Feodosii at His holy grave for the health of myself and my family and for [our] deliverance from the trespasses of our enemies. Till now I have turned many times to the Prelate Feodosii and every time I have been delivered of many misfortunes through the petitioning of His prayers, and so now, finding myself in misfortunes once again, I turn again to him with prayer, as my constant intercessor before the Throne of the Most High, believing that this time the Prelate will [again] bestow his mercy on me and see fit that [one day] I myself may personally offer a moleben of thanksgiving at His holy relics.[119]

Semi-monthly accounts of moneys pledged to Saint Feodosii were published in the Chernigov diocesan press in the early 1890s.[120] Because in most cases the relevant data is missing, we can say little about the social origins of donors; a typically terse entry reads simply "F. Lisov, Kiev." Although there is a preponderance of priests in the donor rolls, this does not necessarily mean that the money actually came from priestly pockets. Several published receipts note that the moneys in question were forwarded to the cathedral by clerics on behalf of unnamed parishioners "in fulfillment of a sacred commission."[121] While some donors included extra money to pay for vials of holy oil from Feodosii's icon lanterns or to order multiple prayer services, more than half pledged a single ruble, which would have been enough to pay for a panikhida or moleben to be sung at Feodosii's shrine.[122] Such notices, submitted in writing, made the obet official and closed the books on whatever debt believers owed to their saints; it also freed up their heavenly accounts for the receipt of future miracles through the saint's intercession.

Although it was performed by Orthodox believers of all estates, obet was largely a gendered practice, with women playing the most prominent role in making sure that Orthodox households fulfilled their sworn obligations to a helpful saint. In her study of religious practices in the Russian north, I. A. Kremleva notes that gestures performed po obetu were most commonly carried out by Orthodox women not only on behalf of themselves but also for their families, friends, and loved ones.[123] Thus saintly shrines provided a place where women could practice in public their traditional roles as custodians of domestic morality.[124] Although women functioned as mediators between the saint and the family unit, this does not necessarily mean that Orthodoxy was "feminized" over the course of the nineteenth century.[125] As Christine Worobec has observed, miracle stories demonstrate that men and women had equal access to saintly shrines in the imperial period, appealed to the saints for the same sort of miraculous interventions, and were equally likely to have their prayers answered by the saints.[126]

The gendered nature of obet, however, does explain a phenomenon commented upon by nearly every late imperial observer of saintly shrines—namely, the preponderance, indeed, the overrepresentation, of women at the graves of the holy dead. While women worshipers made up a clear majority of all Orthodox who visited saintly shrines, they did not account for a statistically significant percentage of the miracles received and recorded. Figures for 1911 from Voronezh Province indicate that women accounted for a full 68 percent of the 21,000 pilgrims who traveled beyond the borders of the province to visit holy places.[127] Yet women accounted for only 51 percent of all miracles reported at the shrine of Saint Tikhon Zadonskii in the 1860s, and for a slightly higher 55 percent of the miracles performed during the ceremonial opening of Ioasaf Belgorodskii's relics at his canonization in September 1911.[128] Of the fifty-five miracles attributed to Patriarch Saint Germogen between 1911 and 1913, 56.4 percent of them were received by women.[129] If women were overrepresented at holy graves it was in part because they were the ones who handled the spiritual bookkeeping of the Orthodox household in the late imperial period. Women came to the shrine to pray not only for themselves but for the health and protection of their loved ones and family members and to thank the saints for the miraculous help rendered them.

Pledges to visit a saintly shrine or to have prayers sung at a saint's grave were undertaken voluntarily, but with an awareness that the continued goodwill of the saint depended upon their fulfillment. Many miracle stories tell of the troubles that would befall believers who reneged on an obet. Heaven, it would seem, knew no fury as that of a saint scorned. In 1913, for example, V. V. Tsyganova, a Moscow woman who lived on Vozdvizhenka Street, just blocks away from Germogen's holy relics, gave a statement to the clergy of the Uspenskii Cathedral describing how the saint had punished her for failing to honor her promise to him:

> I . . . had an abscess develop on my knee on the Wednesday of Holy Week (1913), and the doctor wanted to have it removed, but I didn't. On Holy Saturday, my whole leg began to swell up, the abscess turned black, the pain grew quite strong, and I didn't know what to do, so I took some oil from the lantern of God's Saint [Germogen] and rubbed it on, and it was so soothing that I fell asleep and the abscess ruptured. When I anointed [my knee] with the oil from [the shrine], I promised to go to the Cathedral and tell [people about the cure], but when my leg healed completely I forgot all about my promise and I thought, "Well, it's just an abscess, it's no big deal," but God's Saint saw fit to punish me and I hurt my eyes and couldn't see for two weeks, and I went to the doctor's but I called on God's saint all the same, after which I was as good as new.[130]

The saints were not above holding a petty grudge against believers who ignored their obet. In 1890 Father Georgii Rossinskii, a village priest from Surazhskii district, Chernigov Province, wrote a lengthy letter to the archpriest of the Chernigov cathedral recounting the tangled history of his dealings with Saint Feodosii. In November 1887 apparently, Rossinskii was suffering from a toothache so painful he could not eat hot food for several days. No home remedies or medicines helped and there was no dentist in the village, so the priest decided to pray his pain away: "While sitting at the table, I imagined myself at the shrine of the Prelate Feodosii Uglitskii—whom I've considered my own prayerful intercessor before God since I was just a child—and I prayed to God's Saint [for a cure]." At the close of his prayer, Rossinskii added that he would personally write down an account of the miracle and submit it for publication if Feodosii granted his request and healed his aching tooth. After making this promise, the priest's pain passed away "instantly," much to his delight. That evening, however, as he was sitting down to write an account of what had happened, he was beset by doubts: "I yielded to temptation: notions of not fulfilling my pledge began surfacing one after the other. . . . I said to my wife, 'How will my acquaintances look at this? Maybe they won't believe [my story], or else they'll explain away the miraculous cure, etc.'" Rossinskii decided to postpone writing the story, whereupon his toothache returned more painful than before. He prayed again to Saint Feodosii for a cure, this time without promising him anything in return, and once again the saint healed him and the pain passed.

Months went by and the priest had still failed to make good on his promise to Feodosii. In September 1889, while traveling to a nearby village to perform a funeral and a baptism, Rossinskii was seized by a terrible headache, which lasted for days. In his agony he prayed once again to Feodosii, but this time the saint ignored his prayers and the pain remained. Sensing that the saint was upset with him, Rossinskii prayed to Saint Nicholas the Wonder-Worker, asking him to intercede on his behalf and convey his apologies to Saint Feodosii. Saint Nicholas's mediation appears to have been unsuccessful. That night, the priest dreamed he was standing before a shadowy figure sitting in an armchair in the middle of a dimly lit room. "Though I couldn't see his face," Rossinskii recalled, he was certain that it was Feodosii himself. His suspicions were confirmed when the figure began to upbraid him for not fulfilling his earlier promises. The next morning, he woke up with the firm resolve to recite prayers to Feodosii every day, to donate a small sum toward the "adornment of the Prelate's grave," and finally, to write the long-awaited miracle story.

Yet the priest—who should have known better, all things considered—still postponed putting his promise into action. In March 1890 Feodosii appeared to him once again in a dream and was decidedly standoffish. It was only after some pleading that Rossinskii could coax a blessing out of the saint, but even this was done "grudgingly." Two months later, with all of his promises still unfulfilled, the priest dreamed he was standing before Feodosii's open coffin. "[The saint's] face was showing; it seemed full and fresh, as if [he] were only sleeping. His hands seemed white and fresh, made translucent by the blue veins—as if they were the hands of a sleeping man." Rossinskii recalled that he cautiously stepped up to the saint's body, but as he bent down above the coffin, Feodosii sharply turned his head away, snubbing the priest for two and a half years of broken promises. The next morning, fearful that the saint had literally turned his back on him and would withhold his intercession forever, Rossinskii sat down to write the miracle story, including a self-critical account of his own inexcusable foot-dragging and irresponsibility in the affair.[131]

Such cautionary tales invite us to step back and think about how obet figured in the relationship between believers and their saints. Why should Feodosii, Germogen, and their fellow saints care whether the faithful thanked them, came to visit their shrines, or brought them presents? More to the point, why did Orthodox believers think that their saints cared about such matters? These tales of promises pledged and fulfilled speak to the human qualities that Orthodox believers saw in their saints. While the saints were acknowledged to possess miraculous powers that transcended comprehension, believers interacted with them also as human figures with needs, demands, and personal idiosyncrasies. As Peter Brown has argued, the relationships that believers entered into with the holy dead replicated human ties of friendship, loyalty, and obligation.[132] In the Russian Orthodox case, too, where believers and saints interacted intimately and spoke familiarly, believers understood that the continued patronage of their heavenly friends was dependent on meeting a set of expectations and requirements.[133] In order to receive miracles from the saints in heaven, believers had to be sure that they performed the proper gestures of respect and thanksgiving toward their bodies and graves on earth.

On the occasion of the two-hundredth anniversary of Saint Feodosii Chernigovskii's "blessed passing," a priest in the diocese reminded his parishioners that "through his prayers, [Feodosii] brings down the grace of God in abundant miraculous cures and speedy help to all who seek his intercession. He is the heavenly protector of Chernigov, to whom all sorts of people come every day, as to a father for advice, with prayers for their spiritual and daily needs."[134] The cleric's audience would have needed little reminding. As Kremleva has aptly observed, "constant appeal to the world of the saints was the norm for the believing person."[135] As we have seen, however, there were certain standards and practices that governed how believers lodged these appeals with their saintly champions. While the "spiritual hearing" of the saints was such that believers could speak to them and ask favors from the comfort of their own homes, Orthodox devotional practices were concentrated largely around the saint's grave, where the miracle-working power inherent in the saint's holy body was most immediate and most powerful. By kissing holy relics, touching saintly shrines, anointing themselves with oil from a saint's lanterns, or even drinking it, believers sought physical contact with the saint as the most immediate means to absorb and obtain his miraculous powers.

That Orthodox believers felt no qualms about trying on saintly slippers or donning the mitres of sainted prelates speaks not only to the miraculous efficacy they ascribed to such practices but also to the comfort and familiarity that the faithful felt in the presence of their holy friends. As we have seen, however, these miraculous favors did not come free of charge. Believers recognized the responsibility incumbent on them to render thanks for miracles received, to repay the debts they owed to the saints by frequenting the graves where they lived, offering them praise and worship, and bringing them gifts and donations. Russian Orthodox believers imagined their relationship with the saints as both intimate and personal, yet simultaneously bound up with requirements and obligations that had to be met in order to ensure the continued favor of one's saintly protectors.

While prescriptive Church texts exhorted pilgrims and readers to contemplate the uncorrupted bodies of the saints as signs that spoke to the truths of bodily resurrection and the life of the world to come, miracle stories demonstrate that Orthodox individuals focused their energies more on how the holy dead could assist them in coping with sickness, family matters, and the needs of everyday life. Russian Orthodox miracle stories reflect, then, ordinary believers' overarching concern with the pragmatic and the mundane. Individuals who worshiped at saintly shrines did so with very practical goals in mind. While the invocation of the saints through prayer or pilgrimage is, indeed, a "traditional" mode of recourse, it is significant that by the late nineteenth century we find believers also adapting customary practices to meet new needs. The cult of the saints proved wonderfully able to meet the needs of ordinary Orthodox of all estates, men and women alike, as they coped with the exigencies and uncertainties of late imperial life. At the end of the old regime, as saintly résumés expanded to include a variety of new qualifications alongside their tried and true abilities, a saint's expertise was limited only by the imagination of those who sought out his assistance.

3
Making Saints

CANONIZATION AND COMMUNITY

> "When it shall please the Lord God to give glory to
> His saint on earth, then the Lord shall grant unto
> [the saint's] uncorrupted body the power to perform
> healings and miracles. . . . When there accrue many
> instances of grace-given healings from holy relics,
> then all the Orthodox people of that region ask
> their archcleric to open the relics of this Saint [for
> veneration] and to number him among the ranks of
> the saints and to serve *molebny* to him."[1]
>
> —*DUKHOVNAIA BESEDA*, 1913

On 12 June 1909, worshipers and pilgrims from all across the Russian empire assembled on the square facing the Voskresenskii Cathedral in the small provincial town of Kashin, some seventy miles northeast of Tver, to celebrate the ceremonial opening of the holy relics of the newly glorified Orthodox saint, Princess Anna Kashinskaia. Estimates put the crowds at upward of a hundred thousand, more than twelve times the population of Kashin. Metropolitan Vladimir of Moscow blessed the multitudes with holy water and an orchestra played *Kol' slaven* (How glorious is our Lord) to the accompaniment of the cathedral bells, as the jeweled shrine containing Anna's relics, covered in a purple velvet shroud, was borne through the crowds by a retinue of clerics headed by fifteen bishops and eighty archimandrites. A parade line of police and mounted gendarmes from Moscow and Tver attempted to keep order as the sea of worshipers threw white ribbons and scarves into the air and strained to touch the shrine as it made its way into the cathedral. Ticketed guests and invited dignitaries, princes, governors, and bureaucrats from the capital were swiftly ushered into the cathedral for the ceremonies, while thousands of peasants, cripples, and hysterics stood single file in a line that stretched up and down the two main thoroughfares of downtown Kashin, waiting their turn to enter the church and kiss the miracle-working relics of their "little mother." Pilgrims en route to the celebration reported two radiant beams of light shining above the cathedral domes and visible from more than a mile outside of town—a sign interpreted by all in attendance as clear proof of God's favor for this blessed event.[2]

While secular newspapers in Tver gossiped about which royal personages and local celebrities had been spotted at the gala reception that followed the celebration and regaled readers with reports of the fireworks display and outdoor concerts in the city gardens, the religious press waxed poetic on the moral significance of such a rare and wondrous occasion.[3] Anna's canonization was the first celebrated in Russia in nearly six years, and only the fifth since the beginning of the nineteenth century. What made 12 June 1909 even more remarkable, however, was that Anna had been through the process once before. Demoted by order of the Church Council of 1678, Anna Kashinskaia was reinstated to the ranks of the saints by the Holy Synod in 1908 and her veneration officially reintroduced the following year, thus making her the first (and, to date, only) saint to be, in effect, re-canonized by the Russian Orthodox Church.

The question of just how saints were "made" in imperial Russia has been somewhat contended in the literature. Although the word "canonization" is commonly used to describe the process whereby holy men and women receive official recognition of their sanctity from an institutional church, it should be noted that the Russian Orthodox concept differs somewhat from the more rigorous and formalized system that developed over many centuries in the Roman Catholic Church. In the 1890s Golubinskii explained that, while the Roman Church spoke of the "canonization of saints" (*kanonizatsiia sviatykh*), the more common Orthodox designation for the process was "numbering [one] among the ranks of the saints" (*prichtenie k liku sviatykh*).[4] In other words, the Russian Church claimed that it did not "make" saints so much as it recognized them, giving sanction to the veneration on earth of men and women to whom God had already granted glory in heaven. In the official formulation, then, God Himself makes saints, and the role of the Church and the faithful is restricted to one of reiteration—acknowledging in the visible world that which has already been resolved in the world unseen, namely, that the candidate in question is undoubtedly a saint who stands at the throne of God.[5]

Theology aside, however, human beings make saints, and for very human reasons. Although the Russian Orthodox Church had been reluctant to recognize new saints throughout the eighteenth and nineteenth centuries, the reign of Nicholas II witnessed a sudden surge in the number of holy dead all across the Russian empire, beginning with the canonization of Saint Feodosii Chernigovskii in 1896. In all, the Holy Synod and the emperor sanctioned a total of seven canonizations during the last two decades of

Romanov rule, as compared with only four in the preceding two centuries. Not since the Muscovite period had the Russian Church produced as many saints in so short a time. By the time the Bolsheviks came to power in 1917, the cases of at least half a dozen more saintly candidates had been brought for consideration before the Church Sobor.[6]

Gregory Freeze has put forward a convincing argument that the flurry of canonizations under Nicholas II should be viewed in the context of the last emperor's efforts to find a usable national myth that could galvanize and unite an increasingly fractured polity while bolstering the monarchy's faded charisma. Although Nicholas's personal participation at some of these ceremonies was, in part, an expression of the monarch's genuine piety, the presence of the emperor and his entourage was also a political gesture intended to "reify the mythic union of tsar and people from all classes and all regions" and forestall any further "erosion" of autocratic legitimacy. The highly stylized and ritualistic nature of these canonization ceremonies has prompted Freeze to dub them "great social dramas of religious politics," whose choreographers sought to revitalize the ailing body politic by associating it with the miraculous uncorrupted bodies and holy relics of the newly elevated saints.[7]

These very visible attempts to re-sacralize the autocracy were, however, largely unsuccessful. Try as it might, the ruling dynasty was unable to co-opt or capitalize on the air of sanctity that surrounded the holy relics of God's saints. The reasons go beyond the personal shortcomings of Nicholas himself and his high-handed disregard for the proper procedure of canon law. Sanctity failed to transfer on a national level—and missed the emperor's person entirely—because the saints were, ultimately, too closely bound to specific localities. The saints functioned first and foremost as local heroes, protectors, champions, and friends. As we saw in Chapter Two, the miracles that the saints worked for the living were focused around the sites where their holy relics resided, and these latter were the most direct conduits through which believers could channel the power of the divine. Removed from the local soil in which their cults had flourished to be suddenly transplanted and repackaged as saviors of the nation, new saints tended to perform poorly. As Richard Wortman notes, even so prominent and popularly revered a holy man as the recently canonized Serafim Sarovskii "proved a total failure" at mobilizing Russian troops to fight the Japanese at Port Arthur. The soldiers, it seems, could not rally round a saint whose face they did not recognize and with whose résumé of miraculous intercession they were unfamiliar.[8]

This chapter examines canonization procedure from the bottom up, with particular attention to the role played by ordinary believers and communities in inventing, perpetuating, and promoting the cults of local saints at the end of the imperial period. My focus here is on the cults of Anna

Kashinskaia in Tver Province and the Siberian miracle-worker Sofronii Irkutskii—two saints with distinguished records of miraculous intercession, but who lacked uncorrupted relics (*netlennye moshchi*). For individuals, reporting miracles to parish priests and diocesan canonization committees in support of their candidates' causes were acts of reciprocity performed po obetu, gestures of gratitude offered in exchange for favors and miracles granted to them, to their families and the local Orthodox community more broadly. Similar sentiments of sacred duty and reciprocal obligation were expressed also in the resolutions of the city dumas, confraternities, and provincial zemstvo organizations, whose members joined their voices to the call for canonization and worked tirelessly to form committees, draft petitions, secure signatures, and lobby patrons in St. Petersburg on their candidates' behalf. To focus on the local dimension of sanctity shifts the narrative of late imperial canonization away from the cloakrooms of the Holy Synod and courtly politics of the capital and back to the local communities where the saints and their relics had been revered for generations. Locally revered miracle-workers had histories of their own, well before their causes came before the Synod and the emperor. In late imperial Russia, canonization began at home.

Making, Unmaking, and Remaking Saints

THE CASE OF ANNA KASHINSKAIA

Princess Anna Kashinskaia, widow of the martyred Grand Prince Mikhail Iaroslavovich, died in 1368 at the close of a most pious life. The earliest evidence for her veneration dates to the Time of Troubles. In 1611, nearly 250 years after her death, the Princess Anna was said to have appeared in a dream to a man named Gerasim, the ailing sacristan of the Uspenskii Cathedral in Kashin. Dressed in the robes of a *skhimonakh* nun (the highest and most austere rank of female religious orders) and calling herself only Anna, the princess rebuked Gerasim and his fellow townspeople for failing to render due reverence to herself and her relics:

> My grave is ignored by the narod, you people consider it to be but an ordinary thing, and you hold me in disdain. [People] fling their hats upon my grave, they sit atop it, and no one forbids them this. . . . Do you not know that I pray to the All-Merciful God and the Mother of God so that your city may not fall into the hands of your enemies, and that I preserve you all from many evils and calamities?[9]

Anna then proceeded to give Gerasim instructions for the care and well-being of her grave, which over centuries of neglect had begun to rise up from beneath the cracked and broken floorboards of the wooden cathedral, and entrusted the sacristan with relaying her message to his fellow clergymen. When Gerasim rose from his sickbed, he discovered that his illness had passed and duly informed the prior of the cathedral that the dilapidated stone grave was no common hat rack but the resting place of a proven miracle-worker.[10]

Like other dead bodies rediscovered in seventeenth-century Tver diocese and across Muscovy, Anna swiftly became the object of popular veneration.[11] In light of Gerasim's miraculous recovery and the town's recent deliverance from invading Polish and Lithuanian armies, the Orthodox faithful, encouraged by the episcopal elite in Tver, were inclined to credit these wondrous occurrences to some unseen supernatural force protecting Kashin and its residents.[12] Shortly thereafter, panikhidy were being performed regularly at Anna's grave, now tidied up and adorned with candles and icon lamps left by the sick and crippled who came to touch the princess's coffin in hopes of a cure. Thirty years and eight miracles later, the clergy of the Uspenskii Cathedral saw fit to bring their local healer to the attention of Tsar Aleksei Mikhailovich, who relished the discovery of new miracle-workers.[13] In 1649 the tsar ordered Archbishop Iona of Tver and two Moscow monks to inspect Anna's relics and report on their condition. When the princess's body was discovered to be in a state of divinely ordained incorruptibility, measures were taken for Anna's canonization. A zhitie of the soon-to-be saint was commissioned from a local deacon, and a liturgical church service to be sung in her honor on her feast days was written by the Kievan monk and scholar Epifanii Slavinetskii.[14] That same year, a council of Orthodox bishops proclaimed Anna's canonization, and on 12 June 1650, Tsar Aleksei himself traveled to Kashin and helped shoulder the coffin containing the princess's relics as it was borne in procession through the city streets from the Uspenskii Cathedral to the more lavishly appointed Voskresenskii Cathedral. The ceremonial translation of the princess's relics (*perenesenie*) and their *okrytie* marked Anna Kashinskaia's official elevation to the ranks of the saints.

Anna's saintly status was to prove short-lived. Following the Church Schism of the 1660s, Patriarch Ioakim harbored a hostile suspicion toward any rituals and practices not in compliance with the liturgical reforms of his predecessor, Nikon. When rumors reached Moscow that Anna Kashinskaia's right hand was bent into the shape of the Old Believers' two fingered cross (*dvuperstie*), the patriarch dispatched a clerical commission to investigate the matter. Arriving in Kashin in February 1677, the delegation, headed by Metropolitan Iosif of Riazan, launched a thorough investigation of Anna's relics, her zhitie, and the collection of miracle stories that had served as the basis for her canonization more than two decades earlier. The commission discovered a total of thirteen instances in which the zhitie failed to correspond to events and details given in the chronicle accounts of Anna's life and death. Most of these inconsistencies were minor, but some were more troubling than others.[15] When pressed by the commission, the author of the zhitie replied that he had simply written down the stories and biographical details supplied him by the locals of Kashin (all of whom lived 250 years after the princess's death).[16] To cast further suspicion on Anna's cause, the visiting commission found another dozen inconsistencies in the miracle cures attributed to her. The third and final strike against her came when the commission members opened Anna's shrine for examination and discovered that the saint's body was in far worse shape than the zhitie would lead one to believe; not only had the princess's chasuble and vestments rotted away but her body itself had undergone corruption.[17]

After reviewing the commission's findings, Ioakim convened a preliminary council of all Orthodox hierarchs then present in Moscow. The council resolved that the discrepancies and inconsistencies surrounding Anna's sanctity were serious enough to warrant demotion—especially in light of the saint's apparent endorsement of the two-fingered cross. Anna's grave was ordered sealed pending further notice; her feast days were henceforth to go uncelebrated; the divine liturgy was not to be performed in the chapel church consecrated in her honor; finally, and most tellingly, the special prayers of praise sung to a saint (molebny) were to be replaced by the ordinary requiem prayers (panikhidy) rendered to any deceased Orthodox Christian.[18] In January 1678, a full council upheld the preliminary resolutions of the previous year. The Archbishop of Tver was instructed to collect all of Anna's icons from the diocese and send them to Moscow. The reading of her zhitie was forbidden in churches, along with the celebration of any prayer services in her honor. Evoking the statutes of the Sixth Ecumenical Council, the delegates threatened with excommunication any lay faithful or cleric who continued to revere the former saint, warning that "if anyone has in his possession images of the pious princess Anna, or her zhitie or hymnals, let him bring them to the Most Holy Patriarch or to any of his archclerics, lest he be under the anathema of the holy fathers."[19] Thus, less than thirty years after her canonization, the veneration of Anna Kashinskaia was officially proscribed, her relics sealed to would-be worshipers, and her name struck from the rolls of the Russian Orthodox saints.[20]

While prelates and patriarchs could issue thunderous injunctions against Anna's cult, the Muscovite Church was institutionally ill-equipped to prevent manifestations of popular devotion.[21] Nineteenth-century sources note that although the news of Anna's demotion was met with bitterness and sorrow by believers in Tver diocese, her veneration continued unabated in and around Kashin. By the turn of the twentieth century, a clerical author remarked with evident satisfaction that the Orthodox faithful of Kashin had never lost faith in their saint:

> Two hundred and thirty years have passed from the time of the Council's deliberations, but among the residents of the city and the surrounding districts the memory of the pious princess, the veneration of her sainted remains and of this [place], the site of her deeds, did not cease even for a single day. All the feast days in her honor are celebrated joyously, in every peasant hut her icon stands alongside those of the other saints, and it is the rare house in town that does not have an icon of the pious princess Anna. Parents bless their children with this icon both at weddings and on the sickbed.[22]

A contemporary source concurred, observing that though "not a single church service had been performed in [Anna's] honor" for over two centuries, devotion to the princess was "deeply widespread" among the local Orthodox population.[23] A popular dictionary of saints that went through multiple printings in the mid-nineteenth century not only included an entry on Anna Kashinskaia, with no mention of her demotion, but stated matter-of-factly that "the memory of the Pious Princess Anna is celebrated locally on 2 October."[24]

Thus while Church hierarchs in Moscow could outlaw the singing of molebny at Anna's grave, they could not prevent the Orthodox laity and clergy of Kashin from continuing to honor her memory through extraliturgical means. Believers continued to seek miracles and healing cures at her shrine throughout the nineteenth century—a matter of no small importance in a town that could claim only one hospital and a mere thirty beds by the turn of the twentieth century.[25] According to a 1907 article in the popular journal *Pravoslavnyi sobesednik* (The Orthodox conversationalist), the relationship between the Orthodox of Kashin and Saint Anna extended beyond the liturgical space of the church proper to encompass nearly every aspect of town life: "In her honor, names are given to little girls at holy baptism. In days of rejoicing and in times of hardship, the pious citizenry of Kashin hurry with prayers to their protectress, for the town of Kashin is said to be the town of the pious princess Anna. Newlyweds are blessed with icons bearing her image. Those who desire to take monastic vows pray passionately before her."[26]

At the beginning of each school year, parents brought their children to the Voskresenskii Cathedral to pray at Anna's shrine for saintly help with their studies. Businessmen and merchants in the town and district would commonly swear sacred oaths in Anna's name before entering into contracts or binding agreements.[27] Miracle stories depict men and women of all estates praying to Anna for help in money matters or for assistance in finding work, either in town or outside the city—no small concern at the end of the nineteenth century as Kashin's local textile industry went into decline.[28] As one author explained, "The name of the pious [princess] is with the local residents from cradle to grave."[29]

The grace and heavenly assistance of "little mother Anna" were, in theory, available to all Orthodox, men and women, who sought her help in prayer. But Anna appears to have possessed a special spiritual resonance for Orthodox women in Tver diocese. The majority of the thirty miracles attributed to Anna and recorded by the Tver diocesan consistory from 1897 to 1909 were reported by women (or, in some cases, by fathers or husbands on behalf of their healed daughters or wives).[30] Anna was such a popular name for young girls in the vicinity of Kashin that one observer counted more than thirty Annas in one small village in Kashinskii district alone. Annas in the region celebrated their name days on either one of the two principal feast days dedicated to the saint's memory: some on 2 October (the date of Anna's "blessed end"), others on 12 June (the feast day marking the translation of Anna's holy relics in 1650), and most alternating between the two dates from year to year.[31]

The special affinity that Orthodox women displayed for Anna Kashinskaia may have had something to do with the gender-specific way in which Church sources and ordinary believers talked about the princess saint's particular love for the people of Kashin. As her re-canonization drew near, the diocesan and provincial press published a number of articles and biographical sketches of Anna that emphasized her role as loving mother, faithful wife, and exemplar of feminine piety. The Tver diocesan press described Anna as "the very image of a Christian woman . . . a loving, suffering woman, ready to sacrifice her strength and means for the well-being of those near to her."[32] One popular religious writer extolled Anna's tearful farewell to her husband, en route to the court of the Mongol khan and martyrdom, as "the apotheosis of the Russian woman"—a combination of unconditional love and a resigned endurance to God's will.[33] Church sources explicitly singled her out as a patron saint of the married life: "All who are unhappy in marriage find help at the holy relics of Anna Kashinskaia; the saint persistently obtains from God the blessing of a quiet and peaceful married life, the blessing of 'counsel and love' between men and women."[34]

Stories of Anna's love and protection for the Orthodox faithful of Kashin (see Figure 4) extended beyond individuals to encompass the entire community, serving as a central myth that bound the community together and provided a sense of local identity. Tradition credited Saint Anna with having intervened to save her town and people countless times over the centuries, first from Lithuanian invaders during the Time of Troubles. Anna's expertise expanded over the nineteenth century, not only helping to fend off the French in 1812 but staving off cholera epidemics in 1831 and 1848.[35] The special relationship between the town and its saint continued to operate into the early twentieth century. Certain "pious citizens," for example, were inclined to believe that "the prayers and protection of the devout princess Anna" had spared the town from upheaval and revolution during the "troubled years" of 1905–1906.[36]

FIGURE 4—View of Kashin from the bridge of the Dmitrovskii monastery, 1910. Library of Congress, Prints & Photographs Division, Prokudin-Gorskii Collection, LC-DIG-prok-02333 DLC.

In return for such loving care, the Orthodox of Kashin felt obliged to repay the favor when needed. In 1860, for example, when a diocesan committee in Tver recommended that the number of parishes in Kashin be downsized (judging that nineteen parishes were far too many for a city with a population barely over seventy-three hundred), the public outcry was immediate: "It is impossible that a single parish be closed, *the pious princess Anna will not forgive us.* She helps us so much. We will provide the moneys for the maintenance of the churches and the parish clergy in perpetuity and we will thus preserve all the parishes intact."[37] The petitioners thought it an unspeakable affront to the dignity of their local patron saint if they allowed so-called outsiders to close down one of their "own" parishes. Being the recipients of Anna's assistance carried with it also the reciprocal obligation of protecting the saint's interests and defending her honor as needed.

If Anna herself stood as a symbol and reminder of Orthodox Kashin's special relationship with the divine, her shrine and relics were the central point around which this community cohered. In everyday speech, for example, citizens of Kashin commonly referred to the Voskresenskii Cathedral where Anna's relics were housed as "the princess's cathedral." One source reports that "it was not uncommon to hear: I'm going to the Pious Princess's for the vigil service. . . . I just came from the Pious Princess's. . . . We'll be married at the Pious Princess's."[38] By the late nineteenth century, Anna's memory was celebrated on four different feast days, observed as public holidays in the town and surrounding districts. The grand religious processions staged on these feast days—with the clergy and laity of all estates marching through the city streets bearing icons and banners with Anna's likeness—not only satisfied the religious needs of individuals but served also to sacralize the community's civic and public space.[39] In 1899 the city fathers banned all commercial activity and trading during these processions, and in 1907 the city duma successfully petitioned the Ministry of Education to let children have the day off from school on 17 November so that they, too, could participate in the festivities.[40]

Civic organizations also sought to affiliate themselves with the community's sacred champion. In 1899, for instance, the Kashin city volunteer fire brigade passed a resolution designating 12 June as its annual holiday, a date chosen to coincide with the anniversary of the translation of Anna's relics.[41] When prominent personages and members of the royal family passed through Tver, provincial authorities would often go out of their way to organize an excursion to Kashin so that the visitors could worship at the shrine of Anna Kashinskaia. Such spiritual sightseeing was a matter not just of religious devotion but of civic pride.[42] So too were the icons of Anna often handed out as gifts by the governors of Tver Province to commemorate special occasions or anniversaries. In 1883, for example, Alexander III and Mariia Feodorovna received an icon of Anna Kashinskaia to mark their coronation. In 1900 the Moscow Dragoons Regiment was presented with a similar icon on the occasion of the two-hundredth anniversary of its founding.[43] In 1908, when a delegation of dignitaries from Kashin traveled to St. Petersburg to petition the tsar and Synod for Anna's restoration to the ranks of the saints, they brought with them an "ancient" icon of Anna Kashinskaia to give to Nicholas II.[44] Although such gestures can be seen, of course, in the context of the turn-of-the-century trend toward historicizing Russia's glorious past, they are reflective of the degree to which individuals and organizations in Kashin (and Tver Province more broadly) consciously sought to identify themselves with the image and reputation of their local saint.[45] By the late nineteenth century, Anna Kashinskaia was the symbol not only of Kashin's Orthodox faith but of the community's very identity. Nothing "said" Kashin more than its local miracle-worker and champion.

Anna's relics had been charred in a church fire in 1711, an unfortunate accident that Orthodox commentators attributed to "spiritual carelessness and negligence on the part of us sinful humans." Although her relics could no longer be spoken of as "uncorrupted," miracles continued to be reported at her shrine.[46] The miracle stories submitted by the faithful of Kashin and the surrounding districts in support of Anna's re-canonization demonstrate how average believers described their relationship with Anna as one based on intimate friendship and bound by close ties of place. The tale of a seventy-seven-year-old townswoman from Kashin, Liubov' Gavrilovna Feodorova, is a case in point. In June 1908, as the question of Anna's official recognition was being raised with great excitement in the city duma and provincial zemstvo organizations, Feodorova was busy planning a summer pilgrimage. After narrowing her choices to either the Troitskaia Lavra or the shrine of Saint Makarii at the nearby Kaliazinskii monastery, southeast of town, Feodorova decided to sleep on it. In her dreams that night, she imagined herself standing before Anna Kashinskaia's shrine in the Voskresenskii Cathedral. Seeing that the shrine was open, Feodorova bent down to kiss the saint's hand. Suddenly, Anna's hand turned warm and the saint said to her in a clear voice: "Pray here" (*Moli zdes'*). When she woke in the morning, Feodorova resolved to cancel her travel plans and follow Anna's advice. In a letter written that same month to Father Ioann Amenitskii, the prior of the Blagoveshchenskii Cathedral and an ardent collector of Anna's miracle stories, Feodorova swore she was telling "the holy truth" and reported that she now attended the regular vigil services at Anna's shrine "with joy in [her] spirit."[47]

Another miracle story submitted in 1909 tells of a young married student, Nikolai Ivanovich Prokhorov, who feared that the "tight conditions" of his financial situation would force him and his wife to give up their rented house in Kashin and move in with his father, some twenty miles away. When Prokhorov told his wife that this would mean they might miss Anna's re-canonization ceremonies that summer, she exploded with rage: "What's the matter with you, Kolya? Other pilgrims will be coming in droves from other provinces, and we can't be troubled with a distance of just some thirty versts? Will we really not be able to find a place to stay?" That night, Nikolai dreamed he was in the cathedral, standing before Anna's shrine. He described a great longing to reach down and touch her relics, but shrunk back "with pain in my heart . . . since at that moment I was not pure enough of body to touch the shrine." In the second half of his dream, Nikolai found himself sitting in a room with his wife, his parents, and his sisters when Anna Kashinskaia walked in, clad in white robes, "radiant and robust, though an old woman." Nikolai fell to his knees to beg the saint's pardon for not kissing her relics: "Little mother, Saint Princess Anna, forgive me, a sinner, and have mercy." Anna flashed a "bright and tender smile" and told Nikolai that she was touched by the discretion he had shown and the "sincere grief" he now felt. She bid him rise and, as Nikolai later described in his letter to Father Amenitskii, said that "she had come to tell me that I 'must' be present during the glorification of Her Holy Relics, 'for which,' she said, 'I have waited for so long.'" Nikolai promised Anna that he would be in Kashin without fail, whereupon the saint vanished "like a shadow."[48]

In a letter to Father Amenitskii dated 9 April 1909, Aleksandra Irodova—the wife of a church elder in the town of Bezhetsk, some forty-five miles northwest of Kashin—described the miraculous cure of her two-year-old daughter from pneumonia. Doctors pronounced the child's case as grave and suggested that, should she recover, she "would be left an idiot forever." Shortly after receiving this dreadful diagnosis Irodova dreamed she was back home, "in Kashin before the relics of the pious Saint Anna." She heard a voice coming from Anna's tomb but was unable to make out the saint's words. Upon waking, she interpreted the mysterious words as a divine summons to call on Anna for help and immediately sent word to her parents in Kashin to go and pray at Anna's shrine for their granddaughter's recovery. "At the same time," she wrote to Amenitskii, "I too turned with prayer to the pious Saint Anna, whose image I had brought from Kashin." As the wife of a church elder, Irodova must have had a whole house full of icons, any one of which could conceivably have done the job. But the ties of family and faith, though stretched somewhat by distance, still bound Irodova to Kashin, and it was to the familiar figure of Anna that the desperate mother, naturally, first turned in prayer. Placing Anna's icon on her sick child, Irodova prayed for a cure. Miraculously, she reported, her daughter recovered fully soon after and suffered no side effects from her serious illness.

As is the case with almost all miracle stories concerning as-yet-uncanonized saints, Irodova claimed it was her responsibility to document and report this miracle and thus provide the Church authorities with further evidence that the candidate saint was deserving of canonization. In the opening paragraph of her letter, Irodova asked Father Amenitskii to make sure that her story was published in the Tver diocesan newspaper. Like other recipients of Anna's miraculous intercession, Irodova felt that publicity was a proper show of thanks for services rendered. As she explained to Amenitskii, it was her Christian duty to share her story with other local believers "for the sake of the glorification of . . . the relics of the pious great princess and for the sake of increasing the faith among the narod."[49]

The submission and publication of miracles like Irodova's played a large role in Anna's eventual re-canonization. So, too, did the support of parish priests, diocesan officials, and provincial administrators, who not only tolerated but even encouraged devotion to Anna's cult. Despite the rulings of Ioakim's council, the cathedral clergy in Kashin continued to keep inventories of miracles attributed to Anna, recording a dozen such miracles in the half century following her demotion.[50] As early as 1728, the city administration in Kashin began submitting regular petitions to the archbishops of Tver for permission to stage religious processions with Anna's icons on her feast days. These petitions were routinely granted.[51] In 1817, for example, Archbishop Serafim allowed the faithful of Kashin permission to bear Anna's relics in public procession throughout the city streets in preparation for Anna's reinterment in the newly refurbished Voskresenskii Cathedral; the anniversary of this translation, 17 November, became a local holiday celebrated annually in Kashin.[52]

FIGURE 5—At the shrine of Saint Anna Kashinskaia, 1910. Note the hanging lanterns, gifts of donors to mark the saint's re-canonization. Library of Congress, Prints & Photographs Division, Prokudin-Gorskii Collection, LC-DIG-prok-02342 DLC.

Endorsement at the diocesan level went hand in hand with a local grassroots campaign to restore Anna to the ranks of the saints. In 1853 the rural gentry of Kashinskii district secured over two hundred signatures to a petition requesting the Synod to authorize the singing of molebny to Anna at her shrine (see Figure 5). Because Orthodox canon law stipulated that only saints designated for all-Church veneration could receive molebny, this petition was in effect tantamount to asking that the Synod reverse the rulings of the 1678 Council and re-canonize Anna. When this effort met with failure, in 1859 a second petition was drafted, this time with the support of Archbishop Filofei and submitted directly to the new emperor, Alexander II. The over-procurator of the Holy Synod, A. P. Tolstoi, consulted Metropolitan Filaret of Moscow for his opinion on the matter. After careful study of the 1678 resolutions, Filaret concluded that the council's rulings still held force until such time as God should "see fit to glorify the pious princess Anna by signs"—that is, miracles. Undeterred, in 1861 the citizens of Kashin sent a third petition to the ranking member of the Synod, Metropolitan Grigorii of St. Petersburg, this time pointedly referring to blatant inconsistencies in synodal policy. The petitioners noted that even though the Orthodox Church had never canonized Prince Daniil Aleksandrovich, molebny were regularly sung to him at his shrine in the Danilovskii monastery in Moscow, and that the Great Princess Evdokiia—like Anna, a victim of the Ioakim crackdowns—enjoyed similar favor at the Voznesenskii monastery. If the petitioners hoped that Grigorii, a former archbishop of Tver, would display some sympathies toward the cause of a local holy woman from his old see, they were mistaken. Once again the Synod reiterated the conciliar position of 1678, and the matter was dropped.[53]

Although Synod members in distant Petersburg remained unreceptive to calls for Anna's reinstatement, diocesan officials in Tver increasingly embraced the saint's cause and encouraged her devotion among the Orthodox laity. In the second half of the nineteenth century, three successive archbishops of Tver made a point of including Anna's name in the divine liturgy, both during the benediction prayer blessing the bread and wine (*litiia*) and in the concluding prayer of commendation to the faithful (*otpust*).[54] Priests and prelates in Tver diocese routinely dodged the restriction on performing molebny to Anna by singing services "to all the saints" and then including Anna's name at the close of the prayer: "Venerable Mother Anna, pray to God for us."[55] After Metropolitan Filaret's suggestion that documented miracles would demonstrate whether God possessed special favor for Anna, Archbishop Dmitrii instructed the ecclesiastical superintendents of the diocese to once again begin collecting miracle stories concerning Anna. In the decade from 1899 to 1909, thirty miracle stories were collected and archived by Father Amenitskii at the Voskresenskii Cathedral, as compared with a total of forty over the course of the entire preceding century.[56]

While eighteenth-century petitioners had sought permission from their bishop to stage religious processions in town, nineteenth-century petitions addressed to the Synod and the emperor himself sought nothing less than the full restoration of Anna's saintly status. Not only did supporters set larger objectives for themselves, but from the middle of the nineteenth century the social base of support for Anna's cause broadened as well, both in Kashin and across the diocese of Tver. The earlier petitions from city officials and provincial noblemen had given way, by century's end, to appeals from more socially diverse and inclusive bodies and organizations—civic associations, district zemstvos, and municipal dumas. The institutional structures created by the Great Reforms thus played a key role in mobilizing the Orthodox populace as the movement for Anna's re-canonization spread beyond parish walls and gentry palaces and into the public sphere.

In May 1908, in an address to the Kashin city duma, I. Ia. Kunkin, a member of the Tver Scholarly Archival Commission and a longtime supporter of Anna's cause, posed the question: "Has the time not come for the restoration of full liturgical veneration for the pious princess Anna Kashinskaia?" The duma members were sympathetic to Kunkin's arguments but voted to table any discussion until August, when the delegates were to reconvene following the summer holidays. Kunkin then appealed directly to the mayor who, in turn, called for an extraordinary session of the city duma on 19 June. Once spurred into action, the duma voted unanimously to accept Kunkin's proposal and appointed a committee to travel to St. Petersburg and directly petition the emperor and the Synod in person. Within weeks, the Kashin district zemstvo had seconded the city duma's motion, and the marshal of the nobility for the district had also come out in support of the measure. Later that month, the entire clergy of Kashin city and representatives from the rural parishes met in a Kashin schoolhouse to discuss the question. Chaired by the vicar bishop Aleksandr, the assembly voted to support the efforts of the city duma and zemstvo and resolved to use sermons and homilies to keep their parishioners informed of developments as they unfolded. In the provincial center of Tver, members of the municipal lay confraternities and brotherhoods named for Prince Saint Mikhail, anxious that their patron's wife should join her spouse in the rolls of the saints, joined parish priests in the city and spoke out in favor of Anna's cause. A district-wide meeting of lay church sextons in Kashin on 8 July pledged its support as well. Within two days, delegates had set up tables in the vestibule of the Voskresenskii Cathedral to distribute pamphlets and brochures on the life and miracles of Anna and to collect signatures from worshipers in support of her canonization. Meanwhile, in St. Petersburg, the duma delegation met daily with Archbishop Aleksii of Tver (a member of the Holy Synod) to discuss possible strategies for the realization of their common goal.[57]

After decades of dead ends and terse refusals, Anna's cause was making remarkable headway in the summer of 1908. In July Metropolitan Antonii, the ranking member of the Holy Synod, put the question before a congress of thirty bishops assembled in Kiev, perhaps as a way of testing the waters and gauging the opinion of hierarchs with no ties to Tver diocese. The congress of bishops voted unanimously to support the effort and noted with approval that "the special faith in the sanctity of the pious great princess Anna Kashinskaia remains unshakeable in the Tver region and far beyond its borders to the present day, passed down from generation to generation, from age to age, fortified by the numerous signs and miracles that issue forth from her holy remains." That same month, delegates to the Fourth All-Russian Missionary Congress, also meeting in Kiev, discussed the possibility of Anna's impending canonization, and voted to support the process by whatever means lay at their disposal.[58]

On 30 October 1908, the Holy Synod announced its decision. In what amounted to a complete reversal of its long-held position, the Synod declared that, having considered "the constant and numerous petitions from those who most piously venerate the memory" of Anna Kashinskaia and in view of the "unceasing miracles and healings [performed] through her prayerful intercession," its members now "deemed it proper and fitting to restore liturgical veneration of the pious great princess Anna as a saint, as was so prior to the Moscow Council of 1677."[59] On 7 November, Nicholas II gave his written consent to the Synod's resolution with a tersely worded "Agreed" (*Soglasen*).[60] At the Kashin delegation's request, the date for the public presentation of Saint Anna's relics was set for 12 June 1909, the anniversary of the first translation of Anna's relics by Tsar Aleksei Mikhailovich in 1650.[61] After 230 years, the "little mother" of Kashin, Anna Kashinskaia, was once again a saint of the Russian Orthodox Church.

The Tver diocesan press reported that "a great lively bustling began in the town" as soon as news of the Synod's decision reached Kashin. "People everywhere in the streets, an unusual flurry of carriages and horse-drawn cabs, radiant joy on the faces of all."[62] The Orthodox residents of the town and province were aware that they had played a leading role in the official restoration of their hometown miracle-worker. In an address to the town of Kashin, the members of the Tver city duma described the festivities as an occasion for "general joy" across the province and announced the commission of a silver icon lantern to hang above Anna's shrine in perpetual commemoration of the historic event. "We rejoice," the delegates declared, "along with the residents of the town of Kashin that [we] and all Orthodox have been given the opportunity once more to turn in prayer to the Sainted Protectress of the town and of the Tver region."[63]

A New Saint for Siberia

THE CASE OF SOFRONII IRKUTSKII

Following two centuries of official, though largely unenforced, proscription Anna was now seemingly everywhere. By year's end, the first new church dedicated in her honor was consecrated in an industrial district on the Vyborg side of St. Petersburg, with a second church appearing in the capital in 1910.[64] Icon workshops in Kashin and Moscow began producing images of Anna in great quantities and taking out large notices in *Tserkovnyia vedomosti* (The church gazette) to advertise their hand-painted images of the princess to a nationwide audience. "Work of the highest craftsmanship," a local firm boasted, "delivered on request to all cities and towns in the Russian empire (Blessed at the shrine containing her relics, at the purchaser's request)." Prices started from twenty rubles, though wealthier devotees could spend upward of eight times as much on more elaborate cypress-wood models adorned with gold paint and enamel engraving. Capitalizing on the princess's newfound fame, one entrepreneurial firm in Chernigov even offered 25 percent discounts to customers who bought a matching set of icons featuring Anna and her husband, Prince Saint Mikhail.[65]

The princess turned up even as far away as eastern Siberia. On 1 August 1910, after nearly a week's worth of deliberating how best to enlighten the souls of the native peoples of Siberia, the delegates to the Irkutsk Missionary Congress declared a recess so that they could attend a special service at the Kazanskii Cathedral. After the celebration of the divine liturgy by Archbishop Makarii of Tomsk, the delegates followed the archbishop out into the cathedral square, where they greeted a procession of clerics and lay believers bearing with them a chest containing fragments of Anna Kashinskaia's holy relics. Archpriest Ioann Vostorgov, a prolific Orthodox publicist, harangued the crowds with a lengthy speech on the significance of Anna's life and the moral lessons that the Siberian faithful could learn from her example. With every church bell in the city ringing, it must have been difficult for even this experienced orator to make himself heard above the clamor. The believers who packed the square, however, had not turned out to listen to lectures but to witness the arrival in their town of Anna Kashinskaia, whose reputation as a powerful patron preceded her. One delegate from the congress joyously predicted that the celebration would serve as an overdue summons for the spiritually slothful believers of Irkutsk: "The ceremony roused and awakened Irkutsk society, and they will be talking about it for a long, long time to come."[66]

Siberia had a poor reputation for piety at the end of the old regime, and religious leaders fretted that their flock was much in need of spiritual renewal. A 1912 study commissioned by the newspaper *Sibir'* (Siberia) revealed the unsettling statistic that Irkutsk ranked first in drunkenness among seventy provinces and oblasts in the empire, much to the embarrassment of its archbishop.[67] Church officials and lay brotherhoods scrambled to construct churches and establish functioning parishes in order to meet the general religious needs of the thousands of new arrivals who yearly made the long and difficult trek to Siberia; church construction, however, could not keep up with the growing population.[68] Saints were in such short supply in the vast Siberian expanse that the Holy Synod was obliged to ship relic fragments from Kiev and Moscow so that new churches could be consecrated in accordance with canon law.[69] The scarcity of relics and holy men would later prompt the Old Bolshevik and antireligious activist Emel'ian Iaroslavskii to joke that "Siberia has had no luck when it comes to saintliness."[70] In the half-decade preceding the First World War, however, this would soon change. While the elevation of Anna Kashinskaia was being celebrated on the other side of the empire, Orthodox believers in Irkutsk were busily making plans for the canonization of their own saint, the prelate Sofronii Irkutskii, at whose shrine miracles had been reported with increasing regularity for the past half century.

Born in Poltava Province to Ukrainian parents, Sofronii Kristalevskii was, like many of his later devotees, himself an immigrant to Siberia. In 1753 the Synod confirmed his appointment as bishop of Irkutsk at the personal request of the Empress Elizabeth, whose confidence he had earned while serving as her confessor. The new bishop soon found himself at the head of an enormous far-flung diocese encompassing nearly half the land mass of the empire, stretching from the western shores of Lake Baikal northward to the Arctic Sea and all the way east to Kamchatka. Sofronii proved an excellent overseer and spent the next eighteen years training more priests to serve the diocese, opening new religious schools, consecrating churches, and supervising missionary work among the non-Russian native peoples. He died in 1771 at the close of a distinguished career, and his body was laid to rest in the Bogoiavlenskii Cathedral in the city center of Irkutsk.[71] It remained there undisturbed—and largely ignored—for the next sixty years, until in 1833, during restoration work on the cathedral floor, Bishop Meletii took it upon himself to open his predecessor's coffin and examine the contents. The bishop was pleased to discover that Sofronii's body and vestments had been preserved in what he described as a state of divinely ordained incorruptibility, a finding confirmed by three subsequent examinations carried out by the bishops of Irkutsk between 1853 and 1887.[72]

It was during this period that Sofronii's cult began to gain popularity, as the prelate underwent the belated transformation from able administrator to miracle-worker. The very first issue of *Irkutskiia eparkhial'nyia vedomosti* (The Irkutsk diocesan gazette), which appeared in 1863, carried a lengthy biographical essay on Sofronii and his career in Irkutsk, with special attention to the miracles being reported with ever-increasing frequency at the site of his uncorrupted relics. In 1872, convinced now that they had a true saint on their hands, the cathedral clergy began to keep a book of miracles to record all instances of Sofronii's heavenly intercession in the everyday lives of the Irkutsk faithful.[73] Archbishop Veniamin, who presided over the diocese at the end of the nineteenth century, introduced new local holidays into the liturgical calendar to honor the miracle-worker. Annually on 11 March (Sofronii's name day) and again on 30 March (the anniversary of his death), special panikhida services were performed in Sofronii's honor, drawing large crowds to the cathedral.[74] Biographies and printed images of Sofronii flooded the bookstalls and religious shops of Irkutsk. The first five hundred copies of a special four-page booklet on the bishop's life and deeds sold out almost overnight in 1895; another 1,500 copies were swiftly published and eagerly purchased over the next two years, with an additional 5,000 appearing in 1901 to commemorate the 130th anniversary of Sofronii's death. Around this same time, the local artist M. A. Rudchenko began offering mass-produced portraits of the bishop for sale to the faithful. To satisfy the overwhelming demand in the city, the Rudchenko workshops turned out 2,000 paper-and-cardboard images of Sofronii, and another 4,000 on linen and silk.[75]

By 1912 the number of miracles attributed to Sofronii over the past thirty years had already surpassed those of Irkutsk's more senior local saint, Innokentii, and showed no signs of slowing.[76] Sofronii proved so prolific a miracle-worker that from the early twentieth century onward the Irkutsk diocesan press seldom published miracle stories relating to any other saint; where before readers could thrill to the miracles wrought by saints all across the empire, coverage gradually came to concentrate on the activities and intercession of Irkutsk's own hometown saints, Innokentii and Sofronii. This suggests not only that the press was focusing more on Sofronii's miracles but also that local believers, too, were turning with increasing frequency to an accessible and conveniently located saint whose reputation for miracles was on the rise.

As we saw in the preceding chapter, Orthodox believers imagined their saints not as specialists but as general practitioners qualified to treat any number of diseases and sicknesses and to offer solutions to all sorts of human problems. Cases of reported miracles attributed to Sofronii from the turn of the century cover practically every possible ailment, from toothaches, scarlet fever, and diphtheria to chest pains, depression, broken limbs, paralysis, neuralgia, dizzy spells, loss of consciousness, and complications arising from pregnancy.[77] Yet while the prelate proved himself quite skilled in the standard repertoire of miraculous cures and healings, a great many of Sofronii's miracles hinged around the problem of adjusting to a new life in Siberia. With the construction of the Trans-Siberian Railroad and the introduction of the Stolypin land reforms, the early twentieth century witnessed a dramatic rise in population migration across the empire. Siberia, with its ample landholdings and opportunities for personal enrichment, soon outstripped all other regions as the favorite destination for relocation. In 1897–1916, 48.8 percent of all imperial subjects who packed their bags to start a new life in a new location were headed to Siberia. In the period 1907–1911 alone, a total of 1,695,000 men, women, and children arrived in Siberia. These were chiefly land-hungry peasants from the central agricultural region, left-bank Ukraine, and the Volga provinces.[78] Many of these new immigrants settled in Irkutsk, whose population nearly doubled from 51,000 to 90,000 between 1897 and 1917.[79] Though the allure of Siberia was powerful, the real cost of relocation was considerable. In 1912 it was estimated that a family in European Russia would require between three hundred and four hundred rubles to make the move to Irkutsk Province, and at least one hundred more if the family was headed all the way to the Pacific coast.[80]

Thanks to Sofronii, however, Orthodox newcomers to Siberia had recourse to the sacred to ease the difficult transition. From the last quarter of the nineteenth century up until the very end of the old regime, Saint Sofronii served, in essence, as the unofficial welcome wagon for new arrivals in Irkutsk. Miracle stories recorded by the Irkutsk city clergy depict Sofronii helping immigrants—Russians and Cossacks, peasants and townspeople alike—to find lodging and employment and inspiring them to persevere in their new surroundings.[81] A miracle story from 1905, for example, told of how Sofronii's timely intervention saved from suicide a young woman newly arrived in the city. Alone and penniless, with no means of getting home to Tomsk to be at the bedside of her dying father, the distraught woman was on the brink of hurling herself into the Angara River, when a kindly old man appeared before her with words of comfort. "What can you do to help me?" she asked. "I'm not from around here" (*Ia ne zdeshniaia*). "I do not just help my own," the old man replied, "but strangers, too" (*Ia ne vse svoim pomogaiu, no i chuzhim*). He then proceeded to advise the bewildered newcomer how to make optimal use of the city's resources. The old man informed the woman the precise hours when the governor received petitioners; there she could obtain a discounted rail ticket for the journey home. Afterward, he recommended, she should stop by to see the archbishop, who could help provide any incidentals for the trip—"he's a good man, he will assist you." Her tears dried and fears allayed, the young woman asked the man his name and address so she could call on him later and offer proper thanks. He answered, "Ask for Grandpa Sofronii, everyone knows me and everyone will tell you where I live."[82]

When Mikhail Ogorodnikov and his family arrived in Irkutsk in 1877, they too were strangers, with little more than the clothes on their back; all their other possessions had been lost in an accident while crossing the Enisei River. Ogorodnikov later recalled in a letter to the cathedral clergy that they had no one to turn to for help, for "we didn't even know of the relics of the Prelate Sofronii." Soon after, however, the saint introduced himself to the Ogorodnikovs, appearing to one of the daughters in a dream, blessing the family, and offering to help restore their fortunes if in exchange they commissioned an icon with his likeness. "I will give glory to you and raise you up," the saint told them, "if you give glory to me and have my image drawn." The girl told her parents of the dream, but she could not remember the saint's name. Later, when the family made their first trip to worship at the Bogoiavlenskii Cathedral, the girl recognized Sofronii from the icons that hung above his shrine. The family prayed to their new patron for help and were soon able to set aside enough money to have an icon of Sofronii painted for themselves. By 1891, when Ogorodnikov submitted his story to the cathedral clergy, he and his family had prospered and were enjoying a comfortably bourgeois life in the town of Verkholensk, Irkutsk Province—a middle-class miracle that he unreservedly attributed to Sofronii's blessed intercession.[83]

The story of V. A. Petrov, a St. Petersburg native who moved to Irkutsk in the 1890s, illustrates further how new arrivals in Siberia sought Sofronii's help in adjusting to their unfamiliar surroundings. Upon arriving in Irkutsk, Petrov had asked his landlady to tell him everything about the city "and, as an Orthodox, first and foremost about God's holy churches." It was from her, he recalled, "that I first heard of the Prelate Sofronii," whose fame had not yet spread from Siberia to the imperial capital. Petrov decided to enlist the help of Sofronii in his search for a new job. "I stopped by the old cathedral," he recalled, "and prayed at the grave of the Prelate Sofronii, asking him to be my protector and intercessor and to make my life and work in Siberia for the best." One week later, Petrov received word that he had been offered a position in the Chita offices of the Zabaikal railroad company. Overjoyed, he soon returned to the cathedral for another favor, this time to seek Sofronii's assistance in recovering his wife's baggage, which had been lost on the train somewhere near Tomsk. In thanks for this second miracle, Petrov offered a panikhida service to be sung at the prelate's grave and immediately informed the cathedral record-keepers of the favors that had been rendered him: "I feared it a sin to remain silent and so I decided to set everything down, to the glory of the prelate."[84]

Siberian believers who had received the benefits of Sofronii's intercession felt it was their duty to record such instances with the cathedral clergy for "the glory of the prelate" and as a show of thanks for miracles rendered. Feelings of reciprocal obligation allowed believers to forge intimate relationships with Sofronii based on the expectation that the prelate would continue to help them so long as they, in turn, gave him proper credit for his miracles. The result of this, as writers of miracle stories often explained, was that praying to Sofronii became a routine and regular part of their spiritual lives. Indeed, these stories show that once the saint had proven himself powerful enough to grant a miracle, believers would turn to him as a tried and true source time and time again and over the course of many years and across generations. For instance, a 1913 letter from a local merchant published in the Irkutsk diocesan newspaper described how the prelate Sofronii had helped members of his family for three generations; the author's son thanked the saint for healing him from a childhood injury by co-sponsoring a costly renovation project at the cathedral where Sofronii's relics lay.[85]

A mining engineer from Tomsk, A. S. Shakhmaev, wrote to the Irkutsk clergy of how Sofronii had saved him multiple times from the often unforgiving conditions of life in Siberia. The prelate reportedly first rescued Shakhmaev from sliding off a snowy precipice while his team was surveying for coal and oil deposits east of Lake Baikal in 1899. Ten years later, when Shakhmaev's house burned to the ground, Sofronii again came to the engineer's assistance, preserving from the flames a bundle of papers containing invaluable maps and plans of the Sakhalin oil fields. One of the few items to survive the blaze intact was a silk-screen portrait of the prelate, "with only a slight trace of having been singed." Shakhmaev interpreted this as a calling card of sorts, left behind by the saint so that Shakhmaev would know whom to credit for this miracle. "Ever since the unfortunate incident," the engineer recalled, "this image of the Prelate Sofronii has always been with me. I call upon this blessed saint for help in all of my affairs, and he always helps me." Shakhmaev further reported that in between putting out fires and in addition to healing him of various illnesses and sicknesses, Sofronii had once even sent a rescue party of seal hunters to save him and his Kirghiz crew from drowning when their rowboat struck ice and nearly capsized in the Caspian Sea.[86]

Encouraged by the Synod's 1908 decision to re-canonize Anna Kashinskaia, Irkutsk clerics followed suit by mounting their own campaign the following year. In March 1909 Archbishop Tikhon and a team of clerics examined Sofronii's body for the first time in more than two decades and once again discovered it to be uncorrupted:

> [The commission] looked at the grave and relics of the Prelate Sofronii and found them to be uncorrupted, in almost the same form as was found during the inspections conducted earlier. For one hundred and thirty-eight years, despite the proximity to water (the Angara River is nearby), despite the constant dampness in the caverns beneath the cathedral floors, particularly in the summertime—the coffin, the clothing, and the body of the Prelate Sofronii were found uncorrupted. The impression [made] from looking upon the

uncorrupted relics with one's own eyes, and from the distinct sweet-smelling fragrance emanating [from the relics] defies description.[87]

Armed now with seemingly indisputable evidence of uncorrupted relics and a growing stack of miracle stories on file in the city cathedral, the archbishop wrote again to the Holy Synod in 1910, informing its members that Sofronii was most assuredly a true saint. If the accompanying documentation were not proof enough, Archbishop Tikhon suggested that in canonizing the prelate, the Church would win a great spiritual victory all across Siberia, in essence re-Christianizing Russia's wild east:

> I harbor the unshakeable hope that the glorification of the Prelate Sofronii will have a grace-giving effect on the religious and moral condition of the people of Siberia in general, who are not distinguished by the warmth of their religious feelings and who have, in the course of their lives, wandered far from the Christian ideal. I am certain, too, that the numerous non-Russians [*inorodtsy*] and non-Orthodox who populate Siberia, who listen keenly and watch carefully all the events that transpire in the life of the Russian Christian Orthodox Church, who now, in the majority of cases, regard the Christian religion skeptically and even hostilely—that with the glorification of the Prelate Sofronii, [they] will abruptly change their present attitudes toward Christianity . . . and that those who have fallen away will return at once to the bosom of Christ's Holy Church, and that the rest . . . will respond to her truths and unite in one Christian flock under the unseen leadership of the Prelate Sofronii, who labored so hard for the enlightenment of the natives of Siberia through the holy teachings of Christ.[88]

By the time the Synod wrote back to request additional materials and miracles in support of Sofronii's cause, Archbishop Tikhon was dead, and the banner of Sofronii's cause fell to his successor, Serafim. The Synod instructed the new archbishop "to conduct a thorough inquiry" into all reports of Sofronii's miraculous intercession and to submit a detailed report for the Synod's consideration.[89] To assist him in his efforts, Serafim convened a special "Commission for the Verification of the Miracles Performed through the Prayers of the Prelate Sofronii, Third Bishop of Irkutsk," which held its first meeting in the fall of 1912. The archbishop and his fellow clerics were faced with the daunting task of having to sift through the 168 miracle stories attributed to Sofronii since 1872 and track down the whereabouts of all those who had claimed to have benefited from the prelate's intercession over the past forty years. At its second meeting, the commission decided to streamline its mission somewhat, opting to contact only those believers connected with particularly noteworthy or deserving miracles. The commission mailed letters to miracle recipients, asking them to provide sworn testimony "before a parish priest, two laypeople, and a representative of the civil administration" that their stories were, indeed, true.[90] In addition, the commission took out advertisements in Church publications, calling upon believers who had experienced a miracle but not reported it to come forward now and tell their story. Additional notices were sent out to the bishops of the neighboring Siberian dioceses, asking for their cooperation in Sofronii's canonization and for permission to publish a call for miracle stories in diocesan newspapers from Vladivostok to Viatka.[91]

The matter of verifying miracles was treated with great seriousness by commissions in Irkutsk and elsewhere, and surviving documents in the central archival repositories demonstrate a high degree of legalistic rigor and methodological thoroughness. The most immediate problem was a logistical one. Simply tracking down the whereabouts of miracle recipients and obtaining a statement from them proved an arduous task.[92] Witnesses who could be found and who provided oral or written testimony of Sofronii's miraculous assistance then were required to swear a solemn and legally binding oath in the presence of their parish priests and representatives from the municipal administration. Thus, not only legal punishment but eternal damnation threatened those who offered false testimony:

> In the name of the Father, the Son, and the Holy Spirit. I promise and swear by the Almighty God, before His holy Gospels and life-giving Cross, that I will, in good conscience, relate the entire truth concerning God's great and miraculous mercy shown me through the Prelate Sofronii Irkutskii, who lies in peace in the Old Cathedral in the city of Irkutsk, remembering that I must answer for all of this before the law and before God on His day of judgment.[93]

Further evidence for the rigor of these proceedings comes from the town of Astrakhan, half an empire away, where at this very time a similar commission was investigating reports of saintly intercession attributed to their own local miracle-worker, Metropolitan Iosif the Murdered. Had the witness sought medical help prior to the miracle, and if so, were there extant hospital records to support the witness's claims and were the doctors reputable? How serious was the illness in question, and what were the normal chances for recovery in the absence of a miracle? How much time had elapsed from when the witness had first sought the saint's assistance till his or her recovery from the illness?[94] If their faith and desire to see their saints canonized prevented them from playing the role of true devil's advocates, the commission members who deliberated at Irkutsk, Astrakhan, and elsewhere were wrestling with a monumental issue—namely, when is a miracle truly a miracle? Although some critics charged that the course of canonization in the Russian Church had devolved into "a drawn-out, complicated, and sometimes even petty investigation exhibiting all the characteristics of bureaucratic formalities," the leading authority on the process voiced his support. E. E. Golubinskii argued that certain procedural precautions were necessary in order to prevent an unworthy candidate from slipping into the ranks of the saints by means of "fabricated or invented miracles."[95]

Over the next two years, as the miracle commission continued to collect and collate evidence and testimony, the "great cause" of Sofronii's canonization received official endorsement from the Irkutsk mayor and city duma, the governor's office, and various assemblies of the diocesan clergy.[96] The Brotherhood of the Prelate Innokentii, the largest Orthodox confraternity in the diocese, also came out in support of the new saint's candidacy. So many of Sofronii's supporters joined the brotherhood that its membership nearly tripled from 1912 to 1914.[97] The Thursday panikhida performed at Sofronii's grave since the late nineteenth century now became so popular that huge crowds overflowed the cathedral, obliging the clergy to take prayer requests and declarations of thanks by post.[98] Local almanacs and city guidebooks from this period made mention of Sofronii's miracles alongside such other essential information as commercial statistics, the names and addresses of prominent local personages and government figures, and annual cultural events in the province, proudly informing residents and visitors alike that "at the present time, the question of his canonization is under review."[99]

Sofronii's cause suffered an apparent setback on the morning of 18 April 1917, when a fire broke out in the Bogoiavlenskii Cathedral, causing great damage to the interior of the church and completely consuming the saint's coffin and uncorrupted body. A special commission of clerics, jurists, medical experts, and a chemist inspected Sofronii's remains and confirmed that the body had been reduced to charred bones.[100] "The believers of the city are in tears," the Irkutsk diocesan press reported. "Only remnants [*ostanki*] are left from the relics." The city government pledged a full investigation into the cause of the fire, but rumors swiftly spread. Church newspapers pointed out that the fire had taken place on May Day (new style) and suggested that there might be some insidious link between the fall of the tsar, the rise of socialism, and the destruction of Sofronii's relics.[101] At a special memorial service the following day, the new archbishop, Ioann, attempted to defuse the tension by announcing that the sins of all the Irkutsk faithful—not just the radicalized elements—were to blame for this catastrophe. "The Christian faith has begun to weaken in recent times, and nonbelief and vices to flourish," the archbishop thundered, explaining that God had punished the people of Irkutsk for their wicked ways by depriving them of the relics of their new saint, just as He had taken the Ark of the Covenant from the Israelites and chastised proud Byzantium by allowing its sacred treasures to be plundered by the Turks.[102]

The burning of Sofronii's relics served as the impetus for a great upsurge in lay involvement in his cause. Archbishop Ioann informed the Synod with some civic pride that "veneration of the prelate has grown even stronger as a result of the fire," and that Sofronii's icons could now be found in homes all across the city. Indeed, in response to popular demand, the cathedral clergy began holding two panikhida services a week at Sofronii's grave, instead of just one, with believers coming to the cathedral "in greater numbers than before."[103] Within weeks of the fire, the so-called Union of Orthodox Christians was formed in Irkutsk, whose members pledged to restore the cathedral and shrine to their former glory and to strive for "the active defense of the faith and Christ's Church at any time and against anyone, as the situation demands." Working closely with parish organizations, the union collected 18,000 signatures calling for the "immediate elevation of the blessed Bishop Sofronii" to the ranks of the saints and sponsored a diocesan collection drive that brought in pledges totaling 7,000 rubles toward the purchase of a new shrine, lanterns, and icons of the soon-to-be saint.[104] To put this figure in some perspective, Irkutsk donors pledged a mere 400 rubles that same year to purchase oil and an icon lantern to hang above the shrine of the newly canonized Ioann Tobol'skii in the west Siberian city of Tobol'sk. Religious patrons in Irkutsk, as elsewhere, preferred to keep their charity local.[105]

That summer, the annual diocesan congress of clerics and laity in Irkutsk resolved to expedite the canonization process by sending a special delegation to St. Petersburg to plead Sofronii's case before the Synod.[106] Finally, in April 1918, nearly a year after Sofronii's uncorrupted body had been destroyed by fire, Patriarch Tikhon and the newly constituted Church Sobor announced the Siberian cleric's long anticipated elevation to the ranks of the saints.[107] But much had transpired in Irkutsk and the empire at large since the first murmurings of Sofronii's sainthood some eight years before. Russia had experienced world war, the collapse of the monarchy, the reestablishment of the patriarchate, and two revolutions and was now in the midst of civil war. What is more, the strong local consensus that had formed around the saint's cause was now showing signs of unraveling. In April, an assembly of high-ranking clerics in Irkutsk, including the archbishop and representatives from the monastic clergy, decided on 30 June as the date for the ceremonial opening of Sofronii's relics, and resolved to leave the saint's body in the old Bogoiavlenskii Cathedral, "where the name of the Prelate Sofronii is connected with many memories and acts of grace, signs, and miracles performed through his holy prayers."[108] However, a rival faction of laypeople (particularly women), parish priests, and the executive organ of the diocesan congress argued that Sofronii's relics should be relocated from the old cathedral to the recently built and "more spacious" Kazanskii Cathedral. They maintained that the newer church could hold three times as many worshipers as the Bogoiavlenskii, and that its "extraordinarily high ceilings, central heating, electric lighting, and good ventilation" would be a vast improvement over the "dreadful crampedness and closeness" of the old cathedral, where "streams [of condensation] literally pour down the walls on big feast days and the candles burn out from the lack of air." In the end, proponents of tradition carried the day, but heated discussions continued over the date for the ceremonies. If the festivities were held in late June, critics charged, there would not be sufficient time to publicize the event "throughout Siberia and European Russia" and few pilgrims would have the opportunity to attend. "Instead of spiritual joy, there will be grief; instead of love of Christ—dissatisfaction, dissension, and unpleasantness. . . . The times we are now living through," they warned ominously, "are such that the slightest carelessness in this great affair may give cause for censure on the part of the enemies of Christianity and those who are wavering [in the faith]."[109]

With local believers at an impasse, the Sobor was obliged to intervene, eventually deciding that a 30 June ceremony was unfeasible:

> Owing to the closing of the eastern borders and the transportation chaos, there are barely enough candles in the diocesan storehouse for the satisfaction of everyday needs: there is no flour, no lantern oil, no red wine, no images of the Prelate either on paper or on wood, no brochures and pamphlets necessary for such a ceremony. In order to make plans for the influx of pilgrims it is necessary to enter into some sort of agreement with the city administration, but at the present time the city duma and mayor's office are dissolved and Soviet power has replaced them in the persons of commissars. . . . Finally, the situation in the city is extremely tense at the present time, owing to the movement from the Far East of armed forces mobilized against Soviet power, and it is difficult to say what this movement will lead to in a month or two from now.[110]

Sofronii was the last saint canonized by the Russian Orthodox Church till after the Second World War. But the bishop, it seems, came too late to sainthood. The realities of civil war and political unrest made it impossible to stage the sort of grand festivities that had in years past traditionally attended the proclamation of a new saint. Rather than honoring Sofronii's relics with a citywide celebration, the faithful of Irkutsk would soon find themselves obliged to hide them in a secret location to avoid their desecration and exhumation at the hands of the Bolsheviks.[111]

Whose Saints Are They Anyway?

Four days before the celebration of Anna Kashinskaia's re-canonization, the Tver diocesan press predicted that "the city of Kashin will show itself as one big family on 12 June. Every participant in the Kashin ceremonies will feel this, will sense this. Everyone will profess his spiritual kinship in God with one mouth and one heart; everyone will be joyous and light of heart, everyone will be happy on this day."[112] Yet if the canonization efforts in Kashin and Irkutsk show the power of the Russian Orthodox religion as a force to unite local communities, it would also appear that these bonds were becoming increasingly difficult to maintain during the last decade of the old regime, as social divisions grew sharper and the Orthodox empire was obliged to confront its multiconfessional status.

Russian Orthodox clerics in Kashin and Tver freely expressed from the pulpit and in the press their hopes that Anna's re-canonization would repair the centuries-old schism with the Old Believers, who, denying the legitimacy of the Nikonian Church, had never ceased to recognize Anna's sanctity. One Orthodox cleric joyously anticipated that the restoration of Anna to the ranks of the saints "will signify for us the end of the schism and lead to union and peace in the Church."[113] The lofty rhetoric of religious reunion, however, was undermined by actual practice. In preparation for the canonization ceremonies, for example, members of the cathedral clergy in Kashin took it upon themselves to correct a seventeenth-century tapestry of Anna by sewing a scrap of cloth over the saint's hand, thus replacing the two-fingered blessing with a more theologically palatable three-fingered cross. The incident prompted a group of Old Believers in neighboring Tver to protest vigorously "against the inexcusable audacity and criminal defacing of an ancient monument . . . [by] unreasonably jealous lovers of the three-fingered cross." The archbishop bowed to public pressure and ordered that the replacement hand be removed.[114] Such actions on the part of Orthodox clerics did little to facilitate rapprochement with the Old Believers. Their message, however, was clear: if "Holy Rus'" was to be reunited, it would be on Orthodox terms.

Metaphors of healing were also deployed by conservative sources in Tver Province, who applauded Anna's re-canonization and staked great hopes on the chance that this historic moment would help transcend party and class divisions and mend a nation fractured by the recent upheavals of 1905, that "feverish year of political and religious disintegration."[115] Yet, rather than build bridges, the Tver diocesan newspaper used the occasion as an opportunity to attack "our leading intellectuals" in the province, who not only had been conspicuous by their absence at the public celebrations in Kashin but had slandered the proceedings by "present[ing] the festivities in a false light . . . and present[ing] the faithful children of the Church, the laity, as an ignorant mass, crude, incapable of sorting out the facts of the matter 'rationally,' prone to accepting lies and fraud as truth." The article's author, an Orthodox priest, warned readers that the seductive path preached by the radicalized elements of Russian society was, in fact, a spiritual dead end.

The solution to the ills of modern society lay not in reason but in relics: "It is not in the economic morality of our non-believing intelligentsia that the simple folk will find the source for rectifying and perfecting social life, not in the class war for survival, not in the class hostility and hatred that this morality depends on, but in quiet inspirational prayer here—in the saint's own example, at the shrine of [her] holy relics."[116] The same article alleged that certain unnamed "enemies of the Church" were plotting some sort of "unrest" (*bunt*) on the day of the celebration, possibly planning to hurl a bomb into the crowds.[117] Although in the end the festivities proceeded without incident, the presence of mounted gendarmes brought in from Moscow and Kiev to provide security added further dissonance to the key of harmony and unity in which the ceremony's organizers had sought to score the event.[118]

An increasingly vocal contingent of Orthodox publicists used the public opening of Anna's relics as an opportunity to re-imagine sleepy Kashin as an aggressively anti-modern redoubt, a welcome throwback to a simpler time that had no use for secularists, socialists, or schismatics. A visiting priest from Grozny who took part in the canonization festivities described Kashin glowingly as a "small, quiet, peaceful little provincial town" whose residents were "cordial, hospitable, and with old-fashioned morals."[119] The Tver diocesan press concurred, remarking that "in our age of religious sectarianism and disbelief it is most gratifying to witness the upsurge of religious enthusiasm in Kashin."[120] The editors of *Kormchii* suggested that the "Welcome!" sign that hung above the platform at the Kashin rail station to greet pilgrims be amended to read, "Welcome, our Russian people!" In an age of skepticism, relativism, and "open mockeries against the Orthodox Church," the canonization of a saint was proclaimed a solemn—and exclusively Russian—event: "[H]ere in Kashin, at this sacred celebration, there is no place for other peoples, particularly those who try so boldly and with such impunity to tread on everything that is Russian."[121]

In Irkutsk, too, the bickering of rival factions over the proper resting place for Sofronii's relics reflected growing tensions within the Orthodox community, as laypeople sought to exert greater autonomy in religious life and to define the sacred on their own terms.[122] The strident platform of the Union of Orthodox Christians—whose members took it upon themselves "to protect the inviolability of . . . the remains of the prelate Sofronii from disgrace and desecration by the enemies of the Church"—suggests that the fraying of the social fabric becoming endemic everywhere in 1917 played out also in religious and spiritual matters.[123] By the end of the old regime, then, the image of a single community joined in loving harmony at the relics of its saint had become a fiction that was increasingly difficult to maintain, and even so momentous an occasion as the canonization of a saint could not put the polity back together again. The very relics and saints that had once united communities now exposed divisive societal fault lines and would, after the Bolshevik Revolution, threaten to rend these local communities asunder.

While religious writers could claim that Anna's re-canonization depended "on the will of the Lord," her cause, and that of Sofronii Irkutskii, benefited also from the goodwill of the Synod and the indulgence of an emperor more disposed than most to see the hand of God at work in the world.[124] If, however, their official recognition speaks to a shift in priorities in Petersburg and a greater acceptance for expressions of religious piety emanating from below, the persistence of the cults surrounding Anna and Sofronii speaks to the attachment that local believers and communities felt for their saints. Without the efforts of lay believers and clerics in Kashin and Irkutsk, Anna and Sofronii would likely never have received official recognition from Church officials. It was the great rigor and thoroughness of the miracle commission in Irkutsk and the activism of lay committees, for example, that allowed Sofronii's dossier to stand out and receive special attention at a time when the chancelleries of the Church Sobor were swamped with similar, if shoddier, petitions on behalf of local saints whose causes suffered from poorly documented miracles and unsustainable claims to sanctity.[125]

In Tver, Siberia, and across the empire, the Russian Orthodox faithful saw and talked about their saints not as distant figures in another world but as hometown heroes forever present in the community where they had lived, served, died, and were buried. The particular predisposition of the holy dead to serve the needs of their fellow countrymen first and foremost was seen by clerics and lay believers alike as a sign of the saints' special love for their home regions. That both Anna's and Sofronii's charred relics could no longer be spoken of as uncorrupted was of little concern to their devotees; the miracles attributed to them by the Orthodox faithful were interpreted as comforting proof of the saints' continued presence in the community and as a reassuring sign that the holy dead had not withdrawn their love and assistance from the communities where their bodies resided.

4

The Revolution and the Saints

"Great epochs of social upheaval have always been
accompanied by a reappraisal of all values, by the fall
of the idols created over the centuries, and by the
unmasking of the centuries-old lies that had propped
up the old order in the past."[1]

—MIKHAIL GOREV, 1919

"Religion, faith in god, angels, demons, relics—what
an antiquated notion!"[2]

—*REVOLIUTSIIA I TSERKOV'*
(REVOLUTION AND THE CHURCH),
1919

Shortly after four o'clock on the afternoon of 3 February 1919, an impatient assemblage more than forty strong gathered in the snow before the gates of the Mitrofanskii monastery in Voronezh Province. This ad hoc commission under the chairmanship of the aptly named district Cheka commandant, Bessmertnyi ("Deathless"), was comprised of delegates and functionaries all specially selected for their task by the Voronezh Province Congress of Soviets. Among them were officials from the district executive committees, photographers and reporters from the provincial newspaper, a motion-picture camera crew, physicians from the city department of health, peasant witnesses from the surrounding villages, two Orthodox priests, and a detachment of leather-jacketed Cheka officers. After posting an armed guard at the gates to ward off peasant counter-demonstrators, Bessmertnyi led his delegation into the chapel church and presented the monks and priests inside with a resolution from the provincial congress of soviets that called, on behalf of the workers and peasants of Voronezh Province, for the immediate exhumation of the supposedly incorruptible body of the local Orthodox miracle-worker, Mitrofan Voronezhskii.

After examining the text of the resolution and confirming the credentials of the commission, the prior of the monastery, Hegumen Vladimir, led Bessmertnyi's men to the crypt, where a dozen or so worshipers were praying before the saint's shrine, and instructed his fellow monks to comply with the commission's instructions. While photographers snapped pictures of the massive silver coffin, two elderly clerics pulled back the layer of shrouds and vestments that covered the saint's body. A cloud of dust rose up from the coffin as the final shrouds were removed and the holy relics revealed. To the delight of the commission and the embarrassment of the clergy, it was immediately apparent that the remains of Saint Mitrofan had not been preserved in the state of divinely ordained incorruptibility that tradition had claimed. Those in attendance saw a brownish skull with close-cropped, reddish hair lying atop a gold-embroidered velvet pillow; a dry and brittle skeleton fitted inside a frayed and rotted cassock; substitute bones fashioned out of flesh-colored cardboard and cotton wool to fill the gaps in the skeleton; imitation arms and hands sewn from silk gloves; in the chest cavity, a calico sack stuffed with ashes, cinders, and half of the saint's pelvic bone; a nineteenth-century lithograph portrait of the saint; and a lone gilded cross on a silver chain. After the medical experts had completed their forensic examination of the remains, Bessmertnyi and the commission secretary drafted an official protocol of the proceedings and secured the signatures of all in attendance. The monastery gates were then flung open to admit crowds of curious faithful, who filed past the coffins for hours to see with their own eyes what one contemporary Soviet source called "the great centuries-old fraud perpetrated by the churchmen."[3]

During the first decade of Bolshevik rule, more than seventy carefully staged and orchestrated "relic inspections" were performed throughout Soviet Russia and Ukraine. Under the auspices of the VIII Section of the People's Commissariat of Justice (Narkomiust), Soviet power subjected the relics of some of the most revered holy men and women of the Russian Orthodox Church to exhumation, forensic examination, public scrutiny, and museum display in an effort to reveal to the workers and peasants that they had been the victims of a cruel and callous hoax on the part of the tsars and clergy—namely, that the bodies of "God's Beloved" had not, in fact, been preserved in a state of incorruptibility.[4] Lurid articles and even more shocking photographs were printed in party and state newspapers to demonstrate that so-called holy relics were mere matter, subject to the ravages of time and the natural processes of bodily decomposition. Sworn affidavits signed by local officials and clerical figures, reports from medical examiners on-site, and the testimonials of outraged believers whose faith had been shattered by the revelation of "relic fraud" appeared in the press and were subsequently incorporated into the antireligious presentations and speeches delivered by atheist agitators on the lecture circuit.

The so-called exhumation campaign offers a rich field for exploring the ways in which religious values came to be contested publicly after the Revolution. It is somewhat surprising that this topic has received little attention in Western scholarly literature. Most studies of Church-state relations in the early Soviet period relegate the relic campaign to a paragraph or two and then promptly dismiss it as a sensational, isolated episode that preceded the Bolsheviks' eventual adoption of a more rational and systematic strategy of antireligious indoctrination, one that privileged education over exhumation.[5] Russian scholars writing after 1991 have been more attentive to the relic exhumations, although here the problem is twofold. First, the development and implementation of relic policy is framed in a rather monolithic context of state versus society, that is to say, of a single-minded Bolshevik state foisting an unpopular policy on an inert and passive populace. Second, many of these works, like Orthodox relics themselves, are suffused with an "odor of sanctity" that undercuts somewhat their methodological rigor and brings these texts closer to the realm of hagiography than that of history.[6]

Bolshevik luminaries like N. I. Bukharin, V. D. Bonch-Bruevich, E. M. Iaroslavskii, and P. A. Krasikov championed the public exhumation of holy relics as a form of revolutionary theater that could have but one possible outcome: the worker and peasant audiences, having witnessed with their own eyes the "unmasking" (*razoblachenie*) of relic fraud, would create an insurmountable rift between the indignant lay masses and the devious clergy who, with tales of wondrous healings and miraculous cures wrought by the saints, had lured the faithful, with pocketbooks in tow, to reliquaries filled not with perfectly preserved bodies as billed, but stuffed with straw, wax, cardboard, and bones. In a Narkomiust circular of 25 August 1920, People's Commissar of Justice D. I. Kurskii castigated the Orthodox clergy for its role in the "fraudulent activities" brought to light during the first wave of the relic exhumations:

> The silver sepulchers studded with precious stones contain either rotten bones that have crumbled into dust, or else imitation bodies [constructed] with the help of iron frameworks surrounded by cloth, stockings, boots, gloves, cotton wool, flesh-colored cardboard, and so forth. This is what the archpriests and monks forced the hypnotized masses to worship . . . and in whose name they forced them to deposit their hard-earned kopecks into the Church's pockets. . . . These gilded sepulchers with their supposedly incorruptible bodies were used by the old ruling classes as an apparatus for the religious stupefaction of the ignorant, hypnotized, enslaved masses. . . . The revolutionary consciousness of the laboring masses protests against the fact that mummified bodies, or the remains of corpses, or imitation corpses could

be used in Soviet Russia by Church organizations for the exploitation of the masses, [in] violation of the most elementary conventions of social life and in direct insult to the sensibilities of all conscious citizens.[7]

As the Reformation historian Carlos Eire reminds us, iconoclasm is "a revolutionary act . . . a direct act of violence against the accepted social myth."[8] Indeed, as Kurskii's fiery speech suggests, the Bolshevik exhumation of holy relics represented a radical break between the way in which sacrality and political legitimacy had been perceived under the tsarist regime and the way in which these concepts were to be understood by the new Bolshevik government. Whereas the pageantry of imperial canonizations and ceremonial relic transfers had aimed at bolstering the autocracy's right to rule through a direct association with the sacred and at demonstrating the validity of the one true Orthodox faith, the Bolshevik exhumations—or de-canonizations—aimed at discrediting the memory of the fallen monarchy and, more important, at breaking the influence of its alleged "handmaiden," the Russian Orthodox Church.[9] By using science to reveal the holy relics as mere matter, subject to the ravages of time and nature, and by capturing the moment of their unmasking on film, the Bolsheviks employed the instruments of their self-professed age of scientific progress to debunk the artifacts of an old order now derided as superstitious, obscurantist, and fraudulent. Exhumation, itself a gross parody of canonization, was a politically revolutionary attempt to "lift up the veil that had shrouded the cult of relics in mystery," thus transferring the shame and ignominy of decomposed relics squarely onto the shoulders of those churchmen who had sanctioned their worship and of those members of the ruling elite who had so visibly patronized their cult.[10]

By pressing science into the service of spectacle in order to demystify what had once been mystical and to desacralize what had hitherto been sacred, the Bolshevik regime sought to cast itself as the defender of truth and the champion of reason, while exposing the spiritual legacy of the old regime as (quite literally) rotten. What began, then, as a way to diminish the authority of the Church and clergy in the eyes of the faithful was part, also, of the larger pattern of social reconfiguration and cultural reconstruction that marked the Bolsheviks' ongoing efforts to overturn the religious Russia they had inherited and to found a uniquely Soviet culture based on new principles of socioeconomic organization and human values. For the socialist revolution to succeed, the saints would have to be purged from Holy Rus'.

From Veneration to Desecration

The intellectual and ideological foundations of the relic campaign were rooted in the Bolsheviks' functionalist definition of religion as a mirage to mask class interests and exploitation. This materialist position had already been articulated in Bolshevik thought by Lenin and other ideologues well before 1917 and would continue to form the fundamental framework of the party's line on the philosophy of religion throughout the Soviet period.[11] In the Bolshevik equation, saints and relics—like church attendance, reception of the sacraments, the veneration of icons, and other manifestations of piety—were possessed of no real spiritual content and played a purely political role, namely, diverting the proletariat and poor peasantry from their inevitable trajectory of revolutionary development and propping up an increasingly decrepit autocratic regime. The underground Bolshevik press was outspoken in its criticism of the canonization ceremonies staged in the last years of the empire, decrying such maneuvers as political stratagems meant to deflect the masses' attention from the real pressing questions of the day: social injustice and inequality. In the summer of 1903, for example, the Russian Social Democratic Workers' Party (RSDRP) issued a last-minute appeal to the lay faithful planning to undertake the pilgrimage to Sarov for Saint Serafim's canonization:

> You know why the government needs holy relics—so that you will be obedient like dumb animals, so that they can easily fleece you. And that is why, to inspire still more terror among you, they have come up with the glorification of [Serafim's] relics. The inventors of these relics are the landowners and factory owners who rob you so deftly, the governors who give orders to fire into your midst, the metropolitans and priests who bless the soldiers who shoot at you, and the tsar himself who decorates his ministers for fleecing you and his soldiers for firing upon you. . . . Take a good look at them and do not forget that these leeches will continue to suck [your blood] and oppress you until you cast off the parasites' shackles.[12]

After the Revolution, Bolshevik pamphleteers and propagandists continued to focus on the political uses and abuses to which sainthood had been turned under the old regime (see Figure 6). In the early 1920s, the antireligious writer M. F. Paozerskii argued that "no other state question, not even those of the utmost importance, attracted [Nicholas II's] attention so much as the causes for the glorification of new saints." Paozerskii explained the spate of canonizations not as manifestations of popular devotion to local miracle-workers but rather the cynical machinations of a teetering regime desperate to remain in power and stem the rising tide of revolution: "Just as the development of popular self-consciousness . . . proceeded apace with increased speed, so too did the canonization of saints become a real bacchanalia, to the point where the saints were literally coming out of the oven like hotcakes [*bukval'no peklis', kak bliny*]."[13]

FIGURE 6—Religious stupefaction. A well-fed cleric with cross and knout surrounded by peasant women who have come to venerate the relics of Sergii Radonezhskii. The courtyard of the Troitskaia Lavra is stuffed with bags of money. Mikhail Gorev, *Troitskaia lavra i Sergii Radonezhskii* (Moscow, 1920).

For the Bolsheviks, then, the cult of the saints had nothing to do with belief. Sanctity, incorruptible relics, and miracles were whimsical chimeras that would soon fade away once their true and fraudulent nature was exposed to believers through science and reason. By focusing on the political ends to which sainthood had been put in the late imperial period, the Bolsheviks greatly underestimated the real depth of feeling and devotion that the Orthodox faithful placed in their saints and overestimated the ease with which this devotion would dissipate once the socioeconomic institutions upon which it stood were dismantled. They thought the "thread of habit," as Trotsky phrased it, could easily be snipped and the Revolution could soon safely relegate saints and relics to the dustbin of history.[14]

The origins of the exhumation campaign should also be seen in the context of the revolutionary iconoclastic spirit of 1917. Toppling tsarist statues, plundering nobles' estates, and tearing down images emblazoned with Romanov insignia gave shape and form to popular dissatisfaction with the status quo and represented a symbolic break with the old political and social order.[15] The process of "deromanovization," as Richard Stites has dubbed it, carried over into Church matters, as well.[16] In a Russia that had no tsar, what were churches now to do with the dedicatory inscriptions in honor of the Romanovs that graced icons and reliquary shrines across the empire? In April 1917, for example, parishioners in Samara complained to the local militia that an icon of Prince Saint Aleksandr Nevskii in their church bore an inscription "in memory of the unforgotten Tsar Alexander III," while the dedication on an image of Prince Saint Vladimir commemorated the wedding of Nicholas II and Alexandra and expressed the "ardent [prayers] of the parishioners" for the happy couple. Militia officials politely suggested to the parish priest that the offending inscriptions, both dated 1894, be removed from the icons in question. The harried priest turned to his bishop for guidance, who brought the matter to the attention of the Holy Synod. In his report, Bishop Mikhail recommended that the dedications be taken down, "since such inscriptions do not correspond with the historical moment of our state" and "may elicit indignation amongst the parishioners." The bishop further suggested that the Synod issue general orders outlining the proper course of action in such matters, "taking into account that there may be other misunderstandings in other localities."[17] The Samara authorities expressed no objection to the icons themselves, but only to their overtly politicized association with the fallen dynasty. Similar negotiations over the role of politico-religious symbols in public spaces took place throughout the summer of 1917 and even after October. In response to inquiries from local officials in Voronezh Province, the People's Commissariat of Justice gave instructions that only crowns and symbols of kingship "bear[ing] some relation to the tsarist dynasty overthrown by the people" should be removed from church walls, iconostases, and banners. A judicious decision, to be sure, but one that presented authorities with the difficult task of determining which crowns and regal insignia pertained to the house of Romanov and which to the house of David.[18]

As it had more than a century before in France, and would again in Mexico and Spain, revolutionary fervor in Russia found expression in acts of anticlericalism and iconoclasm directed against the authority of priests, churches, and sacred objects.[19] Conspicuous largely by their absence in the nineteenth century, incidents of popular anticlerical violence—or "spontaneous atheism," as Soviet historians were wont to describe the phenomenon—first rose sharply amid the turmoil of 1905 and spiked again twelve years later.[20] M. V. Shkarovskii, for one, has argued that "anti-clerical attitudes were widespread" among "significant sections" of the Russian population by the fall of 1917.[21] In August, for example, the editors of *Dukhovnaia beseda* dourly informed their readers that acts of iconoclasm and sacrilege were on the rise. In an effort to halt the tide, they warned that divine retribution would befall anyone who dared raise his hand against the Church and its sacred objects.[22] Such admonitions doubtless went unheeded, though, as presumptuous iconoclasts were unlikely to be numbered among the most avid readers of *Dukhovnaia beseda*. Diocesan newspapers, a rich source for the study of anticlerical and iconoclastic episodes, suggest that such incidents were indeed frequent in the summer and fall of 1917 but varied greatly in severity and violence—from the sacking of a church sacristy in Voronezh, for example, to the brutal murder by "criminals in soldiers' dress" of a priest and his wife in Astrakhan diocese.[23]

Among the first targets of antireligious and anti-Romanov iconoclasm were the relics and icons of Orthodox saints. In some cases, profit appears to have been the only discernible motive. On the night of 11/12 October 1917, for example, "criminals" picked the lock to the church of the Nikolaevskii monastery in Orel diocese and stole a miracle-working icon of Saint Nicholas the Wonder-Worker in a silver mounting, along with various liturgical vessels and three hundred rubles from the church candle box.[24] More icons disappeared two weeks later during the plundering of a church located on a princely estate in Tula Province. The church's iconostasis was also smashed, and the *antimins* cloth atop the altar—which by canon law would have contained small fragments of holy relics sewn into the stitching—was also stolen.[25]

Other incidents, however, suggest a correlation between the vocabulary and rhetoric of the perpetrators and the discursive techniques of class stigmatization and irreligion deployed by the Bolsheviks and other radical parties in 1917. Again, radicalized soldiers returning from the front lines appear to have played a prominent role in such episodes. On 16 April 1917, the secretary of the Kiev diocesan consistory wrote to Prince V. N. L'vov, the over-procurator of the Holy Synod, of a "scandalous desecration" that had taken place two days before in the catacombs of the Kiev Monastery of the Caves:

> At 3.00 pm, a party of pilgrims entered the catacombs for worship, among them there were approximately fifteen soldiers. The monk Anuvii was walking at the head of the party and in the middle, the sacristan of the Far Catacombs, hieromonk Venedikt. Having separated from the monk Anuvii, six soldiers [approached] the shrine of the Venerable Titus the Warrior, and with the words "Is there really a monk in here?" they lingered behind at the shrine of the Venerable Titus the Warrior for a prolonged period of time, more than is customary, and then noisily continued on toward the exit. When hieromonk Venedikt and the monk Anuvii arrived at the shrine of the Venerable Titus the Warrior they saw with horror that the holy relics of the Venerable saint had been removed from the shrine and placed up against the wall upside down with his feet in the air. Leading the remaining pilgrims on further, the monk Anuvii saw at the relics of the Venerable Paisii that the top-most shroud [covering the saint's] forehead had been cut; the cut was deep enough so that traces from a sharp knife or some other steel instrument were visible on the Venerable [saint's] forehead.[26]

In the first week of October 1917, a detachment of soldiers from the First Cavalry Guard barged into the Uspenskii Cathedral of the Kiev Monastery of the Caves and began ridiculing as class enemies Saint Nifont Novgorodskii, the emperor Constantine, and Prince Aleksandr Nevskii, whose images adorned the walls and columns of the church. According to the prior of the monastery, the soldiers "began to rudely shout out: what did they paint [these saints] for? They called them 'bourgeoisie' and so forth . . . they demanded that the icons be destroyed and threatened to destroy them themselves . . . and they spewed forth vulgarities against the Apostle-Saint Vladimir that are best not to recount."[27] In Belgorod, Kursk Province, on 19 October, a soldier entered the cathedral church of the Sviato-Troitskii monastery and began swearing at the relics of Saint Ioasaf Belgorodskii. When the soldier tried to tear down the shrouds above the saint's shrine, bystanders threw him out of the church.[28] Two days later in the Moscow Kremlin, a pair of drunken soldiers entered the Uspenskii Cathedral at the close of vesper services and proceeded to rip away at the shrouds that covered the open coffin containing the relics of Patriarch Saint Germogen. When a crowd of priests and worshipers dragged the would-be iconoclasts away from the shrine, the soldiers swore at them and answered that everyone was free to do as he wished these days. "There is no tsar," the soldiers shouted, "and we don't want any priestly bones. Why are our comrades rotting in the ground while he is here amidst all this gold? It's not fair—nowadays everyone is equal."[29]

These examples of episodic iconoclasm and anticlericalism reveal a growing tendency among the more radicalized segments of the Russian population to equate Orthodox symbols of sacrality with the old tsarist order, and hence to view them as antiquated superstitions or anachronisms that had no place in a new age of revolution and social equality.[30] At a session of the Orthodox Church Sobor on 20 January 1918, for example, Archpriest A. V. Suvorov reported to his fellow delegates that he had "discerned the marks of Bolshevism on the faces of several [demobilized] soldiers" who had returned home to the village for the holidays; the soldiers' mothers had complained to Suvorov that their sons snuffed out icon lamps and mocked the relics of the saints as "an invention of the priests to obtain revenues."[31]

Such sentiments, however, were hardly universal even after October. Sainthood remained a powerful symbol of faith and tradition throughout the first year of Soviet rule, as Church figures attempted to preserve a historical and cultural link with the past in the face of a frontal assault on their authority and privilege. On 2 June 1917, at a preparatory meeting held prior to the convocation of the Church Sobor, one of its principal organizers, Prince E. N. Trubetskoi, spoke on the importance of Saint Sergii Radonezhskii as a role model for all Orthodox believers in these troubled times. "Only spiritual strength can save Russia from the terrible danger that is approaching," he declaimed, and he urged his fellow delegates to undertake a pilgrimage to Sergii's shrine and pray for the saint's blessing in their holy mission.[32] When the Sobor finally convened in Moscow on 15 August, it was preceded with a solemn liturgy performed by Metropolitan Vladimir in the Uspenskii Cathedral. After the singing of the Credo, the delegates kissed the relics of the saintly prelates Petr, Iona, Filipp, and Germogen and then, as in centuries past, marched in procession down Red Square with the holy relics of Saint Aleksii.[33] Just days before the Bolsheviks seized power in Petrograd, Metropolitan Veniamin declared a general day of prayer for the city and organized a religious procession to the reliquary shrine of Prince Saint Aleksandr Nevskii, "protector of the capital, he who has repeatedly saved it from enemy hands."[34] As the Red Guards lay siege to the Moscow Kremlin, priests and monks blessed the defending soldiers within on behalf of the fortress's resident benefactor, Saint Aleksii, and held prayer services at his shrine.[35]

Faced by the threat of a new regime committed to erasing the spiritual legacy of the past, Church leaders sought to inspire the faithful with sermons and exhortations that emphasized heroic moments from the lives of the saints. When Metropolitan Makarii of Moscow addressed his flock on the fifth anniversary of the canonization of Patriarch Saint Germogen, he called on them to emulate the sainted prelate's defiance of the Polish invaders and "rise up in defense of the holy church against the violence of the Bolsheviks."[36] During his official visit to Petrograd in May 1918,

Patriarch Tikhon delivered a public prayer before the shrine of Saint Aleksandr Nevskii—"an example for us all"—and called upon the warrior-saint to deliver Russia from a new yoke of oppression: "Remember our land, once so plentiful, flowing with 'milk and honey,' and now grown scarce. O Saint of God, save thy true servants, all who take refuge beneath thy sacred roof, as their champion before God's throne."[37] A similar sense of plaintive urgency was expressed in the Church Sobor's resolution of 27 August 1918 (old style), reinstating the lapsed Orthodox holiday "in memory of all the saints," a feast day on which the Church had traditionally sought heavenly assistance in times of war.[38]

The outbreak of civil war also saw the saints turned to overtly political ends. Although, as Peter Kenez has argued, the Orthodox Church was never an "institution" of the Volunteer Army, the Church's "ideological support" did make an "enormous contribution . . . to the anti-Bolshevik cause" during the Civil War.[39] The political aspirations of the anti-Bolshevik faction became increasingly conflated with apocalyptic and religious rhetoric that represented the Civil War as a conflict between rival armies of good and evil, with the White armies engaged in a crusade to protect the sacred. During his drive on Moscow in the summer of 1919, General Denikin urged his men onward with calls to liberate the holy water held hostage within the Kremlin churches. In an order issued on 20 May 1920, Baron General Wrangel sought to garner support among the Orthodox faithful by declaring that his armies were fighting against the Bolsheviks for the defense "of the profaned faith and its violated sacred objects."[40] When Kolchak's White armies entered Omsk in March 1919, Archbishop Sil'vestr blessed the admiral with an icon of Saint Nicholas the Wonder-Worker. "It was not in vain that the prelate kept a sword in his right hand," the archbishop explained to Kolchak's men. "Under his leadership, our Christ-loving forces will liberate the Russian land."[41] In the White-occupied zones of southern Russia, anti-Bolshevik pamphleteers sought to sway popular opinion against their political opponents by denouncing the new regime for its crimes against sacred Orthodox objects. As one clerical propagandist in Rostov-na-Donu argued, the Bolsheviks were "evil enemies of the Orthodox Church" who had declared war on the holy bodies of God's saints: "Have they not fired upon the holy Kremlin, where the founders of the Russian land, the best people of our Motherland, reside in peace eternal?"[42]

From the perspective of the Bolshevik leadership, such rhetoric served only to make explicit the connections between the cult of the saints and counterrevolution. Narkomiust director D.I.Kurskii, for instance, maintained that not only was the Church's timing of the announcement of the canonizations of Sofronii Irkutskii and Metropolitan Iosif the Murdered of Astrakhan not accidental, it was politically opportunistic. Kurskii charged that by promoting the cult of Saint Iosif—who had suffered martyrdom at the hands of rebel insurgents for his vocal support of the tsarist regime during the seventeenth-century Stenka Razin uprisings—the Orthodox leadership was using sainthood to endorse the forces of counterrevolution and "exert political influence on the backward masses."[43] At the very height of the Civil War, a Bolshevik newspaper in Tula Province played with this notion by publishing a mock intercessory prayer (*akafist*) dedicated to the heroes of the anti-Bolshevik coalition. Entitled "*Akafisty* to the Holy Saints, Fathers Denikin and Kolchak, Tsarist Black Hundredists," the satirical verse inverted the rhetoric of sainthood, casting the White military leaders as new Orthodox saints, and ridiculing the class enemies who prayed to them for the Bolsheviks' defeat:

> Holy father Denikin, save us!
> Look upon the loathsomeness of our impoverishment!
> The might of proletarian and peasant hath risen up,
> Our god-preserved patrimonies have been defiled,
> Our lands, forests, and plentiful fields redistributed,
> Godless schools established on our rural estates . . .
> Denikin, mighty autocrat, protect us!
> Our factories and plants have been seized
> And placed in the service of the state.
> Stock shares dashed and scattered to the winds
> Like unwanted papers, like dried autumn leaves.
> And we have been left like crabs on the seashore:
> Without revenues, without the market, without refuge.
> Zealously we fall before thy feet:
> Defend us, Denikin-warrior!
> Holy father Kolchak, steel-nerved admiral,
> Come and rise from the East, like the sun,
> Glory be to thy rifle slings,
> Bend thine ear to our prayers,
> Come and save us.
> In the god-preserved autocracy of Siberia,
> Where the workers are humbled with birch-rods and rifles,
> Hear the voice of our prayers,
> O hangman and flogger from beyond the Urals,
> Come soon and save us
> From the onslaught of the Bolsheviks.[44]

Like all Bolshevik satire, this parody was meant for more than laughs. The anonymous author of this verse captures the familiar rhythmic invocations and intonations of Orthodox prayer to create a piece that is both anti-White and antireligious at the same time, reinforcing an emergent

Bolshevik discourse that grouped together in a single camp the Orthodox clergy, the reactionary opposition, and the saints they enlisted in their fight against the Revolution.

SEPARATING CHURCH AND STATE IN SOVIET RUSSIA

The decree on the separation of Church and state—adopted by the Council of People's Commissars (Sovnarkom) on 20 January 1918 and made public three days later—reflected the new regime's initially optimistic assumption that religious faith could, in essence, be legislated out of existence by shattering the institutional authority and privilege of the Orthodox Church.[45] In one fell swoop, the decree proclaimed that the Orthodox Church was officially separate from the new workers' and peasants' state. Religious education was banned in all public schools, the legally binding status of religious oaths was rescinded, and all state subsidies for the support of the Orthodox Church and clergy were revoked. The recording of births, deaths, and marriages was placed under civil jurisdiction, the right of churches and religious organizations to own property was abolished, and churches and lay associations were stripped of their legal status as juridical entities. Despite imposing restrictions against the Church's right to own property, the decree guaranteed believers the free use of any and all objects of liturgical value, that is, those used in religious rites and ceremonies. To this end, every church and monastery in Soviet Russia was obliged to provide local officials with an inventoried list of all possessions and property on the premises. Once inventoried and catalogued, liturgical objects (communion vessels, clerical vestments, crosses, and the like) could then be loaned out to the faithful for devotional purposes, provided that a group of twenty believers signed a contract (*dogovor*) with the local council of deputies and accepted full responsibility for their proper use and safe return.[46]

Separating Church and state in the midst of civil war proved in practice an arduous task for the new Bolshevik state. Implementation of the decree in the provinces was a logistical nightmare and proceeded only haltingly throughout most of 1918 and 1919. Faced with a host of pressing problems that demanded immediate attention, local officials in the provinces generally placed a low priority on enforcing the strictures of the separation decree. Although Narkomiust's instructional circulars were published repeatedly in the central press and provincial newspapers, they were frequently misinterpreted by local officials, and often ignored.[47] M. V. Galkin, a former Orthodox priest turned Narkomiust consultant, despaired of the disorderly situation he observed during an inspection tour in Petrograd Province in late 1918. Local officials, he lamented, displayed a "total lack of knowledge" concerning the center's instructions on the separation of Church and state and were familiar with the decree itself "in name only."[48]

As bad as the situation was in Petrograd, it was far worse in more remote provinces, where VIII Section reports revealed shocking levels of disorganization and incompetence. Officials in Riazan, for example, alleged that they had not even received instructions on how to carry out the separation decree until nearly thirteen months after it was first issued. In Iaroslavl Province, where authorities were at least vaguely aware of the decree's existence, few measures had been taken toward its implementation even by April 1919. And in Tambov Province, all civil registries remained in the hands of the local Orthodox clergy as late as the fall of 1919.[49] Even in Novgorod, where justice officials had taken the time to collate and publish a handbook containing all of Narkomiust's decrees and instructions on the separation of Church and state, local authorities were obliged to admit that their initial attempts in this field had proved, by and large, fruitless. For all their efforts, local officials confessed, Novgorod remained "the most religious province in all of Russia."[50]

In a revelatory report to the VIII Section, the director of the so-called Church section of the Novgorod provincial department of justice summed up the results of two years of work as marginal at best. The director candidly admitted that "the published decree on the separation of Church and state is in no way sinking into the consciousness of the narod, who are still insufficiently imbued with revolutionary self-consciousness." In what was to become a common refrain from provincial authorities throughout the years of the Civil War and the relic campaign, Novgorod justice officials blamed their inability to implement the letter of the decree on a lack of funding, resources, and manpower. Given his own operational limitations, the director argued, his office was in a poor position to combat "the sad legacy bequeathed to the revolutionary common people by the tsar: ignorance, darkness, [political] unconsciousness, a complete absence of politics, a lack of understanding of culture, inertness, and a strong devotion to the faith bordering on fanaticism." But by far the greatest obstacle to the separation of Church and state, the commissar claimed, was the Orthodox clergy:

> There are still corners of Novgorod Province where a political agitator's fiery revolutionary words may penetrate only with difficulty, and there are still entire regions where antireligious propaganda is known only from the newspapers. . . . It must be assumed that the work of even many hundreds of people conducting antireligious propaganda will not yield immediate results against the thousands of voices of representatives from the Orthodox Church.[51]

In the context of Red Terror and the Civil War, strident calls for vigilance and stern measures against clerical counterrevolution stiffened the resolve of many Orthodox believers to resist what they perceived as hostile outside intrusion into the religious life of their communities. While not every parish, church, or monastery rose up and actively resisted the regime's efforts to separate Church and state, it must be conceded to the Bolsheviks that in 1918 the potential for that possibility seemed very real indeed. Less than a month after the promulgation of the separation decree, Orthodox clerics and members of the local branch of the liberal Kadet party held a meeting outside of Kostroma to voice their opposition to the new regime's efforts to separate Church and state. An Orthodox priest who spoke at the assembly called on believers to take part in a religious procession in protest of the separation decree: "Let this be the procession to Golgotha—there is no greater joy for a Christian than to suffer and die for Christ."[52]

While most Orthodox preached a path of resistance in accordance with Christian teachings of harmony and fraternity, the injunction that Christ came not only to bring peace but a sword, too, was not forgotten. As one Orthodox priest pointedly reminded his readers in a Civil War–era pamphlet, "war is not only *permissible* from a Christian point of view but may sometimes be a moral obligation."[53] The pastoral letters of Patriarch Tikhon and proclamations issued by the Church Sobor likewise impressed upon believers that their commitments to Christ and His Church took precedence over obedience to earthly obligations. At times, however, the message was mixed. In a resolution of 30 August/12 September 1918, for example, the Sobor enjoined Orthodox Christians, on the one hand, to comply with Soviet orders to compile inventories and, simultaneously, threatened believers with anathema and excommunication if they aided and abetted in the seizure of church objects.

In the same resolution, the Sobor reiterated its stance that churches, monasteries, and chapels—"along with all the sacred objects housed therein"—were "the property of God and the exclusive possession of God's Holy Church" and called on believers to rise up and stand united in defense of sacred objects: "On every Orthodox Christian, according to his calling, there is incumbent the duty to defend the Church's sacred objects from blasphemous usurpation and profanation by use of all means at his disposal not contrary to the spirit of Christ's teachings."[54] In April 1918, the Sobor's Commission on the Persecution of the Church recommended that "Brotherhoods for the Defense of the Church" be established in all dioceses. These organizations were to rally lay believers against any perceived threat to the Church's autonomy and inform the Sobor of any violations or infringements of the separation decree, so that the Patriarch and Sobor could lodge official protests with the government.[55] In several dioceses, lay and clerical brotherhoods acted independently to pass resolutions denouncing the terms of the separation decree and to form leagues and unions for the defense of churches and Church property.[56] In Moscow, for instance, following the attempted assault on Patriarch Saint Germogen's relics at the Uspenskii

Cathedral, Archpriest Nikolai Liubimov organized the All-Russian Orthodox Brotherhood for Those Who Ardently Revere the Sacred Objects of the Moscow Kremlin. According to the brotherhood's charter, "All of Holy Rus' must take upon itself the responsibility that services continue unimpeded in the Kremlin churches, that their sacred objects be preserved in splendor, and that church life prosper in the Kremlin."[57] To prevent any further acts of sacrilege, the cathedral staff ordered that the saint's shrine was not to be opened for veneration unless a priest was on hand to supervise. For further precautions, cathedral watchmen were instructed "to maintain order more vigilantly in the cathedral," and a rotation schedule was drawn up so that at least one watchman would "stand near the Holy Relics at all times when the Cathedral is open to worshipers."[58]

In Arkhangel'sk, editors of the official diocesan newspaper described the pending encounter between the Orthodox faithful and the Bolshevik regime as nothing less than a battle between followers of God and the followers of Antichrist. It was the obligation and sacred duty of all Orthodox Christians to defend sacred objects, liturgical vessels, shrines, and relics from profanation at the hands of unbelievers:

> Unite, O Orthodox. . . . These sacred objects are your property! *[Eti sviatyni—vashe dostoianie!]* You and your pious forefathers built and adorned God's churches and dedicated this property to God. . . . The time has come when you, Orthodox, must now rise to their defense. . . . Preserve and defend God's churches, which for centuries have best adorned the Russian land; do not allow the presumptuous and unclean hands of nonbelievers to [defile] them, do not allow this terrible apostasy to come to pass. If this should come to pass, then Holy Orthodox Rus' would revert into the land of antichrist, a spiritual wasteland, where death is better than life. . . . Better to spill your blood, to merit a martyr's crown, than to permit the Orthodox faith to be profaned by enemies.[59]

Such precautions reflect a growing conviction on the part of Orthodox believers and communities that sacred objects in their charge and custody required special care and attention in these times of uncertainty. Indeed, during the early months of Soviet power, many of the most bitter confrontations between supporters of the new regime and defenders of the Orthodox faith were waged over access to miracle-working relics. On 13 January 1918, for example, crowds of clergy and faithful filled the streets of Petrograd to prevent a detachment of Kronstadt sailors from occupying the premises of the Aleksandro-Nevskaia Lavra, home to the relics of Prince Saint Aleksandr Nevskii and one of the most holy sites in the Russian capital. Unlike earlier, isolated acts against Church holdings, the march on the Lavra was undertaken by direct order of the Bolshevik government—in this case, by Aleksandra Kollontai, People's Commissar for Social Welfare, who intended to convert the nationalized monastery into a shelter for homeless soldiers and the war-wounded.[60] Reaction from the Church leadership was swift. In a rousing speech to the Church Sobor one week later, Prince Trubetskoi called for the excommunication of Kollontai and "all those who took part in the implementation of [her] instructions" and assured his fellow delegates that the attempt on the Lavra was "not an isolated, harmful outburst against the Church, but rather [the first steps toward] the implementation of an entire plan for the destruction of the Church's very chances for survival. . . . This is an open war against the Church, one not begun by us."[61]

The incident at the Aleksandro-Nevskaia Lavra was roundly condemned by Church officials as a secular intrusion into the spiritual realm and prompted Patriarch Tikhon to declare anathema and excommunication against the Bolsheviks—"these monsters of the human race"—on 19 January: "The holy temples are subjected to destruction or robbery and to blasphemous insults: the sacred places, venerated by the people, are being taken over by the godless lords of the darkness of this age. . . . [T]he properties of the Orthodox monasteries and churches are being taken away. Where, then, are the limits to these mockeries of the Church of Christ?"[62]

In Voronezh, less than two weeks after the abortive occupation of the Lavra, Archbishop Tikhon met with laymen and -women to discuss possible strategies to forestall the new regime's plans to nationalize the Mitrofanskii monastery. Outraged by rumors that the Bolsheviks planned to convert the principal monastery church into a theater, turn the Troitskii Cathedral into a cinema, and seize the miracle-working relics of Saint Mitrofan for display in the city museum, believers pledged to the archbishop that "for [the sake of] the churches and the sacred objects dear to their heart, [they would] sooner sacrifice their own lives than allow their profanation and desecration." A committee of lay believers pledged to establish a voluntary security force to defend the monastery and protect Mitrofan's relics from "blasphemers and unbelievers." To ensure extra vigilance and guard against a possible assault by the Bolsheviks under cover of night, twenty-four-hour prayer vigils were to be held at the saint's shrine, with the faithful "sing[ing] prayers of thanksgiving to the Mother of God and Saint Mitrofan day and night."[63]

To show that all the Orthodox of the city were united in their resolve, a religious procession was scheduled for 26 January 1918. The night before, lay believers lined up at the monastery cathedral to kiss the relics of Saint Mitrofan and pray for the success of their undertaking. As the archbishop later reported to Patriarch Tikhon, the worshipers were heckled and jeered by groups of nonbelievers and socialists, who had assembled on the square to stage a counterdemonstration of their own "for the propagation of antireligious ideas." Debates and arguments degenerated into insults and fistfights, as believers pummeled the counter-demonstrators. Similar incidents took place that night in neighborhoods across the city, prompting Red Guardsmen to take to the streets and fire warning shots into the air. However, as the archbishop informed Moscow, this attempt at pacification "only agitated and stirred up the residents of Voronezh."[64]

The next morning, after Saturday services in their parish churches, the participants in the procession made their way through the city streets to the monastery courtyard, where they were to regroup, receive the blessing of the archbishop, and then march around the perimeter of the monastery walls accompanied by the miracle-working icon of the Smolensk Mother of God. Archbishop Tikhon estimated the crowds of worshipers on the monastery square to number in the "thousands" and described the scene in his report to the patriarch as "solemn and deeply moving." The solemnity of the occasion, however, was disrupted by rifle shots from Bolshevik snipers positioned on the rooftop of the building adjacent to the archbishop's residence and at the windows of the invalid rest home on the east wall of the monastery. One marcher was struck and wounded by a bullet and several more injured when an altercation broke out between worshipers and Red Guardsmen who appeared on the monastery courtyard to maintain order. In the ensuing panic, many fled for their lives, while the clergy tried to calm the crowds by holding the Smolensk icon aloft over their heads. Sporadic fighting between groups of worshipers and guardsmen took place throughout the city over the course of the day, ending only when the Bolshevik authorities called in an armored car with a mounted machine gun to patrol the streets. In the wake of the Voronezh disturbances several clerics were arrested, including the prior of the Mitrofanskii monastery, and armed soldiers conducted a search of the archbishop's residence hoping to uncover hidden caches of weapons and ammunition.[65]

The level of organization involved and the speed with which Orthodox believers in Voronezh rallied in defense of Saint Mitrofan and his monastery reveal a popular enthusiasm for the sacred undimmed (indeed, strengthened) by the collapse of the old order and the installation of the new Bolshevik regime. Yet these same factors, which worked to the advantage of religious resistors, played into the anxieties of the Bolsheviks, who imagined, with some justification, the existence of a deep-seated nationwide conspiracy orchestrated by clerics in league with class enemies and counter-revolutionaries to undermine the new regime under the banner of the Orthodox religion. Such fears, grossly overstated and exaggerated as they were, nevertheless would play a central role in shaping Bolshevik policy vis-à-vis the Orthodox Church in the decades before the Second World War. In the wake of such disturbances, the Orthodox religion came increasingly to be regarded by the Bolsheviks as more than an absurd anachronism that would fade away of its own accord in the near future. The forces of religion were a threat to the very survival of the new regime and the success of the revolution.

Bolshevik ideologues before and after the Revolution regarded the popularity of saintly cults and uncorrupted relics as manifestations of false consciousness and cultural backwardness incommensurate with the new socialist order. With the political and social soil in which they had flourished now upturned, Orthodox saints and the vestiges of their cult would soon wither away along with such other antiquated practices as the three-field rotation system and village sorcery. The saints, in essence, had been made obsolete by the October Revolution. Yet after nearly a year of Soviet power, the Revolution had not managed to sweep the saints and their relics into the dustbin of history, and while symbols of sanctity remained visible fixtures on the political and cultural landscape of Russia during the first years of Soviet power, the hotly contested issues of sacrality and sainthood soon became ideological fault lines along which the Orthodox Church and the Soviet state were visibly divided. As we shall see in the following chapter, the Bolshevik elite sought to bring this conflict to a speedy conclusion by confronting the material dimension of sanctity head-on, launching a campaign to shake the Orthodox Church to its foundations by striking a double blow against the very notion of bodily incorruptibility and against the miracles on which the cults of the holy dead were founded.

5

Toppling the Saints from Their Thrones

THE BOLSHEVIK EXHUMATION OF HOLY RELICS

> "When the old society dies, its corpse cannot be shut up in a coffin and placed in the grave. It decomposes in our midst; the corpse rots and infects us."[1]
>
> —V. I. LENIN, 1918

> "Open up the sacred relics—straw? . . . Orthodoxy has lived for a thousand years, but it will perish, but it will perish—ha, ha, ha!—in about twenty years, no more, just as the priests will die out. . . . I don't believe it! They must have broken me! They've stuffed the relics with straw!"[2]
>
> —BORIS PILNYAK, *THE NAKED YEAR*

In Pilnyak's episodic novel of the Civil War, *The Naked Year*, a senile archbishop in the provinces loses his mind as the familiar world around him slips into chaos and ruin. His dementia complete and his faith shattered, the cleric responds with deranged laughter to reports that the Bolshevik exhumations have revealed the holy bodies of the saints as forgeries stuffed with straw. Haunted by the sounds of the "revolution howling . . . like a witch in a blizzard," the archbishop settles down to count the loaves of bread brought to him by an ever-dwindling number of parishioners; soon, he fears, the slow trickle of bread will cease altogether once the faithful recognize that their Orthodox religion is as hollow as its saints.[3]

In the real "naked year" of 1919, with the young Soviet state beset on all sides by White armies, foreign expeditionary forces, mass privations and shortages, and a near total collapse of transportation, communication, and production, the Bolsheviks declared war on the Orthodox saints.[4] As we saw in the previous chapter, the Bolshevik elite held to the materialist assumption that religion would soon wither in the less fruitful soil of a socialist society, and like Pilnyak's addled archbishop, they believed initially that devotion to the saints could not survive long after October. Convinced that the exhumation and exposure of holy relics as mere bones and matter would drive believers away from the Orthodox religion in droves, officials at Narkomiust and the People's Commissariat for Internal Affairs (NKVD) drew up plans for what justice commissar D. I. Kurskii called the "liquidation of the cult of dead bodies and dummies" on an all-Russian scale.[5] Intoxicated with revolutionary optimism, the Bolshevik leadership mistakenly believed that they could uproot Orthodoxy by exposing bodily incorruptibility as a scientific impossibility, little suspecting that ordinary believers cared less whether a saintly body was perfectly preserved than whether it worked miracles.

An Exhumation in Olonets

Soviet historians of the separation of Church and state frequently singled out the northern provinces as a region where Orthodox believers and clergy demonstrated a particularly strong level of resistance to the decree.[6] As a resident of the province informed the VIII Section, Orthodox believers in "remote, cold Olonets" received the separation decree "not only without sympathy, but even with hostility."[7] The clergy's general reluctance or unwillingness to comply with the terms of the separation decree and produce inventories of Church property for official perusal, coupled in many instances with local officials' ignorance of the very contents of the decree itself, prompted Narkomiust to issue special instructions for the edict's implementation on 24 August 1918 and again on 3 January 1919. Paragraph 7 of the August instructions granted local representatives of Soviet power the right to compile their own inventory lists of Church property if the clergy should fail to produce the necessary documentation, in triplicate, within a reasonable time frame.[8] In September 1918, after the brethren of the Aleksandro-Svirskii monastery had ignored repeated requests, the Olonets Province ispolkom dispatched a delegation of its members to conduct an inventory of the property and valuables held at the monastery located outside the township of Lodeinoe Pole. Unarmed and unprepared for resistance, the eighteen-member commission was turned back at the gates by a large crowd of peasants, members of the so-called Union for the Defense of the Aleksandro-Svirskii Monastery, whom the monks had summoned by a prearranged alarm signal of pealing church bells. Narkomiust expert M. V. Galkin reported that the local clergy had warned the peasants that the monastery would likely come "under attack from plunderers, and that it was necessary to stand in defense of the monastery and its property." Following this rebuff, five "active members" of the union, which boasted a membership of approximately a thousand peasants from the surrounding villages, were arrested by Soviet officials and shot at Olonets on 14 October. Among those executed were the prior of the monastery, the treasurer, a visiting monk, a student, and a peasant man.[9]

The delegation returned to the monastery on 23 October, this time with reinforcements from the district Cheka battalion, who assisted the commission in the confiscation of all objects of value. Dozens of gilded crosses, incense censers, candlesticks, silver-bound gospels, sacred vessels, brocaded vestments and bishops' mitres, silver icon frames, pearls and other jewels, imperial medals, silver coins, and three reliquary chests were dragged out from the monastery and requisitioned by agents of the state. The monks of the Aleksandro-Svirskii monastery described the scene vividly in a letter of protest addressed to Narkomiust:

> [V]aluable items were taken, the silver coverings were removed from the icons, and all tea, sugar, and foodstuffs were seized. Everything of value was taken from the prior's quarters, even clothes and underwear, and also the samovar and tea service. The more valuable things they took for themselves, the less valuable were reserved for the local committee of poor peasants [*kombeda*].
>
> Afterward, about ten persons, armed, demanded the keys to the sacristy from the sacristan, Hieromonk Palladii, and they took off [for the sacristy] with him. All church objects of value were taken from the sacristy, along with two fireproof chests containing interest-bearing securities and receipts from the State Bank worth 120,000 rubles and an unknown sum of cash money. From the sacristy they set out for the Preobrazhenskii Cathedral and, without removing their hats, went straight to the altar where they opened the altar tables and took out the altar crosses, gospels, and holy vessels. They made for the candle fund and cleaned out all the money within. They opened the candle booth containing the candles and sacramental wine for the monastery and all the parish churches. . . . They seized the wine and several drank themselves drunk. Among the plunderers were some who had earlier lived in the monastery as novices and laborers and who knew of the hidden monastery valuables. . . . Brandishing revolvers, they began to demand that [the sacristan] reveal the hidden valuables; the sacristan was obliged to do so. All of the hidden [valuables] from the sacristy were hauled out and piled on a cart and taken to Lodeinoe Pole at 6.00 a.m. the following day.
>
> On 11/24 October they seized all of the clothing, shoes, leather, and fabrics from the closets in the vestry, and also the ground wheat-flour and other flour from the granary; 40 *pud* [approximately 1,600 pounds] was taken in all, which was then given over to the village cooperative shop.
>
> On 12/25 October searches were again conducted throughout all the attics and in the mill, and everything of value was seized. All this time they were in a state of intoxication.[10]

That evening, commission members confiscated the keys to the cathedral from the monastery sacristan and threatened to return the following day to cart away the holy relics and shrine of the monastery's founder and namesake, Saint Aleksandr Svirskii. At eight o'clock the next morning, on the fourth day of the ongoing requisition, fifteen members of the commission unlocked the cathedral, barged inside "without removing their hats," and demanded that the monks remove Saint Aleksandr's coffin from its massive silver shrine. With no choice but to comply, the monks hoisted the coffin and placed it atop a small table. According to clerical eyewitnesses, the commissars and soldiers "gathered round on both sides and mockingly tore away the shrouds and coverings from the Venerable Saint and bared him to the breast."[11] The authorities were perhaps no less stunned than the clergymen, who watched as the shrouds were pulled back to reveal a wax effigy of the saint in place of an incorruptible body.[12]

Local officials decided to capitalize on the unexpected discovery by inviting residents of the surrounding districts to visit the monastery and gaze upon Saint Aleksandr's relics for themselves.[13] According to an internal report authored by the local Cheka commandant, many Orthodox believers were bewildered by what they saw:

> Dmitrii Stepanovich SLESAREV approached the grave—a seventy-year-old resident of Aleksandro-Svirskaia Sloboda, known to all as one who believes deeply in the saint's sanctity and his Divine power for Christians. Stunned by the absence of real relics as defined by Holy Scripture but not losing hope in a miracle, SLESAREV, before the entire crowd of people, began to ask for a cure from his old illness, to which the "holy" relics responded with notable silence and cold indifference, much to the general shame and surprise. In the end, the old man, insulted, tore at his gray hair and shouted out: "It's a fraud, a scam. . . . I am no longer a believer."[14]

During his inspection tour of the northwest provinces that fall, VIII Section "religious expert" M. V. Galkin informed his superiors in Moscow that the Aleksandro-Svirskii monastery and the relics of its patron saint, which had hitherto enjoyed "particular popularity among the ignorant, half-pagan peasant masses" of the region, had fallen into disrepute. The revelation of a "commonplace wax dummy" in place of an allegedly uncorrupted body had turned local residents against the monastic clergy.[15] Galkin's observations were borne out by a resolution passed at a mass meeting of peasant representatives from the surrounding districts of Olonets Province on 30 October, one week after local officials had put the fraudulent relics on public display at the monastery:

> The obscurantists of the people have been held up to shame—the monastic clergy and other priestly church-servitors who have perverted the holy ideals of our great teacher Christ, the defender of the oppressed masses who preached the ideals of communism. And so at this present time, we deem it necessary to transport the above-mentioned relics to the city of Lodeinoe Pole as quickly as possible, so as to reveal to the broad masses of poor peasants how they were fooled and how they had their last pennies squeezed out of them by means of these relics and by other frauds. The shame of the race of Cain be upon our priest-servitors, who poisoned the minds of the working class and exploited them with the basest and most vile fraud. Down with the dark forces that have defiled the minds of the proletariat! Long live science and enlightenment for the benefit of the radiant future of mankind![16]

It is significant that the peasant signatories to this resolution did not question the sanctity and miracle-working powers of *real* relics; their anger was directed solely against what they perceived to be a particularly odious example of clerical "fraud" uncovered in their own backyard. Equating true Christian gospel with communist harmony, the peasant delegates blamed the local monks and priests who had allegedly subverted Christ's "holy ideals" for prestige and profit.[17] Bolshevik editors excised all mention of Christ's "holy ideals" and their correspondence with socialism when the resolution was published in the national press, but this vocabulary of outrage, indignation, and anticlerical sentiment was to become a common trope in the popularly generated resolutions and decrees that followed in the wake of most subsequent relic exhumations.

"Let the Dead Bury Their Dead"
Exhumations in the Provinces

News of the impromptu exhumation at Olonets spread by word of mouth and the provincial Bolshevik press, prompting district-level state and party organizations to pass a flurry of resolutions calling for public examinations of local relics in order to expose fraud and manipulation on the part of the clergy.[18] During the first two months of 1919, at least twenty more exhumations occurred either at the initiative of local party and state organizations or through the efforts of workers' groups, peasant assemblies, and petition drives. Later that year, the defrocked priest turned antireligious consultant, M. V. Galkin, writing under his adopted pseudonym of Mikhail Gorev, likened this initial wave of relic exhumations to an "epidemic" and applauded the initiative of "the laboring masses themselves, who held meetings and resolved to cast off the shroud of mystery that had surrounded the gilded and enigmatic tombs."[19] Paraphrasing both Christ and Marx,

Gorev proclaimed what was to become one of many mantras for the relic campaign—"Let the dead bury their dead!" As Gorev explained, "those who wish to lead the life of the proletariat" must consign their saintly protectors to the grave and embrace the new ideals of the Revolution. The dawn of a new age required first the dismantling and burial of outmoded symbols, values, and institutions—among them saints and relics.[20]

All of the exhumations from this period were carried out in provincial centers and rural townships and localities. The relic fever that Gorev diagnosed had not yet spread to the urban centers of Moscow and Petrograd. Of the twenty-one exhumations conducted between October 1918 and mid-February 1919, thirteen were performed in Vladimir Province, four in Tver Province, two in Voronezh Province, and one each in the provinces of Olonets and Arkhangel'sk.[21] Stenographic reports and resolutions calling for exhumation were frequently reprinted in the provincial press and offer insight into the decision-making process of local authorities debating the merits of exhuming their towns' most celebrated residents. In Suzdal, Vladimir Province, for example, the matter of exhuming the relics of Saints Ioann and Feodor, housed in twin coffins at the city cathedral, was decided unanimously by resolution of the four-man presidium of the district ispolkom on 10 February 1919:

> On the basis of the exhumations of the relics of Tikhon Zadonskii, conducted in Zadonsk, Voronezh Prov[ince], of Aleksandr Svirskii in Olonets Province, and others, and, further, taking into account that the time has come to dispel the darkness of mystery in which the clergy has held the people—concealing from curious glances that which is within the shrines—[it is] resolved: to form a commission of representatives from the local ispolkom, from the local committee of the Communist Party, of medical personnel, educators, and clergymen for the inspection of the shrine located in the cathedral.[22]

The presidium at Suzdal voiced sentiments similar to those expressed that same month in letters to the editor of the Novgorod *Zvezda*. "In order to open the eyes of all and to show the ignorant narod the truth, I would desire from the bottom of my heart that our authorities here in Novgorod, that is, Soviet power, open all of the 'relics' housed in the monasteries of Novgorod ... to let the ignorant narod understand just what their spiritual mentors taught."[23] Also in February, the Muromskii district ispolkom and district party committee decided to proceed with the exhumation of the princely saints entombed at the Blagoveshchenskii monastery in Vladimir Province because of a typhus epidemic raging in the surrounding regions (see Figures 7 and 8). The Murom *Izvestiia* explained that exhumation was a matter of public health: "These 'relics' could be a source of infection, since the unfortunate, benighted faithful have been kissing this filth [*gadost'*] for centuries in hope of a 'cure,' 'salvation,' and so forth. . . . A heavy weight would lie on the conscience of Soviet power if anyone should be infected from these three-and-a-half scarecrow 'saints,' especially if it were a worker or peasant, since every laborer, everyone who creates greater or lesser value, is precious to Soviet power. . . . [It is] a moral responsibility for Soviet power to unmask this fraud."[24]

In these letters and resolutions, the vocabulary of truth, morality, and enlightenment is juxtaposed with the darkness, ignorance, and secrecy of saintly shrines and priestly machinations. Local officials and letter-writers describe Orthodox believers as deluded or "ignorant," and therefore it is

FIGURE 7—The exhumation commission poses at the shrine of the princely saints of Murom, Blagoveshchenskii monastery, Vladimir Province, 7 February 1919. GARF, f. A-353, op. 3, d. 734, l. 17.

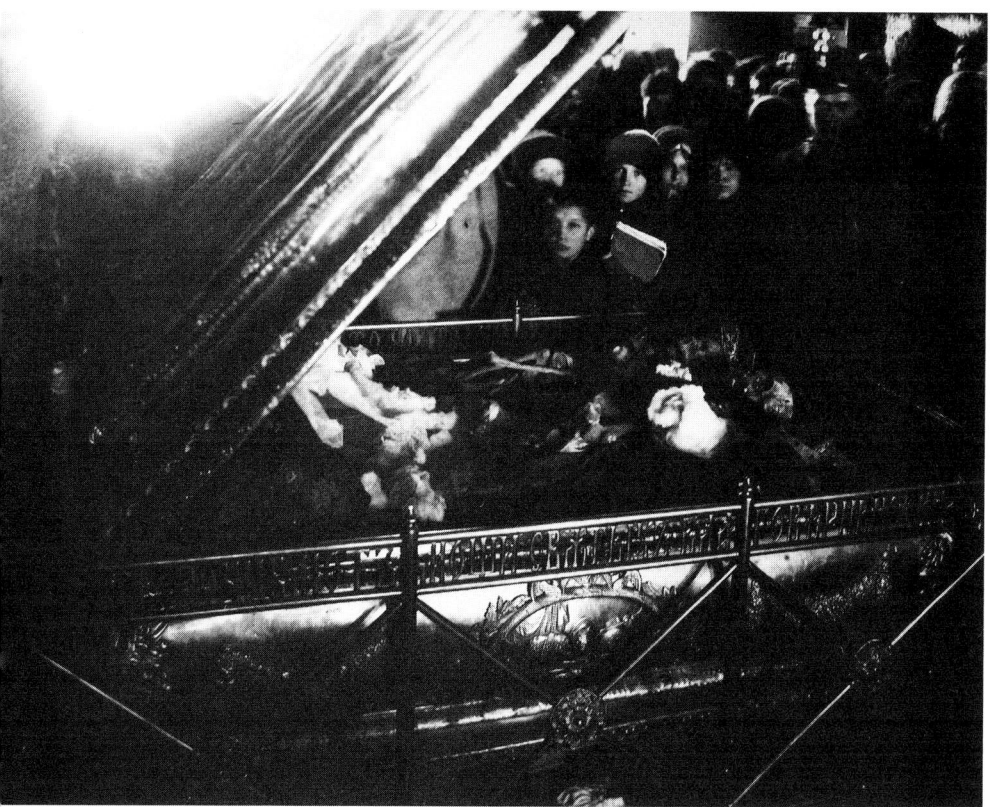

FIGURE 8—Children and soldiers at the shrine of the princely saints of Murom, Blagoveshchenskii monastery, Vladimir Province, 7 February 1919. GARF, f. A-353, op. 3, d. 734, l. 18.

the task of Soviet power to enlighten the benighted masses by throwing open the saintly shrines and subjecting their contents to public scrutiny. Indeed, as the Suzdal daily paper reported, it was the responsibility of Soviet power to take proactive measures in defense of the health and well-being of the laboring population. From the very beginning, then, enthusiasts in the provinces saw exhumation as a revolutionary tactic to "tear away the shroud of spiritual mystery" and lead the ignorant from shadowy superstition into the light of reason.[25]

These subsequent "copycat" exhumations yielded results similar to the first revelatory disinterment at Olonets. The coffin of the sixteenth-century boy saint Artemii Verkol'skii was opened in Arkhangel'sk Province on 20 December 1918, revealing a pile of broken bricks, rusty nails, and a lump of coal—nothing remotely resembling an incorruptible body.[26] The medical experts who examined the remains of Saint Tikhon Zadonskii in Voronezh Province on 28 January 1919 uncovered a heap of moldering bones that crumbled at the touch, arms and legs fashioned out of cardboard, cloth bandages fitted over an iron framework in the shape of a human torso, and a bare skull crowned with a bishop's mitre.[27] When the shrine of Prince Saint Konstantin and his sons was exhumed at Murom on 7 February 1919, it was found to contain four sacks of bones, a torso shaped from cotton wool and rags, a crushed skull, and an ivory brooch.[28]

The exhumation commission sent to inspect the coffin of Saint Makarii Zhabynskii at the Zhabynskii monastery in Tula Province found "nothing inside but spiders." The commission members proceeded to tear apart the cathedral floor, digging more than six feet down in search of holy relics, but failed to find any trace of Saint Makarii's body (see Figure 9).[29] Perhaps the most curious assemblage of random objects and spare parts was discovered in the grave of Saint Makarii Kaliazinskii in Tver Province on 8 February 1919. The official protocol of Makarii's exhumation records the contents of his shrine as "various bones and five pounds of cotton wool . . . 115 various copper coins, 7 silver coins, a broken earring, a button, a small cross, a small nail, a pin, two screws, five lumps of incense, four small beads, a dried pear, a tassel from a shroud, a half pound of laurel leaves, two hooded cowls, and four handfuls of wood shavings"—everything but a saintly body. The eclectic receipt prompted one writer to lament that there was not enough pepper to make a soup from the contents of Makarii's coffin, while a Komsomol antireligious publication scathingly dismissed the inventory of Saint Makarii's shrine as "an entire department store."[30]

Exhumations were heavily publicized in the provincial press and attracted enormous crowds of curious onlookers. According to one newspaper report, more than five thousand attended the exposure of the relics of Saint Nil Stolobenskii in Ostashkovskii district, Tver Province, on 25 February 1919.[31] For those unable to attend in person, the provincial press covered this first wave of relic exhumations in great detail, publishing not only the official exhumation protocols but also the polysyllabic forensic reports from the medical examination teams alongside signed affidavits from clergymen attesting to the truthfulness of the commissions' findings. At the end of January 1919, for four days straight, Voronezh newspapers were filled with full front-page stories detailing the exhumations of Saints Tikhon and Mitrofan.[32] Boldface headlines screamed from the front pages of local newspapers, as in Suzdal, for instance, where readers learned "The Secret of the Relics Revealed!! The Priests' Puppet Show Comedy Has Come to an End!!"[33]

With their scathing and often satirical take on the shocking discoveries unearthed by exhumation, provincial newspapers established the tone of

Toppling the Saints from Their Thrones ~ 131

FIGURE 9—Exhumation of Saint Makarii Zhabynskii, Tula Province, 16 March 1919. GARF, f. A-353, op. 3, d. 734, l. 30.

wry bemusement and lurid sensationalism that was to characterize most press coverage throughout the course of the relic campaign. As one newspaperman in Vladimir put it: "After these most curious unmaskings of priestly machinations, it seems that it is possible only to speak in puns and that one's pen hasn't the strength to write serious articles on this theme."[34] In Vladimir Province, as elsewhere, coverage of the exhumations in the region alternated between the morbid and the absurd, with ample doses of black humor aimed at dispelling the aura of sanctity and piety with which the Church and lay faithful had endowed their saintly protectors. Commenting on Saint Avraamii's unique fashion sense, the editor of the Vladimir *Izvestiia* concluded that the local martyr must, in truth, be the "patron saint of futurist art," after his 12 February 1919 exhumation uncovered a body clad in "stockings . . . women's trousers . . . and a Tatar turban."[35] The same newspaper cheekily proposed selling the surplus contents of saintly coffins at wholesale prices: "Whoever needs several pounds of cotton wool, some horse bones (for soup), and a few skulls for their collection is invited to apply at the women's convent and the Uspenskii Cathedral. The skulls are brand new and of the highest quality, and have been packed in cotton wool for freshness. All of this comes wrapped in the finest material."[36] The Suzdal press feigned bewilderment at the repetitious inventories of corrupted bodies: "Do we have some sort of factory here in Russia for the production of these scarecrows? Some 'relics' look so much like others that it's hard to tell where Mitrofanii ends and Avraamii begins—the difference lies only in the number of bones."[37] Indeed, the superfluous bones discovered in the shrines of the Suzdal saints inspired the city paper to jest that their hometown heroes must have been of "herculean physique." While the martyr-saints of neighboring Vladimir could boast "only" twenty-nine ribs and two jaws apiece, exhumation revealed the physically superior specimens of Suzdal must have had chests and heads large enough to accommodate "at least" forty ribs and four jawbones each.[38] The Vladimir papers demurred, suggesting that the local clergy would do well to export their relics to Egypt for preparation, since the mummies discovered there had proved far better preserved than Russian-made relics.[39]

Provincial newspapers served also as a public forum in which to expose the fraud and deception of the Church and brand the clergy as enemies of the common people. In the pages of the Voronezh press, for example, anticlerical sentiment ran high following the revelation of corrupted bodies at the exhumations of the local miracle-workers Saints Mitrofan and Tikhon. Newspaper articles proclaimed that with the victory of the October Revolution the time had come to purge the province of the "fat-bellied loafers" who had filled their "greasy pockets" with the people's money by telling tales of miracles attributed to saints now shown to be rotten (see Figures 10 and 11). "Communists will not allow the eyes of the people to be closed!" declared the military commissar for Zadonskii district, Voronezh Province. "We will not allow the loafers to make fools of the people and to traffic in churches for the sake of gluttony. . . . Out of the church, tradesmen! Away with false prophets!"[40]

Anxious to capitalize on this opportunity to drive a wedge between the clergy and the faithful, provincial executive committees and press organs experimented with other ways to publicize the findings unearthed by the exhumations. One such method was by staging public debates on the relic question, pitting antireligious lecturers against clerics or lay believers.[41] For understandable reasons, however, local Bolshevik debaters were often hard-pressed to find sparring partners. In February 1919, for example, after the exhumation of Saint Avraamii the Martyr, members of the Vladimir Province ispolkom and justice department extended an unanswered challenge to lay

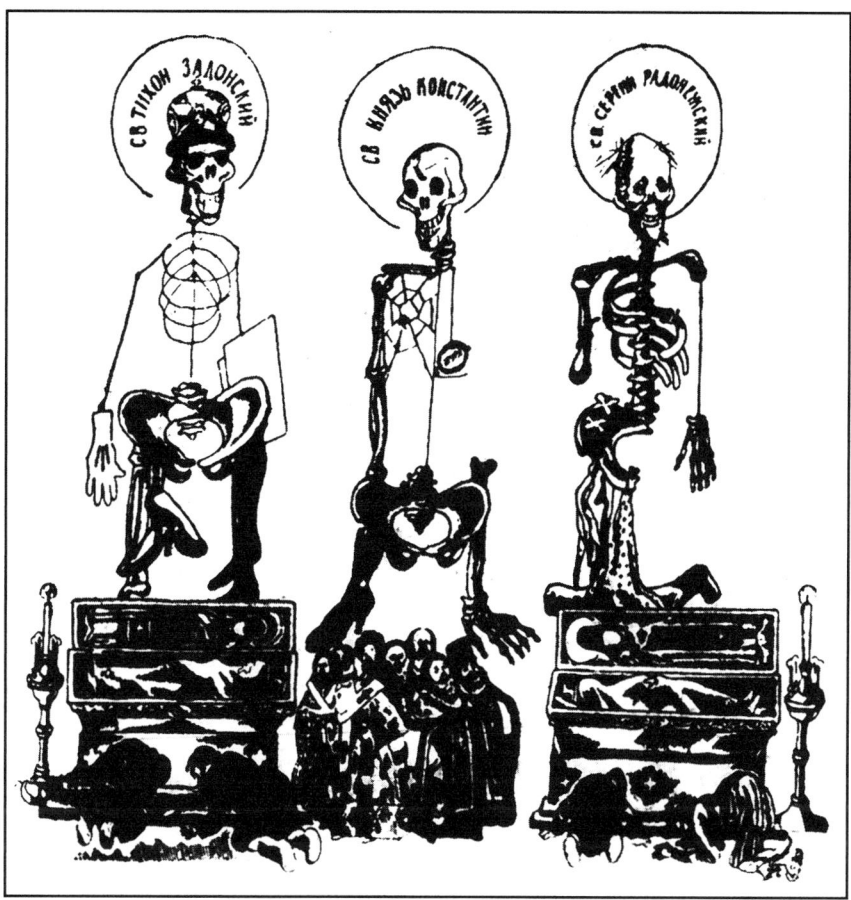

FIGURE 10—Caricatures of the exhumed saints Tikhon Zadonskii, Prince Konstantin, and Sergii Radonezhskii. *Bezbozhnik u stanka*, no. 4 (April 1923): 14.

members of the diocesan council, offering them a chance to defend publicly their arguments in support of incorruptible relics and pledging "assurance[s] that Soviet power would defend the dispute against anything offensive to the clergy."[42] Although newspapers and broadsheets billed these debates as "a purely business-like, objective exchange of opinions and establishment of facts ... in which representatives from the clergy and anyone so desiring can speak their mind about recent events," such forums appear to have garnered predictably little support among Church figures and lay religious leaders, who questioned the timing and necessity of public discussion on such a sensitive subject.[43] Debates that were staged, however, were reportedly well

FIGURE 11—The Incorruptibles. God addresses the assembly of saints: "You've let me down my little saints. I'm ashamed to show my face on earth." *Bezbozhnik u stanka*, no. 1 (January 1924): 17.

attended and often prompted indignant outbursts against the perpetrators of alleged relic fraud. Such was the case in a rural district of Novgorod Province where, in 1920, a former monk and new party member debated the pastor of the local convent church. Members in the audience scored it a victory for the ex-cleric when his opponent acknowledged "that relics may be forgeries, and thereby, albeit indirectly, admitted fraud."[44]

Where clerics proved unwilling to debate, provincial and district officials opted for the simpler strategy of delivering lectures and holding public question-and-answer sessions with local residents. Gorev reported that "many thousands" packed into the Karl Marx Club in the town of Belev, Tula Province, to hear a public reading of the official protocol of the exhumation of Saint Makarii Zhabynskii. "The general mood of the meeting," Gorev reported, "did not remain on the side of the monks for long."[45] Peasants from remote villages traveled hundreds of kilometers to gaze upon the exhumed remains of their heavenly protectors, now on public display in the churches once consecrated in their memory. A peasant letter to the editors of the Samara newspaper *Kommuna* (The commune) summed up the feelings of many erstwhile believers who felt betrayed and hurt in the wake of these first exhumations: "We peasants attach great significance to all kinds of miracles, relics, and shrines. But now it's time we open our eyes and call the clergy's bluff!"[46]

At a citywide meeting held in Suzdal in February 1919, some five hundred townspeople and residents of the surrounding districts passed a unanimous resolution condemning the clergy as "false teachers" and "black gendarmes in cassocks" for their "vile crime" of relic fraud. Claiming to have been "outraged to the very depths of the soul," the participants at the assembly demanded that these "traitors" be handed over "to the people's court for the most severe punishment."[47] In order to further humiliate the clergy in the wake of exhumation, provincial justice administrations did initiate legal proceedings against Orthodox clerics accused of relic fraud. At least four such show trials were held in 1920 alone (three in Moscow and a fourth in Novgorod).[48] As Elizabeth Wood and Julie Cassiday have argued, the highly publicized show trials of the Civil War years served as legal melodramas intended to transform the Soviet courtroom into a venue for education and propaganda.[49] To this end, the purpose of the relic trials was not to determine through legal procedures the guilt or innocence of the accused but, rather, to affirm and proclaim the defendants' guilt in a public forum. Thus, relic trials served as a theatrical showcase for presenting the Bolshevik party's argument against the veneration of the saints. As N. N. Levendal', the prosecutor in the trial of Bishop Aleksii of Novgorod, reported to the VIII Section, "the trial . . . bore less a formal character than it did a meeting-like, ideological one, directed toward a definite goal: the struggle against religious prejudices."[50]

Bishop Aleksii and his clerical co-defendants in the Novgorod trial of 1 November 1920 were charged officially with two crimes: first, that they had deliberately sought to "muddle the minds of the people" (*morochit' narod*) by passing off obviously corrupted remains as incorruptible bodies; and second, that the bishop and his clergy had conducted a secret examination of the holy relics in the Sofiiskii Cathedral prior to their exhumation in order to remove from the shrine any compromising items.[51] During his cross-examination, the bishop refused to admit any guilt and maintained that whatever inspections the clergy may have carried out were "an exclusively Church matter." The prosecution, however, demonstrated little interest in the so-called secret inspection, focusing instead on the opportunity to place on trial the very definition of moshchi and the legitimacy of their veneration. Levendal' and his associates took the audience at the Novgorod House of Arts through a detailed history of the veneration of holy relics, from the earliest councils of the ecumenical Church through the introduction of Christianity in Rus'. Citing the absence of any scriptural basis for the cult in the New Testament ("Neither in the gospels nor in the writings of the apostles do we find a single word about relics and their veneration"), the prosecution argued that relics were frauds invented by the Christian clergy to increase the contents of their coffers at the expense of the laboring masses. Should Christ Himself walk into the courtroom, Levendal' declared in his concluding remarks, He would condemn His faithless servants:

> This present trial has laid bare before you the ulcer of religious poison in all its fullness. You have seen in this historic trial the development of doctrine on the veneration of icons and relics, you have seen all the fraudulent tricks and forgeries to which the clergy resorted for centuries, thus replacing the spiritual, abstract Christian religion with the creed of commerce. And if Christ—who cast the moneychangers out of the temple and who said, "My house is a house of worship"—if this same Christ, a fighter for equality and brotherhood, came once again to earth, then here at this very tribunal, he would be the first to accuse Bishop Aleksii and the other servitors of that church which broke from him [Christ] so long ago. And like the grand inquisitor in Dostoevsky's *Brothers Karamazov*, these princes of the church would say to this imaginary savior come once again—"Why hast thou come to disturb us?"[52]

Aleksii and the other accused clerics pleaded not guilty to charges of "relic fraud," and during their cross-examination they defended the practice of relic veneration. If the prosecution had hoped the defendants would stumble over the definition of moshchi, they were mistaken. Nowhere in Orthodox tradition, Bishop Aleksii maintained, does it say that relics must be complete and uncorrupted bodies. Even though the relics exhumed at the Sofiiskii Cathedral in Novgorod were just bones and body parts, the bishop argued that they were still moshchi:

> Prosecutor Ul'ianskii: "In what condition did you find the relics?"
>
> Bishop Aleksii: "The relics were preserved in the form of bones."
>
> Ul'ianskii: "And did this bother you?"
>
> Aleksii: "No. The degree to which a relic is preserved does not depend on the sanctity of the person to whom the relics belong. Incorruptibility is not a sign of sanctity."

The testimony of a Novgorod monk called to the witness stand also did little to help the prosecution's case: "I don't think that relics necessarily have to consist of a body. During their lifetimes, the saints wore themselves out through fasting and prayer. Thus nothing remained of them but skin and bones. Of course, there couldn't be a belly [*puza*]."[53]

Although the verdicts in these trials were predetermined, the sentences were light. As B. V. Titlinov observed later, "these trials did not entail any special punishments for the accused, but placed the church figures in a severely embarrassing position and subjected them to general mockery."[54] The court pronounced Bishop Aleksii guilty and sentenced him to five years imprisonment in a concentration camp; his co-defendants received prison terms ranging from two to three years. In a show of magnanimity, however, the tribunal immediately commuted the defendants' sentences, declaring that "Soviet power does not intend to fight this centuries-old fraud and superstition by means of force, and that at this present time [Soviet power] is strong enough to disperse this fraud and superstition by means of enlightenment."[55] Such leniency underscored the pedagogical purpose of the relic trials—the aim was not to punish the clergy but, rather, to hold them up to public ridicule and discredit the belief in holy relics.

Yet if the Novgorod trial was supposed to function as revolutionary theater, showcasing the Soviet state's arguments against relic veneration, the audience's reactions to the show were mixed. Assessing the mood of the spectators, Levendal' bitterly informed the VIII Section that "the trial clearly showed how stagnant, ignorant, and undeveloped still is the populace, even in the city of Novgorod: the prosecution's speeches, despite their full correctness and consistency, met with stormy protests from one part of the audience and with sympathetic applause of approval from the other part."[56] As we shall see in the following chapter, the question of how the relic exhumations were being received by the general populace became an increasingly acute concern that divided local authorities and VIII Section officials.

Iconoclasm from Above
Official Endorsement of the Relic Campaign

As Gorev observed, the provinces were proving "more decisive than Moscow or Petrograd" in the elimination of "church fraud in general."[57] Nearly five months had passed since the exhumation of Aleksandr Svirskii in Olonets, with no official word from the central state or party leadership concerning the recent spate of relic inspections. One of the first members of the Bolshevik elite to take note was P. A. Krasikov, an Old Bolshevik and committed atheist (see Figure 12). Petr Anan'evich Krasikov (1870–1939) was raised in the home of his maternal grandfather, the prior of the city cathedral in Krasnoiarsk, where he became intimately familiar with and extremely critical of the Russian Orthodox Church. As a young revolutionary and law student in Petersburg, Krasikov quickly acquired a reputation for his outspoken anticlerical views often surpassing those of his comrades. Krasikov's rhetorical flair and bitter invectives against the Mensheviks won him no friends among the socialist opposition, but his oratory and organizational skills earned the respect of Lenin and other Old Bolsheviks. Krasikov was active in the underground work of the Bolshevik Party, establishing liaisons between the scattered party cells in Russia, Ukraine, and Western Europe. After the Revolution, Krasikov became a key figure in the judicial and antireligious apparatus, serving as the first chair of the Petrograd Soviet's Military-Investigative Commission for the Struggle against Counter-Revolution and Speculation and helping to draft the January 1918 decree on the separation of Church and state.[58]

In May 1918, Krasikov was appointed the first director of the newly founded VIII (later, V) Section of Narkomiust, which office he headed until 1924. As head of the VIII Section, the governmental body entrusted with the implementation of the separation of Church and state, Krasikov quickly recognized that a mass campaign to exhume and expose fraudulent relics could prove a powerful weapon in the new regime's struggle against the supposedly coterminous categories of Church and counterrevolution. The architects of early Bolshevik antireligious policy had learned from the mistakes of the French revolutionaries and the failure of the Paris Commune. As Krasikov explained, the Russian Revolution could not hope to eliminate religious belief so long as the masses placed their trust in a caste of "specialists who claim to be able to perform magical acts that supposedly exert a beneficial influence on gods and demons for humanity's well-being."[59] Premature policies such as shutting down churches and persecuting priests would only cost the new government the already precarious support of the overwhelming masses of peasant faithful and thus threaten to destroy all that the revolutionaries had worked so hard to create. "It is impossible,"

FIGURE 12—P. A. Krasikov, director of the VIII Section of Narkomiust and architect of the relic campaign. Krasikov, *Izbrannye ateisticheskie proizvideniia* (Moscow, 1970).

Krasikov wrote in early 1919, "to force the struggle with popular religious superstitions and prejudices by means of repression."[60] Thus, the question remained as to how to extract the faith from the faithful, without turning the faithful against the government.

The relic exhumations, which were achieving such apparent success in the countryside, seemed to Krasikov an excellent strategy for an assault against the Church and, by extension, against the legacy of the old regime, which had so vigorously promoted the cult of holy relics. Like all Bolsheviks, Krasikov believed that relic devotion was a product of that "religious haze" that clouded the minds of the masses and impeded the progress of economic and social development.[61] Science, not violence, would be the best implement to uproot this "antiquated notion."[62] Krasikov reasoned that if "the forces of tradition and economic and political backwardness" could be expelled and "primitive beliefs and religious fantasy . . . replaced by a scientific understanding of vital and productive processes," the cult of relics could hold sway no longer over the popular imagination.[63] Of course, such a project of scientific education was a long-term goal, unrealizable in the context of economic restructuring and Civil War.[64] More immediate and visually arresting results could be achieved by a sober and systematic unmasking of "relic fraud." Krasikov was confident that the believer's religious psyche could not withstand the breach of trust and righteous indignation that, he assumed, would necessarily follow in the wake of a nationwide campaign to expose saintly relics. The revelation of mass conspiratorial fraud would open the eyes of the faithful to clerical machinations, thus severing their allegiance to the clergy and casting the last remaining bastion of reaction, the Orthodox Church, "into the archive of history."[65]

Shortly after the incident in Olonets Province, Krasikov wrote to Lenin of the "stunning success" that the exhumation of Aleksandr Svirskii had in "discrediting the churchmen."[66] Krasikov suggested that a similar triumph could be replicated among the urban faithful of the capital by exhuming the relics that filled the monasteries and churches of the Moscow Kremlin. Lenin was no less enthusiastic than his lieutenant, and in the spring of 1919 he instructed People's Commissar of Justice D. I. Kurskii to make arrangements for the exhumation of the relics in the Kremlin's Chudov monastery.[67] Like Krasikov, Lenin realized that relic exhumation possessed a dramatic quality that had the potential to discredit the Orthodox Church and sever the deleterious bonds between the faithful and the clergy. V. D. Bonch-Bruevich later recalled that Lenin "repeatedly" emphasized the need "to reveal what these scarecrows [*chuchela*] were stuffed with, to reveal what so-called 'sanctity' was resting within these splendid shrines, to reveal what the people had treated with reverence for so many years and what the servitors of the altar had so cleverly used to fleece the simple folk—this alone would be enough to push hundreds of thousands of people away from religion."[68]

Following Lenin's endorsement, other Bolshevik luminaries were quick to jump on the exhumation bandwagon. In their party primer, *The ABC of Communism*, Nikolai Bukharin and Evgenii Preobrazhenskii hailed relic exhumation as "an excellent weapon in the fight with the church," and an effective means to expose "the base trickery upon which religion in general, and the creed of the Russian Orthodox Church in particular, are grounded."[69] E. M. Iaroslavskii, the future chair of the League of the Militant Godless, personally attended the exhumation of Saint Innokentii at Irkutsk on 25 January 1921 and penned a series of articles on relic fraud that appeared in the Siberian press. Iaroslavskii dismissed Innokentii's miracle-working relics as "twelve pounds of rotten bones, eaten away by moths and maggots," and foretold that exhumations "will help the peasants of Siberia to stop believing in the aid of prayer and relics and will teach them to rely on their own strength. . . . With one less fraud to contend with," he proclaimed, "laboring Siberia will stand even stronger on its own two feet."[70]

Despite their enthusiasm for exhumation, the central authorities were slow to take an active role in the actual implementation of the relic policy. Official endorsement for the relic campaign finally came on 14 February 1919, when Krasikov and members of the Narkomiust collegium issued their first set of regulatory guidelines to all provincial ispolkoms outlining the proper procedure for the conduct of relic exhumations in the localities.[71] In a communiqué dated 1 March 1919, Krasikov informed officials in Iaroslavl Province that relic exhumations should be "welcomed" and "by no means avoided" as a propaganda tactic, since "verification proves that no such 'relics' in fact exist, and clearly reveals to all the centuries-old fraud of the cult servitors and how the exploiting class trafficked in the religious sensibilities of the ignorant and backward masses."[72] Similar sentiments were expressed in the instructions issued to provincial officials in the Ukrainian SSR, who were informed that "the exhumation of relics must not be perceived as a constraint or restriction in the affairs of faith but must appear as the unmasking of a centuries-old fraud."[73]

As with most aspects of religious policy during the Civil War era, the relic campaign fell under the nominal supervision of the People's Commissariats of Justice and Internal Affairs.[74] Directives published in *Revoliutsiia i tserkov'* (Revolution and the church), the official press organ of the VIII Section, repeatedly stressed that local authorities needed no prior permission from the center in order to proceed with exhumation. When local officials in Mogilev Province sought Krasikov's authorization before undertaking a relic exhumation in their district, the VIII Section responded with a special procedural protocol outlining what was to become the center's standard line on the question: "The exhumation of relics is to be carried out at the initiative of the local laboring population, with the authorization of the provincial ispolkom or the provincial congress of soviets. No authorization from the central authorities is required for relic exhumations."[75] The VIII Section maintained that the relic campaign was not being imposed on the masses from above but was a participatory project undertaken by local authorities in response to the wishes and desires of the Soviet citizenry: "The general exhumation of relics in Russia is not being carried out on instructions from the center, but at the initiative of the laboring masses themselves."[76]

Although the impetus for exhumation was expected to come from below, Krasikov's instructions required that certain procedures and rules of etiquette be observed at all times during the campaign. "Relic inspections" (as they were often euphemistically dubbed) were not to be undertaken recklessly; exhumation should be preceded by an agitation campaign of "appropriate revolutionary and enlightenment propaganda" in order to lay the groundwork in preparation for the inevitable shock. Narkomiust officials left the duration of the campaign to the discretion of the local authorities, judging that they "can better assess the mood of the masses" than the central authorities, but officials were strictly enjoined to refrain from any "decisive action if the [agitational] base has not been sufficiently prepared."[77]

The campaign's architects also placed great importance on transparency, emphasizing that exhumation be a public event, performed openly and for all to see. Krasikov's offices required provincial ispolkoms to appoint special "exhumation commissions," chaired and staffed by members of the provincial state and party apparatus. These exhumation commissions, in turn, were obliged to invite representatives from the clergy and faithful to attend the relic inspections, along with local party cadres, workers, peasants, Red Army soldiers, and security personnel. The official exhumation protocols, including a detailed report of the proceedings and an inventory of all items discovered in the shrine during the examination, were to be drawn up by the commission chairman and signed by all witnesses in attendance.[78] In addition, qualified medical experts and physicians were to be on-site "without fail," in order to examine the relics closely and prepare forensic reports on their findings.[79] If at all possible, exhumation commissions should have photographers and camera crews on hand to capture the "unmasking" for posterity and, more immediately, for propaganda purposes.[80] Finally, to "eliminate the possibility of future fraud," exhumed relics were to be kept on display in the church or monastery "for a period of time suitable for the masses to verify the fraud with their own eyes." Krasikov envisioned that, afterward, local officials would ideally order the relics transferred to a nearby museum for permanent exhibition in the "hall of church antiquities."[81]

Knowing that reports and rumors of excesses or abuses could only play into the hands of the clergy and White leadership, the VIII Section insisted that local officials proceed with sensitive caution when staging relic exhumations and observe "certain tact with regards to the religious sensibilities" of the faithful.[82] In a circular of 23 April 1919, the NKVD ordered exhumation commissions "to utilize every unmasking in the press, in lectures, and meetings," and simultaneously to refrain from any inappropriate actions that would require them to "fall back on armed force"; evidence of unseemly behavior on the part of the exhumation commission would be dealt with "most severely."[83] Bukharin and Preobrazhenskii, too, urged would-be exhumationists to carry out the campaign with an "energy and perseverance" tempered by "patience and considerateness," reminding readers that "the credulous crowd is extremely sensitive to anything that hurts its feelings."[84] As Iaroslavskii phrased it, exhumation commissions should conduct themselves in such a way as to give the impression that Soviet power was exhuming holy relics "not for the sake of mockery, not for the sake of ridicule," but simply "to ascertain the truth" and "uncover the centuries-old fraud of the monks."[85]

To avoid accusations of sacrilege and blasphemy from outraged believers, the VIII Section ruled that exhumations were never to be performed on an Orthodox holiday, or when there was a crowd of worshipers inside the church. To avoid any allegations of impropriety, the actual removal of the relics from their shrine should be performed by members of the clergy, ideally the bishop of the diocese or the highest-ranking cleric present (see Figure 13).[86] Although enlisting the cooperation of an understandably unwilling clergy was inherently problematic, the participation of the priesthood had the added bonus of enhancing the performative effect and theatrical flair of the exhumation ritual. As the pamphleteer P. A. Bliakhin, argued, the moment of revelation was made all the more dramatic by forcing the clergy to unmask their own fraud: "Let them admire the work of their own hands and experience shame and humiliation before all the people." Bliakhin argued that the priests and monks—"more cunning than the devil himself"—could then be pinned down helpless under the audience's watchful gaze; once onstage, as it were, there would be "nowhere for the spiritual fathers to run."[87]

For all of its warnings and regulatory guidelines, the VIII Section insisted that every exhumation be carried out with "full decisiveness and consistency."[88] The enthusiasm and martial spirit that local exhumation commissions were enjoined to display in the discharge of their duties was

FIGURE 13—Clergy uncover the relics of Saint Tikhon Zadonskii, Voronezh Province, 28 January 1919. GARF, f. A-353, op. 3, d. 734, l. 4.

reflective of the ethos of élan and esprit that marked the Civil War era more broadly.[89] In July 1920, the III Congress of Soviet Jurists urged officials in the provincial justice departments to treat relic exhumation as a "decisive and conclusive technique" in the struggle against superstition, and "to avoid halfheartedness" in the execution of their duties.[90] As Krasikov reminded local officials: "It is better not to commence with exhumation, than to stand there hesitant and indecisive before a pile of decayed bones and rags. If the liquidation has begun, then it must be carried through to completion, right up to the point when the relics are deposited in the museum."[91]

MOSHCHI UNDER THE MICROSCOPE
SOVIET SCIENCE AND ORTHODOX RELICS

A new wave of exhumations followed in the wake of the regime's endorsement of the relic campaign. A total of thirty-three saints were exhumed between 15 February and 25 May 1919, with over half of these events occurring in or around Moscow and Novgorod.[92] With endorsement also came new opportunities to disseminate these findings to a nationwide audience and to educate the masses as to the scientific principles that disproved divine incorruptibility and, with it, Orthodoxy itself. As the chair of a district party committee in Voronezh Province proudly proclaimed, the telegraph—that modern invention of mass communication—would serve Soviet power by broadcasting news of Saint Tikhon's exhumation "all throughout great Russia, as far as the borderlands and all the way to Siberia." The tens of thousands of pilgrims who had descended on Voronezh yearly to venerate Saint Tikhon's relics would now be replaced by "millions of citizens from all corners of the Orthodox world journey[ing] for weeks, maybe even months, to our peaceful little corner on the Don," anxious to see with their own eyes the false relics of the saint they had once revered.[93] Such predictions failed to materialize into the millions, but the sentiments are indicative of early Soviet utopian reveries. Science and technology in the service of Soviet power would allow the truth of atheist sentiments to traverse wide distances and reach hitherto inaccessible audiences—a grotesque inverse of the very hopes that many Orthodox had held out in the first decades of the twentieth century. Now, however, mass printing, high-speed communication, and ease of travel would not serve the interests of the true faith but, rather, of those who sought to discredit it entirely.

Throughout the course of the relic campaign, the VIII Section's official journal, *Revoliutsiia i tserkov'*, published a series of articles from medical professionals and scholars designed to debunk the supposedly divine ordination of bodily incorruptibility and disprove the belief in the miracles wrought by saints and relics. In the debut issue, People's Commissar of

Health N. A. Semashko discussed the relic question from a "medical-scientific point of view." The commissar explained that the discovery of decomposed bodies and rotten bones inside the shrines of the saints should come as no surprise to "anyone of sound mind and firm consciousness." So-called relics, he stated bluntly, were nothing more than "the remains of corpses." Semashko pointed out that, like all organic matter, the human body undergoes a natural "process of corporeal breakdown," which may be accelerated or retarded by specific climatic, atmospheric, and soil conditions. Semashko wryly maintained, however, that science could offer no rational explanation for the "blatant, undisguised, and insolent fraud" of cotton dummies and "sand-filled mannequins" unearthed in some saints' shrines.[94]

The commissar's arguments were redeployed by subsequent Bolshevik authors who stressed that saintly bodies were perfectly ordinary objects. P. S. Semenovskii, a Moscow forensic physician and witness to several relic exhumations, assured readers of *Revoliutsiia i tserkov'* that "so-called relics are nothing miraculous or supernatural, but simply the remains of corpses that bear the traces of a prolonged process of decay."[95] The fact that holy relics had undergone corruption was simply a testament to the unswervingly mechanistic workings of the universe. Bodily decomposition, Semenovskii argued, is "an extremely important and necessary stage in the process of the biological life cycle on earth."[96] M. F. Paozerskii, an amateur scientist and director of the liquidation division of the Petrograd provincial justice department, concurred with his colleagues' assessments, describing decomposition as one of "the immutable and invariable laws of nature, to which every living creature in the world, including man, is subject."[97]

Bolshevik publicists, however, soon found themselves in a seemingly contradictory position. While they marshaled scientific data and evidence to argue against the possibility of divine incorruptibility, unexpected circumstances obliged them to admit that under certain conditions Paozerskii's "immutable law" of decomposition did not always hold true. As early as 1919, Semashko had warned that relics uncovered in cool, dry, well-ventilated environs, such as the drafty caverns of the Kiev Monastery of the Caves, might very well prove to be naturally mummified. The discovery of such a body, he suggested, might mistakenly be interpreted by deluded believers as a sign of divine favor for the deceased "and may give rise to talk of incorruptibility."[98] It was therefore incumbent on Soviet scientists and local officials to acquaint the faithful with the chemical and atmospheric conditions that allowed a body to be preserved uncorrupted by *natural* means, that is, mummification.

Soviet antireligious authors explained patiently that natural phenomena, not supernatural favor, accounted for why the bodies of certain saints had decomposed entirely, while others had been preserved in a state of natural mummification. Iaroslavskii, for example, pointed out that there was no clear scientific correlation between incorruptibility and sanctity; the bodies of entire mammoths had been preserved for years in the icy tundra, and yet the shrine of Saint Innokentii Irkutskii—subjected to similar climate for a far shorter period of time—contained "shriveled, rotting skin, dust, mold, dirt . . . maggots and dead larvae."[99] Paozerskii, too, doggedly insisted that "there is absolutely nothing miraculous about the preservation of various bodies from corruption and decay, and that it is strange, to say the least, to deem the presence of incorruptible relics as one of the signs of sanctity."[100]

The fact that eight of the sixty-three recorded exhumations for the period 1918–1920 revealed holy bodies in various stages of mummified preservation did present certain difficulties for Bolshevik propagandists eager to disprove the miracle of incorruptibility (see Figure 14).[101] On 1 December 1920, an exhumation commission in Kursk examined the relics of Saint Ioasaf Belgorodskii. The local paper, *Kurskaia pravda*, reported that the crowd "was taken aback by the high degree of preservation of the body, which had been lying in the coffin for one hundred and sixty-six years." An attending physician kept his wits amid the murmuring of the onlookers and swiftly made an incision into the saint's abdomen, "remov[ing] a portion of the intestine, which was completely desiccated, and thus proving that the process of mummification had been natural."[102] To the untrained eye, however, the difference between an uncorrupted body and a mere mummy was slight. When Saint Feodosii Chernigovskii was exhumed in February 1921, for example, his relics were found to be so remarkably well preserved that local agitators were hard pressed to refute the arguments of believers who claimed this was evidence of Fedosii's sanctity. To forestall any popular unrest, Chekists and scientists from Moscow and Kiev were called in to examine the relics and assist local officials in quietly transferring Feodosii's body to the provincial museum of popular education.[103]

Moshchi in the Museum

Spokesmen for the Soviet regime claimed that scientific facts were on their side in their ongoing efforts to expose the truth behind the relic cult. There is little evidence, however, that academic discourses on decomposition and the powers of psychological suggestion were successful in persuading the masses to view the contents of the sacred shrines from a materialist point of view. A more pressing concern for Orthodox believers was what happened to the relics, corrupted or not, once they were exhumed. In August 1921, the editors of *Derevenskaia pravda* (Village truth) wrote to Krasikov and Galkin, informing them that their offices were receiving a great number of letters from rural readers wondering where the relics "disappear to" after the exhumations. The editors pointedly suggested that the staff of *Revo-*

FIGURE 14—The mummified relics of Bishop Saint Nikita Novgorodskii, exhumed at the Sofiiskii Cathedral, 3 April 1919. GARF, f. A-353, op. 3, d. 734, l. 11.

liutsiia i tserkov' might do well to "address this question or write an article on this matter."[104] The point was well taken. Although the VIII Section was quite thorough in detailing the preparatory work required of provincial officials in order to carry out a successful exhumation, it was less helpful in answering the inevitable question of what to do with the relics once they had been exposed. For the first eighteen months of the relic campaign, this most pressing question remained naggingly ambiguous and fostered the first signs of discontent between the VIII Section and provincial authorities.

From the very beginning of the exhumation campaign, Krasikov realized that it was simply impossible for exhumed relics to be placed at the disposal of Orthodox believers or, worse, returned to the churches and monasteries where they had lain for centuries. Instead, Krasikov envisioned the bodies of the saints placed on display in museums throughout Soviet Russia, as artifacts of an archaic religious tradition now made obsolete by the October revolution:

The placement of relics in a museum is the most inoffensive means for the liquidation of the exploitation of popular [religious] prejudices. . . . [S]imilar objects of other religions (for example, those of Egypt, from whence Orthodox relics obviously trace their origins) are now in museums alongside the greatest products of human culture, including the greatest products of religious artistic craftsmanship: images, icons, and statues, including those which formerly served as objects for liturgical use.[105]

At Krasikov's urging, the Narkomiust collegium passed a ruling on 14 February 1919 instructing provincial and district officials to place exhumed relics on display in local museums of antiquity or museums dedicated to local and regional history. The collegium members argued that by transforming holy relics into museum exhibits Soviet power could "eliminate the possibility" of any future "relic fraud" on the part of Orthodox clerics and allow believers to see for themselves the shabby bodies that the Church had passed off as uncorrupted relics.[106]

As was the case with most of the VIII Section's decrees, requiring provincial officials to place holy relics in museums was easier said than done. In Petrograd, for example, many months of neglect during the Revolution and Civil War had caused several smaller museums to fall into grave disrepair, with cold and moisture threatening to damage or destroy the collections. Lack of funding and a shortage of trained personnel hindered provincial museums as well in the first years of Soviet power, and obliged VIII Section officials to make certain concessions to reality.[107] Thus, over the course of 1919, the VIII Section and the NKVD tempered the tenor of their decrees and allowed local officials more latitude in deciding the question of what to do with exhumed relics. The result was little short of chaos.

When the VIII Section requested local officials to report on the steps they had taken to exhume and display holy relics, the responses revealed widespread confusion and ill-preparedness in the provinces. Asked whether his office was familiar with the VIII Section's instructions on museum display for exhumed relics, a respondent from the district ispolkom in the town of Belev, Tula Province, simply drew a line through the space in lieu of an answer. In response to the question of whether there was a museum in the town where relics could be displayed, the same official first wrote, "There is no museum," then crossed it out and changed his answer to the affirmative. In fact, unsure of what to do with Saint Makarii, Belev officials had simply returned his body to the cathedral where they had found him.[108] In Petrograd Province, the local Narkomiust branch informed the VIII Section that its special department for church affairs was encountering certain difficulties in eradicating the relic cult in the province. After careful consideration, provincial officials determined that the chief obstacle to the department's success was the fact that it had "absolutely no employees whatsoever," which made it almost inevitable that "all of [the department's] efforts meet with the same failure."[109]

Faced with a host of pressing problems, the implementation of antireligious policy was generally a low priority for overworked provincial officials. Many came up with innovative ways to carry out or circumvent the VIII Section's instructions on relic display; others interpreted guidelines from the center more as suggestions than requirements. The chairman of the Vladimir Province ispolkom, for instance, decided on his own initiative that only "unusual specimens" would be subjected to medical examination. Arguing that relics fell under the rubric of "liturgical property" as defined by the separation decree, the chairman ruled that saintly bodies could be returned to the care of believers, if they filled out the requisite paperwork. If unclaimed, the relics would be destroyed.[110] In Iaroslavl Province, members of the Poshekhonskii district ispolkom decided it would be more expedient to simply leave the exhumed relics of Saint Adrian Poshekhonskii "exposed forever" under glass in the local cathedral rather than underwrite the expense of relocating the body to a distant museum.[111] Although such an option had been extended to local officials by virtue of a special NKVD circular, this particular method of relic display rankled Krasikov and his colleagues.[112]

By the summer of 1920, with the worst of the Civil War behind them, Narkomiust officials once again pressed forward with the relic campaign. At the urging of Krasikov, the Council of People's Commissars approved a decree that called for the "liquidation of the cult of dead bodies and dummies" on an all-Russian scale. For local officials, exhumation was no longer a voluntary undertaking to be carried out as time or inclination permitted. According to the August 1920 decree, all provincial and district ispolkoms were required to exhume all relics in their districts "systematically and consistently . . . while avoiding any indecisiveness or halfheartedness in the execution of these measures." Henceforth, all holy relics were to be placed in museums without fail. No exceptions could be made, for, as People's Commissar of Justice D. I. Kurskii explained, museum display was "neither an abuse to religious consciousness nor a persecution of any particular faith" but, rather, "the most rational means for the liquidation of future exploitation, prejudices, and superstition."[113]

The decree of 25 August 1920 spelled out unambiguously the new Bolshevik attitude to the sacred that had been implicit, if unstated, since the beginning of the exhumation campaign some eighteen months before. Under the new Soviet regime, Orthodox relics were to be regarded no longer as recipients of religious devotion but objects of public scrutiny. As the VIII Section's senior religious expert, I. A. Shpitsberg, explained in an internal report, relics that remained in churches were impediments to the development of the laboring masses. Transferred to the custody of state museums, however, and placed on public display, exhumed relics could serve useful pedagogical and scientific purposes. Once they were under the scientist's microscope, any lingering debates as to the provenance of supposed saintly bodies could be resolved once and for all. Scientific evidence revealing the saints' bodies as ordinary organic matter could then be used to refute rumors of and claims to their miracle-working powers, thus forcing even the most intransigent believers to break with their faith in the supernatural. Imagining a radiant future in which religion had been finally eradicated, Shpitsberg assured his colleagues at the VIII Section that generations to come would one day owe them all a debt of thanks for having had the foresight to gather together these "curiosities," thus providing "a grateful posterity the opportunity to study the past by means of . . . collected monuments of antiquity."[114]

In the wake of the August decree, Krasikov's VIII Section began issuing orders for provincial officials to ship their holy relics to Moscow for display in the Commissariat of Public Health's (Narkomzdrav) new Museum of Social Hygiene. Although the response from the provinces was still far from overwhelming, exhumed relics began trickling in by the winter of 1920–1921. The first such delivery arrived by rail at Moscow's Kursk Station in the last days of December 1920—a wooden crate marked "top secret cargo," containing the mummified relics of Saint Ioasaf Belgorodskii, "well-preserved" and packed in straw.[115] Ioasaf's relics were sent to the Narkomzdrav museum under Red Army escort; his three-hundred-pound silver shrine was shipped off to the People's Commissariat of Finance.[116]

The Narkomzdrav museum was housed in a converted private residence on Petrovka Street, behind a former flower shop. Filled with glass jars of medical oddities preserved in alcohol and its walls plastered with slogans ("The struggle against religious superstition is as necessary as the struggle against infectious disease!"), the museum's revolutionary content contrasted sharply with the décor of its bourgeois surroundings.[117] Despite an erratic operating schedule complicated by material shortages and several unforeseen closings, the relics exhibit at the Narkomzdrav museum drew an estimated 33,000 visitors in 1922, more than ten times the number of visitors to the more modest and less spectacular antireligious museums in Petrograd.[118] Viewers came in such numbers, however, not to read revolutionary slogans but to visit the hall of holy relics, where, from 2.00 pm to close, six days a week (closed on Mondays), the curious could climb the staircase to the second floor and see for themselves the bodies of Saint Ioasaf Belgorodskii and the three Vilnius Martyrs, Saints Antonii, Ioann, and Evstafii, whose relics had been evacuated to Moscow for safekeeping during the First World War, only to be exhumed after the Revolution. So great were the crowds that Narkomzdrav director N. A. Semashko advised tour groups to book their reservations in advance.[119]

The commissar's recommendation was not simply a case of shameless self-promotion for his museum. Tour groups and organized excursions composed of factory workers, Red Army soldiers, women, and provincial delegates represented the very social demographic that the museum's directors sought to attract. As the commissar explained, the museum's pedagogical purposes could best be met by catering to these "most important" and "most valuable" guests.[120] Organized tour groups would be guided through the exhibit by museum docents, to ensure that the experience the visitors took away with them was both structured and ideologically sound. By contrast, individual visitors were seen as a potential liability. Strolling unattended through the museum grounds, flaneurs were free to draw their own conclusions from the items on display and liable to walk away with misguided impressions.

Architecturally speaking, the hall of relics at the Narkomzdrav museum was structured in such a way as to demystify and desacralize the bodies of the saints and the Orthodox tradition of incorruptibility.[121] Saint Ioasaf, for example, was stripped of his vestments and exhibited naked, save for a small piece of strategically placed cardboard. Prior to exhibition, the saint's hair, worn long in the Orthodox episcopal style, was shaved close to the skull. Robbed of his robes and mitre and with a new short haircut, the naked Ioasaf looked little like a miracle-working saint and more like an ordinary corpse.[122] The saint's image was further deflated by the decision of museum organizers to exhibit Ioasaf's mummified remains alongside the desiccated body of a rat, extracted from a central heating pipe somewhere in the city, and the strikingly well-preserved corpse of a murdered counterfeiter. Strangled after a misunderstanding with his business partners, the counterfeiter had been left in a locked Moscow apartment with the stove running and the windows open, where many months of dry, circulating air had arrested the body's further decay. Museum organizers intended the curious juxtaposition of saint, rodent, and common criminal to disprove the Orthodox correlation between uncorrupted remains and sanctity. As a contributor to the journal *Bezbozhnik* (The godless) remarked, viewers could only draw one of two conclusions from the startling exhibit:

> Either "incorruptibility" does not indicate "saintliness," in which case treating mummies and "relics" with reverence is laughable and ridiculous. Or "incorruptibility" does indicate "saintliness," in which case, then, add counterfeiters, too, to the ranks of the saints (apostles, prophets, great ascetics, and holy fools). Obviously the calling is a highly edifying one. But an "incorruptible rat"? This is a complete embarrassment for the faithful.[123]

In addition to shock value, museum organizers used science to debunk incorruptibility. With the aid of wall posters and some rudimentary chemistry, tour guides treated their visitors to an exposition of the scientific causes underlying the natural processes of decay and decomposition, invoking the all too familiar examples of rotten potatoes and moldy bread to show how natural matter breaks down. From such simple demonstrations, Semashko explained, "the viewer proceeds . . . to more complex ones and is finally acquainted with the decomposition of the corpses of animals and humans." After having been subjected to arcane lectures on the occasional occurrence of natural mummification, the relative merits of being buried in dry sandy soil, and the chemical interaction between fatty acids and soluble calcium salts, visitors would conclude their tour with a viewing of the relics themselves. Armed now with visible proof and scientific knowledge (however hastily acquired and incompletely digested), the viewers could see with their own eyes that there was nothing holy about holy relics. As Semashko confidently predicted, "The similarity of . . . all these corpses . . . is so striking that the scales fall from the eyes of even the most prejudiced and superstitious visitors. Thus the darkness of speculation, fraud, and charlatanism is dispelled by the light of science."[124]

Antireligious officials and museum organizers were certain that a trip to the hall of relics would prove a transformative experience for the faithful and reaffirm the choices of those who had already broken with religion. One tour guide told of an old peasant woman who had traveled from her village to the Narkomzdrav museum, eager to see real holy relics: "Is this where they're showing the saints?" The visitor entered the hall crossing herself but left "defeated, muttering . . . with wide eyes." "What kind of incorruptibles are these?" the woman asked. "It makes you sick to look at them, and to think they made us kiss [them]."

Semashko shared this story in the pages of *Revoliutsiia i tserkov'* as an example of how relic display would serve the larger cause of antireligious education. "Doubtless," he predicted, "this old woman will tell many, many [people] in her village how she saw the fraud with her own eyes. And they will believe her."[125]

Relics continued on display throughout the 1920s, and although the emphasis of antireligious propaganda shifted over the course of the decade, the exhibition of saintly bodies could still evoke a powerful response. A correspondent for *Derevenskii bezbozhnik* (The village godless), for example, marveling at the relics on display at the Central Antireligious Museum in Moscow lamented that his late mother could not have looked upon the exhumed saints for herself: "It's a shame my mother did not live to see this day. Here at the museum she would have seen just what it was she had been kissing and praying to. She would have seen this 'god' without the halo round his head, without the incense smoke, without any miracles and without any sanctity."[126] Another Moscow visitor concurred: "Now I can respond to the old folks who talk about all sorts of miracles and relics. Now

I've seen for myself that all relics are just an invention of the priests and kulaks and so forth."¹²⁷ In the provinces, where museum admission was generally free, testimonials were equally encouraging. Officials in Vitebsk boasted of the large crowds of visitors who poured in to the antireligious wing of the state museum in 1922 to see the relics of Saint Evfrosiniia Polotskaia; the effect produced on the guests, the majority of whom were peasants, was reported as overwhelmingly positive.¹²⁸ As a peasant woman, one of the eighteen thousand visitors to the Vologda antireligious exhibit in 1926–1927, remarked, "Take a look at the exhibition and you'll become an atheist, you can't help it."¹²⁹

Moshchi on Screen

Exhumation as Cinema

With its potential to offer visual proof of "relic fraud" to an audience of millions, cinema held perhaps the greatest allure for Bolshevik officials in their war against the saints. On 28 January 1919, at the behest of local officials in Voronezh Province, Moscow cameraman P. K. Novitskii was sent to Zadonsk to film the "unmasking" of the relics of Saint Tikhon Zadonskii.¹³⁰ Impressed with their initiative and the quality of the finished product, Narkomiust commended the Voronezh officials and urged other provincial exhumation commissions to follow their example. In April 1919, the Photographic and Film Commission of the People's Commissariat of Enlightenment (Narkompros) dispatched a team of such noted filmmakers as Dziga Vertov, Lev Kuleshov, and Eduard Tisse to Sergiev Posad to capture on film the exhumation of Sergii Radonezhskii.¹³¹ Lenin was delighted to learn of this particular project and hastily drafted a memo to his personal secretary, V. D. Bonch-Bruevich: "It is necessary to *track this down* and *check up on it*, so that this film may be shown all across Moscow without delay."¹³² Bonch-Bruevich later recalled that Lenin was "very pleased" with the exhumation films he saw and "always asked whether a film was being shot when the relics of the various 'saints' were being exhumed."¹³³

Although the exhumation films and photographs made for powerfully compelling propaganda, logistical problems and material shortages limited their availability. Krasikov and his staff often had to badger provincial authorities into forwarding copies of exhumation photographs to Moscow so that they could be reproduced for national publication and used on the antireligious lecture circuit. In most cases, a veritable flood of paperwork coupled with bureaucratic inexperience meant that it was months (if at all) before overworked and understaffed provincial offices sent their exhumation protocols and photographs to the VIII Section. When the VIII Section pressed officials in the Vladimir Province justice department for the whereabouts of the photographs and accompanying documentation from the exhumations of Saints Gleb, Georgii, and Andrei, the provincial authorities politely informed Moscow that the original protocols had been misplaced over the course of the past fifteen months and, "despite thorough searches," were presumed lost. At the VIII Section's instructions, local justice officials launched a somewhat halfhearted investigation into the mislaid documents, eventually pinning blame on the chairman of the Vladimir exhumation committee who was himself missing, having left the city for "an unknown address" sometime after February 1919.[134]

Demand for these films and other visual aids greatly exceeded the supply of available copies. The VIII Section was obliged to incur great expense in ordering duplicate reels to accompany Moscow agitators on their periodic lecture tours.[135] During four months in 1919 alone, the VIII Section spent nearly 5,800 rubles on the reproduction of slides, photographs, and films of the exhumations of Tikhon Zadonskii, Sergii Radonezhskii, and Prince Mikhail of Tver.[136] Even then, however, lecturers and films rarely ventured far from the central provinces of European Russia. In the summer of 1919, for example, the Tikhon film appears only to have played in a handful of cities and towns, most in Moscow Province and none more distant than Tver.[137] Moreover, not all requests for copies could be met, particularly those that involved shipping films over great distance and at considerable expense. In the fall of 1920, for example, Krasikov denied the Eniseisk party committee's request for film reels, promising the Siberian officials instead one hundred copies of *Revoliutsiia i tserkov'*.[138] Statistics from the mid-1920s indicate that the total number of antireligious films in circulation in the countryside remained perilously low throughout the decade. By 1925, for example, antireligious productions accounted for a mere 6 percent of the total film footage in Sovkino's lending library, and even then many copies were said to be in such poor condition that entire meters of film were missing from some reels.[139]

Although budget constraints and material shortages meant that few exhumations were actually filmed, those that were quickly became early classics of antireligious propaganda. In accordance with Lenin's wishes, the film of Sergii Radonezhskii's exhumation reached Moscow theaters in time for Easter week.[140] The film of Tikhon Zadonskii's exhumation played to astonished audiences in the towns and villages of Voronezh Province, and an exhibition of photographic stills was staged in the lobby of a prominent downtown movie theater in Zadonsk. Admission was free of charge, and the curious were invited to purchase souvenir postcards with pictures of the exhumed saint.[141] Still photographs from the exhumations of Saints Tikhon, Sergii Radonezhskii, and Mikhail of Tver were similarly reproduced by order of the VIII Section for display in antireligious museums throughout the Soviet Republic.[142] Krasikov's office encouraged provincial authorities to prepare local audiences for upcoming exhumations with a demonstration of visual materials from earlier relic examinations. Photographs and film reels could whet the appetites of curious audiences and prepare them for what they might expect to see inside the exhumed shrines of their own local saints. During a symposium entitled "On Religion and Communism," held at the Petrograd Palace of the Arts on 2–3 September 1919, Krasikov and Galkin treated their audience to photographic stills from various exhumations and a screening of the film of Tikhon Zadonskii's "unmasking." The multimedia presentation resulted in the immediate adoption of a resolution calling for the exhumation of the former capital's patron saint, Prince Saint Aleksandr Nevskii.[143] Krasikov noted with some pride that an elderly woman approached him after the lecture to thank him for his eye-opening lecture: "What a shame that I didn't understand what religion was for such a long time, and that I believed in this fraud! I was lost for so long!"[144]

A "Religious Upheaval"?
Endorsement and Support for the Relic Campaign

In his December 1920 report to the VIII All-Russian Congress of Soviets, Krasikov boasted that the first two years of relic exhumation on a nationwide scale had produced a "religious upheaval [*religioznyi perelom*] everywhere and in all localities, even among the most ignorant and backward elements of our peasantry." He informed his audience that "the populace, particularly the young generation, is losing interest in the cult with amazing speed; the memory of the cult survives only among the old men and women, and among those elements of the populace who made their living 'off of the saints,' that is, the former shopkeepers, restaurateurs, inn keepers, *bliny* vendors, bathhouse owners, and so forth."[145] Bonch-Bruevich made a similar observation at the time, noting that through the exposure of fabricated relics "great numbers of people had pulled away from their saints and from those con artists [*obmanshchiki*] who stood as the guardians of these sacred objects."[146]

As evidence, Krasikov and Bonch-Bruevich cited a series of declarations and resolutions adopted by workers, peasants, and soldiers "awakened" by the relic campaign. Many of these statements appeared in the provincial press and were subsequently republished in *Revoliutsiia i tserkov'* as firsthand testimonials to the successes that exhumation was enjoying among the more socially conscious and politically educated elements of Soviet society. While they should not be read as representative of the populace as a whole, such declarations reveal much about the way in which specific "favored" groups in Soviet society (Red Army soldiers, factory workers, and so on) interpreted, internalized, and subsequently rearticulated the state's official position on the relic question.

In denouncing the relic cult, the authors of these declarations and their signatories proclaimed a new postrevolutionary identity for themselves and their comrades-in-arms and posited their new self-professed values in opposition to the norms and symbols of the old order. A collective resolution adopted unanimously by a group of Red Army soldiers in Vladimir Province vowed that henceforth they would "damn anyone who has preached lies." They railed against the Orthodox clergy as "lickspittles of the capitalists who, by using relics and intimidating the peasantry, have deliberately impeded [the people's] development."[147] A division of cavalry reservists garrisoned in Tver Province expressed their disgust with relic fraud and voted unanimously to exhume Prince Saint Mikhail, husband of Anna Kashinskaia. Their language reflects the confrontational vocabulary of the Civil War:

> We, the Red Army Reserve Cavalry Division of Tver, the "sons of the working people," join the workers of the Morozov factory in calling for the exhumation of the "incorruptible relics," after seeing how those same people who once forced us to worship god and tsar and who deceived us with talk of "incorruptible bodies," the kingdom of heaven, and so on, are now ruthlessly murdering our brothers. We have resolved to join our voice [to the call for] the exhumation of the relics in order to verify the facts behind those lies instilled in us since childhood by the priests and the black [monastic] host who lived off of our blood. Therefore, we salute the workers of the Morozov factory who first took the initiative into their own hands. Down with darkness, injustice, and fraud! Long live light and truth![148]

Not to be outdone, the Third Volga Fire Department issued a summons only slightly less strident, calling for the immediate exhumation of Mikhail's relics. The saint's shrine, the firemen declared, housed "a centuries-old mystery that has brought the laboring people into spiritual slavery. . . . Now, at the beginning of a new life for the Russian people, the politically conscious comrade-proletarians loudly demand the exposure of this mystery, the mystery of a centuries-old fraud. We do not want to leave this evil behind us—we must unmask it; this is our duty."[149]

Similar feelings of "duty" motivated the female delegates to a July 1919 conference for non-party women workers in Vladimir to issue a statement denouncing the cult of the saints. Over the course of the four-day conference, the delegates had been treated to a whirlwind tour of the latest, most progressive innovations and social institutions in Vladimir Province, including the new foundling home, the clinic, and the museum. Vladimir had also witnessed the most relic exhumations of any province (eight already by February 1919), and so, not surprisingly, the delegates' excursion ended with a stop at the Uspenskii Cathedral to examine the exhumed saints on display, accompanied by a physician's lecture explaining the natural process of decay and decomposition. Afterward, the women passed an indignant resolution condemning the corrupted relics uncovered in their province:

> The relics, the so-called "incorruptibles," are a fraud perpetrated by the bourgeoisie to cloud the heads of the laboring masses. Convinced of the justness of their actions, the female delegates to this conference pledge henceforth to struggle against the religious prejudices that exist among the broad masses of working women. Protesting against religious fraud and all of the clergy's inventions, the participants at this conference call upon all working women to renounce religious prejudices—the legacy of the capitalist order.[150]

In an article appearing in the official organ of the Communist Party's women's section (Zhenotdel), a delegate to the conference described the "unexpected results" the relic tour had produced among her peers, many of whom had been believers before. "Upon returning home," she wrote, "the conference participants agitated for the elimination of any and all religious prejudices, speaking out against the uselessness of religious ceremonies and the deception of the priests."[151]

The common thread uniting all these declarations in support of exhumation is, of course, the rearticulation of the Bolshevik mantra that holy relics were nothing but crude forgeries dreamed up by avaricious clergymen to keep the peasants in thrall to the Orthodox faith. But over the course of the exhumation campaign, voicing one's distaste for holy relics came to mean more than just expressing a hatred of clerical hypocrisy. Rejecting relics meant, in essence, rejecting the dead, dark legacy of the old regime itself and the values it had embodied, coupled with the affirmation of something positive. Joining one's voice to the call for exhumation meant publicly professing the ideals of progress and modernity that lay at the heart of the Bolshevik program and confirming one's status as a member of Soviet society. As Igal Halfin and Jochen Hellbeck have suggested (for the later 1920s and 1930s, respectively), the forging of new Soviet identities entailed the self-conscious sloughing off of prerevolutionary selves.[152] One would first have to abandon holy relics and all the negative traits with which Bolshevik rhetoric endowed them—sufferance, forbearance, cravenly cowardice, superstition, ignorance—before one could share in the new socialist paradise.

Throughout 1919 and 1920, while the central and provincial press continued to applaud the masses and local officials for their role in the campaign, published testimonials from outraged ex-believers called attention to the transformative power of exhumation. Iakov Maksimovich Morozov, a peasant and self-described convert to atheism, described in the pages of *Pravda* the experience of witnessing the exhumation of Saint Sergii Radonezhskii at the Troitskaia Lavra on 11 April 1919. Morozov reported that the revelation of "bones and a heap of rotten rags, dirt, moths, and larvae," accompanied by a "strong, awful, stinking smell," produced a profound change in his religious outlook and marked his own break with the traditions of generations of believers before him:

> The fraud that deceived our fathers, grandfathers, and great-grandfathers is now revealed. I myself had gone to worship at the relics many times, both in my youth and as an adult, but I was present at the exhumation. Now the lie has become completely clear to me. For many years, we peasants, carrying our last pennies with us, wasted time in coming to worship these bones, moths . . . and filth now laid bare. And not just us locals, either; people came from thousands of miles away, and will continue to come despite what has been revealed here.[153]

The local press in the northern town of Velikii Ustiug, Vologda Province, recorded the indignant reactions of a peasant woman who ruefully acknowledged that she had long believed in the sanctity of Artemii Verkol'skii's relics: "I came here last year like an idiot, and when I approached the shrine I was shaking all over with fear—I thought, here's a real incorruptible saint. But look what sort of rubbish is lying here!"[154] Reporters and pamphleteers could not resist the impulse to editorialize on "the staggering impression" that the exhumations produced on the witnesses, and they challenged their readers "to think of anything more insolent and shameful than such a mockery of believing simpletons [*prostakov*]."[155] These recorded narratives of former believers may be read as conversion stories with a peculiarly Bolshevik inflection. If prerevolutionary devotional literature rejoiced in the return of errant schismatics brought back to the bosom of the Orthodox Church through some sign of God's mercy at the shrines of the saints, these "Soviet miracle stories" celebrated the conversion of the Orthodox faithful from superstition to atheism as a result of the exposure of decayed relics.[156]

Less than five months after drunken soldiers pulled the relics of Saint Aleksandr Svirskii from his silver shrine in distant Olonets, the VIII Section of Narkomiust had endorsed "relic unmaskings" as the most effective and audacious means to shatter the authority of the Orthodox Church and its clerics in the eyes of the Russian faithful. Henceforth, holy relics were no longer to be objects of pious devotion, but subjects of public scrutiny. The narrators of the exhumation campaign, like its architects, saw the uncovering and exposure of holy relics as a means not only to combat the pernicious influence of the clergy and break the power of the Orthodox Church but also to sweep away all the cultural debris of the tsarist order and awaken the political consciousness of peasants and workers. As the editor of the Vladimir *Izvestiia* explained, Soviet power was laying bare not just rotten saintly bodies but the "decaying corpse of the autocratic order."[157] For Gorev, the relic campaign represented the shared aims and interests of the laboring masses and the Bolshevik vanguard, both locked in mortal struggle with the dark legacy of the past: "Life itself, personified by the benighted, laboring masses, approached the gilded shrines fanned with incense smoke, lifted up the coffin lids, and cast aside all the mysterious shrouds from these rotten human bones; one blast of light and fresh air was all it took to scatter this 'religious mystery' like a dark cloud."[158] The provincial propagandist P. A. Bliakhin, too, saw the metaphoric implications of exhumation. "Smoke from the church chandeliers clouded the light of truth from the poor people and blocked off the path to liberation and happiness.... Only the Great October Revolution," he wrote, "blew this smoke away from Rus', only Soviet power removed the blinders from the eyes of the people." In surveying the successes of the first two years of the exhumation campaign, Bliakhin triumphantly declared that the Russian people had finally begun to stir from centuries of relic-induced slumber: "It is as if we have been asleep like drunkards for a thousand years, and only now have we awakened, only now have we realized just how foolish we were."[159]

As archival and published statements suggest, many believers were shocked and outraged by what they saw when the shrines and reliquaries were opened and their contents examined. Some, like the peasant witness Iakov Maksimovich, claimed to have undergone an instantaneous conversion when bare bones and rags were discovered in place of uncorrupted bodies. But, as we shall see in the following chapter, many more did not. Whether a saint's relics were rotten or exuded a sweet-smelling myrrh, whether his remains were decomposed or untouched by corruption, was largely immaterial so long as the saint continued to work miracles from heaven for his brethren on earth.

6

Relics in Red Russia

ORTHODOX RESPONSES TO THE EXHUMATION CAMPAIGN

> "*Barischna* (Miss), our holy saints disappeared to heaven and substituted rags and straws for their relics when they found that their tombs were to be desecrated by nonbelievers. It was a great miracle."[1]
>
> —MARGUERITE HARRISON, 1921

> "I questioned dozens of witnesses and participants in the unmasking of church fraud: what did they feel when a crudely made dummy appeared before their very eyes, or half-rotten bones were revealed instead of an incorruptible and sweet-smelling body? They said that a miracle had happened: that the saints' bodies, knowing of the desecration being undertaken by nonbelievers, fled their coffins and hid."[2]
>
> —MAXIM GORKY, 1922

At the height of the Civil War, the adventurous American reporter (and spy) Marguerite Harrison traveled back and forth between Moscow and the provinces, relating her impressions of the ongoing Bolshevik experiment to an eager transatlantic audience. In her memoirs, Harrison writes that "I was very much interested in the effect produced by the opening of the 'mostchi' [*sic*] . . . which was undertaken by the Soviet government some two years ago to prove to the people that their sacred relics were dummies of old clothes, papier-mâché, cotton wool and straw." The Orthodox believers that Harrison spoke to displayed a range of emotions. "Some were bitterly disillusioned and turned against the church, others were simply indifferent, and many devout persons believed with touching naïveté." Harrison concluded that the relic campaign "was given the widest possible publicity by pamphlets, newspaper articles, and motion pictures, but on the whole produced very little effect." For Harrison, it was not the religious convictions of the Russian countryside that undermined the success of the relic campaign; rather, it was the backwardness and illiteracy of the village, combined with the inefficiency and incompetence of the young Soviet state: "The great mass of the people never knew anything about [the exhumations], owing to the fact that they could not read, and movies and propaganda workers could not reach the country districts."[3]

Maxim Gorky discovered a similar phenomenon. In his impressionistic study of the Russian peasantry, published abroad in 1922, Gorky recounted the varied reactions of the residents of Sergiev Posad to news of the exhumation of their beloved saint and hometown miracle-worker, Sergii Radonezhskii. The men and women with whom Gorky spoke expressed a variety of opinions on the matter. Some, generally younger, better educated, and irreligious, especially those who sympathized with the Revolution's mission to remake Russian society, were glad to see the relics exposed. "This was a good thing," young people told Gorky, "one less fraud. . . . We don't need any miracles. We want to live in a bright world without fear, without terror." Some were baffled by what they had seen. Some responded "with complete indifference [*ravnodushno*], with silent, vacant curiosity." Others still, like those quoted above, interpreted the *absence* of incorruptible relics as a great miracle, clear evidence that the hand of God had reached down to whisk away the real body of His trusted servant and prevent his desecration by the Bolsheviks. For Gorky, this last interpretation was further evidence, if any were needed, that the backward peasantry, stubbornly clinging to their old traditions and superstitions, were simply unprepared to make the cultural leap into modernity demanded of them by the new Soviet regime. Gorky packed his bags and left for Italy.[4]

Yet the fact that so many men and women held to their traditional beliefs with remarkable tenacity after the revelation of "relic fraud," was not, pace Harrison and Gorky, merely a function of problematic publicization or an illiterate audience. In his magisterial study of popular religious practices in early modern England, Keith Thomas describes the "self-confirming character" of religious faith: "Once [religion's] initial premises are accepted, no subsequent discovery will shake the believer's faith, for he can explain it away in terms of the existing system. Neither will his convictions be weakened by the failure of some accepted ritual to accomplish its desired end, for this too can be accounted for. Such systems of belief possess a resilience which makes them virtually immune to external argument."[5]

Many Orthodox believers and witnesses, when confronted with the potentially faith-shattering evidence uncovered during exhumation, displayed a similar sort of "resilience" and quite readily came up with miraculous explanations to make sense of the presence of a corrupted body. Monks in Voronezh Province, for example, assured believers that Saint Tikhon and Saint Mitrofan had actually ascended into heaven moments before their exhumation rather than suffer outrage at the hands of the Bolsheviks; similar rumors circulated in Zvenigorod concerning the relics of Saint Savva.[6] A monk in attendance at the exhumation of Makarii Zhabynskii explained to one eyewitness that the commission's failure to discover the saint's relics was itself a miracle: "The little father says he will not show himself to you Bolsheviks."[7] The Suzdal papers remarked, tongue in cheek, that "the miraculous transformation of the incorruptible relics of Feodor and Ioann . . . into rotten bones, wood shavings, rags, and cotton wool is most difficult for our sinful minds to grasp."[8] Popular wisdom held that this was precisely the point; the exhumation commission had reported broken bones and rags instead of the uncorrupted bodies of Saints Feodor and Ioann because they were atheists and sinners; only a righteous man, it was said, could truly behold the wondrous bodies of the saints.[9]

How *did* Orthodox men and women respond to the revelation of corrupted bodies and broken bones inside the shrines of their saints? And what does this tell us about how believers understood their relationships with the saints in a changing world where the economic, political, social, and cultural realms were in the process of being reconstructed by a radical new regime? According to official Soviet narratives, the irrefutable evidence uncovered during the exhumation campaign had prompted all but the most unsalvageable witnesses to rebuke the clergy and break with religious superstition. Yet the improvisational ease with which Harrison's and Gorky's interlocutors could explain away the presence of moldered vestments and broken bones in saintly shrines suggests a very different story, one that undercuts the effusive enthusiasm found in the pages of antireligious pamphlets and the local and national press.

As we have seen in the preceding chapters, Orthodox believers, lay and clergy alike, valued incorruptibility as a wondrous miracle and a great sign of God's favor, but the most highly prized relics belonged to saints who were most generous with their miracles, regardless of whether their bodies had undergone corruption. A 1919 petition from Moscow parishioners asking that Sovnarkom cancel the upcoming exhumation of Sergii Radonezhskii underscored a fact that Krasikov and his comrades at the VIII Section seem to have forgotten or never known: it mattered little to devotees whether a saint's relics were corrupted or not. As the petitioners put it, "The Holy Church venerates the remains of God's saints not on account of their incorruptibility, but for their holy lives. Let these remains take the form of dried, half-decayed bones and ordinary dust and they would still [possess] for us a strength that is holy and bountiful."[10] Simply put, Orthodox believers were in search of more than perfectly preserved bodies from their saints; they expected miracles and could overlook corruption or decay provided that cures and healings were forthcoming.

As we saw in Chapters Two and Three, the majority of recorded miracles from the late imperial period involved some degree of physical communication between believers and the sacred—either kneeling at the shrines and graves of the saints, anointing oneself with holy water or oil from the reliquary, or kissing or touching the holy relics themselves. The importance that Orthodox believers placed on tangibility and proximity in their devotions made it all but inevitable that the relic campaign would give rise to conflicts over the right to access, possess, and interact with holy relics. What prompted believers to draft petitions, stage protests, and on rare occasions, resort to violence was not only the act of exhumation itself but also, even more important, the threat, real or imagined, that Soviet power would remove the miracle-working bodies from the community and thus deprive individuals and communities alike of their most powerful means of recourse to the sacred. Relics still mattered to Orthodox men and women even after the Revolution, and so believers sought to retain the services and continued favor of the saints in heaven by safeguarding their bodies and shrines on earth. This meant not only defending relics from exhumation and profanation but also making sure that these powerful sources of assistance, whether corrupted or not, remained in the communities where they belonged.

Because the kind of intimate friendships that lay believers and clergy forged with the holy dead were predicated on patterns of reciprocity and respect, any answer to the question of how Orthodox believers responded to the relic campaign must, to some degree or other, engage the issue of resistance. As William Husband has shown for the period 1917–1932, Orthodox men and women drew from a vast arsenal of resistance strategies—both overt and subtle—in an attempt to protect their sacred objects and traditional religious practices from profanation.[11] Lynne Viola has made a persuasive argument for viewing resistance in the Soviet context as "only one part of a continuum of societal responses" to external pressure, one that could take various shapes and guises depending on the assumptions and expectations of the actors involved.[12] Orthodox resistance to the relic campaign, then, encompasses a broad template of available strategies whereby Orthodox believers could articulate their opposition to the exposure and seizure of holy relics. These strategies ranged from petition drives and official protests registered through the proper Bolshevik channels to such extralegal means of resistance as the spreading of rumors, the staging of demonstrations, and on rare but notable occasions, heated and violent confrontations with Soviet power. This chapter surveys the broad response of reactions that exhumation elicited among Orthodox men and women across Soviet Russia, with particular focus on two local case studies: the small northern town of Vel'sk, home to the miracle-working relics of Saint Prokopii Ust'ianskii, and the Tver region, which had celebrated the canonization of Saint Anna Kashinskaia just a decade before. Such an examination allows us to gauge some measure of the continued relevance that individuals and communities ascribed to their saints as real and ever-present members of the religious collective, even amid times of great turmoil and uncertainty.

Pious Subversion

Violent and Non-Violent Resistance

Just as they had in the imperial Russian countryside and would again during collectivization, Russian Orthodox women often took the lead in defending the boundaries of the moral community from state intrusion. Women could exploit the expectations that patriarchal society placed upon them to act in confrontational ways that their husbands, sons, and brothers could not.[13] Gorev, for example, reported that a crowd of "religious-minded and fanatical" peasant women had tried to forestall the exhumation of Saint Sergii by creating a human barricade outside the gates of the Troitskaia Lavra, boldly challenging the soldiers and Chekists with cries of "Shoot at us, you tyrants!"[14] Incident was averted when the protestors scattered, mistaking for cannons the bulky cameras and lighting equipment being unloaded from the trucks by Kuleshov's film crew. A *samizdat'* account of Sergii's exhumation, however, authored by a young seminarian present at the exhumation, reports that the women "seized this moment to break into the Lavra," charging the wooden gates, which had been opened half-way to allow the trucks to pass through: "They threw themselves onto the file of Red Army soldiers. Horses whinnied, rearing up on their hind legs, the women cried out but they did not fall back until one of the soldiers fired into the air; the barricade was not breached and the gates were once again slammed shut."[15]

In March 1921, two Cheka officers and a professor of chemistry were sent from Moscow to Chernigov to oversee the transfer of Saint Feodosii's relics from the cathedral church to the city museum of popular education. "So as not to give the corpse's transfer . . . an air of thievery and shroud it in secrecy," the experts decided to remove the relics from the church in broad daylight. Despite these precautions, the operation was impaired by protests from the Orthodox faithful: "During the removal a crowd of approximately one hundred people gathered, mostly women. Many of them shouted hysterically, 'Give us back the prelate,' 'Why are you taking [him]?' 'Don't you touch him,' 'Don't you take him,' following the wagon in which the relics

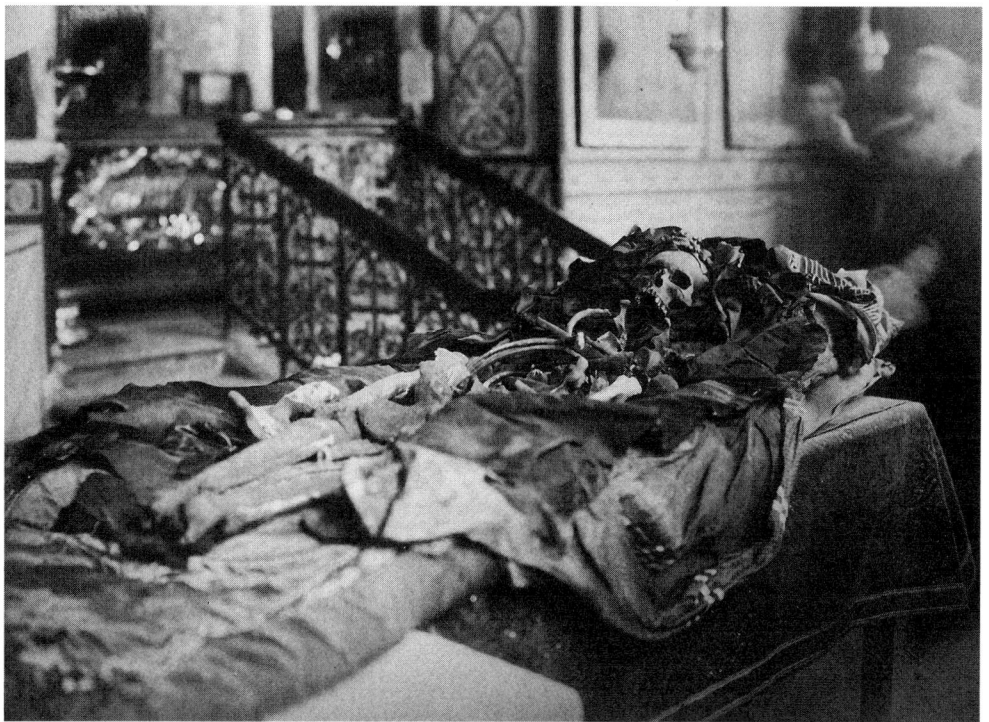

FIGURE 15—The relics of Archbishop Saint Ioann Novgorodskii, exhumed at the Sofiiskii Cathedral, 3 April 1919. GARF, f. A-353, op. 3, d. 734, l. 12.

were brought to the museum with tears and shouting."[16] Older women at times attempted more persuasive means to secure the return of their relics. A Cheka officer in Novgorod reported that a group of elderly women visited his offices to request that the recently exhumed Prince Vladimir and Archbishop Ioann be returned to the Sofiiskii Cathedral (see Figure 15). "We want you to give us our relics back," their spokeswoman boldly told the officer. "What are they to you?"[17]

Monastic communities, diocesan leaders, and rank-and-file clergymen often took upon themselves the initiative to protect holy relics in their custody from exhumation or abduction. One tactic involved simple subterfuge. In August 1919, as Red Army units advanced on White-held Tobol'sk, Bishop Irinarkh ordered the relics of Saint Ioann Tobol'skii buried in their cypress-wood coffin beneath the floorboards of the Pokrovskii Cathedral "in order to avoid desecration and mockery" from the Bolsheviks.[18] Similarly, before fleeing with the White armies in 1919, the brethren of the Nikolaevskii monastery in Verkhotur'e buried Saint Simeon's relics in the monastery courtyard for safekeeping and took the saint's silver shrine with them.[19] In the summer of 1920, an undercover Cheka agent who had infiltrated a group of Orthodox believers centered at the Danilovskii monastery in Moscow reported to his superiors that members of the group were discussing the possibility of saving the monastery's relics from possible seizure by concealing them inside a sealed shrine until "the stormy political struggle dies down."[20]

Some clergymen tried to delay or postpone the exhumations by creating conditions under which relic inspections would be legally impermissible. Taking advantage of the VIII Section's instructions that exhumations were not to be performed while worshipers were inside the church, monks at the Verkhoturskii monastery conducted round-the-clock prayer vigils at the shrine of Saint Simeon so that local officials could not seal the miracle-worker's shrine to worshipers.[21] In Tver on 18 May 1919, clergymen prolonged an already inordinately lengthy noontime liturgy in hopes of preventing Soviet officials from carrying out the exhumation of Prince Saint Mikhail, scheduled for one o'clock. The Tver *Izvestiia* reported that when the authorities finally managed to empty the church of "fanatical worshipers," the clergy simply reassembled the crowd—nearly a thousand strong—on the square in front of the cathedral. A priest called on all the faithful to remove their hats and then led them in the singing of anthems to the saints and shouts of "Christ is risen!" in an effort to drown out the exhumation commission inside.[22] Another tactic occasionally employed by clerics was to inform exhumation commissions that the relic inspection could not be performed, as per VIII Section guidelines, because it coincided with a religious holiday. Here the clergy used to their advantage the preponderance of feast days and festivals in the Orthodox liturgical calendar, knowing full well that almost every day of the year was marked by the observance of some religious holiday or other.[23]

Krasikov's VIII Section had stressed repeatedly the importance of recruiting (or gently coercing) clergymen to personally unwrap the relics from their shrouds and handle the contents of the shrines themselves, thus allowing local officials to avoid any potential allegations of impropriety and sacrilege. On several occasions, however, priests and monks destabilized the proceedings by simply refusing to participate. Some clerics begged off this responsibility altogether, claiming that they were unwilling to run the risk of divine retribution that would befall those who profaned the bodies and bones of the saints. During the exhumation of Saint Sergii, for example, Archimandrite Kronid recused himself of this duty at the last minute and walked out of the church, leaving one of his subordinates to remove the relics from the shrine.[24] Bishop Pavel of Suzdal refused outright the district ispolkom's invitation to attend the exhumation of Saints Ioann and Feodor, scheduled for 10 February 1919 in the bishop's own cathedral church. In an addendum to the official exhumation protocol, Pavel tersely acknowledged that his presence had been requested by the commission but that he had "refrained from attending." The omission of any explanation for his absence underscored the bishop's opposition to the exhumations.[25] A member of the diocesan council in Vladimir similarly declined an invitation to take part in the exhumation of Saint Avraamii, claiming that he could not do so without the council's express permission. This was unlikely to be granted, he argued, since the exhumation was itself an unlawful violation of Narkomiust's own instructions on the separation decree, the fourth paragraph of which forbade actions "not of a necessary nature and which may be construed as insulting" to the religious sentiments of believers.[26] As we shall see, such legal wranglings were deployed frequently, though largely without success, to forestall relic exhumations throughout Soviet Russia.

Other clerics complied with orders to take part in the exhumations but did so in such a way that the proceedings were dragged out to almost interminable lengths. On 16 March 1919, members of the local executive committee in Belev, Tula Province, found themselves engaged in a "lengthy altercation" with the brethren of the Zhabynskii monastery, who refused to allow the Bolsheviks into the church without first seeing proper documentation of the commission's credentials and examining the text of the resolution calling for Saint Makarii's exhumation.[27] According to the chairman of the Zadonskii district ispolkom, Voronezh Province, monks at the Bogoroditskii monastery tried unsuccessfully to sabotage the exhumation of Saint Tikhon by discharging their duties as ordered but with intentional incompetence; one monk allegedly tipped a candle onto a pile of cotton wool, thus sparking a small fire, while another's deliberate clumsiness sent a movie camera crashing to the floor.[28] The prior of the Georgievskii Cathedral in Vladimir regretted to inform the exhumation commission that his church lacked the tools and instruments necessary to pry the lid off the sealed marble shrine containing the relics of Saint Dmitrii; thwarted, the delegates took the cleric at his word that the coffin contained bones similar to those they had seen in other shrines.[29]

Clerics who participated in the relic inspections could subvert the proceedings in ways that completely undermined the intended effect of exhumation. One such example occurred during the exhumation of Saint Evfrosiniia at Polotsk on 13 May 1922. The nun entrusted with removing the saint's shroud did so with such deliberateness and loving reverence that the exhumation assumed the impression of a religious ceremony. When the commission members ordered Sister Neonila to go faster, she continued at her own pace, replying: "Don't rush, you've waited this long."[30] A similarly subversive recoding of the exhumation ritual took place at the Sofiiskii Cathedral in Novgorod in April 1919. After some initial stalling,

Bishop Aleksii duly removed the relics of Saint Nikita Novgorodskii from their shrine but then unexpectedly bent down to kiss the saint's forehead. A Cheka witness reported that many of the faithful who had crowded the cathedral fell to their knees in prayer and followed "the bishop's infectious example," much to the disdain of the exhumation commission.[31] As this incident suggests, Soviet authorities could not always guarantee that curious crowds who strolled into a monastery cathedral or parish church to gaze at exhumed relics would walk away with the intended impression. Reports from Karelia, for example, indicate that dozens of old women crossed themselves piously as they filed past the exhumed remains of Saint Elisei Sumskii.[32]

Possibilities for resistance extended even after the saint's body had been exhumed and photographed. Following the exhumation of Saint Mitrofan Voronezhskii, provincial authorities ordered that his shattered relics be left opened and unsealed so that curious visitors could see how the monks had allegedly fooled them with tales of an uncorrupted body (see Figure 16, the shrine of Gavriil left open for viewing). But as the local Voronezh press reported, the clergy manipulated the opportunity to their advantage, transforming the public viewing into something resembling a religious revival meeting. Instead of simply placing Mitrofan's relics on a table, the monks of the Mitrofanskii monastery and the archbishop of Voronezh arranged the bones with great care and then draped them with a layer of cotton wool and a gilded linen cloth. The clergy encouraged bystanders not only to examine the relics but to step forward and touch and kiss the saintly body for themselves. One afternoon, on a spring day when the monastery church was filled to capacity with onlookers, the monks led a young blind boy from a nearby village to the table. According to an irate letter published in the Voronezh press, no sooner had the child laid his hand on the relics than the monks shouted out that he had been cured by the power of Saint Mitrofan: "The old women and ignorant, unconscious people believed the monks, oohed and aahed, and crossed themselves." When the skeptical letter-writer cornered one of the monastery brethren and asked him why the blind boy had been the only one to receive a cure from touching Mitrofan's bones, the monk answered that the Bolsheviks and doubters "did not approach [the relics] with faith," whereas the child believed and was healed.[33] The historian Iu. V. Got'e noted in his diary that the monks of the Troitskaia Lavra complied with officials' orders to leave the body of Saint Sergii Radonezhskii exposed following exhumation, but in such a way as to corroborate that they had indeed told believers the truth about the age of the relics: "[T]hey have left [Sergii's body] exactly as it was upon exhumation; as I learned today, that is being done deliberately and, in my opinion, correctly; they say that the examining doctors confirmed that the skeleton had lain there for five hundred years. . . . Thus our priests, using

FIGURE 16—Children file past the relics of Saint Gavriil the Martyr, exhumed in Moscow, 1919. GARF, f. A-353, op. 3, d. 734, l. 23.

their wits and leaving the relics uncovered, correctly wish to show: look, we do not conceal what was and what is—and in doing so, of course, they only strengthen religious feeling."[34]

Clerics also used their influence to dispute and discredit the official exhumation reports that appeared in the Soviet press. A monk in Vladimir Province informed worshipers that, despite what they may have read or heard, the bodies of their local princely saints were "untouched by decay" when they were exhumed on 13 February 1919. Gleb's skin was "as soft and elastic as when living," and Iurii's severed head had been discovered miraculously reattached to his torso, wondrous details that the exhumation commission had deliberately omitted from the official protocols in order to deceive the local faithful.[35] The archimandrite of the Verkhoturskii monastery insisted that exhumation officials affix an addendum to their published protocols, noting that he and his brethren disputed the commission's claims that the relics of Saint Simeon gave off a "foul odor" of decay.[36] In Irkutsk, clerics and lay activists simply published and distributed their own accounts of the exhumation of Saint Innokentii. These "counter protocols" disputed the inventory of items found within the shrine and denied charges of bodily corruption, claiming the relics were, in fact, remarkably well preserved.[37]

Some clerics drew on patristic texts and linguistic arguments to make a case that the Soviets were mistaken to sift through saintly shrines in search of uncorrupted bodies. As we saw in Chapter One, Orthodox prelates and prominent lay spokesmen had sparred with Soviet officials from the very outset of the relic campaign over the definition of moshchi, arguing that the word need not refer to whole bodies completely untouched by corruption but could be applied to bones, ashes, or any physical remains. Bishop Aleksii of Novgorod made a similar argument at a pre-exhumation meeting of the commission appointed to examine the relics in the Sofiiskii Cathedral:

> Our Church, in accordance with the Greek Church, has never taught that the relics of the saints are bodies preserved absolutely and entirely. According to the teachings of the Church, relics are the remains of saints, whether they be bodies or bones, there is no difference. We know that some remains have been preserved for longer [periods of time], others for less, but for us it is all the same . . . since we revere the remains for the fact that they belong to saints who are precious to us and in whose prayers and help we believe . . . regardless of in what measure they are preserved, whether only bones [are] left, or entire bodies.[38]

The purpose of such arguments, of course, was to dissuade the Bolsheviks from continuing to exhume the shrines of the saints. As N. D. Kuznetsov, professor of church law at the Moscow Theological Academy, pointed out in a public lecture at the Polytechnic Museum in Moscow, if the Orthodox Church itself did not define *moshchi* to mean exclusively uncorrupted bodies, it was eminently ironic that the godless Bolsheviks should adhere to such a strict fundamentalist definition. Since moshchi could also refer to bones, he asked, why did the Bolsheviks persist in exhuming shrines and then feign outrage when they failed to find whole bodies?[39] Choosing to err on the side of caution, Patriarch Tikhon issued special instructions to his bishops in February 1919, authorizing them to conduct secret relic inspections at their discretion and to remove from the saintly shrines any extraneous objects that might give "grounds for mockery and temptation with regards to holy relics."[40] Judging from the inventories of odd items that continued to turn up in relic shrines, it would appear that the patriarch's instructions were not carried out in most dioceses. Nevertheless, the gesture suggests that the Church leadership was seeking creative ways to comply with the state's demands while continuing to subvert the exhumation project from within.

Despite the very real strains that had surfaced within Orthodox communities at the end of the old regime and during the revolution of 1917, diocesan officials, monastic clergy, parish priests, and lay believers temporarily put aside their differences and rallied round their relics. Such efforts were aided in no small part by the activities of diocesan councils and consistories, which continued to operate during and after the Civil War, though officially outlawed by Narkomiust in the spring of 1920.[41] One of the most broad-based efforts at cooperative resistance took place in Novgorod where lay and clerical groups in the city joined forces in a large-scale effort to secure the proper reinterment of the saints exhumed at the Sofiiskii Cathedral in April 1919. The diocesan council worked together with Metropolitan Arsenii and Bishop Aleksii to print "several thousand" brochures and distribute them in churches throughout the diocese. Within two days of the exhumation, priests were delivering fiery sermons calling on parishioners to sign petitions demanding the reburial of the relics, while teachers in religious schools urged their young students to do likewise. Cheka officers observed cashiers and shopkeepers surreptitiously passing folded petitions to customers along with their change. Highly coordinated as these joint efforts were, resistance was thwarted when Cheka agents raided the home of a Novgorod deacon and discovered a huge cache of contraband petitions and pamphlets. Arrests of the principal figures in the group soon followed. Much to the consternation of Novgorod officials, subsequent investigation revealed that the "counter-revolutionary" circle included not just clerics and shopkeepers but even state employees in the Soviet civil service whose enthusiasm for their hometown saints was undimmed by exhumation.[42]

Museums also became contested sites of resistance to the relic campaign. Although Nikolai Semashko boasted that the "overwhelming majority of visitors [to the Narkomzdrav museum] come to see the fraud with their own eyes . . . [and] voice their indignation with the con artists," the commissar was obliged to admit that there were still "incorrigibles" who refused to subscribe to the museum's programmatic message. One visitor expressed outrage to museum staff that the corpse of the mummified counterfeiter was on display alongside the relics of Saint Ioasaf Belgorodskii; such a "lowlife" (*smerd*) did not belong beside a saint.[43] Stories spread across the city that, while the bodies of Saint Ioasaf and the Vilnius Martyrs continued to exude a sweet-smelling fragrance, the criminal's body gave off the unmistakable odor of putrefaction. On the museum's question-and-answer bulletin board, where visitors could post questions to be answered by museum personnel, a frequent query was "Why does the counterfeiter smell so bad?" Rumor had it that Soviet medical personnel were obliged periodically to whisk away the offending corpse to a laboratory under cover of night and deploy all their skills (always unsuccessfully, it was alleged) to forestall any further decomposition. The implication of the rumor, of course, was that, while

Soviet scientists were unable to keep the counterfeiter fresh with the aid of chemistry and physics, some higher power was looking after the body of Saint Ioasaf.[44]

Despite posted notices that forbade the "performance of ceremonies" in the Narkomzdrav museum, some believers, especially peasant women, would pray openly before the saints on display, crossing themselves, kissing the glass cases, and irritating the tour guides with their defiant gestures.[45] Believers burned candles before the relics of Saint Feodosii Totemskii, on display in the city museum of church antiquities in Vologda. The saint's relics were purported to work miracles inside the museum, and cases were reported of believers trying to bribe museum workers into allowing them to perform a public prayer service. Flooded with petitions signed by tens of thousands of Orthodox believers, the Vologda Province department of justice begged the VIII Section for permission to relocate the relics to an anthropological museum in another city, arguing that it was "completely undesirable and inexpedient" to keep them in the museum of church antiquities: "[T]he placement of the relics amongst icons, sacred statues, iconostases, and other religious cult objects . . . has created among the unconscious masses the illusion that these relics are being exhibited for church veneration."[46] Museum officials in Leningrad hung a placard over the case containing the exhumed relics of Saint Feodosii Chernigovskii, explaining that the saint's mummified body was the product of natural conditions, not divine intervention. Nevertheless, as the Riga correspondent for the *London Times* reported, "The result was not what was expected. Crowds came not to be persuaded of the falsity of their beliefs, but to see the 'holy relics of Saint Theodosius,' the placard being unheeded."[47]

In the early months of the relic exhibition at the Narkomzdrav museum, Orthodox priests in Moscow actively encouraged their parishioners to attend the exhibit and serve as a vocal counterbalance to the antireligious propaganda being spread by the docents. Impromptu debates and heated exchanges would often break out on the museum grounds, pitting priests and believers against lecturers from the Moscow party organization.[48] At the Voronezh museum of local history, where the relics of Saint Mitrofan were on display, Orthodox interlopers infiltrated tour groups and shouted down their guides as traitors telling lies about the miracle-worker.[49] Semashko professed to welcome such diversity of opinion: "We freely admit anyone who comes [to the exhibit] to openly express his outlook and attitude. Sometimes an informative and instructive discussion ensues—let us not worry about this, for the truth always wins."[50] But the presence of believers providing running commentary on the exhibitions undermined and subverted both the mission of the museum and the exhumation project more broadly.[51]

PETITIONS AND LEGAL RESISTANCE

Undoubtedly the most common, though seldom the most successful, mode of nonviolent resistance was through written appeals and petitions to state and party authorities. Clerical and lay opponents of the relic campaign often proved themselves to be legal virtuosi, citing Bolshevik decrees and legal codes verbatim to make the case that the exhumations were in violation of the government's own legislation on the free status of religion in the Soviet Republic. William Husband describes this tactic as a "co-option" of Soviet legality, one in which protestors would challenge the letter of the law "in minute detail."[52] During her short stint in the Commissariat of Justice, the Italian Marxist Angelica Balabanoff observed the phenomenon firsthand. Commenting on the "shrewdness" displayed by believers petitioning Narkomiust officials for the return of Church property, Balabanoff remarked: "It was surprising how quickly they had picked up Bolshevik terminology and newly coined phrases and how well they understood the various articles of the new legislation. They seemed to have lived with it all their lives."[53] The strategy of petition writing reflects not only the tenacious refusal of believers to be parted from their relics but also Russian citizens' growing familiarity with the contours of Soviet legality and their ability to turn and twist those very decrees to their own ends. The former is a testament to the strong ties of religious belief and practice, while the latter may well represent a continuation of the trend toward legal recourse already underway in the Russian countryside since the judicial reforms of the mid-nineteenth century.[54]

Although many petitioners sought to boost their chances for a favorable response by addressing their appeals directly to figures seen as potentially more sympathetic to their plight—for example, the "peasant Bolshevik," M. I. Kalinin, or Lenin himself—most of these were subsequently forwarded by secretarial staff for the VIII Section's consideration.[55] If petitioners routinely sought to bypass the usual chain of command by appealing directly to the top, the administrative apparatus, for its part, did its best to resist any attempts at circumvention. Many would-be petitioners found themselves thwarted by bureaucratic obstacles at every step. An illustrative case in point is that of I. V. Popov, adjunct professor at the Moscow Theological Academy and professor of psychology at Moscow State University. The tale of Popov's tangles with the Bolshevik bureaucracy is a subject worthy of a Zoshchenko short story. In late 1919, Popov, who had served as a lay delegate to the Church Sobor and had close ties with various religious organizations and brotherhoods in Moscow diocese, submitted a petition to Sovnarkom on behalf of lay societies in Sergiev Posad, asking that the exhumed relics of Saint Sergii Radonezhskii be allowed to remain open for veneration in the Troitskaia Lavra. Some days later, when Popov inquired as to the status of the petition, he was languidly informed by a Sovnarkom functionary that it had been forwarded to the VIII Section for consideration. When asked why Sovnarkom's members had not bothered to read a petition directly addressed to them, the bureaucrat assured Popov that in such matters Sovnarkom preferred to act on the basis of the VIII Section's recommendations. The professor turned next to Kalinin, expressing concerns that the government was failing to heed the voice of the common people. Kalinin, to his credit, sent a brief note to People's Commissar of Justice D. I. Kurskii, requesting that he pay particular attention to the petition in question when it arrived at his desk. The following day, however, when Popov appeared at Kurskii's office to plead his case in person, he was told the commissar was too busy to see him. Irritated beyond measure, Popov tried to register a formal grievance with the local bureau of complaints, but there the hapless professor ran up against the same stonewalls he had encountered elsewhere. Having exhausted all his options and with nowhere else to turn, Popov vented his frustrations to his associate and former co-delegate to the Sobor, Archpriest N. A. Liubimov. Liubimov related his friend's unhappy story in a report to Patriarch Tikhon and the members of the Supreme Church Council, who listened to the professor's plight with sympathy and great interest but were utterly powerless to help.[56]

Although by the 1930s petitioning as a legalistic strategy in defense of religious traditions was being practiced frequently even by peasants at both the village and district level, it was principally clerics, lay activists, and the faculty members of Orthodox seminaries and academies who most commonly made use of the practice during the Civil War and the relic campaign.[57] The most prominent proponent of petitions and appeals in protest of relic exhumation was Patriarch Tikhon. In March 1919, Tikhon sought to prevent the upcoming exhumation of Saint Sergii Radonezhskii by appealing directly to Sovnarkom. The patriarch framed his argument in moral and legal terms: not only would exhumation "instill deep distress in the hearts of the faithful" but such an action would be "contrary to the decree on the freedom of religious conscience issued by Soviet power."[58] Again, on 10 May 1920, the patriarch drafted a more sharply worded protest to Sovnarkom concerning the recent decision to put Saint Sergii's relics on display in Moscow:

> [T]he closing of the monastery churches [at the Troitskaia Lavra] and the intention to remove from them relics of the most vital importance impinge on our religious conscience; it is an intrusion by the civil authorities into the internal life and belief system of the Church, an intrusion that runs counter to the decree on the separation of Church and state, counter to the repeated statements from the higher central authorities concerning the freedom of belief, and counter to the [Soviet government's] assurances that there is no general order for the removal of devotional objects from churches.[59]

Three months later, on 9 August, Tikhon submitted another petition to M. I. Kalinin, in which he argued that the exhumation and subsequent confiscation of holy relics was in clear violation of the January 1918 separation decree:

> The fact is that the decree on the separation of Church and state not only prohibits "the promulgation of any laws and resolutions that may inhibit or impinge upon the freedom of conscience" (Paragraph 2) but even guarantees "the free exercise of religious ceremonies, so long as they do not disturb the peace" (Paragraph 5). Given such principles, the desecration of relics is an act that is clearly unlawful from the point of view of Soviet legality. . . . Holy relics are an object of devotion and their place is in a church, not in a museum.[60]

In addition, the patriarch challenged the legal basis for the state's decision to exhibit the relics of the so-called Vilnius Martyrs, on the grounds that the saints' bodies "are not the property of the RSFSR but belong to the Church in the Latvian state and are subject to return to Vilnius."[61] Though legally valid, Tikhon's arguments did not dissuade the Bolshevik leadership. In the margins of the patriarch's petition, Kalinin scrawled "Take no action," and the plea was dismissed.[62]

Other clerics, like Metropolitan Veniamin of St. Petersburg, argued that the exhumations were unlawful insofar as they were being carried out against the wishes of the very same workers and peasants whose interests the Soviet government purported to represent. On 13 September 1919, Veniamin presented G. E. Zinoviev and the members of the Petrograd Soviet with a formal letter of complaint concerning plans to proceed with the exhumation of Saint Aleksandr Nevskii.[63] Claiming that "no small number of workers and peasants" were opposed to such action, Veniamin urged that municipal officials take into account the opinions of the citizenry when deciding the fate of "one of the principal sacred objects of the city of Petrograd." In an editorial response published in *Revoliutsiia i tserkov'*, Krasikov countered the metropolitan's arguments, claiming that the Petrograd Soviet "is nothing more than the organ of the laboring masses of the city of Petrograd and the district." Because the Soviet state stood as the vanguard of the masses, there could, by definition, be no disparity whatsoever between the preferences of the proletariat and the policies of the Petrograd authorities.[64]

Some petitioners formulated quid pro quo arguments to make a case in defense of their relics. One of the most active petitioners and vocal critics of the regime's relic policy was N. A. Liubimov, protopresbyter of the Uspenskii Cathedral in the Moscow Kremlin. As chairman of the Delegation in Defense of the Rights of the Russian Orthodox Church, a watchdog organization established in 1918 by order of Patriarch Tikhon, Liubimov received petitions from parishes across Soviet Russia and registered his constituents' complaints with the proper authorities. In August 1919, Liubimov lodged a protest with the VIII Section on behalf of parishioners in Iaroslavl, who had contacted him in distress over the pending removal of their recently exhumed relics "to parts unknown":

> Such actions by the local authorities deeply offend the religious feelings of the faithful. And this is understandable. For some, [relics] are a sacred object and yet they are hauled away as museum rarities for the public viewing and, sometimes, laughter of others. This is the same as if an image of Buddha were to be taken from a group of Buddhist faithful and sent to a museum, or the tomb of Mohammed from Muslims. Anyone who in any way considers the internal emotions and religious feelings of others can understand just how inexpressible is the pain, spiritual suffering, and heartache that such actions cause the faithful.[65]

Liubimov pointed out that recently an ancient copy of the Koran from the State Public Library had been presented to a group of Muslims in Petrograd and argued that if the government allowed members of one faith to retain their devotional objects it should, by right, grant the same liberty to all believers.[66] Krasikov rejected the cleric's logic as faulty, maintaining that unlike relics the Koran was "a genuine historical document and not a fraud or falsification for some sort of supernatural purpose." Liubimov's petition was dismissed and never brought before the Narkomiust collegium.[67]

While the writers of letters to Soviet newspapers often engaged in discursive acrobatics to phrase their content in the Bolshevik vernacular, the authors of petitions tended to use a more straightforward tone in keeping with the earnest nature of their requests.[68] In some cases, the end result was poignant. In a personal letter addressed to Lenin himself, Mariia Ivanovna Svet, a female lay member of the Brotherhood of Saint Aleksii and an employee in the Moscow City Department of Public Health, requested that plans for the upcoming exhumation of Saint Aleksii at the Kremlin's Chudov monastery be canceled and the saint's relics "be returned to those who love him":

> Comrade Lenin! Dear to You are the bodies and graves of those warriors who fell for socialism and who are buried on the Kremlin Wall! And infinitely dear to us is the coffin of our spiritual leader, Saint Aleksii—for us, his remains are sacred.
>
> Here in free Russia let there be, at last, no loathsome violence on the part of unbelievers toward that which is dear and sacred in the hearts of the faithful.
>
> [I pray] to Saint Aleksii, the prelate of love, that he may touch Your heart and that You, in granting our request, will bring infinite happiness to the three thousand members of our brotherhood.[69]

Despite Svet's prayers, the prelate failed to enter Lenin's heart and the exhumation proceeded as planned.[70]

Collective petitions, often with hundreds or thousands of signatures appended, possessed the authority of large numbers and, though seldom successful in achieving their aims, represented the continued relevance that holy relics had for the Orthodox communities where they resided. Here, too, collective petitions addressed to local officials and central authorities demonstrate the cooperative grassroots efforts of clerics and lay people to mobilize in defense of the sacred. In the spring of 1919, the brethren of the Troitskaia Lavra circulated a petition throughout the surrounding districts protesting the imminent exhumation of Saint Sergii Radonezhskii. Although they managed to secure some 5,000 signatures from the local peasantry and clergy, the Sergiev Posad executive committee ignored the petition and proceeded with Sergii's exhumation as planned. Soviet publicists like Mikhail Gorev dismissed the monks' efforts as counterrevolutionary provocation, claiming that the clergy had simply gone door to door throughout the countryside and "literally extorted signatures from the ignorant masses."[71]

The argument that such petitions were solely the work of a few high-ranking clerics is belied, however, by the archival evidence. Parishes throughout Moscow sent petitions with hundred of signatures to Sovnarkom, pleading that officials rethink their plans to exhume Saint Sergii. Parishioners of the Church of St. Sergii Radonezhskii in Moscow protested "from the very depths of our souls" the upcoming exhumation of their parish's patron saint. As they explained, the exposure and public display of Sergii's relics would be "an insult to our Orthodox faith and our national feeling [*narodnogo chuvstva*]. Let the sacred objects of every religion be respected, and let the relics of the venerable [Sergii] remain untouched." Leaving Sergii Radonezhskii's relics in peace (and in place) was not only a moral issue but a legal one, as well. "The law demands this," the petitioners explained, referring Sovnarkom's members to refer to paragraphs 4 and 5 of their own decree on the separation of Church and state.[72]

Even more petitions circulated in the fall of 1920, when talk turned to removing Sergii's relics from the Lavra and placing them on display in a Moscow museum. Workers and cafeteria employees at the State Aviation Factory No. 2 in Moscow submitted a "most humble request" to their "comrades" on Sovnarkom that Sergii's relics be allowed to remain where they had for the last five hundred years: "We believe that special help and joy in life comes down to us from God through our prayers before the relics of the Venerable Sergii."[73] Orthodox residents of Sergievskii district, Moscow Province, asked that Soviet power "not disturb the holy relics, so that there may be free access [to them] at all times."[74] "Together with You, Comrades, do we endure cold and hunger," wrote workers and housing committee chairmen in Moscow's Blagushinskii district, thus "we would most humbly ask our supreme comrades to satisfy our petition . . . we will follow in the footsteps of our grandfathers and great-grandfathers, who for several hundred years venerated with great feeling [Saint Sergii's] many-centuries' old relics."[75] Petitions were submitted by entire buildings, with the signatures of whole households—husbands, wives, and children alike. In some cases, mothers wrote the names and ages of their children who were still too young to sign their own names.[76] "As free citizens, we ask you to give satisfaction to our religious feelings," wrote residents of a Moscow working-class district. "For us, these sacred objects [Sergii's relics] are more dear than anything on earth; like a fish without water, so too can we not live without [our] sacred objects."[77]

Some Orthodox petitioners argued that the relics belonged to them and that Soviet power should entrust the bodies of the saints to their private care. In March 1919, a lay confraternity in Pereslavl, Vladimir Province, wrote to Lenin himself with a complaint that the relics of the Venerable Daniil, exhumed the month before, were still lying exposed and had not been returned to their proper resting place. The petitioners had asked the district ispolkom for permission to march with Daniil's relics in procession through the town, after which they would personally return the exhumed relics to their shrine. "For some reason," however, local officials had not seen fit to grant this request and so, "on the basis of the VIII Section's own instructions on the separation of Church and state," the petitioners sought Lenin's permission.[78] Lay and clerical members of the diocesan council in Voronezh presented a list of grievances to the provincial ispolkom in the spring of 1919; heading the list was a request that the Bogoroditskii monastery be reopened for worship, the archimandrite be released from prison, and the exhumed relics of Tikhon Zadonskii be transferred to the council's possession, in accordance with Narkomiust's instructions on the use of liturgical property by lay believers. The Voronezh ispolkom sought the advice of the NKVD, whose staff forwarded the question to Krasikov. The VIII Section director replied that he could not speak to the specifics of the local conditions in Voronezh and reiterated that the proper place for relics was in a museum, not in believers' homes.[79]

Petitions requesting that holy relics be entrusted to the care of lay believers or parish communities were routinely ignored or denied.[80] Although their authors cited all of the right edicts and decrees in making their cases, Soviet jurists rejected the argument that holy bodies fell under the rubric of liturgical property. The author of a 1920 antireligious handbook designed for Cossack readers explained the distinction in simple terms: "Soviet power grants freedom of worship to all religious confessions, but it cannot grant freedom of fraud in the name of plunder."[81] Krasikov phrased the matter more bluntly. Rejecting a petition for exhumed relics to be given to a parish council in Iaroslavl, the VIII Section director maintained that "in the twentieth century, in the Soviet Republic, corpses or the remains of corpses or imitation corpses cannot be handed over to private citizens." Krasikov went on to explain that while Soviet power did not prevent "private citizens from venerating the memory of any figure from any period of history," there were certain "boundaries" placed on the exercise of that devotion. Such boundaries, according to Krasikov, did not represent an infringement of the decree on freedom of conscience but, rather, a concession to the dictates of "modern-day science, public hygiene, pedagogy, the revolutionary consciousness of the laboring masses, and so forth."[82]

Clearly, the Orthodox believers who petitioned for the return of their relics saw things very differently. In 1920 city parishes in Vologda, for example, circulated petitions to secure the release of Saint Feodosii's relics from the museum of church antiquities. Among the most astonishing of these documents is the petition drafted by parishioners of the Church of St. Dimitrii:

> It is known that last year, 1919, the relics in question were secretly removed from Tot'ma to Vologda by order of Soviet power and exhibited in a museum, not as a sacred object belonging to the Orthodox faithful, but as an object that supposedly served as a means for the clergy to defraud the religious worship of Christians.
>
> But we are not children that you can trick us, and we know what relics are. We have revered them and revere them still as the remains dear to us of God's saint, who, in his earthly life . . . and by his prayerful assistance in life and after death, comforted and comforts still the hearts of the faithful. Therefore his memory is dear to us, and so too are those objects that remind [us] of his righteous life, especially the remains of his holy relics, which have been and will continue to be for us objects of veneration. Why was it necessary for the authorities to deprive faithful Christians of the objects of their religious worship? And where is that precious freedom of faith and conscience proclaimed by Soviet power and so desired by all? We maintain that such actions as the profanation of the remnants of relics and so forth are blatant violations of the decree on the freedom of conscience, violence and mockery against people of faith, an insult to their religious feelings, and that by no means do they serve to strengthen Soviet power or [ensure] a favorable attitude toward it on the part of the citizenry, who are prepared to obey [Soviet] power in civil matters that have no bearing on objects of faith.[83]

The last lines of this petition suggest that at least some Orthodox protestors were trying to find ways to reconcile their religious belief and obligations to the saints with the responsibilities and rights of Soviet citizenship. But in seeking a middle ground on the relic question, Orthodox Soviet citizens tested the new regime's commitment to the "precious freedom of faith and conscience" and found it wanting. The arguments of Krasikov and other VIII Section experts, who held that the new regime could not simply entrust corpses to the private care of its citizens, were at cross-purposes with the position taken by Orthodox petitioners that they could lay claim to Saint Feodosii's body and that the miracle-worker's relics belonged, by rights, in the community where they had resided for centuries.

"IT WAS A GREAT MIRACLE"
RUMORS, MYTHS, AND LEGENDS

The litany of abuses and atrocities committed by Soviet power against Orthodox clergy and believers throughout the 1920s and 1930s, including the years of the relic campaign, is both a well-documented and prevalent theme in the post-Soviet historiography of the Russian Orthodox Church.[84] Although Krasikov publicly denied that Soviet officials had committed "any sort of excesses [or] disturbances" over the course of the first two years of relic exhumations, his assurances were contradicted by repeated warnings and censures from the VIII Section itself.[85] In 1919, for example, the editors of *Revoliutsiia i tserkov'* criticized party activists in an unnamed provincial town who had torn down the silk canopy from a reliquary shrine and hung it in the offices of the local education department. Irresponsible incidents such as the case of the purloined canopy baffled cooler heads at Narkomiust, who understandably regarded these rash actions as counterproductive and even perilous to the regime's chances for success in the struggle against religion in the provinces. Such actions, the VIII Section declared, were not only "completely illegal" but also "inexpedient," as if reckless officials were seeking "to deliberately discredit Soviet power."[86] Citing Lenin's injunction to use caution when "fight[ing] religious prejudices," VIII Section officials found themselves obliged to issue repeated instructions that provincial authorities refrain from any actions that could be interpreted as offensive by the faithful.[87]

Nevertheless, despite all warnings, Narkomiust received numerous protests concerning alleged improprieties committed during the relic campaign. To be sure, most complaints were dismissed promptly by the VIII Section for lack of evidence. In February 1919, for example, when a private citizen in Tver submitted an angry denunciation of the "blasphemous" exhumation of Tikhon Zadonskii, Krasikov took pains to assure the letter-writer that the saint had been exhumed "with observance of all formalities." Citizen Povedskii was encouraged to submit any "facts that would corroborate illegal actions by the authorities." Absent any evidence, of course, the VIII Section regretted to inform that it could make no investigation into charges of possible misconduct.[88] Vague allegations of impropriety brought forward that same month by the Tver diocesan council were also rejected. According to the council chairman, Archpriest Ioann Znamenskii, local officials in Ostashkov had engaged in and permitted certain unspecified illegal activities during the exhumation of Saint Nil Stolobenskii on 25 February 1919. Krasikov denied the chairman's request for a full investigation into the matter: "[T]he VIII Section needs to be informed *concretely* as to *who* committed these actions, *what* they consisted of . . . and *whether witnesses can corroborate these actions.*" Without such information, the VIII Section director argued that he had no grounds whatsoever to find the local ispolkom's actions either "illegal or contrary to revolutionary legal consciousness."[89]

Protests that outlined specific grievances in detail, however, were deemed serious enough to warrant official investigation from the VIII Section. In April 1919, monks and lay believers in Zvenigorod, Moscow Province, sent a letter of protest to Narkomiust charging local officials with outrageous behavior during the exhumation of Saint Savva Storozhevskii on 17 March. The petitioners alleged that members of the commission had laughed openly at the relics and cast aspersions on their provenance, afterward allowing "the curious" to enter the monastery church and handle the saint's bones themselves: "Look, comrades, aren't these just dog bones? The monks gathered them from all over and placed them here [in the shrine]." When a monk spoke in defense of the saint and reminded the commission of the many miracles worked through Savva's relics, one delegate responded by grabbing the skull and shaking it in the face of the church sacristan: "Take a look at your protector now." Shocked and appalled at the treatment of their beloved saint, the sixty signatories asked Narkomiust that the shrine and relics of Savva, their "gracious helper," be entrusted to a group of local believers for safekeeping.[90]

The VIII Section refused to permit the relics' transfer but promised to launch an investigation into "the actions that supposedly took place."[91] After eight weeks of waiting for the investigation to materialize, canon law professor N. D. Kuznetsov bypassed Narkomiust altogether and sent a second protest directly to Lenin and the members of Sovnarkom. Kuznetsov confirmed the charges of sacrilege levied in the original petition and suggested that such outrageous incidents could very well turn the rural religious against Soviet power:

> [O]ne of the members of the [commission], having taken the skull of the Venerable Savva and raised it up before the confessor, asked him—"Is this a sacred object for you or what?" When he received an answer in the affirmative, he spit about five times on the sainted head of the Venerable [Savva] with these words—"Well, for me it's this." Several other members . . . conducted themselves most irreverently, spewing horrible blasphemies and touching the altar.

> If local agents of [Soviet] power, *who openly mock* the religious feelings of the narod, go unpunished, it may give the impression that they *are supported in these [actions] by Soviet power*, and this may elicit among the narod a dissatisfaction for the Soviet system *in general*.[92]

As an experienced petitioner Kuznetsov must have been aware that his ominous hints regarding the potential for popular unrest would likely elicit a speedy response from Moscow. Indeed, within one week of Kuznetsov's petition, the Narkomiust Collegium ordered VIII Section "religious expert" I. A. Shpitsberg to travel to Zvenigorod and launch a full investigation into the events of 17 March. Shpitsberg, the scion of a prominent Petersburg naval family and a former legal consultant on divorce matters to the Holy Synod, had reinvented himself as an antireligious consultant after the Revolution and already possessed a notorious reputation in Orthodox circles as one of the more vituperative and combative lecturers on the VIII Section's staff. His appointment to the case could hardly have inspired hopes for a fair and balanced investigation.[93] Not surprisingly, Shpitsberg found no evidence of any wrongdoing on the part of local officials, concluding that the exhumation commission and the district ispolkom had conducted themselves "in accordance with revolutionary discipline." The real culprits, Shpitsberg argued, were the local clergy and lay believers who had presented "false testimony, false affidavits, and engaged in agitation to discredit the actions of the representatives of Soviet power."[94] At Shpitsberg's recommendation, the monastery was forcibly shut down and its holdings nationalized, while Kuznetsov and company were placed on trial and sentenced for "disseminating slanderous hearsay among the populace."[95]

As Kuznetsov's fate suggests, formal protest was not without its perils—and, moreover, largely unsuccessful. A more surreptitious avenue of opposition was through rumors of divine intervention and retribution. Reports of visions, apparitions, and miracles were a common religious response to external pressures—political, social, and economic—throughout Europe in the nineteenth and early twentieth centuries.[96] Provincial newspapers are a rich source for studying popular rumors from the years of the relic campaign. Most of these subversive rumors, passed on orally by marginalized groups, would undoubtedly have been lost to historians had Soviet officials not expended a great deal of ink and energy in refuting them. Although it is difficult in some cases to pinpoint the exact origins of these reported rumors, almost all of them conveyed the same moralistic message—to dissuade the faithful from participating in exhumations by recounting the horrors visited upon those who violated the holy relics and thereby reaffirming the vengeful power of a saint when scorned.

In some cases, these rumors were preventative efforts to forestall planned exhumations. For example, in May 1919, the delegation charged with exhuming the relics of Saint Arsenii the Miracle-Worker in Tver Province discovered an anonymous note slipped inside the saint's shrine: "Bolsheviks, come to your senses, reconsider, do not exhume [the relics] tomorrow. The Bolsheviks will suffer [a fate] worse than worms. God will punish you; hell hath not room for you all; you will be struck blind tomorrow." When asked by the commission how these "hooliganish" threats had ended up inside the shrine, Bishop Serafim replied only that the shrine had been opened for veneration and that he had no way of knowing who might have deposited them.[97] In Petrograd, priests warned parishioners that madness, blindness, ulcerous sores, or a "heavenly thunderbolt" would greet those who presumed to profane the shrine of Aleksandr Nevskii, and they urged the faithful to keep a safe distance from the exhumation site.[98] Similar rumors surfaced a decade later in Karelia, where popular opinion appears to have been divided as to whether Saint Elisei Sumskii would paralyze the limbs of those who attempted to remove him from his coffin or whether he would be content to beat the exhumationists senseless with his wooden staff.[99] The Lord worked in mysterious ways, and some rumors suggested that retribution might come from unusual channels. In the summer of 1919, for example, the military revolutionary tribunal in Voronezh informed Narkomiust of widespread rumors in town that Commissar Bessmertnyi, who had presided over the exhumation of Mitrofan Voronezhskii six months before, was now facing trial for his actions "by order of comrade Lenin" himself.[100]

Rumors served also to remind believers that if their holy relics were exhumed and profaned, the community stood to lose not only the presence but also the protection of its local saint. In Voronezh Province, for example, monks at the Bogoroditskii monastery countered the barrage of newspaper editorials calling for the exhumation of Saint Tikhon by spreading strange tales of the holy man leaving his shrine at night to wander the monastery grounds by moonlight. According to the rumors, Tikhon no longer wished to reside at the monastery now that the ungrateful citizens of Zadonsk had insulted him by entertaining plans to exhume his body.[101] Similar stories in Sumskii Posad claimed that Saint Elisei would "rise up into the heavens like the prophet Elijah" rather than suffer disgrace at the hands of the Bolsheviks. Some believers, however, regarded this as highly doubtful. It was more likely that Elisei would cause his body to be swallowed up by the sea. In either case, the offended saint would forever deprive believers in Karelia of his presence and of access to his miracle-working relics.[102]

While most rumors seem to have been localized and geographically specific, other tales that sprung up in the wake of relic exhumations spread like wildfire. Siberian stories of Bolsheviks paralyzed by a vengeful Saint Simeon Verkhoturskii reached as far as Tver Province within weeks of the alleged incident.[103] Gorev wrote of overhearing a group of clerics in Sergiev Posad, hours before Saint Sergii's exhumation, whispering that a commission member from an unnamed province had been struck dead by the hand of God for spitting on holy relics. The Bolshevik blasphemer was said to have demonstrated further disdain for the sacred by approaching the shrine with a cap on his head and a hand-rolled cigarette clenched in his teeth. "Yes, God does not tolerate profanity," one priest nodded in approval. It seems quite possible that the rumors at Sergiev Posad were inspired by the notorious incident at the Storozhevskii monastery in Zvenigorod, which had taken place less than four weeks earlier. If this is indeed the case, it is a testament of sorts to the speed with which such rumors could circulate and the implications that believers drew from them.[104]

In some localities, exhumation was accompanied by millenarian rumors that saw the militantly atheist regime's assault on holy relics as a harbinger of the apocalypse. The desecration and public disgrace of the bodies of the righteous was a clear sign that the end of the world was at hand. In Zvenigorod, for example, Orthodox clerics preached that so blasphemous an act as the exhumation of Saint Savva Storozhevskii could only be the work of Antichrist, who had come to earth in Bolshevik dress to perform this sacrilege.[105] A hieromonk at the Troitskaia Lavra also claimed that the relic campaign marked Antichrist's arrival in Russia, warning parishioners in a sermon that the Bolsheviks were "crucifying Christ for a second time" by exhuming and insulting the bodies of God's saints.[106]

Most Soviet publicists and newspaper writers typically responded to rumors of divine vengeance or imminent apocalypse with derision and ridicule. The district newspaper in Zadonsk laughed away the stories of the roaming Saint Tikhon, claiming that tall tales of the saint's nighttime wanderings had been dreamed up by clever monks in order to explain the absence of an uncorrupted body.[107] The local press in Murom, Vladimir Province, mockingly denounced in a front-page editorial the fantastic rumors repeated by believers following the exhumations of Prince Saint Konstantin and his sainted sons:

> For example, they say that during the exhumation two Bolsheviks were struck blind and one's arm was torn away, that the "relics" hid themselves underground and did not show themselves to the arch-sinful Bolsheviks, that the Bolsheviks tossed out the relics the night before and put bones there in their place. Only the frightened mind of a fanatic, an old senile woman, or a small child could believe all of these contradictory rumors.[108]

In similar fashion, newspapers in Novgorod Province refuted rumors that the exhumation of Saint Kirill Belozerskii had been conducted in secret, behind closed doors. Rumor had it that the exhumation commission had taken this precautionary measure out of fear, so that if divine punishment did, in fact, befall them, Orthodox believers would not be on hand to witness their comeuppance. In truth, the papers claimed, Kirill's exhumation was open to the public and Bolsheviks were not afraid of relics. "Everyone expected a miracle," the Novgorod *Zvezda* reported, tongue in cheek, "and a miracle did indeed happen: the Bolshevik godless exhumed the shrine, and inside, in place of relics, there was found a skull packed in cotton wool, several bones, rotted rags, and metal trinkets."[109]

Although the local press seems to have taken great relish in ridiculing the most far-fetched tales and mocking the priests who allegedly invented them, provincial authorities regarded rumors as no laughing matter. The presidium of the Vladimir Province ispolkom, for instance, felt obliged to issue an open letter to the diocesan clergy in the local *Izvestiia*, refuting the "most improbable and monstrous rumors" that were circulating around the city concerning alleged improprieties committed during the exhumation of Saint Avraamii the Martyr.[110] Local justice officials frequently included a brief overview of the most current rumors in their reports on the mood of the populace. In May 1919, for example, justice officials in Voronezh shared with the NKVD their concerns that "the stirring up of rumors concerning miracles . . . may elicit undesirable consequences [in the form] of popular disturbances."[111] Two months later, when the situation had not improved, the Voronezh prosecutor's office begged Kurskii to send a lecturer from Moscow to help dispel rumors of "mass healings" being reported at the shrine of the exhumed Saint Mitrofan Voronezhskii and to assure the populace that the exhumation had not been a violation of the separation of Church and state.[112] Given its budgetary restraints and limited personnel, however, the VIII Section typically could do little to quell provincial rumors, beyond dispatching the occasional lecturer with a packet of agitational materials. A full three years after the exhumation of the Voronezh saints, antireligious agitators in the province were still countering peasant rumors that members of the exhumation commission had been struck deaf, blind, and mad for disinterring Saint Mitrofan back in 1919.[113] In the decade prior to collectivization, old rumors died hard in the Soviet countryside.

The Contours of Religious Resistance

VEL'SK AND TVER AS CASE STUDIES

On 3 March 1919, the delegates to the district party conference in Vel'skii district, Vologda Province, debated the merits of exhuming the relics of Saint Prokopii Ust'ianskii, a mysterious seventeenth-century saint who, despite the absence of a vita or any biographical details whatsoever, had been revered for centuries by local Orthodox believers as a powerful miracle-worker and valued resident of the community.[114] Almost all of the delegates to the conference enthusiastically supported the motion, confident that

Prokopii's exhumation would be "the best agitation and propaganda for the separation of church and state," and "could serve only to achieve the unmasking of priestly escapades and elevate the teachings of communism." Optimists assured their more hesitant comrades that "there should be nothing to fear," and that they "ought not to be afraid, for the young people are impatiently awaiting this move." In the end, a resolution calling for immediate exhumation passed by a comfortable majority. However, convinced that "the population will show hardly any opposition" and that "no obstacles will be encountered," the delegates voted down an accompanying resolution from the chairman that would have dispatched agitators to the surrounding countryside to conduct preparatory propaganda work among the Orthodox faithful. Also defeated was a proposal for an armed Red Army detachment to escort the twenty-two commission members to the church in Bestuzhevo village where Prokopii's relics were housed. In retrospect, the failure of these latter motions proved a grave error.[115]

Although the Vel'skii district ispolkom later informed its superiors in Vologda that the "mood of the masses was hostile at the time of exhumation," no incidents took place on the morning of 7 March, when the commission uncovered Prokopii's relics before an audience of some three hundred local residents.[116] Believers and clergymen staged no opposition to the removal of the saint from his shrine, nor did they interfere when Prokopii's body was photographed and subjected to a thorough medical examination. No complaints were registered when a full front-page story in the Vel'sk district newspaper mocked Prokopii's relics as "a most ordinary and badly preserved mummy" with missing body parts and flesh the consistency of "smoked whitefish."[117] Though the relics had been exposed, examined, and photographed, believers could take solace in the fact that Prokopii was still physically present to work miracles on behalf of believers who came to him with true faith in times of need and trouble. Indeed, no sooner had the exhumation commission inspected the relics, secured the signatures of witnesses, and left the church, than the clergy whisked Prokopii's body back into the coffin, placed the coffin inside the silver shrine, and performed a moleben service to the saint.[118]

Had Prokopii's relics been left in Bestuzhevo, any further estrangement between local officials and believers could probably have been avoided. Tensions, however, broke out into full-fledged revolt when district officials and a small group of Red Army soldiers returned to the village three weeks later, on 1 April, to transport Prokopii's relics and his silver shrine from Bestuzhevo to the district seat at Vel'sk. When the commission arrived in town, the peasants armed themselves and surrounded the church where Prokopii's relics lay, demanding that their saint's body be left in peace. With neither side willing to budge, the standoff carried over to the following day. At an emergency meeting of the parish council the next morning, villagers pledged "never to surrender the holy relics of the Venerable Prokopii to anyone under any circumstances and to defend them by all lawful means, not even sparing [our] own lives."[119]

As the mood of the crowd grew more hostile, political grievances began to be expressed alongside religious demands. If the Bolsheviks were so eager to take the saint's shrine from the church, the peasants argued, then they should deduct the value of the silver from the extraordinary taxes levied on the village. Other voices from the crowd shouted that the taxes should be abolished altogether, a proposition that seems to have won over the majority of the protesters. The crowd—by this time numbering upward of fifteen hundred—stormed the jails, freeing all prisoners arrested by Soviet power, and then proceeded to capture and beat senseless the members of the local Bestuzhevo party cell. Greatly outnumbered, the soldiers were hesitant to fire into the crowd. The director of the district agitation department later informed his colleagues on the district ispolkom that peasant women, sensing the soldiers' fear, had deliberately taunted them by positioning their bodies right in front of the rifles: "Shoot us, we're the wives of Red Army men, our husbands will have something to say to you."[120]

The soldiers retreated, at first, but returned shortly with some five dozen of their comrades, reinforcements sufficient to convince all but the most irate protesters to lay down their weapons. With order restored, provincial authorities quickly dispatched military revolutionary committees to Bestuzhevo and the surrounding area, granting the commissars plenipotentiary powers to root out and imprison the ringleaders. In the end, punitive measures were taken only against the priests of the parish church where Prokopii's relics were housed. Behind the scenes, however, provincial authorities blamed their overzealous underlings in Vel'sk for the debacle. Officials in Vologda censured the district ispolkom for its "thoughtlessness," inability to handle the development of events, and criminal negligence.[121] Although the extraordinary tax stayed in effect, chastened officials in Vel'sk promised to return moneys confiscated from parish groups and other religious organizations in the village and, more important, issued orders allowing the relics of Saint Prokopii to remain in Bestuzhevo.[122] "Playing around with relics," the provincial ispolkom concluded, "is not worth the trouble [*Igra s moshchami sovershenno ne stoit svech*]."[123]

In the end, then, the protesters may be said to have won the day. The ispolkom backed down, Prokopii's remains stayed in the parish church, and worshipers could continue to seek the benefits of the saint's intercession in their daily lives. The resolution of the conflict suggests the reasons that the relic campaign proved, in the end, a failure. Chief among these was the arbitrary and often contradictory way in which local officials implemented relic policy in the provinces. The ispolkom's well-intentioned efforts to remove Prokopii's remains indicates that local officials were in receipt of the VIII Section's instructions for placing holy relics on display in state-run museums, but the methods employed to execute these orders suggest that local officials had not read what were arguably the most important parts—namely, the paragraphs proposing that such action be undertaken only after a preliminary propaganda campaign, and even then with great caution and tact. Such ungainliness and incompetence in the implementation of central directives was hardly what Narkomiust had in mind when its directors entrusted local and provincial officials with taking the initiative in exhuming holy relics. Incidents like this led to the VIII Section's eventual clamping down on the autonomy of local officials and the adoption of strict guidelines from Moscow with which provincial- and district-level authorities were obliged to comply.

The very real threat posed by such uprisings to regional stability made the relic campaign understandably unpopular with local officials, who found themselves in precarious positions during the Civil War. In March 1919, one of the few dissenting voices on the Vel'sk ispolkom who had spoken out against exhuming Prokopii in the first place warned that meddling with the religious practices of the peasantry under such "difficult conditions" could only lead to problems. As he explained to his comrades, the exhumation of Prokopii's relics may well lead "ignorant minds among the populace to undermine the ispolkom's work in supplying the army and in the construction of strategic roads from Konosh to Vel'sk."[124] His argument, then, was that it was better to postpone these policies until such time as the more pressing problems of the advance of the White armies and the utter collapse of the Russian infrastructure had been successfully resolved; better to grant temporary concessions to the faithful than run the risk of losing all that the Revolution had sought to achieve. As we shall see below, the overcoming of religious superstitions was a secondary concern to local commissars preoccupied with the more immediate demands of consolidating their foothold in the provinces. The low priority that officials placed on the relic campaign ultimately undercut its effectiveness in the provinces.

What does the demonstration at Bestuzhevo tell us about the mentalities of Orthodox believers in early Bolshevik Russia? First, there would likely have been no incident at all had district authorities not taken it upon themselves to remove Prokopii's relics from the village church. The official protocols of Prokopii's exhumation make no mention of any disturbances or murmurings of discontent on the part of local believers or clergymen until soldiers showed up in the village weeks later to seize the saint's body by force. Only then did events spiral rapidly out of control. Had the demonstration been limited to only clerics and kulaks, the district ispolkom would undoubtedly have indicated as much in its correspondence with Vologda, insofar as local Soviet officials seldom missed an opportunity to single out the role of these most incorrigibly counterrevolutionary elements when describing any disturbances in their district. In fact, however, the attempted seizure of Prokopii's relics was opposed not by elements occupying increasingly marginal roles in Soviet society (that is, priests and rich peasants), but by nearly everyone in the village community, including men, women, soldiers' wives, and the very same poor peasants in whose name Soviet power claimed that it was exposing and unmasking holy relics.

If all or most of the community wanted the relics to remain in Bestuzhevo, we should ask ourselves why. Why was it that Prokopii's relics could be exhumed safely and without incident in March, and yet their removal be resisted so forcefully in April? The principal reason (as we have seen in earlier chapters) is that, while Orthodox believers could pray to the saints in the comfort of their own homes or sing anthems to the saints in church, the most immediate and efficacious means to channel the immense miracle-working power of the holy dead was by going to the shrines and kissing or touching the saints' bodies and coffins. Even though his relics had been subjected to the humiliation of exhumation, and even though medical examination had found them to be in a distressingly advanced stage of decomposition, Prokopii's body still remained in the village church and his presence in the community could still be felt. If, however, Prokopii were to leave Bestuzhevo, admittedly not of his own free will but by force, it would be a staggering blow to the Orthodox faithful in the village and the surrounding countryside. Given the reciprocal terms in which most believers understood and articulated their relationship with their saintly protectors, many believers who had received help from Prokopii in years past must have felt it their duty to come to his defense now. In this sense, challenging or resisting the forcible seizure of Prokopii's relics would have been the ultimate expression of obet—the vow or promise made to a saint in return for, or anticipation of, divine favors rendered.

By resisting the attempted removal of the reliquary, the villagers in Bezstuzhevo were expressing the conviction that the saint's tomb was *their* property, that Prokopii's silver shrine and his holy remains belonged to *them* and were not subject to seizure by outsiders, armed or otherwise. Similar questions concerning the custody of sacred objects arose also in Tver Province, where newspapers and archival evidence offer a useful corrective to the traditional Soviet account of overwhelming crowds voting unanimously for exhumation. Confronted with demonstrations and a flood of angry letters following the exhumation of Saint Efrem in the small town of Torzhok, the Tver Province ispolkom resolved sometime in early 1919 to initiate no future exhumations by fiat, for fear of "plac[ing] an unnecessary trump card in the hands of the clergy." Provincial officials pledged henceforth to undertake relic inspections only in those cases where the initiative clearly came from the laborers themselves, "lest we ensure that counterrevolutionaries, on the basis of some premise or another, stir up new agitation against Soviet power, not only in Russia but throughout the whole world." The Tver Province ispolkom's "tip-toeing approach to 'holy relics'" came under heavy criticism in the pages of the official press organ of the NKVD, but the decision stood.[125]

Taking literally the VIII Section's instructions that exhumations should be conducted only with the consent of the workers and peasants, officials in Tver Province decided it was more prudent to put the question before the citizens themselves. In an editorial published on 4 March 1919, the chair of the Tver Province ispolkom declared that while he personally did not believe in the miraculous power of holy relics, exhumation was not a matter for his office to decide. Soviet citizens should take the initiative and make up their own minds: "Relics are not our business. . . . Discuss it [the relic question] at assemblies, in factories, plants, and workshops; come to one decision or another."[126] The public debates and meetings that took place all across the city and in various towns throughout the districts reflect the deep contestations over holy relics in the new Soviet society. Since the Orthodox Church was forbidden to own property by order of the January 1918 separation decree, to whom did holy relics actually belong? And who had the authority to decide their fate?

On 12 March 1919, an assembly of workers from the Morozov factory voted overwhelmingly to exhume the relics of Prince Saint Mikhail, martyred husband of Saint Anna Kashinskaia. This decision prompted the church council of the Preobrazhenskii Cathedral in Tver to respond with a letter of protest to the provincial ispolkom. "We think that the relics of Saint Mikhail the Pious Prince belong to all of the faithful, and in particular to all the faithful who live within the borders of Tver Province and the city of Tver, and not only to those workers who met at the assembly in question."[127] Although it was too late to save Saint Nil Stolobenskii, whose relics had been exhumed in the province already in late February, Orthodox clerics and parish organizations in Tver decided to hold their own meetings to discuss the relic question. They secured permission from the provincial Cheka administration for believers to assemble in their parish churches across the city on the Feast of the Annunciation and vote on whether to exhume their holy relics. The feast day, however, fell on a Friday, when the city's working-class population would be unable to leave their places of employment and participate in the vote. The Tver Province Council of Trade Unions filed a protest, charging that conspiratorial clerics had deliberately scheduled the meeting to coincide with a workday in order to disenfranchise the city's proletarian majority, whom union delegates assumed were more likely to favor exhumation. The union leadership declared that the meeting had to be held on a holiday when everyone was able to attend, and that individual factories, workshops, and city offices be allowed to send specially chosen delegations to the meeting and present their case for exhumation. Although the Tver Province ispolkom sided with the trade union, a standoff ensued in the end, with both factions holding rival meetings in different locations and passing completely contradictory resolutions.[128]

Of the flurry of relic resolutions passed in Tver Province during the spring of 1919, perhaps the most curious comes from an assembly of believers in Loginovo village. Professing to adhere to the ideals of both socialism and Orthodoxy (and discerning no contradiction whatsoever in such a stance), the villagers voted in favor of exhumation so that once and for all the question could be settled of what lay inside the shrines of the saints:

> The church is separate from the state, and though the authorities explain to us that relics are nothing more than a weapon of the clergy for frightening faithful and [politically] unconscious comrades, we think that this may not be the case. Is it really true that relics are just a pile of rotten garbage? Is this really so? The Workers'-Peasants' power must not lie, for it is our power, our defender.
>
> It is necessary for all the faithful, with one voice all together, to declare to [Soviet] power that it must open up the relics, [in the presence of] our assembly of the faithful. Our wish is for the opening up of the relics of the prelate Arsenii.... If we see that the relics are, in fact, incorruptible bodies, then we'll say to the authorities, "Why did you trick us?" And if we see that the relics are just bones and cotton wool, then we'll say to the priests: "Where is your conscience, where is your shame?"[129]

The relic question, it seems, was an issue on which everyone in Tver had an opinion, and although the ispolkom's decision was aimed at consensus-building and compromise, charged emotions often impeded the exchange of reasoned argument or rational discussion. Pro-exhumationists infiltrated church meetings to cast controversial votes. A woman worker who had spoken out in favor of exhuming the relics of Prince Saint Mikhail and Saint Arsenii was beaten by opponents of exhumation during a discussion meeting held at the church of the Devich'ii monastery. In a letter to the editor published in the Tver *Izvestiia*, a worker from the Morozov factory described a similar, if less violent, scene:

> After morning services, the priest held a discussion about the relics, which in his opinion were now being subjected to all sorts of mockery. So then he proposes to take a vote: "Who says the relics should not be exposed?" They almost all raised their hands, since it's almost exclusively old women and old men who go to church. Who is against? [that is, in favor of exhumation]—six people. Then the fanatics raised a big ruckus and like wild animals they yanked down the comrades' hands.[130]

Scenes from the factory meetings, where trade union delegates had predicted almost unanimous support for exhumation, reveal similar discontent and difference of opinion. Tver officials soon learned that workers and poor peasants doggedly refused to operate exclusively within the progressive mental categories to which Marxist-Leninist ideology assigned them. In early May, the Russko-Baltiiskii factory in Tver hosted a general assembly of workers and peasants to discuss the most pressing questions of the day—the latest maneuvers of Kolchak's White armies, mobilization for the front, the desertion question, and relief for soldiers' families. The Tver *Izvestiia* reported that when talk turned to the question of exhuming the relics of Prince Saint Mikhail, the hall erupted in exasperation. A group of city firefighters wanted to discuss further a proposed tariff that would fund their cash-strapped offices, sparking a heated exchange with angry peasants in attendance who were convinced that the levy would mean an increase in grain requisitions. The wives of soldiers at the front shouted down all the speakers: "What's there to say about relics? Talk about relief measures [*Chego tam tolkovat' o moshchakh, tolkuite o posobiiakh*]." Just when order was temporarily restored, the chairman called for a vote on whether to exhume Saint Mikhail's relics, and the proceedings plunged once more into chaos: "One side cried out, 'We have more [votes],' and the other declared, 'We do!' A third side claimed that they had not understood the vote." With nothing resolved, the meeting broke up in disorder.[131]

At a follow-up meeting on 26 April, a consensus was finally reached and the delegates decided overwhelmingly by a vote 496 to 4 to exhume the relics of Saints Mikhail and Arsenii. The demographics of this second meeting, however, were slanted heavily toward factory committee representatives, trade union delegates, members of the local proletkult organizations, and delegates of the city soviets, a fact that may well account for the extreme margin in the voting tally. The Tver Province ispolkom speedily approved the meeting's resolution, and the exhumations were scheduled for 18 May. In the interim, the chair of the newly appointed exhumation commission met with a personal representative of Archbishop Serafim. The two parties hammered out a working agreement whereby the actual removal of the relics from their shrine would be performed by Orthodox clerics, not commissars, and with the understanding that the proceedings would be carried out with an appropriate air of gravity and solemnity. In the end, the archbishop's ambassador proved a more wily negotiator than his Bolshevik counterpart, however, and managed to secure assurances from the commission chairman that a moleben could be sung to the saints before their exhumation, that priests could give speeches and sermons in the church immediately prior to the commission's work, and most important, that the relics would not afterward be taken away from the churches where they lay.[132]

These scenes from Vel'sk and Tver shed some light on how communities reimagined their relationships with holy relics in the wake of the Revolution and at the height of the exhumation campaign. In both cases, local Soviet authorities deployed radically different strategies for implementing the VIII Section's directives on exhumation. Officials in Vel'sk decided on a full-fledged interventionist approach, with almost disastrous consequences, whereas Tver administrators sought to establish some broad-based civic consensus before proceeding with exhumation. Yet the lessons that officials in both cases seem to have taken away from their experience was that exhumation was often more trouble than it was worth. As we saw in Chapter Five, ispolkoms and provincial party apparatuses across Soviet Russia were gradually coming separately to similar conclusions over the course of the campaign. Chafing under the VIII Section's increased efforts to tighten central control over the campaign and disillusioned by the minimal tangible results that exhumation seemed to offer, many already overworked local administrators chose to place relic exhumation very low on their list of priorities.

What is more, the examples of Vel'sk and Tver show how the responses of peasants, workers, soldiers, and believers to the exhumation of holy relics did not always break down into neatly compartmentalized categories. Among the Orthodox faithful, for example, the range of responses was varied. If the villagers of Vel'sk were willing to take up arms and even lay down their lives to ensure that the holy relics remained in their possession, opponents of exhumation in Tver were content to express their dissent through resolutions, petitions, and other legal, nonviolent means. The extraordinary case of the villagers of Loginovo, too, shows that even some believers thought the time had come to open the shrines of the saints—not to discredit the Orthodox religion but to see for themselves what lay within. By the same token, neither did all socially progressive elements hail exhumation as a welcome release from spiritual enslavement. Some, in fact, like the workers of the Russko-Baltiiskii factory in Tver and the poor peasants of Bestuzhevo, seemed quite willing to let the relics lie in peace, arguing that the mission of Soviet power lay not in the confiscation of reliquaries but in guaranteeing social relief measures and lightening the load of the laborers. Others still saw no conflict of interests between their religious faith, their class identity, and their sympathy to the socialist revolution. The refusal of workers to behave like workers—that is, to wholeheartedly embrace exhumation as a revolutionary tactic—suggests that devotion to the cult of holy relics, which had reached across class and estate boundaries prior to 1917, did not evaporate immediately after October. The growing awareness of high-ranking Bolsheviks that the relic policy was regarded with either disfavor or disinterest by even the most socially progressive elements of Soviet society was to have a crippling effect on the course of the campaign, leading ultimately to its abandonment after 1921.

On 9 June 1920, the members of the Ostashkovskii district ispolkom, Tver Province, took a day off from work to commemorate the feast of the translation of the relics of Saint Nil Stolobenskii. State employees in the district also received a holiday, and many accompanied the ispolkom members on their pilgrimage to pray before the saint's relics, located in an island cloister in Lake Seliger. The steamships that plied the adjoining lakes feeding into the Volga River were relieved of their timber transport duties that day so that they could be used to shuttle pilgrims back and forth between the hermitage and the lakeshore. Krasikov and Galkin were outraged by such "disorderliness" on the part of local officials and were incredulous that card-carrying communists could still venerate the relics of the "ex-saint Nil" (*eksprepodobnogo Nila*), exhumed in public just one year before. Can it be, the editors of *Revoliutsiia i tserkov'* asked, that "the comrade communists of Ostashkov still believe in religious prejudices . . . and occlude [the consciousness] of the peasants and workers at a time when a party member must energetically struggle with all [religious] prejudices and lead the benighted masses toward the path of truth?"[133]

The image of leather-jacketed commissars going on pilgrimage to kiss the exhumed relics at Ostashkov serves as a reminder that even provincial party members were not immune to the strong tug of tradition and the allure of the saints.[134] As we have seen in this chapter, the relic campaign produced complicated and often contradictory results among the populace. Some, principally the younger generation and especially those whose worldviews had been radicalized by the experience of world war, revolution, and civil war, embraced the exhumation campaign as a cleansing of Russia's supernatural legacy; a Russia rid of relics was better poised to make the passage into the socialist future. Bolshevik publicists and the campaign's architects assumed that this opinion would be held universally by the most progressive classes in Soviet society—urban workers, poor peasants, and revolutionary soldiers, while only clerics, counterrevolutionaries, and kulaks would cling to their relics. Yet popular support for the campaign did not always fall in line with neatly demarcated Marxist categories of class. When the new regime targeted the cult of the saints as the summation of superstition, defenders of the saints came together from across the social spectrum, often making for strange ideological bedfellows whose allegiances cut across class and estate boundaries—factory workers and parish priests, poor peasants and well-off villagers, old women and Red Army recruits, and even, as at Ostashkov, clerics and commissars.

The unreasonably high hopes that the Bolshevik leadership had placed on the relic campaign were not fully realized among the millions of Orthodox faithful. Most Bolsheviks thought that believers would soon dry their eyes after their saints were swallowed "in the stormy tides of the Revolution" and dutifully embrace the new cult of reason put before them.[135] Such convictions, however, underestimated the depth of the relationship that individual believers and communities had forged with their saints. Krasikov, for one, seems never to have fully grasped the attachment that Orthodox believers had for their relics. As late as the summer of 1921, in the twilight months of the exhumation campaign, the VIII Section director breezily assured Petr Smidovich of the VTsIK (All-Union Central Executive Committee) that the relics of Saint Serafim Sarovskii could be removed easily from the Sarovskaia hermitage in Tambov Province: "[T]he organization of a painless removal of the relics presents no particular difficulties, since the individuals and groups who have an active interest in the exploitation of relics are an insignificant lot and, as example shows, the populace very quickly reconciles itself to the uprooting of the relic cult."[136]

For Orthodox believers, however, who had come to rely on the miracles of their saintly defenders, there was no such thing as a "painless removal" of holy relics. While VIII Section publicists and antireligious agitators preached the impossibility of bodily incorruptibility and pointed to wrecked and ruined relics as the best proof for their arguments, ordinary believers were, on the whole, unresponsive to such logic. In the minds of the Orthodox faithful, a saint was still a saint, so long as he produced miracles and bestowed help on the living. And it was for this reason—to defend their means of access to the divine and to uphold their reciprocal obligations to their saintly protectors—that Orthodox believers protested, petitioned, and resisted the Bolsheviks' attempts to ridicule their relics and, more important, remove them from the communities where their miraculous powers were made manifest.

Epilogue and Conclusion

THE PASSING OF THE SAINTS?

> "Now this whole fairy-tale world, the world of saints, devils, goblins, and the talking dead is dying. No more do the dead speak from their graves. . . . The priests themselves go to doctors and clinics when they get sick, they don't rush off to the 'heavenly healers.' They know that there is nothing supernatural in this world."[1]
>
> —MIKHAIL GOREV, 1925

When an elderly peasant woman burst into tears before the empty coffin of Saint Makarii Zhabynskii in Tula Province, a bystander tried to reassure her with words of comfort. "He probably flew away," the witness suggested. "He is a saint, you know." The woman, however, was inconsolable. "It doesn't matter if he *was* here; he's supposed to *stay* here, where he was buried," she wept.[2] Just months into the campaign, many prominent Bolsheviks were also beginning to wonder whether the saints should not simply stay where they were buried. As the exhumation campaign proceeded, isolated murmurings grew louder from members of the Bolshevik leadership who expressed doubts regarding its necessity or its efficacy.

Perhaps the most pointed critique of the campaign came from the Old Bolshevik and educator S. I. Mitskevich. In the decade before the Revolution, while many party members had formulated abstract notions of the peasantry from the comfortable distance of Switzerland or Germany, Mitskevich had worked as a doctor in the provincial towns and districts along the Volga and had gathered firsthand knowledge of the rural populace and its religious beliefs. In a letter of April 1919, Mitskevich pleaded with Lenin to forestall the imminent exhumation of Saint Sergii Radonezhskii and to put an end to the relic campaign once and for all:

Dear Vladimir Il'ich,

I am writing to You concerning the exhumation of relics.

I think it impossible to propose anything more ridiculous and injurious for us than this notorious exhumation. No one will be convinced by it, legends are spreading that the real relics are being hidden, that counterfeit [relics] will be exhumed. Animosity is growing.

> All this is particularly harmful at the present, critical moment, given the mobilization and advance of Kolchak.
>
> Moreover, this is an infringement of the principle of the separation of church and state.
>
> If they are thinking to exhume relics in Moscow [Province], this will be an act that can inspire only counterrevolution. It will lead to disturbances and extraordinary animosity against us in our very center.
>
> It is necessary to issue instructions at once that these [exhumations] be stopped everywhere and, in general, against such actions as are crudely offensive to the religious feelings of the populace: smoking in church and wearing hats at the altar, which are being committed by people who are communist hangers-on, often drunkards.
>
> It is necessary to announce the [end to the campaign] publicly, in the form of a decree or instruction from Sovnarkom.[3]

Lenin, however, was unconcerned by Mitskevich's warnings. "I think Mitskevich is in a state of panic," he remarked in the margins of the letter, which was passed on to Krasikov's VIII Section. "Excesses during exhumation are, of course, impermissible. This is clear. And it is impossible, of course, to change the minds of old women. But there are masses of letters and reports from the localities that [the populace] is not in favor of superstitions, but quite the contrary."[4]

Despite the cool reception that Mitskevich's letter received in the Kremlin, other Bolsheviks were beginning to voice similar concerns. Among them was one of the exhumation campaign's earliest champions, V. D. Bonch-Bruevich, Lenin's personal secretary and administrative director for Sovnarkom. In early 1919, appalled by episcopal complaints concerning the alleged conduct of drunken local officials during the exhumation of Saint Aleksandr Svirskii, Bonch-Bruevich had pressed the VIII Section to open a full investigation into this "extraordinarily pressing and serious" matter.[5] One year later, when petitions to save the Troitskaia Lavra and the relics of Saint Sergii began pouring in to Sovnarkom, it was Bonch-Bruevich again who urged Krasikov and Kurskii to proceed with caution.[6] Mikhail Kalinin, too, made a case for prudence. In a December 1919 note to Kurskii, Kalinin thought it best to let the relics of Saint Sergii remain open for veneration in the Troitskaia Lavra: "Taking into account religious feelings, it seems to me that there is no basis—barring serious cause—to incite inflammation amongst the masses of the populace."[7] In February 1921, Commissar of Enlightenment A. V. Lunacharskii requested point-blank that the exhumations be ceased: "I have repeatedly warned comrades of the necessity of calling a halt to this operation, which has already made a sufficient impression and yet often meets with such unpleasant surprises."[8] Another critic of the campaign, VTsIK secretary Avel Enukidze, held the purse strings and was therefore in a position to do more than most. In a January 1921 memo to Krasikov, Enukidze criticized as "inconvenient" a request from the Tatar Republic asking that a film commission from Moscow be sent to Sviazhsk to attend the exhumation of Saint Germogen Kazanskii. Enukidze left the matter open to Krasikov's judgment but made no secret of his own hostility to the project: "Personally, I consider this question . . . to be immaterial and a waste of time." In the absence of funding, Krasikov was obliged to concur, informing Tatar officials that the "dispatch of a special commission at this time [was] difficult" and advising them to appeal to other government offices for available cameramen.[9]

More troubling, though, than the reservations of Kremlin moderates was the obvious disinterest showed by local officials for the relic campaign. Given the difficult circumstances faced by provincial Soviet administrators during the Civil War, the wonder was not that so many exhumations were staged well but, rather, that they were staged at all. On 21 February 1919, the presidium of the Kashinskii district ispolkom voted down a proposed resolution for the exhumation of the relics of Saint Anna Kashinskaia, explaining that such an act would constitute a violation of the separation decree and "an intrusion into the [private] life of religious organizations."[10] In the fall of 1919, after the Sergiev Posad council of deputies only narrowly passed a resolution to transfer Saint Sergii's relics to a Moscow museum (with fifteen members voting in favor, fourteen opposed, and one abstention), Bonch-Bruevich again questioned the existence of any real popular support for the exhumation campaign: "If this is not popular with the council of deputies, then what about the masses?"[11]

As the VIII Section fought to keep the campaign alive, enthusiasm for exhumation was clearly wearing thin among provincial and district-level officials across Soviet Russia. Skeptical officials in Viatka Province begged off exhumation altogether, reasoning that the VIII Section's instructions applied only to saints whose bodies were aboveground. As they explained to Krasikov, the bodies of the Venerable Trifon and the Blessed Prokopii were buried on the premises of a monastery that had already been shut down by order of Soviet power, and hence they were inaccessible to worshipers. Digging up the saints' graves, local officials argued, would only draw undue attention to their cult.[12] District officials in Pskov Province dodged the responsibility of exhuming a relic fragment attributed to Saint Sergii Radonezhskii on the grounds that such an action would be pointless. The politically conscious element of the populace, they explained, had already come to view relic veneration "as a vestige of the old regime," whereas "the minority is so rooted in its religious prejudices that any action [taken] toward the relics would doubtless elicit a storm of indignant protests and yield no real results."[13] In Tobol'sk, too, officials informed the VIII Section that they had decided to delay indefinitely any further relic exhumations in the province on account of the "extreme backwardness and ignorance of the populace."[14] In Irkutsk, less than one week after exhuming the relics of Saint Innokentii, a majority of the provincial ispolkom voted to return the saint's body to the city clergy, citing a backlash of protests and appeals from believers. The chair of the ispolkom overturned the decision, but begged his superiors in Omsk to take the relics off his hands. It was impossible, he explained by telegram, to display Innokentii's body in Irkutsk: "Placement [of the relics] in a museum would give rise to unavoidable pilgrimage and excitement of the crowds." In the end, the Irkutsk officials decided to solve the problem by packing the body on a train and shipping it to the Narkomzdrav museum in Moscow.[15]

Evidence suggests that the reluctance of provincial authorities was motivated less by outright insubordination than by a cautious fear of sparking disturbances among the Orthodox in their district. Such concerns became especially acute following the outbreak of peasant rebellion in Tambov Province in 1920. The mass uprisings in the Central Black Earth region coincided most inexpediently with the VIII Section's August 1920 decree calling for a concerted nationwide push to purge all relics from Soviet Russia.[16] In light of recent events in his own district, the director of the Novgorod Province church liquidation section concluded that a total liquidation of the relic cult was "untimely." He pointedly reminded the VIII Section that "all these positive results still give no guarantee . . . that religious fanaticism will not take the form of suffering and martyrdom 'for the persecuted faith and the desecration of the sacred.'"[17] Similarly, the justice department in Pskov confided to Krasikov that "the time has not yet come when relics may be removed from their sites of veneration without incident. They will be cast aside by their adherents themselves when [they] are enlightened and see how the teachers of the church defraud them. This time will come very soon, once we return to the constructive work of peace time."[18]

Elsewhere, though, local officials made no secret of the fact that they could simply not be bothered to comply with the center's instructions to exhume and display holy relics. The Moscow and Petrograd city soviets voted down draft resolutions of the VIII Section's August 1920 decree on the grounds that it would be impossible to implement.[19] As Avel Enukidze, acting chair of the Petrograd Soviet, explained:

> The present moment is unsuitable for this campaign, since the city soviet and party organizations are occupied with the fuel and ration campaigns and are allocating much of their strength to the Wrangel and Polish fronts. Having focused all agitation and attention toward these most important questions, they cannot devote sufficient strength and attention to work on the liquidation of relics and, principally, cannot engage in serious preparatory agitation for the campaign, without which the liquidation of relics will yield not positive but, rather, negative results.[20]

Provincial officials were often more blunt and less politic in their appraisals. Krasikov's VIII Section spent the better part of 1921 trying to persuade the department of justice in Eniseisk Province to exhume the relics of Saints Daniil and Vasilii Mangazeiskii and to send the finger of Innokentii Irkutskii to Moscow so that it could be reunited with the rest of the saint's body, already on exhibition in the capital. Exasperated officials in Eniseisk announced that they had their hands full with liquidating churches in the province and were unable to devote sufficient time and energy to digging up holy relics. "In any event," they pointedly reminded Krasikov, "[closing churches] demands greater preparation than the exhumation of what are already known to be rotten corpses."[21] In January 1920, justice officials in Arkhangel'sk reminded Krasikov that their province was still caught in the crossfire of military action, tersely assuring him that once the Civil War had been won, the procurement crisis resolved, and measures taken to implement the separation of Church and state, then officials would proceed with counting and exhuming holy relics. Until that time, agitation would have to suffice.[22]

In short, provincial officials realized sooner than their superiors that the exhumation campaign was not meeting with the successes predicted. In Novgorod Province, where at least eight saints had been exhumed in the early months of the campaign, local justice officials informed the VIII Section that exhumation by itself could not overcome the faith believers placed in their saints. Nine hundred years of Orthodoxy had penetrated "the very flesh and blood" of the faithful so deeply, they argued, that undertaking any further exhumations in the province would be "premature" and "bound to result in inflamed relations with the ignorant masses." Pilgrimage to the shrines of the saints was "massive" even after exhumation, they claimed, and the Sofiiskii Cathedral where the bodies of the most prominent saints of Novgorod lay was still "overflowing with worshipers." The end result was that exhumation had failed: "[W]ithout closing our eyes to the truth . . . it is possible to conclude that relic exhumation has not diminished the religious feelings of the citizenry of the city of Novgorod, but to the contrary has served as the impetus for the intensified display of religious feelings among the citizenry of the city . . . and its surrounding regions."[23]

On 1 April 1921, the architects of the relic campaign conceded grudging defeat. In a top secret circular dispatched to all provincial and city ispolkoms in the Russian Republic, the VIII Section chastised local officials for their "intolerable confusion and inconsistency" in the prosecution of the relic campaign. "Feebleness and short-sightedness" had resulted in a number of "unprepared [and] unplanned" exhumations, "completely unsupported by a solid portion of the laboring masses and without the sympathy of the entire population." The VIII Section admitted that "unanticipated opposition and agitation from churchmen, kulaks, and locals" had undercut the success of the campaign. But Moscow made it abundantly clear that the burden of responsibility lay squarely on the shoulders of local officials for failing to precede the exhumations with the requisite agitation and propaganda blitzes explaining Soviet power's motives and rationale for digging up the corpses of the saints.[24] To remedy these unforgivable lapses in judgment, the VIII Section stipulated that its offices henceforth be apprised in advance of any future exhumations; whereas grassroots enterprise and initiative "from below" had been celebrated at the beginning of the relic campaign, permission from the center now became a prerequisite for exhumation. The VIII Section's decree effectively brought the initiative of local officials to a screeching halt; a mere six exhumations were conducted sporadically over the next nine years, from April 1921 to February 1930.[25] For all intents and purposes, the relic campaign had come to an end.

Following the mass peasant uprisings throughout the Central Black Earth Region and the sailors' mutiny at Kronstadt, the Bolsheviks backed away from an overtly confrontational policy vis-à-vis the Russian Orthodox Church, focusing their energies instead on creating and maintaining a *smychka* between town and countryside. With the XII Party Congress of 1923, Soviet antireligious policy officially shifted its emphasis away from the aggressively confrontational style of the Civil War and toward the more pragmatic assessment that the final victory over religion, though inevitable, would, like the ultimate victory of the international proletariat, be indefinitely delayed. Lunacharskii expressed the regime's new turn by likening religion to a nail; the harder one strikes it, the deeper it is driven in to the wood. In the era of the New Economic Policy (NEP), gradualists maintained that pliers, not hammers, were needed to extract the faith from the faithful.[26]

The regime's laissez-faire attitude, combined with what Helmut Altrichter has described as the "toughness of tradition," allowed Orthodox devotional practices to flourish under the benign neglect of NEP.[27] Confronted with mounting evidence that religious observance was on the rise in rural localities, Bolshevik antireligious figures began voicing nagging doubts that initial predictions of Orthodoxy's untimely demise had been greatly exaggerated. The relic campaign, critics charged, had not gone far enough and had failed to live up to its potential. Writing in 1923, and with the added benefit of hindsight, the Bolshevik antireligious publicist I. I. Skvortsov-Stepanov conceded that Soviet power had missed out on a golden opportunity to capitalize on the exposure of holy relics as corrupted bodies and extraneous rubbish. "The blow was felt," he wrote, "but we made use of it weakly: a few newspaper articles—rather fleeting references—a couple of belated brochures, a reprinting of the exhumation protocols."[28] Another antireligious writer mused, "If only it had been possible to verify all the church calendars and the historical legends of the miracles of male and female saints and miracle-working icons, then the priests' frauds would have appeared in their full magnitude."[29]

Such self-criticism, though refreshing, misses the point. Church calendars were not the problem; bodies were. Krasikov's call for "full decisiveness" in the conduct of the campaign seldom translated into actual practice. With provincial- and district-level ispolkoms and party cells scrambling to address problems of far more immediate import than the exposure of holy relics, the vast majority of saintly bodies were exhumed, photographed, and promptly forgotten by local officials. While the grisly details of exhumation were written up faithfully in local newspapers, these stories, within a week or less, receded quietly from bold headlines on page 1 to mere mentions on page 4 before disappearing altogether, usually within a month at most. Similarly, overworked Bolshevik officials seldom followed through with the VIII Section's instructions on museum display or prolonged public exhibition. In many localities, commissars simply left the saints' shrines open for casual viewing, for periods ranging anywhere from a matter of days to a few months. Afterward, officials re-interred the bodies, resealed the coffins, and moved on to address a new set of directives from Moscow or the provincial center. Thus, despite the VIII Section's vision of a "total liquidation of the cult of dead bodies and dummies," Soviet power exhumed only a small percentage of holy relics in Russia during the relic campaign, and only a fraction of these ever found their way to state-run museums or antireligious exhibits. As late as 1936, local officials had left untouched a full twenty-two of the thirty-one holy relics residing within the city limits of Novgorod.[30] Thus, for most of the 1920s, the majority of holy bodies remained in the same churches and monasteries where they had been for years before and remained still accessible to Orthodox worshipers.

The result of this, as the antireligious publicist V. Shishakov remarked at the end of the 1920s, was that unexhumed relics continued to be venerated, and exhumed relics "left in the hands of the churchmen . . . once again slowly passed back into [devotional] use." Much to Shishakov's chagrin, the brethren of the Mitrofanskii monastery in Voronezh had added "new bones of completely different provenance" to the shrine of Saint Mitrofan, and equipped with a new body, the saint enjoyed a resurgence of popularity in the 1920s.[31] Behind the commissars' backs, all across European Russia, believers resumed their devotional practices as before. In April 1919, as the winter snows receded, monks at the Spaso-Sumorin monastery in Vologda Province scheduled a religious procession to pray for rain and ensure propitious weather for the spring sowing season. On the Feast of the Ascension, some five thousand Orthodox residents from the surrounding districts assembled on the monastery grounds and watched as a retinue of clerics shouldered the relics of Saint Feodosii Totemskii—clad in full vestments for the occasion and looking no worse for wear, considering that his relics had been exhumed by local Soviet officials only six weeks before. The faithful had simply broken the seals on Feodosii's shrine, removed his body, and proceeded with their customary devotional practices as if nothing had changed.[32] In February 1920, the district militia in Belevskii district informed the Tula Province department of justice that the excavations undertaken in search of Saint Makarii the year before had long since been filled in, the ornate shrine placed back atop the saint's putative grave, and now, once again, "the faithful venerate Makarii" as before. The shrine was said to draw "very many believers" on Makarii's feast day of 22 January.[33]

In Voronezh, exhumation gave rise to a new sort of economic speculation—trafficking in sacred items that had been salvaged—or pilfered—from the coffins of the saints. Shortly after Saint Mitrofan's exhumation, one of his holy gloves was allegedly purchased by an unnamed *"intelligent"* for the enormous sum of fifty rubles; envious bidders offered the buyer twice what he had paid if he would part with his newly acquired treasure. Just one of Mitrofan's cardboard slippers, which had served as a substitute for the saint's missing foot, was said to have fetched a price worth more than five hundred pairs of silk slippers.[34] In some localities, too, new saints made their debut to replace those whose relics had been exhumed or confiscated. In 1921, for example, officials in Chernigov reported that the Orthodox clergy had rolled out the relics of a new saint to replace Feodosii Chernigovskii, currently under glass in a city museum.[35] In Voronezh, just weeks after the exhumation of Tikhon and while the film reel of his exhumation was still playing in city theaters, the brethren of the Bogoroditskii monastery had received permission from the patriarch to open for worship the reliquary of a new holy man, a monk named Georgii. The new saint's cult was short-lived, however. When provincial officials caught wind of the monks' plans, they hastily dispatched a second exhumation commission to the monastery to expose the relics in the basement of the monastery church. The episode prompted the Voronezh press to observe bitterly, "Another day, another new 'forged' saint."[36]

Even as the relic campaign sputtered to a close, it had become apparent to many Bolshevik observers that two years of work and some seventy exhumations had done little to change the ways in which the majority of believers in the Soviet Republic, especially the rural population, understood and acted out their relationship with the saints. As briefings and intelligence reports from the provinces confirmed, the faithful still turned to their saints—even exhumed ones—for miracles and assistance. In Voronezh, monks and priests continued to take requests for prayer services in memory of the exhumed saints Tikhon and Mitrofan and diligently recorded new miracles attributed to their intercession.[37] Believers in Smolensk Province claimed that the locally venerated relic fragments belonging to the Vilnius Martyrs, Saints Antonii, Ioann, and Evstafii, continued to work miraculous cures more than a year after the bulk of their bodies had been exhumed and presumably "discredited" in Moscow, where the relics remained for some time on display in the Donskoi monastery. Abbess Serafima, who had secured portions of these relics for her convent, reiterated these claims from the witness stand when she was put on trial in 1920 on charges of relic fraud. Among the recently cured, she claimed, were a crippled fourteen-year-old boy who had been made to walk and an eighty-year-old woman healed of her paralysis through the intervention of the Vilnius Martyrs.[38] Nor had exhumation managed to defeat the popularity of the Lithuanian saints in Moscow. In a preliminary deposition prior to the trial, the abbess's co-defendant, Hieromonk Dosifei of the Donskoi monastery, testified that so many worshipers came to kiss the saints' feet that the monks were obliged to change the relics' slippers and stockings every month.[39]

Although Gorev predicted that the exhumation of Saint Sergii Radonezhskii would extinguish once and for all the thousands of flickering candles that burned at the saint's shrine, Orthodox pilgrims continued to come to pray before Sergii's relics, albeit now from the opposite side of a glass partition placed atop his lidless coffin. An antireligious writer who visited the Lavra during the 1920s was appalled to see excursionists lagging behind their tour guides so that they could press their lips to the glass and pay their respects to the saint.[40] According to testimony established at the trial of Abbess Serafima, the patriarch's chancelleries received a total of 1,500,000 rubles in revenue from the Troitskaia Lavra during the nine-month period *following* the exhumation of Saint Sergii—in large part through receipts of candle sales and donations made at the offering boxes that still stood, inexplicably, alongside the saint's shrine.[41] Even if exaggerated by the Soviet procuracy, these figures demonstrate that a large percentage of Orthodox believers—perhaps even the majority—still placed their faith in the intercessory powers of Sergii and his fellow saints. Such evidence belies the assertions of Bolshevik publicists that only "decrepit and senile old women, hysterics [*klikushi*], and the psychologically abnormal . . . choose to believe in the sanctity and incorruptibility of so-called relics."[42] When Novgorod city officials finally exhumed and confiscated the relics of the monk Moisei from the Skovorodskii monastery, they discovered ruble- and kopeck-coins minted as late as 1929 inside the shrine, money left behind by believers who continued to visit the saint and thank him for his intercession with offerings of Soviet currency.[43] By decade's end, one antireligious publicist concluded bitterly that "in several localities, the cult of relics is flourishing as before."[44]

By 1929, with the First Five Year Plan in full swing, the ethos of gradualism came under increased criticism from impatient party activists eager to speed up victory on the so-called antireligious front. The enthusiasm for full-scale collectivization was replicated in the drive for full-scale secularization, which involved shifting the tactical center of gravity away from the Orthodox Church as an institution and toward the parishes and lay organizations on the grassroots level. In the late 1920s and 1930s, a new cohort of provincial- and district-level cadres over-fulfilled their directives by closing down churches and eradicating the parish organizations that had flourished during the preceding decade.[45]

Soviet officials also set about to exhume saintly shrines that had escaped their attention the decade before.[46] Local officials who had forgone exhumation in their district now came under intense public criticism for their negligence. *Bezbozhnik*, the official organ of the League of the Militant Godless, led the charge, attacking local administrators in Kashin for leaving the relics of Anna Kashinskaia untouched since the Revolution. It was "the sheer permissiveness" of such "compromisers" that had undermined the effectiveness of the relic campaign. A cohort of local officials were placed on trial in Kashin in late 1929 on charges of "allow[ing] serious distortions of party policy."[47] Saint Anna herself was eventually exhumed by more enthusiastic comrades on 24 February 1930. The inspection uncovered a sack of charred bones, an eighteenth-century copper coin, and a scrap of red-dyed canvas cloth "of recent make." Anna's was the last major relic exhumation staged in public.[48]

The late 1920s witnessed also a redefinition of how saints figured in the larger picture of Soviet antireligious strategy. By the end of the decade, Bolshevik propagandists had shifted their tactics, placing less emphasis on the saints as fraudulent bodies and focusing greater attention on the holy dead as class enemies and "former people" (*byvshie liudi*). In a 1929 pamphlet, the former chairman of the commission that had exhumed the saints of Murom ten years before waxed indignant that, of the nineteen saints in Vladimir Province, ten were princes or princesses, seven were bishops or monks, and two hailed from ranks of the landed gentry. "Each and every one, without exception, class enemies of the laborers! What a selection! Could not a single righteous man be found from among the millions of laborers?"[49] Antireligious museums in the provinces and the capital exchanged their displays of holy relics for exhibits featuring the ornate jewels, crosses, and vestments worn by the so-called princes of the church and purchased, as the captions read, with the blood and sweat of the narod.[50] In Rostov, for example, museum officials staged an exhibition that featured a collection of class-biased miracle stories attributed to the former miracle-worker and current class enemy Dimitrii Rostovskii. The exhibition's organizers charged that from the eighteenth century onward, Dimitrii had opted almost exclusively to render his "miraculous" assistance not to the peasants and workers who needed it most but to clerics, merchants, noblemen, and state officials.[51] Soviet studies uncovered similar bias in the nineteenth-century miracles attributed to Saint Tikhon Zadonskii, which prompted one writer to calculate that the sainted bishop "clearly loved the nobility eighty times more than the peasantry."[52]

Medical experts, too, shifted their position on the saints, focusing less on the condition of their corpses and more on the regrettable example of poor hygiene and bodily care they set for the faithful:

> And who are these saints, whose example the laborers must imitate? Among them there are those who do not wash, who do not cut their hair, who live in uncleanliness, who wear . . . hair shirts, who walk around in rags and fetters. . . . Mortifying their flesh, these people passed their nights in the same kennel with the dogs, smeared their faces with the dung of animals, and rejoiced all the while that they [stood] near to the "kingdom of heaven."[53]

During collectivization, the saints came under especially heavy criticism for their feast days, which kept rural agriculture in thrall to the rhythms of an antiquated calendar.[54] As Sergei Kirov explained, the time had come for the Russian peasantry to dispense with its saintly specialists and embrace science: "How can it be considered necessary to mow the hay after St. Peter's Day without fail, or to harvest grain on St. Elijah's Day? Do you think that Peter and Paul know the conditions of Leningrad oblast better than you or I? Nowhere does it say that Peter and Paul ever frequented Leningrad oblast."[55] In short, by the First Five Year Plan, saints were no longer just fake bodies but privileged charlatans whose miracles were scientific impossibilities and whose veneration was an impediment to socialist construction.

This shift involved also a shake-up and reorganization of the content of antireligious museums. Out of step with new trends in antireligious policy, the Narkomzdrav relic exhibit closed its doors in 1929, and most of its holdings were relocated to museums in Moscow and Leningrad.[56] As late as 1935, the relics of Saint Serafim Sarovskii could still be seen at the Central Antireligious Museum in Moscow, where they appeared as "a shapeless mass of rotten bones."[57] Although a handful of relics did continue on exhibition throughout the 1930s, these few were no longer the centerpieces they once had been. Saints exhumed during and after the First Five Year Plan were seldom put on public display but more often were locked away and, in certain cases, simply destroyed.[58] By the end of the Second World War, most relic exhibitions gathered dust in storage rooms and cellars, all but forgotten by museum personnel.[59]

This did not, however, signify an abandonment of the antireligious museum project per se but, rather, a refinement of the model under which it was to operate. The number of working antireligious museums across the country increased from eleven in 1927 to seventy-three just five years later.[60] Thanks to increased activism on the part of the organizers of workers' clubs and student groups, museum attendance figures also continued to grow steadily over the course of the 1920s and spiked sharply after 1929. During the winter of 1924–1925, for example, nearly 2,500 people, mostly students and schoolchildren, attended organized tours of the Museum of Antireligious Propaganda in Leningrad.[61] By contrast, in 1931 more than 100,000 people passed through the doors of the State Antireligious Museum (the former St. Isaac's Cathedral in Leningrad) during its first year of operation. The special opening night festivities alone, dated deliberately to coincide and compete with Orthodox Easter celebrations, brought in a crowd of some 7,200.[62] By this time, however, the central attraction was no longer a ghoulish collection of saintly corpses but an enormous pendulum suspended inside the church from the top of the one-hundred-meter-high domed cupola. As a new generation of museum docents explained to their visitors, Foucault's Pendulum, named for the nineteenth-century French physicist Jean Foucault, demonstrated both the rotation of the earth and the backwardness of those Christians who had condemned Copernicus.[63] By the First Five Year Plan, the pendulum had replaced holy relics, as Soviet antireligious propaganda shifted from the sensational to the scientific.

As the Protestant Reformation and the French Revolution demonstrate, the dismantling of one social myth carries with it the corollary need to erect another in its place. So too in the Bolshevik relic campaign can we discern a certain productive force at work. The revolutionary regime's long-term goal was not only to obliterate the "religious superstitions" surrounding the saints but to create a new society on earth, to refashion Russia in its own image. In exhuming the bodies of the Orthodox saints, the Bolshevik state did indeed seek to discredit the Church as a rival institutional locus for the social and cultural identities of the Russian Orthodox populace, and in that sense it undoubtedly met with less than total success in the short term. But, more broadly, the relic campaign was also part of the new regime's repeated efforts to define itself in opposition to what had come before: the new Communist society would not be predicated on dead bodies and decay, on incense smoke and asceticism, on secrecy, fraud, and chicanery. By exhuming saintly bodies from gilded shrines, exposing the scientific impossibility of incorruptibility, and consigning relics to museums as vestiges of an outmoded past made obsolete by humanity's historical development, the Bolsheviks sought to celebrate the vibrant power of science and reason in the service of human progress and the realization of a socialist society.

The oppositional relationship between the superstitions of the old regime and the accomplishments of the Soviet state was vividly expressed in a satirical antireligious piece from 1924 depicting a fantastic encounter between a young Komsomol activist and an unlikely trinity made up of the fairy-tale witch Baba-Yaga, the devil, and Saint Nicholas the Wonder-Worker. The three are on their way to the Simonov monastery in Moscow to attend Easter services when they are stopped at the gates by the *komsomolets*: "Where are you going, citizens?" After the trio identify themselves, the Komsomol youth asks them if they plan on performing any miracles while in town. When they answer yes, he proceeds to debunk each figure's claims to power. Baba-Yaga explains that she can fly. The komsomolets laughs. So can Soviet pilots, he retorts, and they can even take passengers and luggage up into the skies with them. The devil claims he can make writing appear on walls in fiery letters. The gas lights and electric signs on Moscow's Teatral'naia Square burn just as brightly, the young man responds, shaking his head. When Saint Nicholas boasts of his ability to cast out demons, the komsomolets is less than impressed:

> "Demons, eh? That's nothing. Over the last five years we've cast out all sorts of unclean spirits—the tsar, Kolchak, Denikin, and Wrangel. Who the hell knows the rest, I can't remember them all. Not to mention all their hordes and bands too, and here you are talking about demons."
>
> "I'll heal the infirm . . ." [Nicholas says].
>
> "What, piece by piece? You can't top us on this one either. We're not exactly amateurs. The whole transportation system, and industry too, they were left cripples after the Civil War but now we're beginning to straighten them out. And we won't be asking for your help. The scourge of miracles is right here in this calloused hand," and with that the komsomolets stuck his fist right in the miracle-worker's nose.
>
> "I'll feed five thousand people with bread seven times over," Nicholas the Wonder-Worker continued.
>
> "So what? That's old news. In Moscow, our MPO [Moscow Ration Department] has let the cat out of the bag on that little trick. Once they exposed the ration-card scam all those miracles came to an end. And the GPU nabbed all the ration-card miracle-workers [*kartochnye chudotvortsy*] and shot them."
>
> "I'll show you a real miracle. The miracle of miracles. I'll turn water into wine."
>
> "It won't work. The MUR [Moscow Criminal Investigation Department] is already on to it. Measures are being taken against home-brew [*samogon*]. Try it more than once and you'll wind up in the courtroom for sure, you'll see."
>
> "I'll show you some relics, then. Incorruptible ones lying hidden for a thousand years."
>
> "What relics? Give it up, brother. Over the last five years we've checked out I-don't-know-how-many relics and taken a lot of them away from the little workshops where they were made. A whole bunch of them. This is nothing for us anymore. . . . Over the last five years we've worked miracles the likes of which the old humanity never dreamed."

Crestfallen at finding their miracles redundant in the new Russia, the three "out-of-work miracle-workers" slink off in defeat. At last report, the author tells us, Nicholas the Wonder-Worker was contemplating a career in the black market, using his miraculous job skills to traffic in hard currency.[64] The moral of the story is clear: Soviet Russia had demystified the world, stripped it of the supernatural, and outgrown its religious past; Soviet power had put the miracle-workers out of business by making the saints superfluous. Enumerating the advances Soviet power had made in the countryside over the past decade, a Leningrad antireligious activist concurred: "Village agricultural schools, books, newspapers, conversations with agronomists, model farms—all these are undermining the activity of the Christian saints."[65]

The Bolshevik campaign against Orthodox saints and holy relics was thus an integral part of the Soviet enlightenment project. With an arsenal of science, technology, knowledge, and learning at its disposal, the Soviet state sought to banish the supernatural from its borders, while claiming for itself the ability to change the material world and to work "miracles." The state assumed for itself the wondrous qualities that Orthodox believers had long attributed to their saints. Nowhere was this more clearly exemplified than in the embalming of V. I. Lenin, whose uncorrupted body lay in state in a glass shrine on Red Square after his death in 1924. The preservation and display of Lenin's body was not a heavy-handed attempt on the part of the Bolsheviks to co-opt Orthodox religiosity or to suffuse the party with a sacred aura but, rather, a demonstration that Soviet power—not the Orthodox faith—held the keys to unlocking the mysteries of the material world. The preservation of Lenin's body was attributed not to the inscrutable workings of supernatural powers or divine grace but to chemistry, biology, and mankind's mastery of nature. Lenin's body was not a holy relic, nor did Vladimir Il'ich perform healing cures for the benefit of those who filed past his tomb. In essence, Lenin's body was an "anti-miracle"—if holy relics embodied the physical presence of supernatural forces and heavenly powers that defied rational explanation, Lenin's body represented the victory of reason over faith. Thus, Soviet power showed that it could accomplish what the exhumation campaign had shown God Himself incapable of—preserving the body of a chosen one from corruption and decay.[66]

"Can they really be considered Russian Orthodox?" the ethnographer Ol'ga Tian-Shanskaia asked of her rural subjects in Riazan Province in the 1890s. "Not at all. They are confused, helpless, and terrified, and have no idea what to do 'to gain salvation.'"[67] This book has argued that Russian Orthodox lay believers were anything but helpless when it came to interacting with their saints. If they were not always clear where the road to salvation lay or how to gain it, Orthodox believers were well aware of the material, earthly benefits they could obtain from the intercession of the saints. The requests that believers made and the miracles they sought when they prayed at saintly shrines demonstrate that the Orthodox faithful imagined their saints not as distant entities but as friends, guardians, and neighbors, ever-present, all-powerful, and ready to bestow miracles on the living. Pace Tian-Shanskaia, Russian believers were, indeed, Orthodox. That they turned to the saints more for earthly assistance than for salvational guidance suggests that Orthodox believers saw their faith not as something remote but as an integral part of their everyday lives and of the world around them. In the bodies and relics of their saints, Russian Orthodox believers found powerful avenues of recourse to assist them in mediating the perils and pitfalls of modern life.

Insofar as Bolshevism and Orthodoxy represented two diametrically opposed ways of seeing the world, a clash between these rival ideological systems was inevitable after the Revolution of 1917. As Emel'ian Iaroslavskii put the question, "If the world is controlled by God, if the fate of the people is in the hands of God, His saints, angels, devils, and fiends—then what sense is there in the organized struggle of the workers and peasants, in the creation of a Leninist Party? What sense is there in the Socialist reconstruction of society?"[68] Yet, while the Bolsheviks had chosen well in setting their sights on the saints as targets in a full-scale war of reason versus superstition, they misfired by focusing exclusively on the notion of bodily incorruptibility. As we saw in the first three chapters of this book, Orthodox believers placed great value on the bodily incorruptibility of their saints, but they did not require pristine corpses as prerequisites to sanctity. The sine qua non of sainthood in the popular religious imagination was not so much incorruptibility as miracles, and the more of these the better. The great popularity commanded by the cults of Saint Anna Kashinskaia and Saint Sofronii—neither of whom could boast relics that were uncorrupted at the time of their canonization—demonstrates that believers cultivated their patronage for reasons that transcended the saints' bodily coherence (or lack thereof). Their moshchi were important and treasured, true, but this was because they worked miracles with great frequency and regularity, for all believers who came in faith to seek out their powerful intercession.

If the condition of a saint's body was ultimately of little consequence to believers, however, its physical presence was of the utmost importance. The devotional practices associated with the cult of the saints were rooted above all else in the located presence of the saint himself or herself. Russian Orthodox believers were firm in their conviction that the most immediate avenue for accessing the healing power of the saints was by frequenting their graves, kissing their relics, touching their shrines, anointing themselves with holy oil from the icon lanterns that flickered above their tombs, and even, on occasion, donning articles of their clothing. Although these devotional practices were subject to improvisation and experimentation on the part of the faithful, who turned to the saints to work new "modern" miracles in the last decades of the old regime, they were also circumscribed by a deep sense of place and location. Evidence from miracle stories suggests that the faithful believed the gestures and oblations they performed at the saint's grave were the surest and most efficacious means of interacting with the sacred. Although the saint stood in heaven before the throne of God, the faithful could cultivate his friendship and intercession so long as he retained his tangible and tactile presence on earth; of the saint's two bodies, however, believers were far more concerned with the one he had left behind.

As Vera Shevzov has demonstrated, Orthodox believers felt a sense of propriety and possession (*sobstvennost'*) toward their sacred objects. In their view, icons, banners, churches, and chapels belonged not to "the Church," understood as some distant institution, but to the believers who comprised the ecclesial community at the parish level.[69] In the same way, believers imagined that holy relics belonged *to* and *in* the community where those relics resided. Because Orthodox believers understood their relationship with the saints in reciprocal terms, when commissars came to confiscate holy relics, Orthodox men and women repaid their debts to the holy dead by resisting the removal of their bodies. The greatest expressions of outrage to the relic campaign came not from believers distraught at the notion of their beloved saints being exposed to public view but, rather, from those faithful who were incensed at the very idea of the saints' shrines being sealed to worshipers and their bodies uprooted from the communities where they had lain for generations. The violent outburst that ensued in Vel'sk when district officials attempted to abscond with Prokopii's body demonstrates that believers were committed to keeping the saint's relics in the village and in their possession; even though it had been exhumed, the saint's body was still a sacred object of devotion and veneration, and most important, a source of miracles. Hardliners at Narkomiust came to realize too late that exhumation itself could only do so much to change the minds of the faithful; to be successful in eliminating a cult based on the material presence of the saints, the Soviets would need to seize and remove holy relics from churches and monasteries. Krasikov's dreams of a demystified Russia rid of relics, of a Russia where saints would exist only alongside other historical artifacts and behind the confines of museum display cases, were unrealizable in the context of the Civil War and the period of reconstruction and consolidation that followed.

Notes

Abbreviations

d. — *delo* (file)

f. — *fond* (collection)

g. — *god* (year)

l., ll. — *list, listy* (leaf, leaves)

no. — *nomer* (number)

ob. — *oborot* (obverse)

op. — *opis'* (inventory)

otd. — *otdelenie* (section)

st. — *stol* (department)

t. — *tom* (volume)

vyp.— *vypusk* (issue)

Introduction

1. J. G. Kohl, *Russia: St. Petersburg, Moscow, Kharkoff, Riga, Odessa, the German Provinces on the Baltic, the Steppes, the Crimea, and the Interior of the Empire* (London, 1844), 230–31 (emphasis in original).

2. Ibid., 233.

3. Ibid.

4. Ibid., 262. Consider Kohl's comments on the Orthodox liturgy itself: "The most disagreeable part of the Russian service is the astonishing inactivity of the congregation. The only thing done by them during this whole three hours' ceremony, is repeated crossing and touching the floor with the forehead. . . . They have no books in their hands either to follow the reading or the singing, they are merely spectators, and the whole service a pompous spectacle. There is nothing to enlighten the mind, or awaken perception; nothing to better the heart or rouse up the slumbering conscience" (ibid., 254). For a thoughtful and theologically informed discussion of the physicality of Orthodox worship, see Kallistos Ware, "'My Helper and My Enemy': The Body in Greek Christianity," in *Religion and the Body*, ed. Sarah Coakley (Cambridge, England, 1997), 90–110.

5. The Russian word *sviatoi* is equivalent to the English "saint." The Russian language, however, contains various terms of endearment for the saints, direct translations for which are absent in English. The most common, *ugodnik* (alt., *sviatoi ugodnik* or *bozhii ugodnik*), translates literally as "he who pleases/is pleasing to [God]." Clerical figures and lay believers alike commonly used *ugodnik* as a more intimate form of address to a particular saint, as in "Nikolai-ugodnik, moli o nas" (Saint Nicholas, pray for us). In the text, I have translated *ugodnik* and *bozhii ugodnik* as "saint" and "God's saint," respectively.

6. *Russkaia sviatynia* (St. Petersburg, 1873), 97–137. It should also be mentioned that the Church does not possess relics of every saint in the Orthodox liturgical calendar. In his magisterial study of extant Greek Orthodox relics, Otto Meinardus uncovered

more than 3,600 holy relics belonging to 476 saints; these 476, however, amount to only 12.5 percent of the 3,800 saints listed officially in the Byzantine Hagiologion. See Otto Meinardus, "A Study of the Relics of Saints of the Greek Orthodox Church," *Oriens Christianus* 54 (1970): 130–278.

7. Priest Tarasii Seredinskii, "Opredelenie razlichiia mezhdu vostochnoiu i zapadnoiu tserkoviiu otnositel'no ucheniia o sostoianii dush sviatykh do vseobshchago voskreseniia," *Dukhovnaia beseda*, t. 11, no. 39 (24 September 1860): 98–105.

8. William James, *The Varieties of Religious Experience: A Study in Human Nature* (New York, 1902), 324.

9. On the iconoclast controversy in Byzantium (c. 726–843 AD), see J. M. Hussey, *The Orthodox Church in the Byzantine Empire* (Oxford, 1986), 30–68.

10. *The Russian Primary Chronicle: Laurentian Text*, ed. Samuel Hazzard Cross and Olgerd P. Sherbowitz-Wetzor (Cambridge, MA, 1953), 116. There is a large literature on saints and relics in Kievan Rus' and Muscovy. See, for example, G. P. Fedotov, *Sviatye drevnei Rusi* (Paris, 1931); Gail Lenhoff, "The Notion of 'Uncorrupted Relics' in Early Russian Culture," in *Slavic Cultures in the Middle Ages*, ed. Boris Gasparov and Olga Raevsky-Hughes (Berkeley and Los Angeles, 1993), 252–75; Jean-Pierre Arrignon, "Le rôle des reliques dans la *Rus'* de Kiev," in *Les reliques: Objets, cultes, symboles*, ed. Edina Bozóky and Anne-Marie Helvétius (Tournhout, 1999), 57–63; and O. G. Postnov, "Netlennye moshchi i mertvye dushi: smert' v Rossii," in *Traditsiia i literaturnyi protsess* (Novosibirsk, 1999), 349–64. Vladimir's transfer of holy relics to Kiev mirrors similar processes in Western and Eastern Christendom, whereby rulers and bishops made use of the bodies and bones of the saints to legitimate their own authority and strengthen devotion to the new faith among their subjects. See, for example, Patrick J. Geary, *Furta Sacra: Thefts of Relics in the Central Middle Ages* (Princeton, 1978), 3–30; Lionel Rothkrug, "Religious Practices and Collective Perceptions: Hidden Homologies in the Renaissance and Reformation," *Historical Reflections/Réflexions Historiques* 7 (1980): 1–264; and Danila Popovic, "The Political Role of Relics in Medieval Serbia," in *Relikvii v iskusstve i kul'ture vostochnokhristianskogo mira*, ed. A. M. Lidov (Moscow, 2000), 58–61.

11. On the vitality of lay piety in Muscovy, see Eve Levin, "Supplicatory Prayers as a Source for Popular Religious Culture in Muscovite Russia," in *Religion and Culture in Early Modern Russia and Ukraine*, ed. Samuel H. Baron and Nancy Shields Kollmann (DeKalb, 1997), 96–114.

12. Daniel H. Kaiser, "Naming Cultures in Early Modern Russia," *Harvard Ukrainian Studies* 19 (1995): 271–91. In the Catholic West, naming children after saints had been made mandatory a century before, as per the Council of Trent. See Stephen Wilson, *The Means of Naming: A Social and Cultural History of Naming in Western Europe* (London, 1998), 190–93. On baptism and Russian naming practices in the imperial period, see P. I. Nechaev, *Prakticheskoe rukovodstvo dlia sviashchennosluzhitelei, ili sistematicheskoe izlozhenie polnago kruga ikh obiazannostei i prav*, 12th ed. (Petrograd, 1915), 229.

13. On publishing and reading trends in imperial Russia, see Gary Marker, *Publishing, Printing, and the Origins of Intellectual Life in Russia, 1700–1800* (Princeton, 1985), 41–69; and Jeffrey Brooks, *When Russia Learned to Read: Literacy and Popular Literature, 1861–1917* (Princeton, 1987). On the popularity of the lives of the saints among the Russian *narod*, see Iv. Ivin, "O narodno-lubochnoi literature. K voprosu o tom, chto chitaet narod (Iz nabliudenii krest'ianina nad chteniem v derevne)," *Russkoe obozrenie*, t. 22, no. 9 (September 1893): 242–60, and t. 23, no. 10 (October 1893): 768–85; F. Simonov, "Chto chitaiut nashi sovremennye krest'iane?" *Permskiia eparkhial'nyia vedomosti*, no. 13 (May 1914): 231–35. On religious prints and images, see T. A. Voronina, *Russkii lubok 20–60-x godov XIX veka: Proizvodstvo, bytovanie, tematika* (Moscow, 1993), 116–24; T. A. Voronina, "Russkii religioznyi lubok," *Zhivaia starina*, no. 3 (1994): 6–11.

14. On the prevalence of this utilitarian understanding of sanctity among Ortho-

dox believers in Muscovy, see Eve Levin, "From Corpse to Cult in Early Modern Russia," in *Orthodox Russia: Belief and Practice under the Tsars*, ed. Valerie A. Kivelson and Robert H. Greene (University Park, 2003), 81–103.

15. A. N. Kurtsev, "Palomnichestvo v Tsentral'nom Chernozem'e (1861–1917 gg.)," in *Materialy dlia izucheniia selenii Rossii*, 2 vols. (Moscow, 1997), 2:142–46; P. N. Zyrianov, *Russkie monastyri i monashestvo v XIX i nachale XX veka* (Moscow, 1999), 72–77.

16. The classic English-language examples of this literature are by John Shelton Curtiss, *Church and State in Russia: The Last Years of the Empire, 1900–1917* (New York, 1940), and *The Russian Church and the Soviet State, 1917–1950* (Boston, 1953). In more recent decades, Gregory L. Freeze has made immense contributions in the field of the social and political history of the Russian Orthodox Church and the clergy, while offering a much needed corrective to the once dominant view of the Church as a placid subordinate of the imperial state. See, for example, Gregory L. Freeze, *The Parish Clergy in Nineteenth-Century Russia: Crisis, Reform, Counter-reform* (Princeton, 1983), "Handmaiden of the State? The Orthodox Church in Imperial Russia Reconsidered," *Journal of Ecclesiastical History* 36 (1985): 82–102, and "The Orthodox Church and Serfdom in Preform Russia," *Slavic Review* 48 (1989): 361–87.

17. For a typically tendentious view of the Church's counterrevolutionary record after 1917, see R. Iu. Plaksin, *Krakh tserkovnoi kontrrevoliutsii, 1917–1923 gg.* (Moscow, 1968). Since the fall of the Soviet Union, Russian scholars have produced some important studies that not only deal with the Orthodox Church and the Soviet state but also take believers, clerics, parish societies, and lay organizations into account. See N. A. Krivova, *Vlast' i tserkov' v 1922–1925 gg.: Politbiuro i GPU v bor'be za tserkovnye tsennosti i politicheskoe podchinenie dukhovenstva* (Moscow, 1997); M. V. Shkarovskii, *Russkaia pravoslavnaia tserkov' pri Staline i Khrushcheve: Gosudarstvenno-tserkovnye otnosheniia v SSSR v 1939–1964 godakh* (Moscow, 1999); and Tatiana A. Chumachenko, *Gosudarstvo, pravoslavnaia tserkov', veruiushchie, 1941–1961 gg.* (Moscow, 1999).

18. Gregory L. Freeze, "Recent Scholarship on Russian Orthodoxy: A Critique," *Kritika* 2 (2001): 277 (emphasis in original).

19. Recent contributions include Chris J. Chulos, *Converging Worlds: Religion and Community in Peasant Russia, 1861–1917* (DeKalb, 2003); Jennifer Hedda, *His Kingdom Come: Orthodox Pastorship and Social Activism in Revolutionary Russia* (DeKalb, 2008); Nadieszda Kizenko, *A Prodigal Saint: Father John of Kronstadt and the Russian People* (University Park, 2000); and various works by Vera Shevzov, "Chapels and the Ecclesial World of Pre-Revolutionary Russian Peasants," *Slavic Review* 55 (1996): 585–613, "Miracle-Working Icons, Laity, and Authority in the Russian Orthodox Church, 1861–1917," *Russian Review* 58 (1999): 26–48, and *Russian Orthodoxy on the Eve of Revolution* (Oxford, 2004). See also the essays collected in Mark D. Steinberg and Heather J. Coleman, eds., *Sacred Stories: Religion and Spirituality in Modern Russia* (Bloomington, 2007).

20. Arguing that Orthodoxy should be understood as an ecclesial community that encompasses both clergy and laity, the recent work of Vera Shevzov exemplifies the application of this approach to the Russian case. See Vera Shevzov, "Letting the People into Church: Reflections on Orthodoxy and Community in Late Imperial Russia," in Kivelson and Greene, *Orthodox Russia*, 59–77. On "great" and "little" traditions generally, see Robert Redfield, *Peasant Society and Culture: An Anthropological Approach to Civilization* (Chicago, 1956). Examples of this bifurcation abound in the older literature on Russian Orthodoxy. See, for example, I. P. Kalinskii, *Tserkovno-narodnyi mesiatseslov na Rusi* (St. Petersburg, 1877); Vladimir Dal', *O pover'iakh, sueveriiakh i predrassudkakh russkago naroda*, 2nd ed. (St. Petersburg, 1880); and E. G. Kaiander, *Russkie sviatye* (Moscow, 1930). For a critical reassessment of the utility of this model, see Eve Levin, "*Dvoeverie* and Popular Religion," in *Seeking God: The Recovery of Religious Identity in Orthodox Russia*, ed. Stephen K. Batalden (DeKalb,

1993), 29–52; Stella Rock, *Popular Religion in Russia: "Double Belief" and the Making of an Academic Myth* (New York, 2007); and Christine D. Worobec, "Death Ritual among Russian and Ukrainian Peasants: Linkages between the Living and the Dead," in Frank and Steinberg, *Cultures in Flux*, 11–33.

21. Pierre Delooz, "Towards a Sociological Study of Canonized Sainthood in the Catholic Church," in Stephen Wilson, ed., *Saints and Their Cults: Studies in Religious Sociology, Folklore and History* (Cambridge, 1983), 194, 196, 199 (emphasis in original).

22. Peter Burke, "How to Be a Counter-Reformation Saint," in *Religion and Society in Early Modern Europe*, ed. Kaspar von Greyerz (London, 1984), 45–55.

23. Levin, "From Corpse to Cult," 84. Late imperial historians of canonization generally supposed a far greater degree of standardization and centralization in the Kievan and Muscovite periods than surviving evidence allows. See Vasilii Vasil'ev, *Istoriia kanonizatsii russkikh sviatykh* (Moscow, 1893); and E. E. Golubinskii, *Istoriia kanonizatsii sviatykh v Russkoi tserkvi*, 2nd ed. (Moscow, 1903). See also P. Peeters, "La canonisation des saints dans l'Eglise russe," *Analecta Bollandiana* 33 (1914): 380–420, and 38 (1920): 172–76. For a critique of Golubinskii's argument that a recognizable and coherent process for the canonization of saints existed in Muscovy, see Paul Bushkovitch, *Religion and Society in Russia: The Sixteenth and Seventeenth Centuries* (Oxford, 1992), 74–99.

24. On the Orthodox Church's efforts to improve the level of lay piety, see Gregory L. Freeze, "The Rechristianization of Russia: The Church and Popular Religion, 1750–1850," *Studia Slavica Finlandensia* 7 (1990): 101–36. Similar attempts to co-opt and purify popular devotional practices, festivals, and saintly cults were undertaken in the eighteenth and nineteenth centuries by Catholic hierarchs, with varying levels of stringency and differing degrees of success. See, for example, S. J. Connolly, *Priests and People in Pre-Famine Ireland, 1780–1845* (New York, 1982); Jonathan Sperber, *Popular Catholicism in Nineteenth-Century Germany* (Princeton, 1984); and Brian R. Larkin, "Liturgy, Devotion, and Religious Reform in Eighteenth-Century Mexico City," *Americas* 60 (2004): 493–518.

25. Alexander V. Muller, trans. and ed., *The Spiritual Regulation of Peter the Great* (Seattle, 1972), 13, 15.

26. Eve Levin, "False Miracles and Unattested Dead Bodies: Investigations into Popular Cults in Early Modern Russia," in *Religion and the Early Modern State: Views from China, Russia, and the West*, ed. James D. Tracy and Marguerite Ragnow (Cambridge, 2004), 253–83; Simon Dixon, "Superstition in Imperial Russia," *Past and Present*, no. 199, supplement 3 (2008): 207–28.

27. For an exemplary overstatement of the differences between the "offical" religion of the seminaries and the "popular" religion of the village, see Moshe Lewin, "Popular Religion in Twentieth-Century Russia," in *The Making of the Soviet System: Essays in the Social History of Interwar Russia* (New York, 1994), 57–71.

28. A thoughtful exploration of this point is developed in Scott M. Kenworthy, "The Revival of Monasticism in Modern Russia: The Trinity–Sergius Lavra, 1825–1921" (Ph.D. diss., Brandeis University, 2002), ch. 6. On the similarities between "elite" and "popular" religious worldviews and opinions on the powers of the saints in Western Christianity, see André Vauchez, *Sainthood in the Later Middle Ages*, trans. Jean Birrell (Cambridge, England, 1997), esp. 535–39.

29. Gregory L. Freeze, "Institutionalizing Piety: The Church and Popular Religion, 1750–1850," in *Imperial Russia: New Histories for the Empire*, ed. Jane Burbank and David L. Ransel (Bloomington, 1998), 235.

30. The policies of the Catholic Church in Third Republic France offer an instructive case for comparison. In the late nineteenth century, Catholic religious elites became increasingly receptive to miracle stories attributed to the Virgin Mary

and the saints, in part to bolster allegiance to the Church against the intellectual challenges of secularism and socialism. See Thomas A. Kselman, *Miracles and Prophecies in Nineteenth-Century France* (New Brunswick, 1983); Brian Brennan, "Piety and Politics in Nineteenth-Century Poitiers: The Cult of St. Radegund," *Journal of Ecclesiastical History* 47 (1996): 65–81; Ruth Harris, *Lourdes: Body and Spirit in the Secular Age* (London, 1999); and Paul d'Hollander, "Les ostensions en Limousin au XIXe siècle," *Revue de l'Histoire des Religions* 217 (2000): 503–16.

31. Laura Engelstein, "Old and New, High and Low: Straw Horsemen of Russian Orthodoxy," in Kivelson and Greene, *Orthodox Russia*, 30.

32. E. N. Voronets, *Ob angelakh-khraniteliakh i o podrazhanii sviatym, imenami kotorykh my nazyvaemsia* (Khar'kov, 1877), 6–7. See also A. A. Nevskii, *Russkaia dukhovno-nravstvennaia khristomatiia*, 3rd ed. (Moscow, 1874), 225. The theology of the guardian angels in the Orthodox tradition dates back at least as far as the ninth century, when Saint Theodore of Edessa wrote in praise of their assistance. See the discussion in Ivan Pankeev, *Obychai i traditsii russkogo naroda* (Moscow, 1999), 60.

33. I. Klimiuk, "Slovo o pochitanii sviatykh," *Irkutskiia eparkhial'nyia vedomosti* (hereafter *IEV*), no. 9 (1 May 1913): 292.

34. Priest Evlampii Biriukov, *Katikhizicheskiia besedy k sel'skim prikhozhanam* (Kamyshlov, 1900), 58–59.

35. These stories are treated at greater length in Chapters One and Two. On dreams and visions as a specific genre or motif in the Russian religious tradition more generally, see E. K. Romodanovskaia, "Rasskazy sibirskikh krest'ian o videniiakh (k voprosu o spetsifike zhanra videnii)," *Trudy Otdela drevnerusskoi literatury* 49 (1996): 141–56.

36. On saintly cults and relic veneration in the early Christian Church, see Peter Brown, *The Cult of the Saints: Its Rise and Function in Latin Christianity* (Chicago, 1982); Lionel Rothkrug, "The 'Odour of Sanctity' and the Hebrew Origins of Christian Relic Veneration," *Historical Reflections/Réflexions Historiques* 8 (1981): 95–142; and Béatrice Caseau, "Sacred Landscapes," in *Interpreting Late Antiquity: Essays on the Postclassical World*, ed. G. W. Bowersock, Peter Brown, and Oleg Grabar (Cambridge, MA, 2001), 21–59. The canons of the Council of Gangra (dated variously from 340 to 376 AD) pronounced anathema on any Christian who "out of pride regards with abhorrence the assemblies of the martyrs and the services there held, or the commemoration of the martyrs." See J. Stevenson, ed., *Creeds, Councils and Controversies: Documents Illustrative of the History of the Church, A.D. 337–461* (New York, 1966), 6.

37. In their study of Western sainthood, Weinstein and Bell note the oft-cited paradox that the very bodies that most ascetic saints had spent their earthly lives renouncing and mortifying should become a conduit for God's grace: "Where saints had regarded their bodies as reservoirs of sin and mortal enemies of the spirit, their remains were treated as vessels of miracle. The saint who had spent a lifetime resisting the importunities of the world became a dispenser of worldly favors." See Donald Weinstein and Rudolph Bell, *Saints and Society: The Two Worlds of Western Christendom, 1000–1700* (Chicago, 1982), 240. The Buddhist relic cult offers a suggestive avenue for comparison. As Kevin Trainor has observed, there is a "fundamental tension" in the veneration of relics of the Buddha and his enlightened followers. The "religious power" that these relics possess and the materiality of the cult are counterposed to the inherent values of Buddhist nonattachment and renunciation of the material world. See Kevin Trainor, *Relics, Ritual, and Representation in Buddhism: Rematerializing the Sri Lankan Theravāda Tradition* (Cambridge, England, 1997), 119–20; Robert H. Sharf, "The Idolization of Enlightenment: On the Mummification of Ch'an Masters in Medieval China," *History of Religions* 32 (1992): 1–31.

38. In the Catholic tradition, such relics are properly called "tertiary" or "third-class" relics. The Orthodox Church has no such classification system. The use and

popularity of "proxy relics" in imperial Russia is treated at greater length in Chapters Two and Three.

39. Laurie Kain Hart, *Time, Religion, and Social Experience in Rural Greece* (Lanham, 1992), 194.

40. M. M. Gromyko, *Mir russkoi derevni* (Moscow, 1991), 111–25. On the reciprocal relationship between believer and saint in rural northwest Portugal, see João de Pina-Cabral, *Sons of Adam, Daughters of Eve: The Peasant Worldview of the Alto Minho* (Oxford, 1986), 165–71.

41. I. A. Kremleva, "Obet v religioznoi zhiznoi russkogo naroda," in *Pravoslavie i russkaia narodnaia kul'tura*, 2 vols. (Moscow, 1993), 2:152.

42. Such phrases were commonly articulated in Orthodox sermons and in published conversations (*besedy*) with parishioners. See, for example, Archpriest Ioann Platonov, "Slovo v nedeliu Syropustnuiu i den' 200-letiia so vremeni blazhennoi konchiny Sviatitelia Feodosiia Uglitskago, Arkhiepiskopa Chernigovskago, 4 fevralia 1896 goda," *Chernigovskiia eparkhial'nyia izvestiia* (hereafter *ChEI*), no. 4 (15 February 1896): 122.

43. See Brown, *Cult of the Saints;* and "'Kosti, kotorye dorozhe dragotsennykh kamnei i blagorodnee zolota . . .': O pochitanii sviatykh moshchei v drevnei tserkvi," *Danilovskii blagovestnik*, no. 10 (1999): 19–23. The first Christians gathered at the graves of their martyred brothers and sisters to partake of the Eucharist; their example inspired the practice of requiring that all consecrated churches contain holy relics in the foundation. See "Ob obychae sovershat' liturgiiu na moshchakh sviatykh," *Danilovskii blagovestnik*, no. 10 (1999): 23–25.

44. On local saints in the early modern period, see Kalinskii, *Tserkovno-narodnyi mesiatseslov*, 9–14; and Richard Bosley, "The Changing Profile of the Liturgical Calendar in Muscovy's Formative Years," in *Culture and Identity in Muscovy, 1359–1584*, ed. A. M. Kleimola and G. D. Lenhoff (Moscow, 1997), 26–38.

45. See, for example, *O krestnykh khodakh sovershaemykh iz Moskovskago Uspenskago sobora* (Moscow, 1893); and Georgii Georgievskii, *Prazdnichnye sluzhby i tserkovnye torzhestva v staroi Moskve* (St. Petersburg, 1899), 233–55. On medieval and early modern Catholic religious processions as expressions of the sacred community, see Richard Trexler, "Florentine Religious Experience: The Sacred Image," *Studies in the Renaissance* 19 (1972): 7–41; and Natalie Zemon Davis, "The Sacred and the Body Social in Sixteenth-Century Lyon," *Past and Present*, no. 90 (1981): 40–70.

46. *Chernigovskaia pamiatka. Spravochnaia knizhka na 1898/9 god* (Chernigov, 1898), 339–40.

47. Moshe Sluhovsky, *Patroness of Paris: Rituals of Devotion in Early Modern France* (Leiden, 1998), 65.

48. William A. Christian, Jr., *Person and God in a Spanish Valley* (New York, 1972), 46. On the local dimension of Russian religiosity, see Gromyko, *Mir russkoi derevni*, 111–25.

49. *Ocherk istorii goroda Chernigova, 907–1907* (Chernigov, 1908), 64. Just three years later another local source put forward an even bolder claim, maintaining that Feodosii's canonization was the "most important event in the life of Chernigov diocese" since the beginning of the eighteenth century. See *Kartiny tserkovnoi zhizni Chernigovskoi eparkhii iz IX vekovoi eia istorii* (Kiev, 1911), 161. On the importance of the local dimension in Orthodox identity, see also Chris J. Chulos, "Orthodox Identity at Russian Holy Places," in *The Fall of the Empire, the Birth of a Nation: National Identities in Russia*, ed. Chris J. Chulos and Timo Piirainen (Aldershot, 2000), 28–50.

50. Geary, *Furta Sacra*, 7.

51. On the canonizations of new saints in the late imperial period, see Robert L. Nichols, "The Friends of God: Nicholas II and Alexandra at the Canonization of Serafim of Sarov, July 1903," in *Religious and Secular Forces in Late Tsarist Russia: Essays in Honor*

of *Donald W. Treadgold*, ed. Charles E. Timberlake (Seattle, 1992), 206–30; and Gregory L. Freeze, "Subversive Piety: Religion and the Political Crisis in Late Imperial Russia," *Journal of Modern History* 68 (1996): 308–50.

52. On the relationship between mass media, consumer culture, and religion in the modern age, see R. Laurence Moore, *Selling God: American Religion in the Marketplace of Culture* (Oxford, 1994), 204–37; Colleen McDannell, *Material Christianity: Religion and Popular Culture in America* (New Haven, 1995), 132–62; Helena Waddy, "St. Anthony's Bread: The Modernized Religious Culture of German Catholics in the Early Twentieth Century," *Journal of Social History* 31 (1997): 347–70; and Suzanne K. Kaufman, "Selling Lourdes: Pilgrimage, Tourism, and the Mass-Marketing of the Sacred in Nineteenth-Century France," in *Being Elsewhere: Tourism, Consumer Culture, and Identity in Modern Europe and North America*, ed. Shelley Baranowski and Ellen Furlough (Ann Arbor, 2001), 63–88.

53. Recent scholarship has moved away from the teleological implications of the secularization thesis and is now focused more on how religious practices and beliefs changed, developed, and persisted over the modern period. See, for example, Tamás Faragó, "Seasonality of Marriages in Hungary from the Eighteenth to the Twentieth Century," *Journal of Family History* 19 (1994): 333–50; Frans van Poppel, "Seasonality of Work, Religion and Popular Customs: The Seasonality of Marriage in the Nineteenth- and Twentieth-Century Netherlands," *Continuity and Change* 10 (1995): 215–56; Sarah Williams, "Urban Popular Religion and the Rites of Passage," in *European Religion in the Age of Great Cities, 1830–1930*, ed. Hugh McLeod (New York, 1995), 216–36; and Barrie M. Ratcliffe, "Workers and Religion in Mid-Nineteenth-Century Paris: The Evidence from the Timing of Weddings and Baptisms," *Historical Reflections/Réflexions Historique* 24 (1998): 283–327. For the Russian case, see Jeffrey Burds, *Peasant Dreams and Market Politics: Labor Migration and the Russian Village, 1861–1905* (Pittsburgh, 1998); Simon Dixon, "The Orthodox Church and the Workers of St. Petersburg, 1880–1914," in *European Religion in the Age of Great Cities, 1830–1930*, ed. Hugh McLeod (New York, 1995), 119–41; and Page Herrlinger, "Orthodoxy and the Experience of Factory Life in St. Petersburg, 1881–1905," in *New Labor History: Worker Identity and Experience in Russia, 1840–1918*, ed. Michael Melancon and Alice K. Pate (Bloomington, 2002), 35–63.

54. Paul Froese, *The Plot to Kill God: Findings from the Soviet Experiment in Secularization* (Berkeley and Los Angeles, 2008), chs. 3–4.

CHAPTER ONE: IN THE EYE OF THE BEHOLDER

1. N. S—n, "O netlenii sviatykh moshchei," *ChEI*, no. 19 (1 October 1896): 651.
2. *O netlenii sviatykh moshchei i chudesa ot nikh* (Moscow, 1902), 29.
3. Bishop Aleksandr of Vologda to M. K. Vetoshkin, chairman of the Vologda gubispolkom (letter dated 30 April 1919) in L. N. Miasnikova, "Dokumenty svidetel'stvuiut," in *Tot'ma: Kraevedcheskii al'manakh*, vyp. 2 (Vologda, 1997), 558.
4. Vetoshkin to Aleksandr, 6 May 1919, ibid., 561–62.
5. Aleksandr to Vetoshkin, 13 May 1919, ibid., 562–66.
6. Ibid. Modern Orthodox authorities echo the argument that moshchi need not be incorrupt. See Archimandrite Feodosii (Perevalov), *Tserkovnyi entsiklopedicheskii slovar'. Posobie pri izuchenie Zakona Bozhiia i Tserkovnoi Istorii* (Harbin, 1931), 140–41; Hieromonk Afanasii (Kudiuk), "O pochitanii sv. moshchei," *Zhurnal Moskovskoi Patriarkhii*, no. 8 (1956): 59–63; Archpriest Aleksii Mechev, "O moshchakh ugodnikov Bozhiikh," *Zhurnal Moskovskoi Patriarkhii*, no. 12 (1993): 68–71; V. M. Zhivov, *Sviatost': Kratkii slovar' agiograficheskikh terminov* (Moscow, 1994), 46–57; "Moshchi," in L. N. Mitrokhin, ed., *Khristianstvo: Slovar'* (Moscow, 1994), 292; N. I. Barsov, "Moshchi," in S.

S. Averintsev, ed., *Khristianstvo: Entsiklopedicheskii slovar'*, 2 vols. (Moscow, 1995), 2:183; and *Kanonizatsiia sviatykh v XX veke* (Moscow, 1999), 30.

7. Aleksandr to Vetoshkin, 13 May 1919, in Miasnikova, "Dokumenty svidetel'stvuiut," 562–66. Aleksandr's letter of 13 May 1919 was published in *Krasnyi sever*, no. 23 (28 May 1919), but it appeared in expurgated form, with all of the bishop's numerous references to patristic texts excised by the editorial board.

8. Vetoshkin to Aleksandr, 28 May 1919, in Miasnikova, "Dokumenty svidetel'stvuiut," 568–69.

9. "Moshchi," in *Bol'shaia sovetskaia entsiklopediia*, 1st ed. (Moscow, 1926–1947), 40:530.

10. Lenhoff, "Uncorrupted Relics," 256. Lenhoff argues that this position represented a fundamental and self-conscious break with Greek and Byzantine views of relics, which tended toward suspicion of any bodies that appeared resistant to corruption. A case for the Scandinavian origins of the Kievans' fascination with uncorrupted bodies is made in F. B. Uspenskii, "Netlennost' moshchei. Grecheskaia, russkaia i skandinavskaia traditsii," in *Relikvii v iskusstve i kul'ture vostochnokhristianskogo mira*, ed. A. M. Lidov (Moscow, 2000), 42–45.

11. Bushkovitch, *Religion and Society in Russia*, 92.

12. *Kafedral'nye Chernigovskie monastyri: Il'inskii, Eletskii i Borisoglebskii* (Kiev, 1860), 168.

13. On the rise of the diocesan press in the 1860s and the creation of parish schools in the 1880s, see Freeze, *Parish Clergy*, 233, 429–30. On the pedagogical tasks of the new religious press, see Archpriest Ioann Iakhontov, "Zadacha dukhovnago zhurnala," *Dukhovnaia beseda*, no. 22 (2 June 1862): 514–22.

14. The phrase in the subhead is taken from *O netlenii sviatykh moshchei i chudesa ot nikh*, 29.

15. For a sampling of patristic texts in support of the incorruptibility of holy relics, see "Kosti, kotorye dorozhe dragotsennykh kamnei," 19–23.

16. P. M. Vlastov, *O netlenii sviatykh moshchei. Kratkoe istoricheskoe izsledovanie* (Moscow, 1890), 5–6.

17. Archimandrite Antonii, *Dogmaticheskoe bogoslovie pravoslavnoi kafolicheskoi vostochnoi tserkvi, s prisovokupleniem obshchago vvedeniia v kurs bogoslovskikh nauk* (St. Petersburg, 1862), 252.

18. Archimandrite Misail (Smirnov), *Sviatyi blagovernyi kniaz' Konstantin, prosvitel' Muromskago kraia, i chada ego: Mikhail i Feodor* (Vladimir, 1896), 12.

19. Golubinskii, *Istoriia kanonizatsii sviatykh*, 297–308, 516–27.

20. See, for example, the "proper notion" of relics expounded in Archimandrite Evgenii [Mertsalov], *Kak sovershalas' kanonizatsiia sviatykh v pervoe vremia sushchestvovaniia russkoi tserkvi?* 2nd ed. (Murom, 1910), 10n1.

21. S. D. Bulgakov, *O pochitanii netlennykh moshchei sv. ugodnikov Bozhiikh: K predstoiashchemu torzhestvu proslavleniia Sviatitelia Iosafa, Episkopa Belgorodskago, v 4-i den' mesiatsa sentiabria 1911 goda* (Kursk, 1911), 24.

22. Miasnikova, "Dokumenty svidetel'stvuiut," 562–66. See also Archpriest Stefan Ostroumov, *Pis'ma o pravoslavnom blagochestii*, 2nd ed. (St. Petersburg, 1907), 361–70.

23. E. Poselianin, "O sviatosti, proslavlenii i netlenii sviatykh," *Volynskiia eparkhial'nyia vedomosti*, no. 23 (11 August 1903): 661.

24. Aleksandr Golosov, *Osnovy pravoslaviia (Kurs VIII-go kl. zhenskikh gimnazii Ministerstva narodnago prosveshcheniia)*, 5th ed. (Moscow, 1912), 88.

25. M. A. Kal'nev, *O pochitanii sv. moshchei i drugikh ostankov ugodnikov Bozhiikh* (Odessa, 1912), 4.

26. Priest A. N. Efimov, *Razmyshlenie o torzhestvennom otkrytii sviatykh moshchei Sviatitelia i Chudovortsa Chernigovskago Feodosiia Uglitskago* (Chernigov, 1897), 7.

27. Vlastov, *O netlenii sviatykh moshchei*, 50.

28. On the impossibility of assigning natural causes to explain incorruptibility, for example, see Bulgakov, *O pochitanii netlennykh moshchei*, 12–13; Vlastov, *O netlenii sviatykh moshchei*, 6, 15–28; Archpriest Evfimii Ostromyslenskii, "Perepiska syna dukhovnago s dukhovnym ottsem svoim o netlenii sv. moshchei," *Strannik*, t. 4, otd. 2, no. 11 (November 1861): 225–39; N. S—n, *O netlenii sviatykh moshchei* (Kiev, 1896), 1–8; A. I. Sokolov, *Kul't, kak neobkhodimaia prinadlezhnost' religii. Polemiko-apologeticheskoe bogoslovskoe izsledovanie* (Kazan, 1900), 329–30; Archpriest Petr Smirnov, *U moshchei Sviatitelia Feodosiia v Chernigove. Vpechatleniia i vospominaniia* (St. Petersburg, 1902), 9; V. M. Skvortsov, *O pochitanii moshchei sv. ugodnikov Bozhiikh* (St. Petersburg, 1910), 10–15; and Priest Olimp Diakonov, *O sv. moshchakh* (Saratov, 1914), 4. For an early refutation of the arguments made by opponents of incorruptibility, see Archbishop Feofan Prokopovich, *Razsuzhdenie o netlenii moshchei sviatykh ugodnikov Bozhiikh, v Kievskikh peshcherakh, netlenno pochivaiushchikh* (Moscow, 1786).

29. *O netlenii sviatykh moshchei i chudesa ot nikh*, 8–9; K. Ponomarev, *Netlenie sv. moshchei i znachenie ikh dlia khristianina* (Chernigov, 1915), 8.

30. *O netlenii sviatykh moshchei i chudesa ot nikh*, 20.

31. Priest G. Kliucharev, "V zashchitu pochitaniia netlennykh moshchei sv. ugodnikov Bozhiikh," *Pravoslavnyi putevoditel'*, no. 7 (July 1903): 27.

32. Priest Ioann Popov, *V Kashin i Poltavu, na vserossiiskiia torzhestva i "mimoezdy moi" (Nabliudeniia, vpechatleniia i zametki palomnika-turista)* (Vladikavkaz, 1909), 7.

33. Ponomarev, *Netlenie sv. moshchei*, 17. On the incorruptibility of the Kazan miracle-workers, see also A. N., *Moshchi sviatykh Sviatitelei i Chudotvortsev Kazanskikh Guriia i Varsonofiia* (Kazan, n.d.), 1–4. For a contrary view, see Nikolai Abramov, "O pochitanii sv. Ugodnikov i chestnykh moshchei," *Volynskiia eparkhial'nyia vedomosti*, no. 35 (11 December 1904): 1128–30. Although his left toe had been "subjected to decay," his shoulders and knees were "a little detached, though . . . not entirely separated," and the skin on his body had "darkened," Saint Tikhon Zadonskii was deemed uncorrupted when examined by a Synodal commission in 1861. See the commission's report in Chulos, *Converging Worlds*, 71.

34. *O netlenii sviatykh moshchei i chudesa ot nikh*, 29.

35. Rothkrug, "Odour of Sanctity," 95–142; Caseau, "Sacred Landscapes," 42–44. According to one source, uncorrupted bodies "often," but not always, gave off a fragrant odor. See Skvortsov, *O pochitanii moshchei*, 7.

36. Archpriest D. Troitskii, "Torzhestvo 19-go iiulia 1903 goda," in *Serafim Sarovskii: Al'bom*, ed. V. A. Iurchenkov (Saransk, 1998), 115–17; see also Archimandrite Nikanor, *Sv. German, vtoroi arkhiepiskop Kazanskii* (Kazan, 1890), 6–7.

37. "Chudesa po molitvam Blazhennago Episkopa Sofroniia," *IEV*, no. 16 (15 August 1914): 522.

38. Skvortsov, *O pochitanii moshchei*, 7.

39. D. D. Ivanchenko, *K sviatym mestam. Zapiski palomnika* (Saratov, 1911), 64; Skvortsov, *O pochitanii moshchei*, 7; Golubinskii, *Istoriia kanonizatsii sviatykh*, 36–37. Uncorrupted or not, the oil-dripping heads in the Kiev Monastery of the Caves were popular destinations for miracle-seekers. One woman wrote to the journal *Kormchii* in 1909 to ask the editors whether they could publish an article on the subject "for the benefit of my husband, who has doubts as to [their] sanctity." See "Otvety voproshaiushchim," *Kormchii*, no. 6 (1909): 71.

40. The phrase in the subhead is taken from Vlastov, *O netlenii sviatykh moshchei*, 62.

41. Efimov, *Razmyshlenie o torzhestvennom*, 3.

42. On the imperial Church's self-styled civilizing mission, see articles by Freeze, "Rechristianization of Russia" and "Institutionalizing Piety."

43. The image of saints as radiant lights, beacons, or candles shining to show the

faithful's path to heaven was a common trope in late imperial religious literature. See the introduction to Archpriest M. Khitrov, *Svetochi khristianstva* (St. Petersburg, 1898).

44. Bishop Vissarion, *O khristianskikh imenakh*, 2nd ed. (Moscow, 1890), 21.

45. Abramov, "O pochitanii sv. Ugodnikov," 1122. See also "O pochitanii Sv. ugodnikov (Na nedeliu Syroputnuiu, v den' pamiati sv. Feodosiia Uglitskago, 5 fevralia)," *Dukhovnaia beseda*, no. 2 (February 1912): 73–76.

46. Priest I. Kutepov, "Beseda o podrazhanii Sviatym," *Pastyrskii sobesednik*, no. 28–29 (13–20 July 1896): 469. See also *Zhizn' i podvigi sviatitelei Moskovskikh: Petra, Aleksiia, Iony, Filippa i Germogena* (Moscow, 1903), 12–13; S. I. B., "Pouchenie v nedeliu vsekh Sviatykh," *Kormchii*, no. 24 (1894): 340–41.

47. Bishop Evdokim, *Sviatye minuty: Primery blagochestiia i dobrodetelei izvlechennye iz zhitii sviatykh* (Sergiev Posad, 1909), 3–7.

48. "Dlia chego khristianam daiutsia imena sviatykh ugodnikov Bozhiikh? (Na nedeliu 1–iu Piatidesiatnitse)," *Dukhovnaia beseda*, no. 5 (May 1909): 165–66. See also "Po stopam ugodnikov Bozhiikh (Na nedeliu 1-iu po Piatidesiatnitse," ibid., no. 5 (May 1912): 280–83; Bishop Nikodim of Belgorod, "Kak mozhno podrazhat' Sviateliu Ioasafu?" ibid., no. 9 (September 1915); and "O podrazhanii sv. ugodnikam Bozhiim," ibid., no. 11 (November 1915): 712–14.

49. Brooks, *When Russia Learned to Read*, 22–27. See also Simonov, "Chto chitaiut nashi sovremennye krest'iane?" 231–35.

50. "O prigodnosti chteniia na utreni dlia prikhozhan zhitii sviatykh," *Kavkazkiia eparkhial'nyia vedomosti*, no. 22 (16 November 1880): 715.

51. "Knigi poleznyia dlia chteniia narodu," *Kormchii*, no. 4 (1888): 10–11. See also Priest D. Favorskii, "Chto chitat' narodu?" published as a special pamphlet supplement to *Kormchii*, no. 48 (1895).

52. "O vypiske v tserkovnyia biblioteki zhitii sv. ottsov," *Donskiia eparkhial'nyia vedomosti*, no. 21 (1 November 1884): 791–92. The author of the proposal, an ecclesiastical superintendent for Kagal'nitskii district, claimed that there was a huge demand among the *narod* for stories and lives of the saints: "[I]t is remarked by many priests that if their *besedy* with parishioners do not open up with some tales from the lives of the holy fathers, the parishioners' attention quickly fades, they begin to get bored, and they slink away from the meeting in an inconspicuous manner." Ibid., 791.

53. See, for example, Priest P. Shumov, "Kak khristianinu otnosit'sia k molve liudskoi?" *Kormchii*, no. 26 (1895): 342–44; "O prichashchenii Sviatykh Tain," *Kormchii*, no. 41 (1895): 527–28; and Priest A. Grammatin, "Dogmaticheskie i nravstvennye uroki, zaimstvovannye iz zhitii sviatykh," *Tobol'skiia eparkhial'nyia vedomosti*, no. 19–20 (1–16 October 1892): 417–22.

54. Priest Ioann Iakimov, *Besedy iz zhizni sviatykh. Posobie pri vedenie pastyrskikh vnebogosluzhebnykh sobesedovanii s sel'skimi prikhozhanami* (Moscow, 1895), 252–56. See also Priest V. Krylov, "Uroki blagochestiia iz zhitii sviatykh (Besedy sviashchennika s prikhozhanami)," *Kormchii*, no. 38 (1889): 456–58; and Archpriest V. G. Bazhanov, *Primery blagochestiia iz zhitii sviatykh*, 11th ed. (St. Petersburg, 1914).

55. V. Ermilov, *Ugodnik Bozhii Sviatitel' Tikhon Zadonskii*, 2nd ed. (Moscow, 1899), 7; Iakimov, *Besedy iz zhizni sviatykh*, 229–32.

56. Iakimov, *Besedy iz zhizni sviatykh*, 349.

57. Voronets, *Ob angelakh-khraniteliakh*, 15.

58. "Ot chego chasto ne ispolniaiutsia molitvy nashi?" *Tverskiia eparkhial'nyia vedomosti* (hereafter *TEV*), no. 18 (15 September 1880): 332.

59. Gerd Theissen classifies this genre of miracle story as a "rule miracle," which "seek[s] to reinforce sacred prescriptions either through punishment or exhortation." See Gerd Theissen, *The Miracle Stories of the Early Christian Tradition*, trans. Francis McDonagh (Edinburgh, 1983), 106, also 107–12.

60. See, for example, Platonov, "Slovo v nedeliu Syropustnuiu," 119–23; *Sviatiteli-podvizhniki novago vremeni, proslavlennye v XVIII–XIX stoletiiakh* (Moscow, 1903), 10–11; and Leonid I. Denisov, *Chudesa Bozhii. Sovremennyia nam znameniia milosti Bozhiei, iavlennyia za posledniia gody chrez sv. moshchei i ikony*, 2nd ed. (Moscow, 1904), 80–89.

61. N. N. Esipov, *Sviatitel' i Chudotvorets arkhiepiskop Chernigovskii Feodosii Uglitskii* (St. Petersburg, 1897), 105. Victims of demonic possession in imperial Russia were predominantly female. While Saint Feodosii was quite active in healing possessed women, this appears to be the rare case in which the saint frees a man from demons. See Christine D. Worobec, *Possessed: Women, Witches, and Demons in Imperial Russia* (DeKalb, 2001), 53–54, 207–9.

62. *Sviatiteli-podvizhniki novago vremeni*, 12.

63. Platonov, "Slovo v nedeliu Syropustnuiu," 122.

64. Pavel Ostrov, *O pochitanii sviatykh moshchei* (Moscow, 1847), 36.

65. "Neuvazhenie k sviatyne," *Dukhovnaia beseda*, no. 3 (March 1914): 252–54.

66. "Nakazanie raskol'nika Sviat. Dimitriem Rostovskim," *Kormchii*, no. 37 (1891): 438–39.

67. Bulgakov, *O pochitanii netlennykh moshchei*, 70–71. Though he had lain in state for more than two months, Ioasaf's (or, alternately, Iosaf's) body was said to be untouched by corruption when he was buried in February 1755. See V. A. Borisov, *Sviatitel' Iosaf Gorlenko, episkop Belgorodskii i Oboianskii: Ego zhizn' i deiatel'nost'* (Sergiev Posad, 1911), 180.

68. "Ne dolzhno somnevat'sia v sviatosti ugodnikov Bozhiikh i netlenii ikh sviatykh moshchei (k sentiabria—godovomu dniu otkrytiia moshchei sv. Ioasafa Belgorodskago)," *Dukhovnaia beseda*, no. 9 (September 1912): 495–96. See also Archpriest Aristarkh Izrailev, *Netlennyia moshchi sviatykh blagovernykh kniazei Feodora i chad ego Davida i Konstantina, v Iaroslavskom Spaso-Preobrazhenskom monastyre, nyne Arkhiereiskom dome*, 2nd ed. (Moscow, 1899), 15; L. Ia. Lavrovskii, *Sv. Blagovernyi Rostislavich Smolenskii i Iaroslavskii* (Smolensk, 1899), 30–34; Bulgakov, *O pochitanii netlennykh moshchei*, 53–72; Archpriest Evfimii Ostromyslenskii, "Perepiska syna dukhovnago s dukhovnym ottsem svoim o netlenii sv. moshchei," *Strannik*, t. 3, otd. 2, no. 8 (August 1861): 70–84; "Nakazannoe somnenie v istinnosti moshchei pecherskikh ugodnikov," *Strannik*, t. 2, otd. 1, no. 4 (April 1863): 67; I. F., "Utverzhdenie very v netlenii sv. moshchei," *Kavkazkiia eparkhial'nyia vedomosti*, no. 4 (16 February 1879): 166–73; "Nakazanie Bozhie za nepochitanie sv. pravednikov," *Kormchii*, no. 1 (1889): 10; and Iv. Babanin, "U groba Sviatitelia Mitrofana (razskaz)," *Kormchii*, no. 47 (1892): 573–74.

69. *Kak ia ubedilsia v netlenii sviatykh moshchei* (Moscow, 1913), a single-page broadsheet in the collections of the Russian National Library, St. Petersburg, originally published in *Voskresnyi den'*. Metropolitan Saint Filipp's massive silver shrine was stolen by the French armies when they fled Moscow after the campaign of 1812 but later recovered by Kutuzov. When Metropolitan Avgustin and his clerics returned to the cathedral after the French retreat, they found Filipp no longer lying on the floor but resting peacefully atop the altar, his body still uncorrupted (despite its rough treatment) as if by some great miracle. See *O sviatykh Ugodnikakh Bozhiikh, koikh netlennyia moshchi pochivaiut v Uspenskom sobore* (Moscow, 1893), 14–15. The relics of Patriarch Germogen were said to have suffered a similar affront at the hands of the French, while a heaven-sent flame kept marauders from the shrine of Metropolitan Saint Iona. See D. S. Dmitriev, *Patriarkh Germogen (ocherk)* (Moscow, 1906), 22; Priest V. Sokolov, *Sviateishii Patriarkh Germogen* (Moscow, 1912), 24; and Archimandrite Iosif, *O sviatykh ugodnikakh Bozhiikh, Moskovskikh chudotvortsakh* (Moscow, 1877), 10–11. On the condition of the holy relics in the Moscow Kremlin following the French retreat, see RGIA, f. 797, op. 2, g. 1812, d. 5295, ll. 1–16.

70. *Kak ia ubedilsia v netlenii sviatykh moshchei*.

71. Brown, *Cult of the Saints*, 119. See also the discussion in Paul Antony Hayward, "Demystifying the Role of Sanctity in Western Christendom," in *The Cult of Saints in Late Antiquity and the Middle Ages: Essays on the Contribution of Peter Brown*, ed. James Howard-Johnston and Paul Antony Hayward (Oxford, 1999), 115–42.

72. V. P., "Nakazanie za neverie (iz vospominanii starika)," *Kormchi*, no. 11 (1888): 6–7.

73. "Sbornik tem i planov pouchenii," *Dukhovnaia beseda*, no. 5 (May 1911): 327–28.

74. On relics as a prefiguring of the bodily resurrection in the post-Nicene Church, see Caroline Walker Bynum, *The Resurrection of the Body in Western Christendom, 200–1336* (New York, 1995), 59–114.

75. Bulgakov, *O pochitanii netlennykh moshchei*, 26. For an exposition of this argument dating to the first third of the nineteenth century, see Dmitrii Sosnin, *O netlenii sviatykh moshchei v Tserkvi Khristianskoi* (St. Petersburg, 1832), 45–53.

76. Priest A. Efimov, "Razmyshlenie o predstoiashchem torzhestvennom otkrytii sviatykh moshchei Sviatitelia i Chudotvortsa Chernigovskago Feodosiia Uglitskago," *ChEI*, no. 17 (1 September 1896): 538.

77. This point was further emphasized by the inclusion of James 5:11 ("Behold, we count them happy which endure") on the list of recommended passages from *Dukhovnaia beseda*. Lutherans and most Protestant denominations rejected the epistle of James as noncanonical, a fact that the journal's editors knew full well. The pointed inclusion of James on the recommended list served again to highlight that there were special truths and promises in Holy Scripture available to the Orthodox faithful but not to errant sectarians.

78. Archpriest Petr Smirnov, *Chudesa v prezhnee i nashe vremia*, 2nd ed. (Moscow, 1895), 27–28.

79. "S kakoiu tseliiu khranit Gospod' moshchi pravednykh," *Kormchi*, no. 40 (1896): 528–29.

80. Archimandrite Zosima, "Pouchenie v prazdnik Sviatitelia Innokentiia, pervago Irkutskago episkopa (26 noiabria)," *IEV*, no. 3 (1 February 1913): 69.

81. "S kakoiu tseliiu khranit Gospod,'" 528–29.

82. Brown, *Cult of the Saints*, 92.

83. "Znachenie otkrytiia sv. moshchei Sviatitelia Feodosiia Uglitskago," *Voskresnoe chtenie*, no. 45 (3 November 1896): 717–19. See also Nikolai Slavin, *O netlenii sviatykh moshchei* (Chernigov, 1896); Priest A. V—skii, "Sviatitel' Feodosii Uglitskii (po povodu 200-letiia so dnia blazhennoi konchiny Sviatitelia Feodosiia)," *ChEI*, no. 3 (1 February 1896): 85–91; N. Feodos'ev, "Torzhestvo dukhovnoi zhizni," *ChEI*, no. 18 (15 September 1896): 622–32; A. Kh., "Iavleniia blagodati Gospodnei v Chernigove," *Rukovodstvo dlia sel'skikh pastyrei*, t. 3, no. 45 (10 November 1896): 251–55; and *Pamiati novoproslavlennago sviatitelia Feodosiia Uglitskago, arkhiepiskopa Chernigovskago* (Tobol'sk, 1899), 15–16.

84. *Zhitie i otkrytie netlennykh moshchei Sviatitelia Feodosiia Uglitskago, arkhiepiskopa Chernigovskago* (Moscow, 1896), 28.

85. "Zachem sviatye (ko dniu proslavleniia sv. Pitirima, episkopa Tambovskago)," *Dukhovnaia beseda*, no. 7 (July 1914): 542–43. See also "Sviatitel' Pitirim Tambovskii (v pomoshch' pastyriam propovednikam k predstoiashchemu proslavleniiu sviatitelia)," in ibid., 493–503.

86. An enormous volume of literature was produced to accompany each of the twelve saints canonized under Nicholas II. Of particular interest for their highly politicized content are the pamphlets and monographs marking the glorification of Patriarch Saint Germogen in 1913, which emphasized his special role as protector of the Russian Fatherland and a model of patriotism and steadfast duty. See, for example, *Programma*

torzhestvennago sobraniia v pamiat' Sviateishago Germogena, Patriarkha Vserossiiskago, 19 fevralia 1912 goda (Moscow, 1912); K. K. Nazarevskii, *Novoproslavlennyi sviatitel' Sviateishii Ermogen, Patriarkh vseia Rossii* (Moscow, 1912); Pavel' Rossiev, *Velikii pechal'nik za rodinu, Patriarkh Germogen: Istoricheskii ocherk* (Moscow, 1912); Boris Shervud, *Skazanie v stikakh o Patriarkhe Germogene* (Moscow, 1912); and, notably, Priest V. Shchukin's prayerful hope that "new Germogens" may emerge to deliver Holy Rus' from its present misfortunes, in his *Patriarkh Germogen kak predstavitel' i pobornik natsional'noi religioznosti (1612–1912 g.)* (Riga, 1913), 17.

87. I. Klimiuk, "Chemu nauchaiut nas moshchi sv. ugodnikov," *IEV*, no. 9 (1 May 1913): 254.

88. I. Klimiuk, "Slovo o pochitanii sviatykh," *IEV*, no. 9 (1 May 1913): 292 (emphasis in original). In the Russian Bible, the relevant passage is Psalms 33:21.

89. "Uroki ot netleniia ugodnikov Bozhiikh," *Dukhovnaia beseda*, no. 9 (September 1909): 278.

90. To cite but a few notable examples: "O pochitanii sviatykh pokloneniem. Otvet preosviashch. Guriia, episkopa Tavricheskago, na vozrazheniia molokanina Z. D. Zakharova," *Kievskiia eparkhial'nyia vedomosti*, no. 18 (16 September 1873): 506–20; Priest P. A. K—v, "Zhizn' vselenskikh uchitelei i sviatitelei: Vasiliia Velikago, Grigoriia Bogoslova i Ioanna Zlatousta, kak primer bor'by s sovremennym napravleniem v delakh khristianskoi very i nravstvennosti," *Donskiia eparkahial'nyia vedomosti*, no. 21 (1 November 1884): 804–8, no. 22 (15 November 1884): 839–53, and no. 24 (15 December 1884): 938–51; Priest Savva Bogdanovich, *Beseda so shtundistom o tom, chto dolzhno pochitat' sviatykh i molit'sia im*, 4th ed. (Kiev, 1907); Skvortsov, *O pochitanii moshchei*, 10–15; Golosov, *Osnovy pravoslaviia*, 26–27, 84–88; Priest I. Kozlov, *V pomoshch' missioneru, pastyriu i revniteliu pravoslaviia. Posobie po noveishei polemike s raskolom, izlozhennoe po predmetam v alfavitnom poriadke* (Petrograd, 1915), 252–53; and *O pochitanii moshchei sv. ugodnikov Bozhiikh* (St. Petersburg, 1912). This last was a small, pocket-sized pamphlet packed with scriptural passages in support of the veneration of the saints that was distributed free of charge to would-be missionaries seeking to win over the souls of sectarians.

91. For an overview of nineteenth-century fears of sectarian incursion and the Church's unsuccessful efforts to respond to this challenge, see A. Iu. Polunov, "The State and Religious Heterodoxy in Russia (from 1880 to the beginning of the 1890s)," *Russian Studies in History* 39 (2001): 54–65. On the particular threat posed by Baptists to the Orthodox order, see Heather J. Coleman, *Russian Baptists and Spiritual Revolution, 1905–1929* (Bloomington, 2005), chs. 4–6.

92. "O pochitanii Bozhiei Materi, angelov i sv. ugodnikov," *Pravoslavno-missionerskii listok*, published as a special supplement to *Kormchii*, no. 15 (1909), unpaginated. See also Kliucharev, "V zashchitu pochitaniia netlennykh moshchei," 9–27.

93. Priest F. I. Titov, *Pouchitel'noe chtenie o znachenii torzhestvennago otkrytiia chestnykh moshchei sviatitelia Feodosiia, Chernigovskago chudotvortsa* (Kiev, 1896), 5–6.

94. Sosnin, *O netlenii sviatykh moshchei*, 55.

95. Chernigov Province in 1915 was home to nearly 79,000 Old Believers, over 100,000 Jews, 6,000 Catholics, and 4,500 Lutherans and other Protestants. A complete confessional breakdown for the province is provided in I. E. Petrovskii, *Chernigovskaia guberniia v etnograficheskom, administrativnom, ekonomicheskom, promyshlennom, uchebnom i drugikh otnosheniiakh. 1915 god* (Chernigov, 1915). The large number of Old Believers in the Urals region may also account for the successes of Saint Simeon Verkhoturskii's uncorrupted relics in bringing the occasional schismatic back to the Orthodox Church. One notable case, in which Saint Simeon healed a lame Old Believer woman who subsequently converted, was widely reprinted in the devotional pamphlets distributed free of charge to pilgrims visiting his shrine. See Priest Ioann Antoninov, *Palomnichestvo iz*

Ekaterinburga v Verkhotur'e, 6–24 maia 1914 g. (Ekaterinburg, 1914), 77–89.

96. On Feodosii's posthumous conversion efforts among Old Believers, see *Blazhennyi Sviatitel' Feodosii Uglitskii, Arkhiepiskop Chernigovskii, i chudesa ot moshchei ego* (St. Petersburg, 1896), 15; Priest A. N. Efimov, *Novoiavlennyi ugodnik Bozhii, Sviatitel' i Chudotvorets Vserossiiskii Feodosii Uglitskii, arkhiepiskop Chernigovskii* (Chernigov, 1902), 49; *Sviatitel' Feodosii, Chudotvorets Chernigovskii* (Chernigov, n.d.), 41. On the conversion of Jews by Feodosii, see "Chudesnyia istseleniia po molitvam k Sviatiteliu Feodosiiu Uglitskomu," in *ChEI*, no. 19 (1 October 1896): 648–49; and of Baptists, "Akt ob istselenii meshchanina g. Voznesenska Vladimira Fedorova u moshchei Sviatitelia Feodosiia," in *ChEI*, no. 14 (15 July 1897): 517–21.

97. "Publichnoe raskaianie sogliadataev raskola i ispovedanie imi very v netlenie, sviatost' i chudotvorenie Ugodnika Bozhiia Sviatitelia Feodosiia Uglitskago," *ChEI*, no. 21 (1 November 1896): 729.

98. Abramov, "O pochitanii sv. Ugodnikov," 1127. See also Biriukov, *Katikhizicheskiia besedy*, 58–59. The great popularizer Father John of Kronstadt explained the union between believer and saint in simpler, more intimate terms: "We live together with them in the same house of the Heavenly Father, only on different floors; we on the ground floor, they in heaven." See "Iz dnevnika ottsa Ioanna Kronshtadtskago: Ezhednevnoe prizyvanie Sviatykh," *Kormchii*, no. 35 (1893): 522.

99. Klimiuk, "Slovo o pochitanii sviatykh," 292.

100. Ostroumov, *Pis'ma o pravoslavnom blagochestii*, 313.

101. Priest Ioann Veriuzhskii, *Istoricheskiia skazaniia o zhizni sviatykh podvizavshikhsia v Vologodskoi eparkhii proslavliaemykh vseiu Tserkoviiu i mestno chtimykh* (Vologda, 1880), 5. See also Priest A. Linchevskii, "Moshchi sviatykh—opora very i dobrodetelei khristianskikh (k 9-mu maia)," *Dukhovnaia beseda*, no. 5 (May 1909): 146–48.

CHAPTER TWO: GOING TO SEE THE SAINTS

1. *Palomnichestvo. Putevyia vpechatleniia* (Tula, 1902), 16.
2. *O netlenii sviatykh moshchei i chudesa ot nikh*, 33.
3. Archpriest K. I. Fomenko, *O russkom palomnichestve k mirotochivym moshcham Sviatitelia Nikolaia* (Kiev, 1901), 1–3.
4. Ibid., 3 (emphasis in original).
5. Ibid. For an earlier account of a Russian pilgrim's journey from Siberia to Bari, see *Puteshestvie Irkutianina v Bargrad dlia pokloneniia moshcham Sviatitelia Nikolaia Chudotvortsa* (St. Petersburg, 1861).
6. M. M. Gromyko and A. V. Buganov, *O vozzreniiakh russkogo naroda* (Moscow, 2000), 152–55; Gromyko, *Mir russkoi derevni*, 116–20; Priest N. I. Smirnov, *O prikhodskikh palomnichestvakh ko sviatyniam* (Moscow, 1911), 4, 22–23.
7. The concept of reciprocity, or exchange, is explored in Laura Stark, *Peasants, Pilgrims, and Sacred Promises: Ritual and the Supernatural in Orthodox Karelian Folk Religion* (Helsinki, 2002), 157–71. On similar relationships between believers and saints in late antiquity and the medieval West, see Brown, *Cult of the Saints*; Wilson, "Introduction," to his *Saints and Their Cults*, 22–26; and Virginia Reinburg, "Praying to Saints in the Late Middle Ages," in *Saints: Studies in Hagiography*, ed. Sandro Sticca (Binghamton, 1996), 269–82.
8. On the importance of saintly shrines as "located images," see Christian, *Person and God*, ch. 2; and Sabine MacCormack, "Loca Sancta: The Organization of Sacred Topography in Late Antiquity," in *The Blessings of Pilgrimage*, ed. Robert Ousterhout (Urbana, 1990), 7–40.
9. On the methodology of reading miracle stories, see Candace Slater, *City Steeple,*

City Streets: Saints' Tales from Granada and a Changing Spain (Berkeley and Los Angeles, 1990).

10. Notable examples of late imperial religious travel literature include A. Iarygin, *Putevoditel' po gorodu Chernigovu* (Chernigov, 1900); and A. Mel'nikov, *Putevoditel' dlia palomnikov v Serafimo-Sarovskuiu pustyn'* (Nizhnii Novgorod, 1903). For an insightful reading of travel literature pertaining to Solovki, see Roy R. Robson, "Transforming Solovki: Pilgrim Narratives, Modernization, and Late Imperial Monastic Life," in Steinberg and Coleman, *Sacred Stories*, 44–60.

11. Vasilii Orlov, *Rukovoditel' Vladimirskikh bogomol'tsev* (Vladimir, 1880), 70–88.

12. Priest K. Iaroslavskii, "Spisok ugodnikov Bozhiikh i drugikh lits podvizavshikhsia v predelakh Iaroslavskoi eparkhii i upominaemykh v raznykh pechatnykh i rukopisnykh sviattsakh i istoricheskikh ukazateliakh," *Iaroslavskiia eparkhial'nyia vedomosti*, no. 20 (18 May 1887): 318–20; no. 22 (1 June 1887): 357–60; no. 23 (8 June 1887): 361–65.

13. *Materialy dlia istorii Tverskoi eparkhii* (Tver, 1898), vi.

14. M. A. Dobrogaev, *Russkomu palomniku na pamiat' o poseshchenie Chernigova, po sluchaiu otkrytiia chestnykh moshchei Ugodnika Bozhiia Sviatitelia Feodosiia, 1896 goda 9-sentiabria* (Chernigov, 1896), 11.

15. A. N. Kurtsev, "Kul'tovye migratsii naseleniia Tsentral'nogo Chernozem'ia v 1861–1917 gg.," in *Iz istorii monastyrei i khramov Kurskogo kraia* (Kursk, 1998), 92–96.

16. I. P. Taradin, *"Sviatoi" Mitrofan, episkop Voronezhskii* (Voronezh, 1926), 18–19.

17. I. P. Bogatov, *Vladimirskie sviatye i ikh chudesa* (Vladimir, 1929), 15–16. For statistics on the prerevolutionary holdings of all 1,257 monasteries in the Russian empire, organized by province, see V. F. Zybkovets, *Natsionalizatsiia monastyrskikh imushchestv v sovetskoi Rossii, 1917–1921 gg.* (Moscow, 1975), 113–96.

18. G. M. Veselovskii, *Voronezh v istoricheskom i sovremenno-statisticheskom otnosheniiakh s podrobnym planom goroda i ego okrestnostei* (Voronezh, 1866), 103.

19. Orlov, *Rukovoditel' Vladimirskikh bogomol'tsev*, 113–15.

20. See, for example, the photograph of the shrine of the Venerable Gerasim and tales of the saint's miracle-working powers in Deacon Sergii Nepein, "Sviatyni drevnosti v g. Vologde," *Russkii palomnik*, no. 49 (3 December 1894): 775–77. On Gerasim, see also Vladimir Mordvinov, *Zhitiia sviatykh ugodnikov Bozhiikh v predelakh Vologodskoi eparkhii, proslavlennykh Tserkov'iu i mestno chtimykh* (Moscow, 1879), 23–25. Photographs of Feodosii Chernigovskii in his coffin were published in national religious publications in 1896, for the benefit of those unable to attend the canonization in Chernigov. See *Kormchii*, no. 41 (1896): 537, and no. 48 (1896): 633.

21. See, for example, the tale of the miraculous healing of a daughter of a captain of the guard in *Stradalitsa, istselennaia moliltvami ugodnika Bozhiia, sv. Mitrofana Voronezhskago* (St. Petersburg, 1874); and the tale of a sick woman healed of rheumatism in Archpriest Nikolai Varushkin, *Istselenie bol'noi pri rake moshchei Sviatago Feodosiia Chernigovskago* (Kazan, 1901).

22. The figures are for 1913. See the advertisement on the back cover of Hieromonk Iraklii, *S bogomol'ia ot "Troitsy-Sergiia"* (Sergiev Posad, 1916). On the publication of the leaflets, see Kenworthy, "The Revival of Monasticism," ch. 6.

23. Roy R. Robson, *Solovki: The Story of Russia Told through Its Most Remarkable Islands* (New Haven, 2004), 170–85; Debra Coulter, "Ukrainian Pilgrimage to the Holy Land, 988–1914," *Ukrainian Review* 43 (1996): 62–77.

24. Kurtsev, "Palomnichestvo v Tsentral'nom Chernozem'e," 144–45.

25. Chulos, "Orthodox Identity," 33; Kurtsev, "Kul'tovye migratsii," 92–96.

26. *ChEI*, no. 10 (15 May 1895).

27. *Chernigovskaia pamiatka. Karmannaia spravochnaia knizhka na 1896/7 god* (Chernigov, 1896). The adjective *karmannaia* was dropped from subsequent annual edi-

tions of the city directory, probably because the dimensions of the thousand-page book made it difficult to fit into all but the largest pockets.

28. Ronald C. Finucane, *Miracles and Pilgrims: Popular Beliefs in Medieval England* (London, 1977), 83.

29. D. N. Bantysh-Kamenskii, *Rossianin pri grobe Patriarkha Germogena*, 2nd ed. (Moscow, 1806), 3–4, 21. See also A. I. Eshenbakh, *Velikii pechal'nik zemli Russkoi, Sviateishii Patriarkh Germogen* (Moscow, 1913); *Sviashchennomuchenik Ermogen, Patriarkh Moskovskii i vseia Rossii Chudotvorets* (Moscow, 1913); N. M. Dement'eva, *Patriarkh Germogen. Razskaz iz istorii Russkoi tserkvi* (Moscow, 1914).

30. The earliest testimony I have found for a miracle performed at the shrine of Patriarch Germogen dates to 1903 and concerns the healing of a young Moscow townswoman named M. S. Pavlova. See *Sviateishii Patriarkh Germogen i chudesa ot ego moshchei. 17 fevralia 1612–1912 g.* (Moscow, 1911), v.

31. *Narodnaia vera v sviatost' Patriarkha Ermogena i plody etoi very—chudesa sovershaiushchiiasia po Ego molitvam* (Moscow, n.d.), 12. A copy of the pamphlet may be found among Patriarch Tikhon's papers in Gosudarstvennyi Arkhiv Rossiiskoi Federatsii (hereafter GARF), f. R-4652, op. 1, d. 1, ll. 41–61ob. (here, l. 44).

32. GARF, f. R-4652, op. 1, d. 1, l. 50ob. (emphasis mine).

33. V. Sokolov, *Sviateishii Patriarkh Germogen*, 27–28.

34. Nazarevskii, *Novoproslavlennyi sviatitel' Ermogen*, n.p. On word of mouth as a means for spreading news of the miracles performed at the shrine of Feodosii Chernigovskii, see *Blazhennyi Sviatitel' Feodosii Uglitskii*, 11; and L. I. Denisov, *Novoiavlennyi ugodnik Bozhii, Sv. Feodosii Uglitskii, arkhiepiskop i chudotvorets Chernigovskii* (Moscow, 1897), 14–19.

35. Kizenko, *Prodigal Saint*, 151–96.

36. S. S. Kharlamova, "Tserkovnye periodicheskie izdaniia kak istochnik izueheniia etnograficheskikh aspektov pravoslaviia," in *Biblioteka i istoriia. Sbornik nauchnykh trudov*, vyp. 2 (Moscow, 1994), 109–20; Louise McReynolds, *The News under Russia's Old Regime: The Development of a Mass-Circulation Press* (Princeton, 1991).

37. "Chudesnyia istseleniia," *Iaroslavskiia eparkhial'nyia vedomosti*, no. 6 (5 February 1861): 55–56.

38. "Chudesnyia istseleniia pri moshchakh Sviatitelia Feodosiia, Arkhiepiskopa Chernigovskago, Chudotvortsa," ChEI, no. 23 (1 December 1896): 803–7.

39. "Novyia proiavleniia milosti Bozhiei po molitvam k sviateliu Feodosiiu Uglitskomu," ChEI, no. 4 (15 February 1892): 135–37.

40. GARF, f. R-4652, op. 1, d. 1, l. 46.

41. "Kak Sviatye slyshat nashi molitvy?" *Kormchii*, no. 29 (1891): 342.

42. In principle, the Synod exercised complete control over the movement of relics. In the event that a cathedral or monastery church was to be remodeled, bishops were required to obtain permission from the Synod before they could relocate any holy relics within to a temporary resting place. See, for example, the correspondence in RGIA, f. 796, op. 180, otd. 3, st. 2, d. 3021, and ibid., op. 181, d. 2510.

43. See the description of the silver coffin containing a mica-studded cypress chest that housed the relic fragments of twenty-seven saints in Priest V. Romanov, *Kratkiia skazaniia o zhitii sviatykh ugodnikov Bozhiikh, koikh chastitsy moshchei pochivaiut v khrame Sviatyia Troitsy, s. Isache, Lubenskago uezda* (Poltava, 1901), 15. Soviet commissars confiscated many of these precious reliquaries in the 1920s but left behind vivid descriptions of their shape and appearance. See, for example, the accounts in GARF, f. A-353, op. 4, d. 378, ll. 18–19 (description of a chest in the Sofiiskii Cathedral, Novgorod, containing fragments of the infant martyrs of Bethlehem slaughtered by King Herod); and GARF, f. A-353, op. 5, d. 262, ll. 18–20 (description of a cross in the Sviato-Troitskii monastery, Iakhnobol'skaia canton, Kostroma Province, containing fragments of the bodies and bits

of cloth from Feodosii Totemskii and half a dozen other saints).

44. An excellent analysis of how medieval pilgrims experienced and interacted with saintly shrines is found in Ben Nilson, *Cathedral Shrines of Medieval England* (Woodbridge, 2001), ch. 4. On the architectural trends surrounding the placement of shrines and the aesthetics of relic display in the medieval West, see John Crook, *The Architectural Setting of the Cult of the Saints in the Early Christian West, c. 300–1200* (Oxford, 2000), 40–209; and Henk van Os, *The Way to Heaven: Relic Veneration in the Middle Ages* (Baarn, 2001).

45. D. D. Ivanchenko, *Zapiski pri poezdke v Sarovskuiu pustyn'* (Saratov, 1908), 2.

46. Archpriest Feodor Vasiutinskii, *Chernigov, ego sviatye khramy, chudotvornyia ikony i mestnochtimyia sviatyni* (Chernigov, 1911), 49–50.

47. *Palomnichestvo*, 16; *Sviatyni Chernigova* (St. Petersburg, 1900), 12–13.

48. V. M. Skvortsov, *Chudesa ot netlennykh moshchei novoiavlennago Ugodnika Bozhiia, Sviatitelia Feodosiia (Uglitskago)* (Kiev, 1896), 4. See also M. D. Pletnev, *U moshchei sviatitelia Iosafa. Vpechatleniia palomnika* (Moscow, 1911), 21–23.

49. Priest A. G. Troitskii, *Palomnichestvo ko Sv. Muromskim Chudotvortsam* (Nizhnii Novgorod, 1917), 15–16.

50. A. Kovalevskii, *Vospominanie ochevidtsa torzhestva otkrytiia sviatykh i mnogotselebnykh moshchei Sviatitelia Feodosiia Uglitskago, Arkhiepiskopa Chernigovskago, Chudotvortsa*, 4th ed. (Moscow, 1908), 11–12.

51. Ivanchenko, *Zapiski pri poezdke*, 42.

52. Scriptural justification for the belief that proxy relics retain the power of the saint comes from the Old and New Testaments. In 2 Kings 2:13–14, the mantle of Elijah, wielded by his disciple Elisha, is made to part the waters of the River Jordan. In Acts 19:11–12, "cloths and aprons that touched [Paul's] skin" are used to heal the sick of Ephesus. See the discussion of proxy relics in the Orthodox tradition in Meinardus, "Study of the Relics of Saints," 131–32. Medieval Iceland presents an interesting case for comparison. Because saints were relatively scarce on the island, believers placed great stock in portable proxy relics. See Margaret Cormack, *The Saints in Iceland: Their Veneration from the Conversion to 1400* (Brussels, 1994), 61–65.

53. GARF, f. R-4652, op. 1, d. 1l. 44ob.–45. See also the account of a young Siberian girl's recovery from diphtheria and scarlet fever in 1899 through clothing placed atop the shrine of Sofronii Irkutskii, in GARF, f. R-3431, op. 1, d. 300, l. 413.

54. RGIA, f. 796, op. 445, d. 346, ll. 294ob., 297–297ob.

55. Archpriest Mikhail Arkhangel'skii, *O taine sv. eleia* (St. Petersburg, 1895), 67–74, 84–87, 102–9.

56. GARF, f. R-3431, op. 1, d. 300, ll. 414–15. Liudmilla Popova, widow of a chancellery employee in Irkutsk, suffered from intense migraines and toothaches that only Sofronii's holy oil could relieve. When she suffered an attack while attending services at the cathedral one day, she knelt before the saint's shrine and rubbed oil over her head, neck, and gums. Shortly thereafter, she reported with great joy that her teeth had begun "to come loose and fall out one after the other," which solved, at least, the problem of her recurring toothaches. For further examples of healing miracles involving holy oil, see the stories submitted by Archbishop Pavel of Chernigov to the Holy Synod in 1850–1851, in RGIA, f. 796, op. 131, d. 301, ll. 5–12, 18–21.

57. GARF, f. R-4652, op. 1, d. 1, l. 12.

58. Ivanchenko, *Zapiski pri poezdke*, 30.

59. *Sv. Feodosii Uglitskii. Znameniia milosti Bozhiei po molitvam Sviatitelia* (Moscow, 1896), 13–14. The silver spoon with which Saint Feodosii took Holy Communion was housed in the Chernigov Archaeological Museum. See "Mestnye izvestiia," *Chernigovskiia gubernskiia vedomosti*, no. 892 (25 August 1896): 1.

60. GARF, f. R-3431, op. 1, d. 300, l. 417. Sofronii's slipper was also used to heal

ailments of the legs and feet. See "Chudotvoreniia, proisshedshiia pri grobe Sofroniia, ep. irkutskago," *IEV*, no. 20 (15 October 1912): 570–74.

61. I. Z—n, *Poezdka v Troitse-Sergievu Lavru ko dniu Prepodobnago Sergiia, 5 iiulia 1885 goda* (Kiev, 1886). A deaf retired clerk living (appropriately enough) in the town of Glukhovo reported a similar recovery of his hearing after his wife poured drops of holy oil from the relics of Feodosii Chernigovskii into his ears. See "Blagodatnaia pomoshch' po molitvam k Sviatiteliu Feodosiiu Uglitskomu, Arkhiepiskopu Chernigovskomu, Chudotvortsu," *ChEI*, no. 4 (15 February 1897): 141.

62. *Shkol'noe puteshestvie v Zadonsk na bogomol'e* (Voronezh, 1890), 9. Monks at the Kiev Monastery of the Caves sang the praises of the miracle-working hat of Ioann the Much-Suffering. One Soviet source claims that the hat, described by the monks to be of "ancient origin," was in fact manufactured in 1847. See V. A. Shidenko, *Peshchery i moshchi Kievo-Pecherskoi Lavry* (Kiev, 1962), 4.

63. RGIA, f. 796, op. 445, d. 346, l. 354.

64. In 1911, for example, Iosif's srachitsa had healed one woman of typhus and a peasant woman from what doctors diagnosed as a "dangerous case of scarlet fever." See the miracle stories in ibid., ll. 112–112ob., 272–272ob.

65. Orlov, *Rukovoditel' Vladimirskikh bogomol'tsev*, 85.

66. "Sviatitel' Feodosii Uglitskii, Arkhiepiskop Chernigovskii. Po povodu 200-letnei godovshchiny so dnia blazhennoi konchiny ego," *ChEI*, no. 8 (15 April 1896): 267.

67. "Blagodatnaia pomoshch' po molitvam k Sviatiteliu Feodosiiu, Arkhiepiskopu Chernigovskomu, Chudotvortsu," *ChEI*, no. 12 (15 June 1897): 453, and no. 3 (1 February 1898): 136; E. Poselianin, *Vpechatlenie bogomol'tsa u moshchei Sviatitelia Feodosiia, novoiavlennago chudotvortsa Chernigovskago* (Moscow, 1897), 30.

68. "Blagodatnaia pomoshch' po molitvam k Sviatym i v chastnosti k Sviatiteliu Feodosiiu Uglitskomu, Arkhiepiskopu Chernigovskomu, Chudotvortsu," *ChEI*, no. 6 (15 March 1896): 214–15.

69. *Sv. Feodosii Uglitskii*, 6–9.

70. "Mozhno li verit' vsiakomu son?" *Dukhovnaia beseda*, no. 8 (August 1911): 525–27.

71. *Sv. Feodosii Uglitskii*, 6. See also "Chudesnaia pomoshch' po molitvam k sviatiteliu Feodosiiu Uglitskomu, Arkhiepiskopu Chernigovskomu, Chudotvortsu," *ChEI*, no. 21 (1 November 1896): 721–26.

72. V. Sokolov, *Sviateishii Patriarkh Germogen*, 28.

73. An 1896–1897 directory of physicians in Chernigov lists seven obstetricians, three "women's doctors," two veterinarians, one dentist, and twenty-one doctors, including a certain Iosif Fratsovich Sikorskii. See *Chernigovskaia pamiatka. Karmannaia spravochnaia*, 87–88. Despite his reputation, Sikorskii seems quick to have diagnosed as hopeless several cases that Saint Feodosii subsequently cured with ease. See, for example, the miraculous cure of a young child from a skin infection (*erysipelas*) in "Blagodatnaia pomoshch' po molitvam k Sviatiteliu Feodosiiu, arkhiepiskopu Chernigovskomu, Chudotvortsu," *ChEI*, no. 10 (15 May 1898): 403–4.

74. *Novye chudesa ot moshchei Sviatitelia Feodosiia Uglitskago, arkhiepiskopa Chernigovskago* (Chernigov, 1890), 17–18.

75. Christine D. Worobec, "Miraculous Healings," in Steinberg and Coleman, *Sacred Stories*, 22–43.

76. V. A. Kovrigina, "Zemstvo i zdravookhranenie v Rossii vtoroi poloviny XIX v. (k voprosu o zemskoi meditsine)," in *Rossiiskaia provintsiia XVIII–XX vekov: Realii kul'turnoi zhizni* (Penza, 1996), 83–84.

77. Statistics for 1913 as given in Neil B. Weissman, "Origins of Soviet Health Administration: Narkomzdrav, 1918–1928," in Susan Gross Solomon and John F.

Hutchinson, eds., *Health and Society in Revolutionary Russia* (Bloomington, 1990), 109.

78. Samuel C. Ramer, "Feldshers and Rural Health Care in the Early Soviet Period," in ibid., 121–45.

79. Kselman, *Miracles and Prophecies*, 38. See also the discussion in Amanda Porterfield, *Healing in the History of Christianity* (Oxford, 2005), 159–85.

80. "Khristianskii vzgliad na bolezni," *Kormchii*, no. 30 (1893): 457–58; "Golos meditsiny v zashchitu very," *Kormchii*, no. 48 (1895): 623–26; Priest E. Landyshev, "Besedy sel'skago pastyria so svoimi prikhozhanami po gigiene," *Dukhovnaia beseda*, no. 12 (December 1911): 859–66.

81. V. Iu. Leshchenko, *Sem'ia i russkoe pravoslavie (XI–XIX vv.)* (St. Petersburg, 1999), 174–83.

82. "Diven Bog vo sviatykh Svoikh," *Iaroslavskiia eparkhial'nyia izvestiia*, no. 52 (27 December 1909): 1048–49.

83. GARF, f. R-4652, op. 1, d. 1, l. 47.

84. Ibid., l. 48ob.–49.

85. Ibid., ll. 53–53ob.

86. For further examples of miracle stories involving believers turning first to physicians and then to the saints for help, see the healings attributed to Germogen in GARF, f. R-4652, op. 1, d. 1, ll. 43ob. ("terrible head pains"), 44–44ob. ("severe and chronic head cold"), 44ob.–45 (leg pains and inability to walk), 46 (stomach pains), 46ob. (pneumonia), 47–48 (heart problems), 49–49ob. ("strong pains and bleeding"), 51ob.–52 (optical tumor and loss of vision), 56ob.–57 (unspecified illness requiring surgery), 57–57ob. (heart palpitations), 59ob.–60 (abscess in the knee), 60 ("fungal eczema" of the arms and legs), 61ob.–62 (recovery from gunshot wound), 62–62ob. (swelling of the legs).

87. Finucane, *Miracles and Pilgrims*, 59.

88. Porf. Klenus, "Blagodatnaia pomoshch' Sviatitelia Feodosiia Chernigovskago," *Strannik*, t. 2, otd. 1 (1861): 252–54.

89. "Blagodatnaia pomoshch' po molitvam k Sviatiteliu Feodosiiu, Arkhiepiskopu Chernigovskomu, Chudotvortsu," *ChEI*, no. 17 (1 September 1897): 606–7.

90. "Chudesa po molitvam Blazhennago Episkopa Sofroniia," *IEV*, no. 11 (1 June 1913): 321–22.

91. *Pamiat' o Chernigove, 6–9 sentiabria 1896 goda. Sviatitel' Feodosii Uglitskii, arkhiepiskop Chernigovskii i Novgorodseverskii* (Kiev, 1897), 20. For a sampling of Saint Feodosii's miracles, arranged by the type of cure rendered, see *Sv. Feodosii Uglitskii*.

92. *Sviatiteli-podvizhniki novago vremeni*, 13–16.

93. "Chudesa po molitvam k Sviatiteliu Feodosiiu Uglitskomu," *ChEI*, no. 3 (1 February 1896): 91–97.

94. Sokolov, *Sviateishii Patriarkh Germogen*, 26.

95. Nadieszda Kizenko, "Protectors of Women and the Lower Orders: Constructing Sainthood in Modern Russia," in Kivelson and Greene, *Orthodox Russia*, 106–24. For comparison with modern impulses in saintly cults in Catholic Germany and France, see Waddy, "St. Anthony's Bread," 347–70; and Caroline Ford, "Religion and Popular Culture in Modern Europe," *Journal of Modern History* 65 (1993): 152–75.

96. Terry Rey, *Our Lady of Class Struggle: The Cult of the Virgin Mary in Haiti* (Trenton, 1999), 338.

97. Worobec, "Miraculous Healings," 29.

98. On noble indebtedness, see Seymour Becker, *Nobility and Privilege in Late Imperial Russia* (DeKalb, 1985), 28–54.

99. "Chudesa po molitvam k Sviatiteliu Feodosiiu Uglitskomu," *ChEI*, no. 3 (1 February 1896): 94–95.

100. "Chudesnaia pomoshch' po molitvam k sviatiteliu Feodosiiu Uglitskomu,

Arkhiepiskopu Chernigovskomu, Chudotvortsu," *ChEI*, no. 21 (1 November 1896): 725–26. On peasant litigiousness in the late imperial period, see Jane Burbank, *Russian Peasants Go to Court: Legal Culture in the Countryside, 1905–1917* (Bloomington, 2004).

101. "Blagodatnaia pomoshch' po molitvam k Sviatiteliu Feodosiiu, Arkhiepiskopu Chernigovskomu, Chudotvortsu," *ChEI*, no. 2 (15 January 1897): 70–71.

102. After the 1905 Revolution many universities and seminaries purged their ranks by expelling so-called radical elements of the student body. A Moscow mother credited Patriarch Saint Germogen with protecting her two sons during those troubled times. "Thanks exclusively to the prayerful intercession of Patriarch Germogen," she reported, her sons "were not mixed up in the former disturbances" at the Vladimir seminary and had avoided expulsion. See *Sviateishii Patriarkh Germogen i chudesa*, v.

103. On the improvisational nature of early modern Orthodox devotion, see Levin, "Supplicatory Prayers," 96–114.

104. Vasiutinskii, *Chernigov, ego sviatye khramy*, 49–50.

105. Kizenko, "Protectors of Women and the Lower Orders," 115.

106. Kremleva, "Obet v religioznoi zhizni," 128–57.

107. "Chudesa po molitvam k Sviatiteliu Feodosiiu Uglitskomu," *ChEI*, no. 16 (15 August 1896): 503–8.

108. "Blagodatnaia pomoshch' po molitvam k Sviatiteliu Feodosiiu, arkhiepiskopu Chernigovskomu, Chudotvortsu," *ChEI*, no. 12 (15 June 1898): 490–91; no. 4 (15 February 1896): 124–27.

109. "Chudesnyia istseleniia pri moshchakh Sviatitelia Feodosiia Uglitskago, Arkhiepiskopa Chernigovskago, v dni otkrytiia i proslavleniia ikh," *ChEI*, no. 20 (15 October 1896): 669.

110. "Chudesnaia pomoshch' po molitvam k Sviatiteliu Feodosiiu Uglitskomu, Arkhiepiskopu Chernigovskomu, Chudotvortsu," *ChEI*, no. 21 (1 November 1896): 725–26.

111. V. T. Georgievskii, *Raka i oblachenie dlia moshchei Sviatitelia Germogena* (Moscow, 1914), 6–8. On the relationship between pious acts and the assertion of Muscovite tsars' right to rule, see Nancy Shields Kollmann, "Pilgrimage, Procession and Symbolic Space in Sixteenth-Century Russian Politics," in *Medieval Russian Culture*, vol. 2, ed. Michael S. Flier and Daniel Rowland (Berkeley and Los Angeles, 1994), 163–81.

112. Richard Wortman, *Scenarios of Power: Myth and Ceremony in Russian Monarchy*, volume 2, *From Alexander II to the Abdication of Nicholas II* (Princeton, 2000), 235–70, 364–91, 439–80. Georgievskii describes the grand shrine commissioned by Nicholas II to house the relics of Patriarch Saint Germogen in *Raka i oblachenie*, 6–8. By this gesture the emperor was establishing the continuity between his reign and that of Vladimir Monomakh, who ordered ornate sepulchres built for the bodies of Saints Boris and Gleb in the twelfth century. See also the description of the elaborate silver lantern ("done in the ancient style") donated by the Empress Mariia for the shrine of the Prelate Saint Petr in the Uspenskii Cathedral, in *O sviatykh Ugodnikakh Bozhiikh*, 6; and the new jeweled canopy over the shrine of Saint Simeon Verkhoturskii donated by Nicholas and Alexandra in 1914, in Antoninov, *Palomnichestvo iz Ekaterinburga*, 1–2.

113. "U sv. moshchei," *Pastyrskii sobesednik*, no. 38 (21 September 1896): 593–99; *Kartiny tserkovnoi zhizni*, 164. Another source estimates the cost of the silver shrine at 35,000 rubles. See Kovalevskii, *Vospominanie ochevidtsa*, 12. Feodosii's wooden coffin, which lay inside the ornate shrine, was itself a gift, made by a local merchant in 1824 who converted to Orthodoxy from the Old Belief after he had been cured through the saint's intercession. *Blazhennyi Sviatitel' Feodosii Chernigovskii*, 15.

114. *Zhitie i otkrytie moshchei*, 26.

115. *Chernigovskiia gubernskiia vedomosti*, no. 904 (6 September 1896). To mark the nine-hundredth anniversary of the founding of Chernigov diocese, the sisters

of the Vvedenskii convent in Nezhinsk donated a hand-made "velvet shroud with gold embroidery" to adorn Saint Feodosii's shrine. See "Novyia pozhertvovaniia v Chernigovskii kafedral'nye sobor," *ChEI*, no. 24 (15 December 1893): 1006.

116. Priest Pokrovskii, *Sv. blagovernaia kniaginia Anna Kashinskaia. Zhizn', chudesa i molitvennoe pochitanie blagovernoi kniagini Anny Kashinskoi pravoslavnym russkim narodom* (Moscow, 1909), 32; "Opis' podnoshenii, prinesennykh v dar Kashinskomu Voskresenskomu Soboru v den' tserkovnago proslavleniia Sviatoi Blagovernoi Velikoi Kniagini Anny Kashinskoi—12 iiunia 1909 goda," *TEV*, no. 25 (30 June 1909): 275–82.

117. "Sviatitel' Feodosii Uglitskii, Arkhiepiskop Chernigovskii. Po povodu 200-letnei godovshchiny so dnia blazhennoi konchiny ego," *ChEI*, no. 8 (15 April 1896): 267. See also *Blazhennyi Sviatitel' Feodosii Uglitskii*, 15.

118. Platonov, "Slovo v nedeliu Syropustnuiu," 122. Offerings and votive gifts to the saints were encouraged by the Orthodox clergy, so long as they fell within the prescribed norms of decency and propriety. The practice of attaching coins to icons or reliquaries— either in hopes of a cure or as a show of thanks for a miracle rendered— was expressly forbidden, however, by an edict of the Holy Synod dated 10 January 1722.. A late-nineteenth-century gloss on this ruling noted that priests should explain to parishioners that monetary donations should be placed in the proper receptacle, that is, the offertory box. See N. Nikol'skii and M. Izvol'skii, *Sistematicheskii sbornik nedoumennykh voprosov i otvetov na nikh vstrechaiushchikhsia v tserkovno-prikhodskoi praktike, pomeshchennyia v izdavaemom pri S.-Peterburgskoi Dukhovnoi akademii "Tserkovnom vestnike" za poslednii (1875–1895) dvadtsat' let* (St. Petersburg, 1896), 9–10. In Vologda Province, believers would leave silver or wooden miniatures of legs, arms, heads, teeth, and so on, at icons and shrines as votive offerings of thanksgiving. See Kremleva, "Obet v religioznoi zhizni," 142.

119. "Novyia chudesa po molitvam k Sviatiteliu Feodosiiu Uglitskomu," *ChEI*, no. 12 (15 June 1895): 355.

120. Published donor rolls appeared in the back pages of the unofficial section (*neoffitsial'naia chast'*) of *ChEI* between March 1890 and March 1893 under one of two headings: "Ot Chernigovskago Kafedral'nago sobora" or, from January 1892, "Na molitvy pri moshchakh sv. Feodosiia Uglitskago i s drugim naznacheniem polucheny den'gi."

121. See, for example, the five-ruble donation of Priest I. B. on behalf of his parishioners in *ChEI*, no. 24 (15 December 1890): 675.

122. These statistics compare with the record of monetary donations pledged by the faithful to outfit a new shrine and canopy for Anna Kashinskaia's relics in 1909. Although the city government and wealthy individuals made lavish gifts of up to one thousand rubles, 44 percent of all donations received were less than five rubles. See *TEV*, no. 8 (23 February 1909): 92–93.

123. Kremleva, "Obet v religioznoi zhizni," 129, 142, 147. Notable contributions to the study of gender and Russian Orthodoxy include Eve Levin, *Sex and Society in the World of the Orthodox Slavs, 900–1700* (Ithaca, 1989); Brenda Meehan, "The Authority of Holiness: Women Ascetics and Spiritual Elders in Nineteenth-Century Russia," in *Church, Nation, and State in Russia and Ukraine*, ed. Geoffrey A. Hosking (London, 1991), 38–51; Brenda Meehan, "To Save Oneself: Russian Peasant Women and the Development of Women's Religious Communities in Pre-Revolutionary Russia," in *Russian Peasant Women*, ed. Beatrice Farnsworth and Lynne Viola (Oxford, 1992), 121–33; Isolde Thyrêt, "Women and the Orthodox Faith in Muscovite Russia: Spiritual Experience and Practice," in Kivelson and Greene, *Orthodox Russia*, 159–75; and Worobec, *Possessed*.

124. Gary Marker, "God of Our Mothers: Reflections on Lay Female Spirituality in Late Eighteenth- and Early Nineteenth-Century Russia," in Kivelson and Greene, *Orthodox Russia*, 193–209; Robert A. Orsi, *Thank You, Saint Jude: Women's Devotion to the*

Patron Saint of Hopeless Causes (New Haven, 1996); Robert A. Orsi, *The Madonna of 115th Street: Faith and Community in Italian Harlem, 1880–1950* (New Haven, 2002), 204–17.

125. Orthodox monastic orders had become predominantly female by the end of the nineteenth century, but it is not clear whether this sociological trend speaks to a "feminization" of Russian Orthodox piety per se. See William G. Wagner, "Paradoxes of Piety: The Nizhegorod Convent of the Exaltation of the Cross, 1807–1935," in Kivelson and Greene, *Orthodox Russia*, 211–38; and Brenda Meehan, "Popular Piety, Local Initiative and the Founding of Women's Religious Communities in Russia, 1764–1907," in Batalden, *Seeking God*, 83–105.

126. See the discussion in Worobec, "Miraculous Healings." On the limitations that Muscovite culture placed on Orthodox women's access to saintly graves, see Isolde Thyrêt, "Muscovite Miracle Stories as Sources for Gender-Specific Religious Experience," in Baron and Kollmann, *Religion and Culture*, 115–31.

127. Kurtsev, "Palomnichestvo v Tsentral'nom Chernozem'e," 145. Women made up a similar percentage of pilgrims headed for the Holy Land in the period between 1883 and 1899. See Piter Veisensel [Peter R. Weisensel], "Soobshcheniia russkikh krest'ian-palomnikov o Palestine kak otobrazhenie zhizni russkoi sel'skoi obshchiny," *Pravoslavnyi Palestinskii sbornik*, no. 31/94 (1992): 37–44.

128. I. P. Taradin, *Zadonskii Bogoroditskii monastyr' i Sviatoi Tikhon: Istoriko-kriticheskoe issledovanie* (Voronezh, 1927), 87; Pletnev, *U moshchei sv. Iosafa*, 46–56.

129. *Narodnaia vera v sviatost' Patriarkha Ermogena*, in GARF, f. R-4652, op. 1, d. 1, ll. 41–61ob.

130. GARF, f. R-4652, op. 1, d. 1, ll. 59ob.–60.

131. Archpriest I. A. Platonov, *Novye chudesa ot moshchei Sviatitelia Feodosiia Uglitskago, arkhiepiskopa Chernigovskago* (Chernigov, 1890), 20–26. In September 1890 the Chernigov cathedral received five rubles from Rossinskii, with a note attached: "Five rubles for prayers at the relics of Saint Feodosii Uglitskii, for candles, for making a shroud for the holy relics, and for other purposes." See "Ot Chernigovskago Kafedral'nago sobora," *ChEI*, no. 18 (15 September 1890): 409–10. Rossinskii reported another miracle the following year, when Saint Feodosii healed his four-year-old daughter from a severe fever. See "Eshche proiavlenie milosti Bozhiei po molitvam k sviatiteliu Feodosiiu Uglitskomu," *ChEI*, no. 8 (15 April 1891): 279–81.

132. Brown, *Cult of the Saints*, 50–68.

133. Reinburg, "Praying to Saints in the Late Middle Ages," 272.

134. Priest A. V—skii, "Sviatitel' Feodosii Uglitskii (po povodu 200-letiia so dnia blazhennoi konchiny Sviatitelia Feodosiia)," *ChEI*, no. 3 (1 February 1896): 89.

135. Kremleva, "Obet v religioznoi zhizni," 129.

Chapter Three: Making Saints

1. Hieromonk Aleksii, "O proslavlenii sviatykh i ob otkrytii ikh sv. moshchei," *Dukhovnaia beseda*, no. 4 (April 1913): 192.

2. For a description of the events of 12 June, see "U raki Sv. Anny Kashinskoi," *Strannik*, t. 1, otd. 2 (June 1909): 908–10; "Russkaia pechat' po povodu otkrytiia moshchei kn. Anny Kashinskoi," ibid., 910–11; "Chudesa i znameniia nebesnyia v Kashine," *Poslednyia Tverskiia novosti*, no. 13 (14 June 1909): 3; "Torzhestvo vozstanovleniia pochitaniia sviatoi blagovernoi Anny Kashinskoi," *Pribavleniia k Tserkovnym vedomostiam*, no. 25 (20 June 1909): 1140–45; and "Torzhestvo otkrytiia moshchei sv. blagovernoi kniagini Anny Kashinskoi," *Sovremennoe obozrenie* (supplement to *Kormchii*, 1909, no. 25): 98.

3. See, for example, the breathless speculation as to which dignitaries might

attend the celebration and the follow-up reportage in *Poslednyia Tverskiia novosti*, "Mestnaia khronika," no. 11 (31 May 1909): 1; "12 iiunia, den' proslavleniia Sv. Anny Kashinskoi," no. 13 (14 June 1909): 3–4; and "Mestnaia khronika," no. 15 (28 June 1909): 1–2.

4. E. E. Golubinskii, "Zametka o slove 'kanonizatsiia,'" *Bogoslovskii vestnik*, t. 1, no. 1 (January 1895): 166–67.

5. This theological point informs the analysis of all nineteenth-century Russian Orthodox discussions of canonization. See, for example, Golubinskii, *Istoriia kanonizatsii sviatykh*; Vasil'ev, *Istoriia kanonizatsii russkikh sviatykh*; Mertsalov, *Kak sovershalos' kanonizatsiia sviatykh*; and M. E. V., "Istoriia kanonizatsii russkikh sviatykh," *Stavropol'skiia eparkhial'nyia vedomosti*, no. 14 (16 July 1894): 633–59.

6. The seven saints canonized under Nicholas II were Feodosii Chernigovskii (1896); Serafim Sarovskii (1903); Anna Kashinskaia (1909); Ioasaf Belgorodskii (1911); Patriarch Germogen (1913); Pitirim Tambovskii (1914); and Ioann Tobol'skii (1916). See RGIA, f. 797, op. 84, otd. 2, st. 3, d. 372, ll. 100–100ob.; and "Kanonizatsiia sviatykh," *Dukhovnaia beseda*, no. 7 (July 1914): 515.

7. Freeze, "Subversive Piety," 315, 309, 311. See also Nichols, "Friends of God," 206–29.

8. The quotation is from Grand Duke Aleksandr Mikhailovich, cited in Wortman, *Scenarios of Power*, 2:391n92.

9. T. Manukhina, *Sviataia blagovernaia kniaginia Anna Kashinskaia* (Paris, 1954), 110–11.

10. Golubinskii, *Istoriia kanonizatsii sviatykh*, 161.

11. Isolde Thyrêt argues that the cults of Saints Arsenii and Mikhail were introduced by the bishops of Tver in part to help heal a region ravaged by the Time of Troubles. See Isolde Thyrêt, "Accounts of the Transfer of Relics and Cults of Saints in Muscovite Russia: Saints Arsenii and Mikhail of Tver," a paper presented to the conference "Modern History of Eastern Christianity: Transitions and Problems," Harvard University, 26–27 March 2004. On the discovery of holy bodies and the establishment of local cults more broadly, see Levin, "From Corpse to Cult," 81–103.

12. On the legend of Kashin's miraculous deliverance from Lithuanian siege, see Golubinskii, *Istoriia kanonizatsii sviatykh*, 161. Despite Anna's intercession, the city fell twice to Polish armies, however, first in 1609 and again in 1612. The hagiographical literature surrounding Anna makes no mention of the second assault, which followed one year after the healing of Gerasim. On the devastation of Kashin during the Time of Troubles, see G. Ia. Mokeev and I. Iu. Merkulova, "Kashin XVI–XVII vv. i goroda skhodnogo tipa," *Arkhitekturnoe nasledstvo* 36 (1988): 165–74.

13. Eight miracles were attributed to Anna between 1611 and 1649. The cured included the crippled wife of a Kashin blacksmith, the paralyzed son of a nobleman, and the blind wife of a "nobleman of foreign birth." See Priest S. A. Arkhangelov, *Zhitie i chudesa sviatoi blagovernoi kniagini Anny Kashinskoi* (St. Petersburg, 1909), 56–57.

14. Ibid., 62; V. O. Kliuchevskii, *Drevnerusskiia zhitiia sviatykh kak istoricheskii istochnik* (Moscow, 1871), 340–41; N. P. Barsukov, *Istochniki russkoi agiografii* (St. Petersburg, 1882), 41–43.

15. The zhitie, for example, notes that Anna died in 1337, while the chronicle accounts have her living another twenty years. According to the zhitie, Anna was the daughter of a Kashin boyar and a native of the town, whereas the chronicles claim her father was Prince Dmitrii Borisovich of Rostov. The text outlining the thirteen inconsistencies is reprinted in I. Ia. Kunkin, *Gorod Kashin: Materialy dlia ego istoriia*, vyp. 2 (Moscow, 1905), 62–67.

16. A. P. Bogdanov, *Russkie patriarkhi, 1589–1700*. 2 vols. (Moscow, 1999), 2:118–19; Kliuchevskii, *Drevnerusskiia zhitiia sviatykh*, 340–41.

17. Arkhangelov, *Zhitie i chudesa*, 71–72. The commission's findings are reprinted in V. I. Kolosov, *Blagovernaia kniaginia Anna Kashinskaia* (Tver, 1905), 30–46. Most nineteenth- and twentieth-century sources, Orthodox and Old Believer alike, agree that Ioakim's decision to inspect Anna's relics was motivated principally by the Church's desire to discredit the *dvuperstie*. See, for example, P. Koltypin, *Svedeniia o zhizni blagovernoi velikoi kniagini Anny Kashinskoi, suprugi sv. velikago kniazia Mikhaila Tverskogo* (St. Petersburg, 1872), 19; and Archpriest Aleksandr Skobnikov, *Sviataia blagovernaia kniaginia Anna Kashinskaia* (Kashin, 1909), 6–7. Interestingly, though, the commission's report of 1677 makes no mention of the two-fingered cross and even explicitly states that, although Anna's right hand was bent over her breast, "the palm and fingers are straight, and not in the form of a blessing." See Golubinskii, *Istoriia kanonizatsii sviatykh*, 165.

18. Golubinskii, *Istoriia kanonizatsii sviatykh*, 165.

19. *Pamiati sv. blagovernoi kniagini Anny Kashinskoi* (Moscow, 1909), 4.

20. Priest S. A. Arkhangelov, "Opredelenie Moskovskago Sobora 1678 goda o zhitii i podviga Blagovernoi Velikoi Kniagini Anny Kashinskoi," *Strannik*, t. 1, otd. 1 (April 1909): 534–54. On efforts to eradicate (and later co-opt) Old Believer saintly cults, see Georg Michels, "Rescuing the Orthodox: The Church Policies of Archbishop Afanasii of Kholmogory, 1682–1702," in *Of Religion and Empire: Missions, Conversion, and Tolerance in Tsarist Russia*, ed. Robert P. Geraci and Michael Khodarkovsky (Ithaca, 2001), 19–37.

21. On the imperious conduct of Muscovite hierarchs, see Georg Michels, "Ruling without Mercy: Seventeenth-Century Russian Bishops and Their Officials," *Kritika* 4 (2003): 515–42.

22. Archpriest Aleksandr Skobnikov, *Na mogile kashinskoi pravednitsy v Uspenskom sobore* (Elets, 1909), 6.

23. Priest S. A. Arkhangelov, *Sviataia blagovernaia velikaia kniaginia Anna Kashinskaia k dniu—12 iiunia 1909 g.—vozstanovleniia Eia proslavleniia* (St. Petersburg, 1909), 16.

24. D. A. Eristov, *Slovar' istoricheskii o sviatykh proslavlennykh v Rossiiskoi tserkvi, i o nekotorykh podvizhnikakh blagochestiia, mestno chitimykh* (St. Petersburg, 1836), 30; and the second edition of the same title (St. Petersburg, 1862), 23–24. In both editions, Anna was listed alphabetically, with no reference to her disgrace under Patriarch Ioakim.

25. "Kashin," in *Entsiklopedicheskii slovar'*, 41 vols. (St. Petersburg, 1890–1904): 28:820.

26. Quoted in *Sviataia blagovernaia velikaia kniaginia Anna Kashinskaia* (Moscow, 1910), 35.

27. I. V. Bazhenov, *Sv. blagovernaia kniaginia Anna Kashinskaia* (St. Petersburg, 1891), 16.

28. Arkhangelov, *Sviataia blagovernaia kniaginia*, 17. On industry in late imperial Kashin, see Arkhangelov, *Zhitie i chudesa*, 13; and "Kashin," *Entsiklopedicheskii slovar'*, 28:819–21.

29. Arkhangelov, *Sviataia blagovernaia kniaginia*, 17.

30. Ibid., 134–49.

31. Arkhangelov, *Zhitie i chudesa*, 80; and Arkhangelov, *Sviataia blagovernaia kniaginia*, 18.

32. "Dlia chego chestvuetsia sv. Anna Kashinskaia? (K voprosu o znachenii zhenshchiny sovremennom khristianskom obshchestve)," *TEV*, no. 22 (8 June 1909): 438–39.

33. E. Poselianin, "Pred Kashinskimi torzhestvami," *Pribavleniia k Tserkovnym vedomostiam*, no. 23 (6 June 1909): 1061. On the martyrdom of Prince Saint Mikhail, see Priest A. V. Sokolov, *Sviatyi blagovernoi velikii kniaz' Mikhail Iaroslavich Tverskii* (Tver, 1864).

34. N., "U sviatykh moshchei sv. Anny Kashinskoi," *Kormchii*, no. 26 (1909): 309. On Anna as a role model for Christian men and women, see also Prudnikov, *Istoricheskiia svideniia o blagovernoi kniagine Anne Kashinskoi, supruge sv. Mikhaila Tverskago*, 2nd ed. (St. Petersburg, 1859), 18. Gendered representations of the saint are encountered still today. A recent text celebrates Saint Anna for her "quiet" and "humble" character, "as befitting an Old Russian princess." See G. S. Gadalova, "Zhenshchiny Tverskogo kniazheskogo dvora (Velikie Kniagini Kseniia i Anna—mat' i zhena Mikhaila Tverskogo)," in *Velikii Kniaz' Tverskoi i Vladimirskii Mikhail Iaroslavich: Lichnost', epokha, nasledie* (Tver, 1996), 49.

35. Arkhangelov, *Sviataia blagovernaia velikaia kniaginia*, 16–17.

36. Arkhangelov, *Zhitie i chudesa*, 79; and Priest Ioann Zav'ialov, *Gorod Kashin, ego istoriia, sviatyni i dostoprimechatel'nosti. S kratkim zhitiem blagovernoi kniagini Anny* (St. Petersburg, 1909), 13. Despite Anna's intervention, the cholera epidemic of 1848 raged for nearly four months in Kashinskii district and accounted for the deaths of some fifteen hundred people (1.4 out of every hundred people in the district), the second-highest mortality rate in Tver Province. Nevertheless, the residents of Kashin might well have thought themselves fortunate to escape relatively unscathed from a disease that claimed 99,000 victims in the central industrial region alone. See G. I. Arkhangel'skii, *Kholernyia epidemii v Evropeiskoi Rossii v 50-ti-letnii period 1823–1872 gg.* (St. Petersburg, 1874), 251–52.

37. Arkhangelov, *Zhitie i chudesa*, 18 (emphasis mine). In 1866 the population of Kashin city and the surrounding localities was 7,372. See N. R—v, *Ocherk Kashina* (n.p., 1867), 27–28.

38. Manukhina, *Sviataia blagovernaia kniaginia*, 151.

39. These feast days were now 12 June (marking the translation of Anna's relics in 1650); 21 June (the day of the discovery of her relics); 2 October (the day of her death); and 17 November (the date of the second translation of Anna's relics, from the Uspenskii cathedral to the Voskresenskii, in 1817). See Zav'ialov, *Gorod Kashin*, 14. On the use of religious processions to sacralize civic space, see for example, Richard Mackenney, "Public and Private in Renaissance Venice," *Renaissance Studies* 12 (1998): 109–30.

40. Arkhangelov, *Sviataia blagovernaia velikaia kniaginia*, 20–21. The municipal edict of 1899 appears to have been more strict than imperial law, which stipulated only that "eating and drinking establishments be closed and that no one traffic in anything at all, save basic food necessities, until the procession returns to church." See Priest Aleksandr Tresviatskii, *Kalendar' sviashchennika* (Samara, 1893), 161–62.

41. Arkhangelov, *Sviataia blagovernaia velikaia kniaginia*, 22.

42. Among the royal visitors to Anna's grave in the decades before her re-canonization were the Empress Mariia Feodorovna and the Great Princess Ekaterina Pavlovna. See ibid., 23.

43. Arkhangelov, *Zhitie i chudesa*, 83–84.

44. "Neobychainoe religioznoe voodushevlenie v g. Kashine," *TEV*, no. 30 (21 July 1908): 672.

45. Wortman, *Scenarios of Power*, 2:235–70.

46. Popov, *V Kashin i Poltavu*, 7; Arkhangelov, *Zhitie i chudesa*, 89.

47. *Sviataia blagovernaia velikaia kniaginia*, 139.

48. Arkhangelov, *Zhitie i chudesa*, 144, 145–47.

49. Irodova's story was published in Tver diocese and subsequently reprinted in a nationwide religious periodical. See "K proslavleniiu blagovernoi kniagini Anny Kashinskoi," *TEV*, no. 15–16 (20–27 April 1909): 298–99; and "K proslavleniiu blagovernoi kniagini Anny Kashinskoi," *Kormchii*, no. 23 (1909): 266.

50. Manukhina, *Sviataia blagovernaia kniaginia*, 141.

51. Arkhangelov, *Sviataia blagovernaia velikaia kniaginia*, 16.
52. Pokrovskii, *Sv. blagovernaia kniaginia*, 30.
53. Ibid., 144–45; Arkhangelov, *Zhitie i chudesa*, 89; *Sviataia blagovernaia velikaia kniaginia*, 34.
54. Manukhina, *Sviataia blagovernaia kniaginia*, 150.
55. Arkhangelov, *Sviataia blagovernaia velikaia kniaginia*, 28; Skobnikov, *Na mogile*, 6.
56. Manukhina, *Sviataia blagovernaia kniaginia*, 151.
57. A narrative of the events of May–July 1908 is given in "Neobychainoe religioznoe voodushevlenie," 670–73. On support for Anna's cause in Tver, see Manukhina, *Sviataia blagovernaia kniaginia*, 28–30; *TEV*, no. 44 (27 October 1908): 606–7; and "Otkrytie moshchei blagovernoi kniagini Anny Kashinskoi," *Pochaevskii listok*, supp. no. 22–23 (1909): 161–66.
58. "Poslanie Sviateishago Sinoda vozliublennym o Gospode chadam Pravoslavnoi Russkoi Tserkvi o vozstanovlenii tserkovnago pochitaniia blagovernoi velikoi kniagini Anny Kashinskoi," published as a special supplement to *Tserkovnyia vedomosti*, no. 21 (23 May 1909): 3; Manukhina, *Sviataia blagovernaia kniaginia*, 28–30.
59. "Poslanie Sviateishago Sinoda," 3–4.
60. RGIA, f. 797, op. 84, otd. 2, st. 3, d. 372, ll. 100–100ob.
61. See the Synod's subsequent decree of 11 April 1909 (No. 4627), in *TEV*, no. 14 (13 April 1909): 134–35.
62. "Svetlye dni v gorode Kashine," *TEV*, no. 15–16 (20–27 April 1909): 293.
63. "Kashinskiia torzhestva," *Poslednyia Tverskiia novosti*, no. 3 (14 June 1909): 2–3.
64. "Osviashchenie pervago khrama vo imia sv. kniagini Anny Kashinskoi," *TEV*, no. 51–52 (28 December 1909): 1069–70; *Kashin, pravoslavnyi russkii gorod* (St. Petersburg, 1998), 26–27.
65. *Pribavleniia k Tserkovnym vedomostiam*, no. 25 (20 June 1909): 129, and no. 26 (27 June 1909): 136.
66. *Irkutskii missionerskii s"ezd. 24 iiulia–5 avgusta 1910 goda. (Dnevnik uchastnika s"ezda)* (Tomsk, 1910), 75–76.
67. "Slovo Arkhiepiskopa Serafima o neobkhodimosti bor'by s p'ianstvom," *IEV*, no. 23 (1 December 1912): 639–47. The related problems of deviance and crime are treated in Alan Wood, "Russia's 'Wild East': Exile, Vagrancy and Crime in Nineteenth-Century Siberia," in *The History of Siberia: From Russian Conquest to Revolution*, ed. Alan Wood (London, 1991), 117–39.
68. G. V. Oglezneva, "Usloviia deiatel'nosti pravoslavnoi tserkvi v vostochnoi Sibiri vo vtoroi polovine XIX–nachale XX vekov: Regional'nye osobennosti," in *Konfessii narodov Sibiri v XVII–nachale XX vv.: Razvitie i vzaimodeistvie* (Irkutsk, 2005), 128–34.
69. On the shipment of holy relics to consecrate new Siberian churches, see the 1874 correspondence between Bishop Pavel of Kamchatka and the Holy Synod in RGIA, f. 796, op. 155, d. 638, ll. 1–4ob. On relics and church consecration more broadly, see Archpriest V. G. Pevtsov, *Tserkovnoe pravo. Lektsii chitannyia v 1891–92 akad. godu* (St. Petersburg, 1892), 99–100.
70. E. M. Iaroslavskii, "12 funtov sibirskikh moshchei," *Sovetskaia Sibir'*, 28 January 1921, reprinted in E. M. Iaroslavskii, *O religii* (Moscow, 1957), 30–31. See also I. N. Iurasov, "Proverka very," in *O Emel'iane Iaroslavskom: Vospominaniia, ocherki, stat'i*, ed. P. S. Fateev and V. V. Korolev (Moscow, 1988), 207–12.
71. Archpriest Milii Chefranov, *Blazhennyi Sofronii, 3-i episkop irkutskii* (Moscow, 1907); O. E. Naumova, *Irkutskaia eparkhiia XVIII—pervaia polovina XIX veka* (Irkutsk, 1996), 55–69.
72. "Doklad o kanonizatsii sviatitelia Sofroniia, tret'iago episkopa irkutskago," in GARF, f. R-3431, op. 1, d. 303, l. 6 (undated, no later than 8 December 1917). The

incorruptibility of Sofronii's relics was regarded as all the more miraculous insofar as the bishop's un-embalmed body had lain in state for more than six months before his burial—"during the summer, no less," as Archbishop Tikhon informed the Synod. See GARF, f. R-3431, op. 1, d. 300, l. 409ob. (Archbishop Tikhon to the Holy Synod, 19 March 1910).

73. Chefranov, *Blazhennyi Sofronii*, 342.

74. Ibid., 329.

75. Ibid., 343.

76. The miracle books of the Voznesenskii monastery credit Saint Innokentii with 103 attested miracles, three-quarters of which were performed prior to his 1803 canonization. See Priest In. Popov, "O chudesakh Sviatitelia Innokentiia," *IEV*, no. 6 (15 March 1910): 160–64; and Archpriest P. V. Gromov, *Nachalo khristianstvo v Irkutske, i Sviatyi Innokentii, pervyi episkop Irkutskii, ego sluzhenie, upravlenie, konchina, chudesa i proslavlenie* (Irkutsk, 1868), 285–408.

77. See the miracle stories recorded in GARF, f. R-3431, op. 1, d. 300, ll. 413–21; and *Iavlenie blagodatnoi pomoshchi Sviatitelia Sofroniia, 3-go episkopa irkutskago* (Irkutsk, 1915).

78. V. Dashkevich, *Pereselenie v Sibir'* (St. Petersburg, 1912), 51–52; V. M. Kabuzan, *Emigratsiia i reemigratsiia v Rossii v XVIII–nachale XX veka* (Moscow, 1998), 125, 173, 267–68; Donald W. Treadgold, *The Great Siberian Migration: Government and Peasant in Resettlement from Emancipation to the First World War* (Princeton, 1957).

79. N. G. O. Pereira, *White Siberia: The Politics of Civil War* (Montreal, 1996), 27.

80. Dashkevich, *Pereselenie v Sibir'*, 38.

81. On Sofronii's help of non-Russians, see the miracle stories in GARF, f. R-3431, op. 1, d. 300, l. 413 (the healing of a Cossack girl); and d. 301, ll. 109–110 (the healing of an illiterate Cossack widow). The ethnic diversity of the Siberian provinces increased sharply toward the end of the old regime. In 1858 immigrants from the Ukrainian provinces (Cossacks and ethnic Ukrainians) accounted for 0.1 percent of the Siberian population; by 1917, the figure had risen to 9.4 percent. See Kabuzan, *Emigratsiia i reemigratsiia*, 173, 268. On the popularity of Sofronii's fellow Siberian saint Vasilii Mangazeiskii among baptized pagans and non-Russians, see a 1912 account of his miracles in RGIA, f. 796, op. 445, d. 344, ll. 2–3.

82. GARF, f. R-3431, op, 1, d. 300, ll. 419–419ob. This miracle, reported by the young woman's landlady, was one of ten forwarded to the Holy Synod by Archbishop Tikhon of Irkutsk on 19 March 1910.

83. "Chudesa po molitvam Blazhennago Episkopa Sofroniia," *IEV*, no. 24 (15 December 1913): 797–800.

84. Ibid., *IEV*, no. 12 (15 June 1914): 399–403. Indeed, diocesan newspapers reminded readers that it was indeed a sin to keep silent when miracles had been rendered them. Those who had received miracles were expected to share this news with the faithful, just as the blind man healed by Jesus at the pool of Siloam had done in John 9. See "K slave novoiavlennago ugodnika Bozhiia, sviatitelia Feodosiia, Chernigovskago Chudotvortsa," *ChEI*, no. 7 (1 April 1899): 235–43.

85. "Chudo po molitvam Sviatitelia Sofroniia," *IEV*, no. 9 (1 May 1913): 259–62; and "V starom sobore," in the special supplement to *IEV*, no. 1 (1 January 1917): 39.

86. GARF, f. R-3431, op. 1, d. 301, ll. 89–91ob. (letter of Aleksandr Stepanovich Shakhmaev to the Commission for the Verification of the Miracles Performed through the Prayers of the Prelate Sofronii, Third Bishop of Irkutsk, 3 February 1914).

87. GARF, f. R-3431, op. 1, d. 300, l. 411ob.

88. Ibid., l. 412.

89. *Ukaz* no. 7975 from the Holy Synod to the archbishop of Irkutsk (31 May 1912), as published in *IEV*, no. 19 (1 October 1912): 141–45.

90. "Zasedaniia Komissii po udostvoreniiu deistvitel'nosti chudotvorenii po molitvam Sviatitelia Sofroniia, 3-go episkopa irkutskago," *IEV*, no. 7–8 (1–15 April 1913): 59.

91. *IEV*, no. 20 (15 October 1912): 149–52, and no. 7–8 (1–15 April 1913): 58–60.

92. In Chernigov, for example, the local commission investigating the miracle stories attributed to Feodosii Chernigovskii found that "in almost all instances" the recipients of miracles recorded in the cathedral registries were either already dead or could not be located. See "Novyi molitvennik za zemliu Russkuiu pred Gospodom, sviatitel' Feodosii Uglitskii, arkhiepiskop Chernigovskii," *Rukovodstvo dlia sel'skikh pastyrei*, t. 3, no. 41 (13 October 1896): 167–68.

93. GARF, f. R-3431, op. 1, d. 301, l. 55. Orthodox canon law was strict on the sanctity of oaths; anyone who broke an oath sworn on the cross or gospels had violated the commandment against taking the name of the Lord in vain and was declared anathema for ten years, which meant that liars ran the very real risk of dying without first having taken holy communion. See Nechaev, *Prakticheskoe rukovodstvo dlia sviashchennosluzhitelei*, 387–94; "Pouchenie pred prisiagoi," *Dukhovnaia beseda*, no. 9 (September 1909): 304. Imperial law stated that anyone who falsely publicized miracles "for the sake of profit, vainglory, or any sort of personal advantage" could be brought to trial under article 933 of the penal code. See Tresviatskii, *Kalendar' sviashchennika*, 164.

94. On the work of the Astrakhan commission, see RGIA, f. 797, op. 83, otd. 2, st. 3, d. 411, ll. 1–7ob.; and *Ot Komiteta po delu otkrytiia i proslavleniia chestnykh ostankov Mitropolita Iosif Ubiennago* (Astrakhan, 1911). For examples of this commission's deliberations and methodological approach to the investigation of miracles, see RGIA, f. 796, op. 445, d. 346, ll. 112–112ob., 138–39, 172–172ob., 253–253ob., 272–272ob., 279ob., 365, 373, 383. A similar commission was operating at the same time in Tambov diocese to investigate the miracles attributed to Saint Pitirim. RGIA, f. 796, op. 205, d. 262, ll. 8–9ob. (Bishop Kirill of Tambov to the Holy Synod, 7 February 1913).

95. Golubinskii, *Istoriia kanonizatsii sviatykh*, 284–85n1.

96. The phrase is that of the mayor of Irkutsk; see the various statements of endorsement for Sofronii's candidacy in GARF, f. R-3431, op. 1, d. 300, ll. 430–33.

97. See Innokentii Pisarev, "Kratkii otchet Irkutskago tserkovnago vo imia Sviatitelia Innokentiia Bratstva za 1912 g.," *IEV*, no. 16 (15 August 1913): 496–509; and the special supplements to *IEV*, no. 23 (1 December 1913) and no. 24 (15 December 1913). By the end of 1914, in its thirteenth year of existence, the brotherhood boasted 366 active members (five out of every six of whom were laymen); various honorary members, including the governor general of the province, the archbishop, and Metropolitan Makarii of Moscow; and nearly 13,000 rubles in capital. See "Ocherk o sostoianii Irkutskago tserkovnago vo imia Sviatitelia Innokentiia Bratstva za 1914 goda," published as a special supplement to *IEV*, no. 23 (1 December 1914).

98. GARF, f. R-3431, op. 1, d. 300, l. 411.

99. *Kalendar'-spravochnik po g. Irkutsku i Irkutskoi gubernii na 1914 god* (Irkutsk, 1914), 111.

100. "K kanonizatsii sv. Sofroniia," *Golos Iakutskoi tserkvi*, no. 18–19 (September–October 1918): 93.

101. "V starom sobore," *IEV*, no. 7–8 (1–15 April 1917): 268. The article also reported that a "grandiose gathering of soldiers and workers" was under way on the cathedral square on the morning of the fire, casting further suspicion on radical elements in the city. For more on the fire, see the report to the Holy Synod in GARF, f. R-3431, op. 1, d. 300, ll. 436–37 (19 September 1917).

102. Archbishop Ioann, "Rech' pred panikhidoi po Sviatitele Sofronii (19 aprelia 1917 goda)," *IEV*, no. 9–10 (1–15 May 1917): 275–76. On the destruction of holy relics as a message from God, see Archimandrite Evdokim, "U moshchei prep. Serafima

Sarovskago," *Bogoslovskii vestnik*, t. 2, no. 7–8 (July–August 1903): 514.

103. GARF, f. R-3431, op. 1, d. 300, l. 436ob.

104. Ibid., l. 437. The signed petitions are housed in GARF, f. R-3431, op. 1, d. 300, ll. 14–56, 87–338, and d. 302, ll. 1–36. On the formation of the union and its efforts, see "V soiuze pravoslavnykh khristian" and "Ot Soveta soiuza pravoslavnykh khristian pros'ba," *IEV*, no. 9–10 (1–15 May 1917): 326–30; and GARF, f. R-3431, op. 1, d. 303, ll. 7–8.

105. Archbishop Ioann, "Otchet v izraskhodovanii deneg, sobrannykh na lampadu i ikonu Sviatitelia Ioanna, mitropolita Tobol'skago i Sibirskago," *IEV*, no. 3 (1 February 1917): 30–31.

106. *Zhurnaly Irkutskago 49-go ekstrennago eparkhial'nago s"ezda dukhovenstva i mirian Irkutskoi eparkhii 29 maia–11 iiunia 1917 goda* (Nizheudinsk, 1917), 18–20.

107. See the decree of 5/18 April 1918 in GARF, f. R-3431, op. 1, d. 303, ll. 22–25ob.; subsequently republished in *Tserkovnyia vedomosti*, no. 19–20 (1–14 June 1918): 109–14.

108. RGIA, f. 831, op. 1, d. 83, ll. 14–14ob. (Archbishop Ioann to the Holy Synod, 29 April 1918).

109. Petition of Irkutsk parish clergy to Patriarch Tikhon in RGIA, f. 831, op. 1, d. 83, ll. 16–17ob. (undated, likely late April or early May 1918). Earlier in the decade, even before his canonization had been officially approved by the Synod, Patriarch Germogen was the subject of debate among Church publicists who argued whether it would be more fitting to celebrate the patriarch's memory on 22 October (the date in 1612 when he discovered the icon of the Kazan Mother of God, under whose banner Pozharskii's forces defeated the Poles) or 17 January (the anniversary of his death). See A. Lebedev, *V kakoi den' naibolee prilichno chestvovat' pamiat' Patriarkha Germogena* (Saratov, 1910). The difference here, however, is that the debates in Irkutsk were more broad-based and inclusive, involving not just religious thinkers and elites but rank-and-file clerics and lay believers.

110. GARF, f. R-3431, op. 1, d. 303, ll. 28–29 (Sobor protocol of 14/27 May 1918). Revolution and civil war similarly delayed the canonization ceremonies for Metropolitan Iosif the Murdered of Astrakhan. Shortly after the Patriarch's decision to canonize the new saint, the diocese of Astrakhan requested, with a certain poignant optimism, that the festivities be delayed to 11 May 1919, "on account of local conditions [and] in view of the circumstances of these present times." See RGIA, f. 831, op. 1, d. 82, l. 3 (Metropolitan Mitrofan of Astrakhan to Patriarch Tikhon, 12/25 June 1918). Shortages of ecclesiastical staples such as candles, communion wine, and incense were endemic across Siberia during the Civil War and after. See T. N. Kogol', *Vzaimootnosheniia Russkoi Pravoslavnoi Tserkvi i gosudarstva v pervoe desiatiletie Sovetskoi vlasti (Istoricheskii analiz na materialakh Zapadnoi Sibiri)* (Tomsk, 2005), 76–77.

111. According to the 1930s memoirs of a monk who had taught for some time in the Irkutsk seminary before the Revolution, local believers who attempted to hide the relics of Saints Innokentii and Sofronii from Bolshevik desecration were shot. See Archimandrite Feodosii (Almazov), *Moi vospominaniia (Zapiski Solovetskogo uznika)*, ed. M. I. Odintsov (Moscow, 1997), 112.

112. "Dlia chego chestvuetsia sv. Anna Kashinskaia?" 437.

113. Zav'ialov, *Gorod Kashin*, 13–14. Similar sentiments were expressed in the 1908 petition of support drafted by the clergy and laity of Tver; see *TEV*, no. 44 (27 October 1908): 606–7.

114. A. V. Simakov, *Zhitie i podvigi blagovernoi velikoi kniagini Anny Kashinskoi* (Ural'sk, 1909), vi. At the time, the Tver diocesan press noted with pride that Kashin's population was "exclusively Orthodox." See "Neobychainoe religioznoe voodushevlenie," 673.

115. "Svetlye dni," 291. See also Zav'ialov, *Gorod Kashin*, 14.

116. Priest Ioann Il'igorskii, "Po povodu Kashinskikh torzhestv," *TEV*, no. 37 (21 September 1909), 768. See also Archpriest I. Solov'ev, *Kakoi smysl' i znachenie imeet prichtenie Sviateishago Patriarkha Ermogena k liku Sviatykh? V otvet nedoumevaiushchim i voproshaiushchim o znachenii etogo torzhestva i prave na nego Sviateishchago Sinoda* (Sergiev Posad, 1913), 5–7.

117. Il'igorskii, "Po povodu Kashinskikh torzhestv," 761, 765–66, 768.

118. On the security measures at the Kashin ceremonies, see "Ot Tverskago gubernatora," *TEV*, no. 20 (25 May 1909): 237.

119. Popov, *V Kashin i Poltavu*, 4.

120. "Neobychainoe religioznoe voodushevlenie," 670.

121. "Sviatye dni," 101. This article appeared in the periodical pamphlet *Sovremennoe obozrenie*, published as a supplement to *Kormchii*, no. 26 (1909).

122. On the movement for greater lay activism and autonomy in the late imperial period, see P. A. Leont'ev, "Revoliutsiia v tserkvi: S"ezdy dukhovenstva i mirian v 1917 godu," in *Tserkov' v istorii Rossii*, vyp. 2 (Moscow, 1998), 214–48; Mikhail E. Dmitriev, "Riazan Diocese in 1917," *Russian Studies in History* 38 (1999): 66–82; Chris J. Chulos, "Revolution and Grassroots Re-evaluations of Russian Orthodoxy: Parish Clergy and Peasants of Voronezh Province, 1905–17," in *Transforming Peasants: Society, State and the Peasantry, 1861–1930*, ed. Judith Pallot (New York, 1998), 90–112; and Shevzov, "Miracle-Working Icons."

123. GARF, f. R-3431, op. 1, d. 303, l. 7.

124. Bazhenov, *Sv. blagovernaia kniaginia*, 16.

125. In March 1918, for example, the Sobor rejected a petition from a former archbishop of Vladimir regarding the canonization of the holy fool Kiprian. Although Kiprian was credited with thirty-one miracles, the Sobor ruled that strong evidence was lacking and that the petition itself read as if it had been "composed hastily." That same month, the Sobor rejected a proposal to canonize Vasilii Mangazeiskii, arguing that the petition had been brought forward "by one lone individual" (a former bishop of Eniseisk) and "without any information for a proper decision (in the file there is neither a zhitie, nor a book giving an account of [his] miracles)." GARF, f. R-3431, op. 11, d. 304, ll. 6, 11. The Sobor also rejected a motion to canonize Prokopii Ust'ianskii, and sent his dossier back to Vologda for further documentation. Ibid., ll. 1–2ob.

CHAPTER FOUR: THE REVOLUTION AND THE SAINTS

1. Mikhail Gorev, "Vskrytie moshchei Tikhona Zadonskogo i Mitrofana Voronezhskogo" (1919), in *Moshchi: Sbornik materialov, dokumentov i razoblachenii*, ed. Valentin Rozhitsyn (Kharkiv, 1922), 59.

2. "Religiia i kommunizm," *Revoliutsiia i tserkov'* (1919), reprinted in P. A. Krasikov, *Izbrannye ateisticheskie proizvedeniia* (Moscow, 1970), 33.

3. Gorev, "Tikhona Zadonskogo," 59–95; Taradin, *"Sviatoi" Mitrofan*, 23–24.

4. There is no consensus among scholars as to the exact number of relic exhumations conducted during the early years of Soviet power. In his December 1920 address to the VIII All-Russian Congress of Soviets, P. A. Krasikov, director of the VIII Section of the People's Commissariat of Justice, announced that sixty-three relic exhumations had been carried out to date. Although Krasikov's figures were only for the period 1918–1920, subsequent Soviet scholars tended to cite this number as the sum for the entire relic campaign. But the recent publication of hitherto inaccessible documents from the State Archives of the Russian Federation (GARF) and the Archive of the President of the Russian Federation (APRF) reveals that a second, smaller wave of exhumations was

carried out between 1922 and 1924, in conjunction with the Soviet state's campaign to requisition church valuables, and again during the years of the First Five Year Plan. To be sure, these later exhumations were conducted much more sporadically and with far less pomp than the early relic exposures. This new data, however, raises the total to at least seventy-four exhumations, conducted in twenty provinces between October 1918 and February 1936, with more than 75 percent of these occurring in the first eight months of this period. See N. N. Pokrovskii and S. G. Petrov, eds., *Arkhivy Kremlia: Politbiuro i tserkov', 1922–1925 gg.*, 2 vols. (Moscow, 1997), 1:171–73, 515–16n10. For Krasikov's report, see "Otchet VIII-go (Likvidatsionnogo) otdela Narodnogo Komissariata Iustitsii VIII-mu Vserossiiskomu s"ezdu Sovetov," in *Moshchi*, 105–14.

5. A notable, though dated, exception is Bernard Marchadier, "L'exhumation des reliques dans les premières années du pouvoir soviétique," *Cahiers du Monde Russe et Soviétique* 22 (1981): 67–88. References to the campaign and specific exhumations may be found in Dimitry V. Pospielovsky, *Soviet Antireligious Campaigns and Persecutions* (New York, 1988), 19–20; Richard Pipes, *Russia under the Bolshevik Regime* (New York, 1993), 346; Glennys Young, *Power and the Sacred in Revolutionary Russia: Religious Activists in the Village* (University Park, 1997), 97; Jennifer J. Wynot, *Keeping the Faith: Russian Orthodox Monasticism in the Soviet Union, 1917–1939* (College Station, 2004), 41–45.

6. Post-Soviet treatments include V. A. Alekseev, *Illiuzii i dogmy* (Moscow, 1991); V. A. Alekseev, *"Shturm nebes" otmeniaetsia? Kriticheskie ocherki po istorii bor'by s religiei v SSSR* (Moscow, 1992); Vladimir Stepanov (Rusak), *Svidetel'stvo obvineniia*, 3 vols. (Moscow, 1993); V. A. Iurchenkov, "Likvidatsiia moshchei sviatykh kak faktor obshchestvenno-politicheskoi zhizni 20-x godov," in *Obshchestvenno-politicheskaia zhizn' rossiiskoi provintsii, XX vek*, vyp. 1 (Tambov, 1993), 55–58; A. I. Nezhnyi, *Komissar d'iavola* (Moscow, 1993); and "'Nepobedimye soprotivnymi silami': Sud'ba sviatykh moshchei russkikh ugodnikov Bozhiikh v XX veke," *Danilovskii blagovestnik*, no. 10 (1999): 31–39. Notable exceptions to the prevailing trend of hagiographic treatments are A. V. Kashevarov, *Gosudarstvo i tserkov': Iz istorii vzaimootnoshenii sovetskoi vlasti i russkoi pravoslavnoi tserkvi, 1917–1945 gg.* (St. Petersburg, 1995), 70–78; A. V. Kashevarov, "Kampaniia sovetskoi vlasti po vskrytiiu sviatykh moshchei v 1918–1920 gg.," in *Tserkov' i gosudarstvo v russkoi pravoslavnoi i zapadnoi latinskoi traditsiiakh* (St. Petersburg, 1996), 77–97; M. Iu. Krapivin, *Nepridumannaia tserkovnaia istoriia: Vlast' i tserkov' v Sovetskoi Rossii (oktiabr' 1917-go–konets 1930-x godov)* (Volgograd, 1997), 48–50; and A. Rogozianskii, *Strasti po moshcham: Iz istorii gonenii na ostanki sviatykh v sovetskoe vremia* (St. Petersburg, 1998).

7. D. I. Kurskii, "Tsirkuliar NKIu ot 25 avgusta 1920," in *Otdelenie tserkvi ot gosudarstva: Sistematizirovannyi sbornik deistvuiushchego v SSSR zakonodatel'stva*, ed. P. V. Gidulianov, 3rd ed. (Moscow, 1926), 66–68.

8. Carlos M. N. Eire, *The War against the Idols: The Reformation of Worship from Erasmus to Calvin* (Cambridge, 1986), 151.

9. A typically "Soviet" view of the mutually constitutive relationship between the old regime and the Orthodox Church is P. A. Krasikov, "Sovetskaia vlast' i tserkov'" (1919), in Krasikov, *Izbrannye ateisticheskie proizvedeniia*, 19–28.

10. M. Dolginov, "'Sviatye' moshchi i blagochestivaia spekuliatsiia," in M. Dolginov, ed., *O sviatykh moshchakh: Sbornik materialov* (Moscow, 1961), 40.

11. See, for example, M. I. Shakhnovich, *Lenin i problemy ateizma: Kritika religii v trudakh V. I. Lenina* (Moscow, 1961).

12. A. V. Belov, *Pravda o pravoslavnykh "sviatykh"* (Moscow, 1968), 115–16. These late imperial canonizations and the political overtones surrounding them were a popular theme in the Soviet antireligious press throughout the 1920s and 1930s. See S. Kondrat'ev, "Nikolai II-i i ego sviatye ugodniki," *Nash bezbozhnik*, no. 14 (26 November 1925): 3; Mikhail Gorev, *Poslednii sviatoi: Poslednie dni Romanovskoi tserkvi* (Moscow,

1928); G. Venediktov, "Tsarskaia okhrana i moshchi Serafima Sarovskogo," *Ateist*, no. 56–57 (1930): 1–35; Z. Gurskaia, "Istoriia kanonizatsii 'startsa' Serafima Sarovskogo," *Antireligioznik*, no. 4 (July–August 1935): 34–36.

13. M. F. Paozerskii, *Russkie sviatye pred sudom istorii* (Moscow, 1923), 10. An almost identical argument is made in M. F. Paozerskii, *Prepodobnyi Serafim Sarovskii* (Moscow, 1924), 3–10.

14. Leon Trotsky, "Vodka, the Church, and the Cinema" (1923), in *Bolshevik Visions: First Phase of the Cultural Revolution in Soviet Russia*, ed. William G. Rosenberg, 2 vols. (Ann Arbor, 1984), 2:108.

15. Richard Stites, "Iconoclastic Currents in the Russian Revolution: Destroying and Preserving the Past," in *Bolshevik Culture: Experiment and Order in the Russian Revolution*, ed. Abbot Gleason, Peter Kenez, and Richard Stites (Bloomington, 1989), 1–24.

16. Richard Stites, *Revolutionary Dreams: Utopian Vision and Experimental Life in the Russian Revolution* (Oxford, 1989), 65.

17. RGIA, f. 796, op. 204, otd. 6, st. 3, d. 82, ll. 1–2 (Bishop Mikhail of Samara to the Holy Synod, 20 April 1917). Similarly contentious debates broke out as to whether the tsar's name should be included in the traditional prayer sung during the divine liturgy. See B. I. Kolonitskii, *Simvoly vlasti i bor'ba za vlast': K izucheniiu politicheskoi kul'tury rossiiskoi revoliutsii 1917 goda* (St. Petersburg, 2001), 59–62.

18. GARF, f. A-353, op. 3, d. 737, ll. 56, 58 (correspondence between the Voronezh provincial justice department and Narkomiust).

19. Bruce Lincoln, "Revolutionary Exhumations in Spain, July 1936," *Contemporary Studies in Society and History* 27 (1985): 241–60; Adrian A. Bantjes, "Idolatry and Iconoclasm in Revolutionary Mexico: The De-Christianization Campaigns, 1929–1940," *Mexican Studies/Estudios Mexicanos* 13 (1997): 87–120; and Julio de la Cueva, "Religious Persecution, Anticlerical Tradition and Revolution: On Atrocities against the Clergy during the Spanish Civil War," *Journal of Contemporary History* 33 (1998): 355–69.

20. On anticlericalism and antireligious iconoclasm as "spontaneous atheism" (that is, as the first step in a Leninist teleology that would lead eventually and inexorably to a society organized along the principles of atheism), see L. I. Emeliakh, "Antiklerikalizm i ateizm russkikh krest'ian nakanune Velikoi Oktiabr'skoi sotsialisticheskoi revoliutsii," in *Po etapam razvitiia ateizma v SSSR* (Leningrad, 1967), 59–85; and L. I. Emeliakh, *Antiklerikal'noe dvizhenie krest'ian v period pervoi russkoi revoliutsii* (Moscow, 1965).

21. Mikhail V. Shkarovskii, "The Russian Orthodox Church," in *Critical Companion to the Russian Revolution*, ed. Edward Acton, Vladimir Iu. Cherniaev, and William G. Rosenberg (London, 1997), 424–27. On nineteenth-century anticlericalism (or lack thereof), see Gregory L. Freeze, "A Case of Stunted Anticlericalism: Clergy and Society in Imperial Russia," *European Studies Review* 13 (1983): 177–200; and Chris J. Chulos, "Peasant Perspectives of Clerical Debauchery in Post-Emancipation Russia," *Studia Slavica Finlandensia* 12 (1995): 33–53.

22. "Glumlenie nad sviatyneiu ne prokhodit darom," *Dukhovnaia beseda*, no. 8 (August 1917): 379.

23. To cite but a few examples: "Ubiistvo sviashchennika khut. Bukatina Grigoriia Govzdeva i ego zhena," *Astrakhanskiia eparkhial'nyia vedomosti*, no. 17 (30 August 1917): 571–72; "Uroki i primery iz zhizni," *Dukhovnaia beseda*, no. 10 (October 1917): 479–81; and "Sviatotatstvo," *Vestnik tserkovnago edineniia*, no. 27 (22 October 1917): 4.

24. GARF, f. R-3431, op. 1, d. 563, l. 134 (Bishop Serafim of Orel to the Holy Synod, 24 October 1917).

25. GARF, f. R-3431, op. 1, d. 563, ll. 135–135ob. (Bishop Iuvenalii of Tula to the Holy Synod, 27 October 1917).

26. RGIA, f. 796, op. 204, otd. 6, st. 3, d. 73, ll. 1–1ob. On the relics in the Far

Catacombs, see P. L., *Kievo-Pecherskaia Lavra v eia proshedshem i nyneishnem sostoianii, s fasadami velikoi Lavrskoi tserkvi, planom eia i planom peshcher* (Kiev, 1894), 85–89.

27. GARF, f. R-3431, op. 1, d. 563, ll. 144–145 (Hieromonk Martirii to Archbishop Evlogii of Volynia, 21 October 1917). "Bourgeois" as a sociopolitical slur in the context of 1917 is discussed in Boris I. Kolonitskii, "Antibourgeois Propaganda and Anti-'Burzhui' Consciousness in 1917," *Russian Review* 53 (1994): 183–96.

28. S. N. Emel'ianov, *Vlast' i tserkov': Evoliutsiia gosudarstvennoi religioznoi politiki i institutov tserkovnogo upravleniia v guberniiakh Tsentral'nogo Chernozem'ia: 1917–1922* (Kursk, 2001), 58.

29. M. I. Vostryshev, *Patriarkh Tikhon* (Moscow, 1995), 139–40; and "Koshchunstvo v Uspenskom sobore," *Vestnik tserkovnago edineniia*, no. 31 (5 November 1917): 4.

30. The Protestant Reformation provides a useful comparative framework within which to view the transition from image-making to image-breaking (to paraphrase Hermann Heimpel's famous phrase). See, for example, Natalie Zemon Davis, "The Rites of Violence," in her *Society and Culture in Early Modern France* (Stanford, 1975), 124–51.

31. A. I. Vvedenskii, *Tserkov' i gosudarstvo: Ocherk vzaimootnoshenii tserkvi i gosudarstva v Rossii, 1918–1922* (Moscow, 1923), 133.

32. Ibid., 41–42.

33. Archpriest Vladislav Tsypin, *Istoriia Russkoi tserkvi, 1917–1997* (Moscow, 1997), 16.

34. Plaksin, *Krakh tserkovnoi kontrrevoliutsii*, 169.

35. In a 22 November 1917 report to the Holy Synod, Archpriest Aleksandr Dernov noted that the Cathedral of the Annunciation had taken several artillery hits during the fighting, particularly along the southeast wall "where the large shrine with fragments of holy relics is housed." GARF, f. R-3431, op. 1, d. 563, ll. 150–51.

36. M. Ia. Latsis, *Dva goda bor'by na vnutrennem fronte* (Moscow, 1920), 48.

37. Vvedenskii, *Tserkov' i gosudarstvo*, 228–29.

38. Plaksin, *Krakh tserkovnoi kontrrevoliutsii*, 167–68.

39. Peter Kenez, *Civil War in South Russia, 1919–1920* (Berkeley and Los Angeles, 1977), 78–79.

40. Plaksin, *Krakh tserkovnoi kontrrevoliutsii*, 97.

41. Ibid., 111–12. The following year the archbishop called upon the faithful of his diocese to accept Soviet rule and work peaceably to rebuild Russia in the wake of the Civil War. See Sil'vestr's pastoral letter of 14 January 1920, reprinted in *Russkaia pravoslavnaia tserkov' i kommunisticheskoe gosudarstvo, 1917–1941 gg.: Dokumenty i fotomaterialy* (Moscow, 1996), 46–47.

42. Archpriest Sergii Shchukin, *O "volkakh v ovech'ei shkure"* (Rostov-na-Donu, 1919), 11, in GARF, f. A-353, op. 2, d. 717, l. 45.

43. Plaksin, *Krakh tserkovnoi kontrrevoliutsii*, 167; Belov, *Pravda o pravoslavnykh "sviatykh"*, 137. The special liturgical service commissioned in Iosif's honor in conjunction with his May 1918 canonization mentions the metropolitan's death at the hands of "lawless evildoers," "mutineers," and "brigands." RGIA, f. 831, op. 1, d. 82, ll. 1–1ob., 12–25.

44. "Akafisty sv. ugodnikam, tsarskim chernosotennym ottsam Denikinu i Kolchaku," *Belevskii proletarii*, no. 63/89 (24 August 1919): 2.

45. For the text of the separation decree, with a history of the events leading up to its composition and promulgation, see M. M. Persits, *Otdelenie tserkvi ot gosudarstva i shkoly ot tserkvi v SSSR (1917–1919 gg.)* (Moscow, 1958), 98–109.

46. As per Narkomiust's supplementary decree of 24 August 1918. The Narkomiust archives contain hundreds of inventories, often with signed agreements contracting for the use of liturgical property. See, for example, the inventory of the Uspenskii-Trifonov monastery (Viatka Province) and the accompanying *dogovor* in GARF, f. A-353, op. 4, d. 408, ll. 391–401.

47. A typical informational brochure is Ia. M. Burov, *Chto oznachaet zakon o svobode sovesti i otdelenii tserkvi ot gosudarstva? (Podrobnoe, postateinoe rasmotrenie dekreta o svobode sovesti s prilozheniem samogo dekreta)* (Moscow, 1918).

48. GARF, f. A-353, op. 2, d. 691, l. 254 (Galkin to VIII Section of Narkomiust, undated but no earlier than December 1918). Mikhail Vladimirovich Galkin (? –1948), the son of a Petersburg priest, was exiled to Ufa in 1906 for revolutionary activities. Upon his graduation from the history faculty of St. Petersburg University in 1913, Galkin remained in the capital and became a parish priest at the Spaso-Preobrazhenskaia church. After the October Revolution, Galkin, who had a reputation for reformist views, was named by V. D. Bonch-Bruevich to the five-man commission that drafted the January 1918 decree on the separation of Church and state. His work on the commission brought him into contact with P. A. Krasikov, whom he came to work under at the VIII Section in the summer of 1918. Throughout that year, Galkin traveled extensively throughout the northwest provinces in the capacity of a "religious expert," reporting to Moscow on the implementation of the separation decree in the localities. Galkin defrocked himself in late 1918 and joined the Communist Party the following year. Writing under the pen name of Gorev, he contributed many articles for the antireligious press, authored several pamphlets and brochures, and was present at several relic exhumations, including that of Saint Sergii Radonezhskii on 11 April 1919. The most complete biographical information on Galkin may be found in Daniel Peris, "Commissars in Red Cassocks: Former Priests in the League of the Militant Godless," *Slavic Review* 54 (1995): 345–48. See also "'Tserkov' otdeliaetsia ot gosudarstva': Doklady eksperta Narkomiusta M. V. Galkina, 1918 g." (Part I), *Istoricheskii arkhiv*, no. 6 (1993): 162–70; and Hedda, *His Kingdom Come*, 194.

49. B. V. Titlinov, *Tserkov' vo vremia revoliutsii* (Petrograd, 1924), 150. On the problems of implementing the decree during the Civil War, see also Persits, *Otdelenie tserkvi ot gosudarstva*, 110–30; N. P. Krasnikov, "Velikaia Oktiabr'skaia sotsialisticheskaia revoliutsiia i provozglashenie svobody sovesti," in *Po etapam razvitiia ateizma v SSSR* (Leningrad, 1967), 7–21; M. L. Neitman, "Iz istorii provedeniia v zhizn' Leninskogo dekreta ob otdelenii tserkvi ot gosudarstva i shkoly ot tserkvi (1918–1920 gg.)," in *Zabaikal'skii kraevedcheskii ezhegodnik*, no. 2 (Chita, 1968), 46–61; M. I. Odintsov, *Gosudarstvo i tserkov' (Istoriia vzaimootnoshenii. 1917–1938 gg.)* (Moscow, 1991), 13–18; and Mikhail V. Shkarovskii, *Peterburgskaia eparkhiia v gody gonenii i utrat, 1917–1945* (St. Petersburg, 1995), 41.

50. GARF, f. A-353, op. 3, d. 757, ll. 26–26ob. (Novgorod gubispolkom to VIII Section, received 6 August 1919). The handbook, published as *Polozhenie ob otdelenii tserkvi ot gosudarstva* (Novgorod, n.d.), is housed in ibid., ll. 289–300.

51. Ibid., ll. 101–101ob. (Kuprianov, director of the Novgorod gubispolkom department of justice, to VIII Section, 3 January 1920).

52. A. N. Evstratova and G. G. Bril', "Sovetskaia vlast' i dukhovenstvo: K voprosu o vzaimootnosheniiakh v 1917–nachale 20-x godov (Na materialakh Verkhnego Povolzh'ia)," in *Intelligentsiia, provintsiia, otechestvo: Problemy istorii, kul'tury, politiki* (Ivanovo, 1996), 326–27.

53. Priest Valentin Sventsitskii, *Voina i tserkov'* (Rostov-na-Donu, 1919), 10, in the collection of émigré and White Guardist pamphlets at the State Public Historical Library (GPIB) in Moscow (emphasis in original). Some sense of the religiously inflected rhetoric of the White movement, often anti-Semitic and always inflammatory, may be assessed from the large collection of broadsheets and pamphlets in GARF, f. A-353, op. 2, d. 717.

54. "O meropriiatiiakh po okhrane tserkvei i sviashchennykh predmetov," in RGIA, f. 831, op. 1, d. 71, ll. 2–3.

55. GARF, f. R-3431, op. 1, d. 564, ll. 13–15ob. (report of Archpriests P. N. Lak-

hostskii and G. I. Bulgakov to the Church Sobor, 26 March/10 April 1918).

56. For examples of parish opposition to the separation decree, see "Ot Pravleniia Moskovskoi dukhovnoi seminarii," *Moskovskiia tserkovnyia vedomosti*, no. 4 (1–14 March 1918): 3–4; "Postanovlenie," *Arkhangel'skiia eparkhial'nyia vedomosti*, no. 8 (2/15 May 1918): 2; and "Rezoliutsiia obshchago sobraniia prikhodskoi obshchiny Petrozavodskago kafedral'nago sobora 24 (11) fevralia 1918 g.," *Olonetskiia eparkhial'nyia vedomosti*, no. 5–6 (1–15 March 1918): 40–42. This latter resolution was signed by 1,500 Orthodox believers in Petrozavodsk.

57. The brotherhood's charters and mission statements are in GARF, f. R-4652, op. 1, d. 1, ll. 170–170ob.; and RGIA, f. 796, op. 445, d. 350, ll. 13–18ob.

58. GARF, f. R-3431, op. 1, d. 563, ll. 132–132ob. (report of Archpriest N. Liubimov to the Holy Synod).

59. "Vozzvanie Pomestnago Sobora po povodu dekreta o svobode sovesti," *Arkhangel'skiia eparkhial'nyia vedomosti*, no. 6 (2/15 April 1918): 1.

60. See Archpriest F. N. Ornatskii's report to the Church Sobor, 22 January 1918, as quoted in Vvedenskii, *Tserkov' i gosudarstvo*, 170–76.

61. Ibid., 124–25.

62. Tikhon's anathema against the Bolsheviks is reprinted in *The Russian Revolution and Religion: A Collection of Documents concerning the Suppression of Religion by the Communists, 1917–1925*, ed. and trans. Boleslaw Szczesniak (Notre Dame, 1959), 36–37. Petitions against the attempted seizure of the Lavra were drafted and signed in many dioceses. In Arkhangel'sk, for example, activists managed to secure 3,000 signatures in protest. See "Sekvestr Aleksandro-Nevskoi lavry," *Arkhangel'skiia eparkhial'nyia vedomosti*, no. 2 (1 February 1918): 52–53; and V. Bakhmet'ev, "Gonenie na Tserkov'," *Vestnik tserkovnago edineniia*, no. 9 (28 February 1918): 1–2.

63. GARF, f. R-3431, op. 1, d. 563, ll. 35–39 (report of Archbishop Tikhon of Voronezh to Patriarch Tikhon, 5/18 February 1918). See also "Vsenarodnoe molenie" and "V Mitrofanskom monastyre," *Vestnik tserkovnago edineniia*, no. 9 (28 January 1918): 3; and "Krestnyi khod v Mitrofanskom monastyre," in the following issue, no. 10 (1 February 1918): 3.

64. GARF, f. R-3431, op. 1, d. 563, ll. 35–39 (report of Archbishop Tikhon of Voronezh to Patriarch Tikhon, 5/18 February 1918).

65. Ibid.

Chapter Five: Toppling the Saints from Their Thrones

1. V. I. Lenin, "Doklad o bor'be s golodom" (4 June 1918), in Eric Naiman, *Sex in Public: The Incarnation of Early Soviet Ideology* (Princeton, 1999), 160. The quotation in the title is from Titlinov, *Tserkov' vo vremia revoliutsii*, 175.

2. Boris Pilnyak, *The Naked Year*, trans. Alexander R. Tulloch (Ann Arbor, 1975), 74–75.

3. Ibid., 75.

4. Donald J. Raleigh, *Experiencing Russia's Civil War: Politics, Society, and Revolutionary Culture in Saratov, 1917–1922* (Princeton, 2002).

5. See Narkomiust's 25 August 1920 circular in P. V. Gidulianov, *Otdelenie tserkvi ot gosudarstva. Sistematizirovannyi sbornik deistvuiushchego v SSSR zakonodatel'stva*, 3rd ed. (Moscow, 1926), 69.

6. See, for example, N. Blinov, *Popy i interventsiia na severe* (Arkhangel'sk, 1930).

7. GARF, f. A-353, op. 2, d. 719, ll. 23–25 (letter from G. P. Enokhov to *Revoliutsiia i tserkov'*, received 4 February 1919).

8. Szczesniak, *Russian Revolution and Religion*, 40–48; P. V. Gidulianov, *Tserkov'*

i gosudarstvo po zakonodatel'stvu R.S.F.S.R.: Sbornik uzakonenii i rasporiazhenii s raz"iasneniiami V Otdela NKIu (Moscow, 1923), 14.

9. "'Tserkov' otdeliaetsia ot gosudarstva': Doklady eksperta Narkomiusta M. V. Galkina, 1918 g." (Part II), *Istoricheskii arkhiv*, no. 1 (1994): 137.

10. GARF, f. A-353, op. 3, d. 731, ll. 63–65ob. Similar outrages were reported during the search of the Spaso-Preobrazhenskii monastery in Staraia Rus on 2 December 1918. According to a report heard by Patriarch Tikhon and the Supreme Church Council, soldiers and commissars "dug around for holy relic fragments in the shrine," manhandled some clerical vestments, and threw a heavy glass bottle at an icon of the Mother of God; the icon sustained a "deep scratch" but the relic fragments were said to be unharmed, despite their rough treatment. RGIA, f. 831, op. 1, d. 23, ll. 7–13ob.

11. GARF, f. A-353, op. 3, d. 731, ll. 63–65ob. Bishop Ioannikii's report of the incident to Patriarch Tikhon is found in ibid., op. 4, d. 383, ll. 69–69ob.

12. Kurskii, "Tsirkuliar," 66; Krasikov, "Otchet," 105; P. Bliakhin, *Kak popy durmaniat narod!* (Petrograd, 1920), 36. The monks' report makes no mention of the condition of Aleksandr Svirskii's relics.

13. Titlinov, *Tserkov' vo vremia revoliutsii*, 175; Julius F. Hecker, *Religion under the Soviets* (New York, 1927), 76–77.

14. GARF, f. A-353, op. 4, d. 380, l. 62ob. (Olonets Cheka to Olonets gubispolkom, copy, no earlier than 4 February 1919).

15. See Galkin's 29 November 1918 report to Narkomiust following his visitation tour of Olonets and Petrozavodsk provinces in "Tserkov' otdeliaetsia ot gosudarstva" (Part II), 137–38.

16. Ibid., 138. The expurgated text appeared as "Rezoliutsiia," *Golos trudovogo krest'ianstva*, no. 280 (26 November 1918): 2. On the discursive style of popularly authored resolutions, see the discussion in Ekaterina Betekhina, "Afterword: Style in Lower-Class Writing in 1917," in Mark D. Steinberg, *Voices of Revolution, 1917* (New Haven, 2001), 309–38.

17. Statements invoking the similarities between the socialist mission and the gospel ideals of harmony and equality are commonly encountered both in prerevolutionary radical texts and the early Soviet press, particularly in the provinces. For examples from the Central Black Earth region, see V. D. Orlova, "Massovye politicheskie prazdnestva 1917–1918 godov v guberniiakh chernozemnogo tsentra," in *Obshchestvenno-politicheskaia zhizn' rossiiskoi provintsii, XX vek*, vyp. 1 (Tambov, 1993), 28–32. On the poetics of Russian revolutionary-religious imagery, see Mark D. Steinberg, *Proletarian Imagination: Self, Modernity, and the Sacred in Russia, 1910–1925* (Ithaca, 2002); Jay Bergman, "The Image of Jesus in the Russian Revolutionary Movement: The Case of Russian Marxism," *International Review of Social History* 35 (1990): 220–48.

18. Gorev, "Tikhona Zadonskogo," 65; "O moshchakh netlennykh, bol'shevikakh, derznovennykh i krest'ianakh udivlennykh," *Golos pravdy*, no. 1 (2 January 1919): 3.

19. Gorev, "Tikhona Zadonskogo," 65–66, 95 (emphasis in original).

20. Ibid., 95. As a former priest and present party member, Gorev could not have been unaware of the dual reverberations of this phrase. In the New Testament, the words are spoken by Jesus to chide a young man who says he must see to his father's funeral before he can follow Christ (cf. Matthew 8:21–23 and Luke 9:59–61). Marx stripped the words of their scriptural context and used them most famously in the opening chapter of his *Eighteenth Brumaire of Louis Bonaparte* (1852): "The social revolution of the nineteenth century cannot take its poetry from the past but only from the future. It cannot begin with itself before it has stripped away all superstition about the past. The former revolutions required recollections of past world history in order to smother their own content. The revolution of the nineteenth century must *let the dead bury their dead* in order to arrive at its own content." *The Marx-Engels Reader*, ed.

Robert C. Tucker, 2nd ed. (London and New York, 1978), 597. In a 1914 polemic against Kautsky and again on the eve of October, Lenin also used the phrase to make the point that historical events had overtaken the now obsolete Second International. Insofar as he used it to suggest that the dawn of a new age requires the dismantling and burial of outmoded symbols, values, and institutions, Gorev's invocation of the phrase may be said to owe more to Marx and Lenin than to Christ. For Lenin's use of the phrase, see "Dead Chauvinism and Living Socialism: How the International Can Be Restored" (1914) and "The Tasks of the Proletariat in Our Revolution" (1917) in V. I. Lenin, *Collected Works*, 4th ed., 45 vols. (Moscow, 1974), 21:94–101, 24:55–91.

21. "Tablitsa vskrytii 'moshchei,' proizvedennykh po pochinu trudiashchikhsia v predelakh Sovetskoi Rossii v 1918, 1919 i 1920 g.g.," in GARF, f. A-353, op. 4, d. 379, l. 4.

22. *Golos pravdy*, no. 19 (15 February 1919): 1–2.

23. F. Ovchinnikov, "Otkroite glaza narodu," *Zvezda*, no. 53 (20 February 1919): 4.

24. V. L., "Vekovoi obman," *Izvestiia* (Murom), no. 15/112 (11 February 1919): 1. The "three-and-a-half" saints mentioned are Konstantin, his sons Mikhail and Feodor, and their mother Irina, whose disembodied head was found inside the shrine in a "decorative bundled sack of green silk." See "Osmotr 'moshchei' v gor. Murome," *Izvestiia* (Vladimir), no. 34/194 (14 February 1919): 1. The insidious link between Orthodox ritual and infectious disease would become a common trope in subsequent antireligious propaganda. Notable examples include M. F., "Narodnye sueveriia i detskie bolezni," *Bezbozhnik u stanka*, no. 6 (1924): 19; N. Semashko, "Sifilis i tserkovnye obychai," *Nash bezbozhnik*, no. 5–6 (17 May 1924): 6; and "Ne khristosusia!" *Nash bezbozhnik*, no. 7 (18 April 1925): 2.

25. A. Sheenkov, "Dukhovnaia podlost'," *Golos pravdy*, no. 19 (15 February 1919): 1.

26. On the origins of the cult of Saint Artemii (canonized in 1640), see Levin, "From Corpse to Cult," 87–89, 94, 98. For the contents of Artemii's shrine see Dolginov, "'Sviatye' moshchi i blagochestivaia spekuliatsiia," 41.

27. I. V. Liukov, *Taina serebrianoi grobnitsy* (Lipetsk, 1963), 22–23; and *Revoliutsiia i tserkov'*, no. 9–12 (1920): 76. Black-and-white photographs from Saint Tikhon's exhumation appeared in *Revoliutsiia i tserkov'*, no. 2 (1919): 11–17.

28. *Bezbozhnik u stanka*, no. 4 (April 1923): 14. Bliakhin archly suggested that the brooch had been a lover's gift to the young monk in charge of the shrine's upkeep and maintenance, which token the monk had accidentally dropped into the coffin while checking on the saint's remains. See P. Bliakhin, *Doloi chertei, doloi bogov, doloi monakhov i popov!* 2nd ed. (Odessa, 1920), 25.

29. M. Gorev, "Pod spudom," *Revoliutsiia i tserkov'*, no. 3–5 (1919): 28–32; N. Meshcheriakov, *Popovskie prodelki* (Samara, 1919), 17. Similarly, the exhumation of Saint Nikodim Kozheozerskii's crypt in Onezhskii district, Arkhangel'sk Province, on 19 March 1919 failed to discover any traces of the saint's relics whatsoever. GARF, f. A-353, op. 4, d. 380, ll. 44–44ob. Orthodox custom dictated that churchyard graves be dug to a depth of three arshins (approximately seven feet). See Tresviatskii, *Kalendar' sviashchennika*, 107.

30. M. Zhakov, "Dva Makariia," *Bezbozhnik u stanka*, no. 5 (May 1923): 15; V. Zhekulin, "Kak tvoriat chudesa," in *Molodym bezbozhnikam: Materialy k komsomol'skomu rozhdestvu* (Moscow, 1924), 101–2. The Kaliazinskii district ispolkom mailed a "parcel with items found in [Makarii's] coffin" to the VIII Section's Moscow offices in April 1919; the present whereabouts of the dried pears and beads are unknown. See the correspondence in GARF, f. A-353, op. 3, d. 749, ll. 3–4.

31. "Vskrytie moshchei 'prepodobnogo' Nila Stolobenskogo," *Krasnyi Ves'egonsk*, no. 8/21 (16 March 1919): 4.

32. See the coverage in *Sovetskaia gazeta* for the end of January 1919.

33. *Golos pravdy*, no. 19 (15 February 1919): 1.

34. Andrei Rublev, "O moshchakh i prochikh veshchakh," *Izvestiia* (Vladimir), no. 38/198 (19 February 1919): 2.

35. I. Zavadskii, "Velikii sharlatan," ibid., no. 42/202 (23 February 1919): 3. The official protocols of Saint Avraamii's exhumation were published as "Osmotr Devich'ego monastyria v g. Vladimire," in ibid., no. 33/193 (13 February 1919): 1. The medical examiners observed "no sign of trauma damage" to the skull, a finding inconsistent with the fact that Avraamii is said to have died a martyr's death at the hands of the Kama Bolgars.

36. "Gor'kim smekhom moim posmeiusia," ibid., no. 34/194 (14 February 1919): 1.

37. K. Kuznetsov, "Paki i paki o moshchakh," *Golos pravdy*, no. 21 (20 February 1919): 2.

38. A. Sheenkov, "Neuzheli ustupim?" ibid., no. 20 (18 February 1919): 2–3.

39. Kin., "O moshchakh netlennykh," *Izvestiia* (Vladimir), no. 23/183 (1 February 1919): 2. Following the discovery of Tutankhamen's tomb in 1922, invidious comparisons between well-preserved Egyptian mummies and less impressive Orthodox relics became more common in the antireligious press. See, for example, "Faraon v grobu," *Bezbozhnik*, no. 11 (June 1926): 13; V. G. Bogoraz-Tan, *Khristianstvo v svete etnografii* (Moscow, 1928), 100.

40. M. Boldyrev, "Vtoroe otkrytie 'moshchei' Tikhona," *Sovetskaia gazeta*, no. 11/107 (2 February 1919): 1. Boldyrev's final peroration is a reference to Christ's casting the moneychangers from the temple in Jerusalem (Matthew 21:12, Mark 11:15), implying that the Orthodox clergy was occupied more with mercenary interests than spiritual concerns. The image of unscrupulous clerics "pulling the wool over the eyes of the faithful" and lining their "deep pockets" with the laborers' "last pennies" (or in some versions, "sweaty" or "blood-stained" pennies) was a trope often repeated over the course of the relic campaign. See, for example, I. Lomakin, *Moshchi* (Moscow, 1919), 8–12.

41. Public debates on religious questions were common during the early years of Soviet power; the most famous contests of this period featured such celebrity participants as People's Commissar of Enlightenment A. V. Lunacharskii versus the Renovationist cleric A. V. Vvedenskii. The popularity of public debates as a method of antireligious education waned during the latter half of the 1920s, however, when it became clear that clerics were more or less consistently trouncing their Bolshevik opponents. In 1926, a prolific antireligious publicist called for an end to such debates on the grounds that "the priests know the texts of the gospels better than ninety-nine out of a hundred antireligionists, and in response to one text they will cite dozens of others." See Vl. Sarab'ianov, *Ob antireligioznoi propagande*, 3rd ed. (Moscow, 1926), 65.

42. G. Turkin, "Pis'mo Vladimirskomu dukhovenstvu," *Izvestiia* (Vladimir), no. 38/198 (19 February 1919): 2.

43. Gorev, "Tikhona Zadonskogo," 91–92.

44. GARF, f. A-353, op. 3, d. 737, ll. 230–230ob. (notes of a 21 October 1920 debate in Borovichi canton, Novgorod Province); and op. 4, d. 378, l. 3 (notes of a December 1920 debate in Kresets, Novgorod Province).

45. Gorev, "Pod spudom," 100. For a more skeptical assessment of the success that such debates enjoyed in rural localities, see Young, *Power and the Sacred*, ch. 2.

46. *Revoliutsiia i tserkov'*, no. 9–12 (1920): 82.

47. "Rezoliutsiia," *Golos pravdy*, no. 21 (20 February 1919): 3.

48. Accounts of the 1920 trials are given in "Sudebnye protsessy o poddelke moshchei," in Rozhitsyn, *Moshchi*, 124–67. See also "Delo ob"edinennogo Soveta prikhodov Moskvy" and "Protsess Griaznova," *Revoliutsiia i tserkov'*, no. 9–12 (1920): 89–91, 92; and the discussion in Wynot, *Keeping the Faith*, 43–45.

49. Elizabeth A. Wood, *Performing Justice: Agitation Trials in Early Soviet Russia*

(Ithaca, 2005); Julie A. Cassiday, *The Enemy on Trial: Early Soviet Courts on Stage and Screen* (DeKalb, 2000).

50. GARF, f. A-353, op. 4, d. 378, l. 6ob. (annual report for 1920 from the Novgorod Province church liquidation section to Krasikov).

51. Six Novgorod clerics (five monks and an archpriest) were charged along with Aleksii. See the trial transcripts in Mikhail Gorev, "Tserkovniki i ikh agenty pered narodnym revoliutsionnym sudom," *Revoliutsiia i tserkov'*, no. 9–12 (1920): 52.

52. GARF, f. A-353, op. 3, d. 757, ll. 241–241ob.

53. Gorev, "Tserkovniki i ikh agenty," 46, 48.

54. Titlinov, *Tserkov' vo vremia revoliutsii*, 178.

55. Gorev, "Tserkovniki i ikh agenty," 53. Bishop Aleksii (Simanskii) became patriarch of the Russian Orthodox Church in January 1945, a position he held until his death in 1970.

56. GARF, f. A-353, op. 4, d. 378, l. 6ob.

57. Gorev, "Pod spudom," 28–32.

58. Krasikov also served as chief prosecutor for the Supreme Court of the USSR (1924–1933) and chairman of the All-Russian Executive Committee's Standing Commission on Religious Cult Questions (1929–1938); as deputy chairman of the Supreme Court (1933–1938) he participated in the drafting of the Soviet Constitution of 1936. Krasikov survived the Great Purges and died of natural causes in 1939. In a eulogy published in *Bezbozhnik*, Emel'ian Iaroslavskii described Krasikov as "a dear friend, a good Bolshevik, and a mighty opponent of religion . . . who put all his energy into the construction of a new classless, religion-less society." E. M. Iaroslavskii, "Pamiati P. A. Krasikova" (1 September 1939), in E. M. Iaroslavskii, *O religii* (Moscow, 1957), 318. See also Peris, "Commissars in Red Cassocks"; A. M. Gindin and G. M. Gindin, *S Leninym v serdtse: Zhizn' Petra Krasikova* (Moscow, 1968); A. M. Gindin and G. M. Gindin, *Petr Krasikov: Zhizn' i revoliutsionnaia deiatel'nost'* (Krasnoiarsk, 1972).

59. P. A. Krasikov, "Sovetskaia politika v religioznom voprose" (1919), in *Izbrannye ateisticheskie proizvedeniia*, 17–18.

60. "Praktika antireligioznoi bor'by," *Revoliutsiia i tserkov'*, no. 1 (1919): 11.

61. A succinct discourse on the nature of this "religious haze" and the social ills which were believed to follow in its wake is V. D. Bonch-Bruevich's 31 March 1919 letter to Father Leonid Feodorov, Catholic exarch to Russia. See "Iz pis'ma sviashchenniku," in V. D. Bonch-Bruevich, *Izbrannye ateisticheskie proizvedeniia* (Moscow, 1971), 307–11.

62. P. A. Krasikov, "Religiia i kommunizm," in *Izbrannye ateisticheskie proizvedeniia*, 33.

63. P. A. Krasikov, "Sovetskaia politika v religioznom voprose," ibid., 17–18.

64. For classic Bolshevik expositions of this argument, see A. V. Lunacharskii, *Pochemu nel'zia verit' v boga? Izbrannye ateisticheskie proizvedeniia* (Moscow, 1965); and I. I. Skvortsov-Stepanov, *Izbrannye ateisticheskie proizvedeniia* (Moscow, 1959).

65. P. A. Krasikov, "Komu eto vygodno?" *Izvestiia VTsIK* (4 December 1919); reprinted in Krasikov, *Izbrannye ateisticheskie proizvedeniia*, 56.

66. Krasikov cited in Alekseev, *Illiuzii i dogmy*, 132.

67. *Russkaia pravoslavnaia tserkov' i kommunisticheskoe gosudarstvo*, 36.

68. Bonch-Bruevich cited in Plaksin, *Krakh tserkovnoi kontrrevoliutsii*, 172–73.

69. N. Bukharin and E. Preobrazhensky, *The ABC of Communism: A Popular Explanation of the Program of the Communist Party of Russia* (Ann Arbor, 1988), 255.

70. Iaroslavskii, "12 funtov sibirskikh moshchei," 30–31.

71. GARF, f. A-353, op. 3, d. 841, ll. 34–34ob. (protocols of the 14 February 1919 session of the Narkomiust collegium).

72. Ibid., op. 2, d. 690, ll. 22–22ob. (VIII Section Protocol No. 369, 1 March 1919), as published in *Revoliutsiia i tserkov'*, no. 1 (1919): 42.

73. "O provedenii dekreta ob otdelenii tserkvi ot gosudarstva," in Gidulianov, *Otdelenie tserkvi ot gosudarstva*, 70.

74. On the leading role played by these two bodies in the conduct of early Soviet antireligious policy, see Arto Luukkanen, *The Party of Unbelief: The Religious Policy of the Bolshevik Party, 1917–1929* (Helsinki, 1994), 64–68.

75. VIII Section Protocol No. 389 (5 March 1919), in *Revoliutsiia i tserkov'*, no. 1 (1919): 42. Entrusting the implementation of relic policy to local officials was largely a pragmatic policy decision, allowing Narkomiust's chronically understaffed offices to devote more time, money, and manpower to the multiple responsibilities that fell under the purview of their commissariat. Given that the VIII Section in 1918 accounted for a mere 3.6 percent of all Narkomiust personnel, and that a shocking 43.2 percent of the commissariat staff were diagnosed in "weak" health, it is not surprising that Justice officials would be eager to conserve their already meager resources. See Vitalii Nikolaevich Sadkov, "Narkomat iustitsii RSFSR i sovetskoe zakonodatel'stvo (1917–1922 gody)" (Doktor ist. nauk. diss., Rossiiskii gosudarstvennyi gumanitarnyi universitet, 1996), 195–98.

76. *Revoliutsiia i tserkov'*, no. 1 (1919): 51.

77. Narkomiust Directive No. 616 (23 May 1919), in *Revoliutsiia i tserkov'*, no. 2 (1919): 44; and *Revoliutsiia i tserkov'*, no. 6–8 (1919): 117.

78. VIII Section Protocol No. 369 (1 March 1919), in *Revoliutsiia i tserkov'*, no. 1 (1919): 42. See also the undated NKVD circular on the conduct of exhumations addressed to all provincial and city ispolkoms in *Trudovaia nedelia*, no. 15/38 (7 April 1919): 4–5.

79. In the last years of the relic campaign it was not uncommon for a half dozen medical experts and scientists to be in attendance during an exhumation. An archaeologist was called in to witness the exhumation of Saint Evfrosiniia Polotskaia on 13 May 1922, and officials from the People's Commissariat of Health participated in the forensic examination of the Catholic martyr Saint Andrei Bobola on 23 June 1922. The archaeologist, Deinis, was unimpressed with the condition of Evfrosiniia's relics, claiming to have studied Egyptian mummies that were much better preserved. See "Akty o vskrytii t.-n. moshchei katolicheskogo sviatogo Andreia Boboli," and "Vskrytie moshchei Evrosinii Polotskoi," in *Revoliutsiia i tserkov'*, no. 1–2 (1924): 90–94, and 94–95.

80. As per VIII Section Protocol No. 369, in *Revoliutsiia i tserkov'*, no. 1 (1919): 42. The motion was enthusiastically endorsed by provincial authorities. See V. M. Marasanova, "Izmenenie otnoshenii tserkvi i gosudarstva ot grazhdanskoi k Velikoi Otechestvennoi Voine (na materialakh Volgo-Viatskogo i Iaroslavskogo kraia)," in *Religiia i tserkov' v kul'turno-istoricheskom razvitii Russkogo Severa (k 450-letiiu prepodobnogo Trifona, Viatskogo chudotvortsa)*, 2 vols. (Kirov, 1996), 1:344–48.

81. GARF, f. A-353, op. 3, d. 841, ll. 34–34ob. (Protocol No. 145 of the 14 February 1919 session of the Narkomiust collegium). Security was always an issue with the exhumed relics. For example, the relics exhumed at Novgorod on 3 April 1919 were placed under armed guard for the duration of their public display. In principle, permission from the central offices of the NKVD was required before any relics could be transported to a museum from their original site of exhumation, though it is unclear whether local officials complied with this stipulation. See "Protokol zasedaniia Rasshirennoi Komissii po Otdeleniiu Tserkvi ot Gosudarstva, 3 aprelia 1919 goda," in GARF, f. A-353, op. 3, d. 757, ll. 8–8ob.; and NKVD Circular No. 2456 (23 April 1919), as published in *Russkaia pravoslavnaia tserkov' i kommunisticheskoe gosudarstvo*, 59.

82. VIII Section Protocol No. 369, in *Revoliutsiia i tserkov'*, no. 1 (1919): 42.

83. *Russkaia pravoslavnaia tserkov' i kommunisticheskoe gosudarstvo*, 59. See also Titlinov, *Tserkov' vo vremia revoliutsii*, 176–77; and the NKVD circular of 28 February 1919, reprinted in *Revoliutsiia i tserkov'*, no. 2 (1919): 39.

84. Bukharin and Preobrazhensky, *The ABC of Communism*, 255.
85. Iaroslavskii, "12 funtov sibirskikh moshchei," 31.
86. VIII Section Protocol No. 369, in *Revoliutsiia i tserkov'*, no. 1 (1919): 42.
87. Bliakhin, *Kak popy durmaniat narod!* 29–30.
88. Krasikov, "Otchet," 111.
89. On the wartime mentality of early Soviet officials, see E. G. Gimpel'son, "Sovetskie upravlentsy: Politicheskii i nravstvennyi oblik (1917–1920 gg.)," *Otechestvennaia istoriia*, no. 5 (1997): 44–54.
90. Titlinov, *Tserkov' vo vremia revoliutsii*, 178.
91. Krasikov, "Otchet," 111–12.
92. "Tablitsa vskrytii 'moshchei,'" in GARF, f. A-353, op. 4, d. 379, l. 4.
93. Salat, "Kukla Tikhona v monastyre," *Sovetskaia gazeta*, no. 9/105 (31 January 1919): 1–2. This piece was reprinted in pamphlet form soon after the exhumation; the first edition numbered a thousand copies. See *Kukla Tikhona v Zadonskom monastyre* (Zadonsk, n.d.).
94. N. Semashko, "Vopros o 'moshchakh' s nauchno-meditsinskoi tochki zreniia," *Revoliutsiia i tserkov'*, no. 1 (1919): 16–17.
95. P. Semenovskii, "Dannye nauki o mumifikatsii trupov," *Revoliutsiia i tserkov'*, no. 9–12 (1920): 44. Semenovskii was one of three experts called in by the Moscow militia to examine the exhumed relics of the martyred boy saint Gavriil, from St. Basil's Cathedral on Red Square. Semenovskii and company confirmed that the remains in question were human, but that it was impossible to determine their age or provenance: "Bones or parts of bones are very easy to obtain, for example, from technicians in an anatomy lecture hall, during the razing of old gravesites, the restoration of old buildings, etc." GARF, f. A-353, op. 3, d. 739, ll. 58–59 (report of the forensic committee, 3 December 1919).
96. Semenovskii, "Dannye nauki," 36.
97. Paozerskii, *Russkie sviatye pred sudom istorii*, 67.
98. Semashko, "Vopros o 'moshchakh,'" 17. Semashko's prediction proved correct; thirty-three mummified relics and fourteen "partly mummified" relics were discovered after a 1922 investigation of the catacombs. See M. Z. Petrenko, *Pravda pro pechery i moshchi Kyïvs'koï lavry* (Kiev, 1957), 33–40; P. "Torgovlia moshchami," *Bezbozhnik*, no. 3 (15 February 1932): 16; V. Ginzburg, "Chto predstavliaiut soboiu 'moshchei' byvshei Kievo-Pecherskoi lavry," *Antireligioznik*, no. 7 (1939): 48–50.
99. Iaroslavskii, "12 funtov sibirskikh moshchei," 30–31.
100. Paozerskii, *Russkie sviatye pred sudom istorii*, 68.
101. B. P. Kandidov, "Antireligioznaia agitatsiia v gody grazhdanskoi voiny," *Bezbozhnik*, no. 19–20 (October 1932): unpaginated article.
102. "Vskrytie moshchei Ioasafa Belgorodskogo," *Kurskaia pravda*, no. 270/304 (10 December 1920): 2.
103. GARF, f. A-353, op. 5, d. 252, ll. 5–6ob. (report from Dr. P. S. Semenovskii and Cheka agents Nikitin and Shtukin to the Moscow Cheka, after 21 March 1921). Saint Feodosii's relics did not remain long in Chernigov. By early 1923, the saint's body had been relocated to the Narkomzdrav museum in Moscow, from whence it was taken to Leningrad sometime in the later 1920s. See V. I. Silant'ev, *Bol'sheviki i pravoslavnaia tserkov' na Ukraine v 20-e gody* (Khar'kov, 1998), 130–31. Monks in Tver reportedly gloated that the "kike doctors" were unable to explain why the relics of Saint Arsenii the Miracle-Worker had been preserved. "They spread out their hands in surprise." "Esche 'netlennye moshchi.' Vskrytie 'moshchei' episkopa Arseniia," *Izvestiia* (Tver), no. 114 (28 May 1919): 5.
104. GARF, f. A-353, op. 5, d. 258, l. 37 (letter of 23 August 1921).
105. Ibid., op. 3, d. 731, ll. 55–56 (VIII Section to Archpriest N. A. Liubimov,

16 September 1919). On the "primitive" origins of relic veneration, see Prof. Valentin Rozhitsyn, "Kogda i pochemu poiavilas' vera v moshchi," in *Moshchi*, 3–29; and A. Ranovich, *Proiskhozhdenie khristianskogo kul'ta sviatykh* (Moscow, 1931).

106. GARF, f. A-353, op. 3, d. 841, ll. 34–34ob. (protocol of the 14 February 1919 session of the Narkomiust collegium).

107. I. I. Shangina, "Etnograficheskie muzei Leningrada v pervye gody sovetskoi vlasti (1918–1923 gg.)," *Sovetskaia etnografiia*, no. 5 (1987): 71–80.

108. GARF, f. A-353, op. 2, d. 700, ll. 100–101 (Belevskii district ispolkom to VIII Section, 21 May 1919).

109. Ibid., d. 714, ll. 77–77ob. (Petrograd Province justice department to VIII Section, received 10 February 1921).

110. "Vsem Komissiiam po obsledovaniiu moshchei vo Vladimirskoi gubernii," *Izvestiia* (Vladimir), no. 39/199 (20 February 1919): 1.

111. GARF, f. A-353, op. 3, d. 731, ll. 93–93ob. (protocol of the 5 May 1919 session of the Poshekhonskii-Volodarskii district ispolkom).

112. According to the additions made by the NKVD administrative department to the VIII Section's original instructions on relic exhumations, local officials had three choices of what to do with holy relics: they "may either be left for several days in their new state [that is, exhumed and exposed] for viewing and then afterward returned to their previous location in their previous state; or the 'relics' may be left for good in their previous location and in their unmasked form; or, finally, they may be delivered to a museum or other public building for permanent public viewing." Although this last option was "most desirable," the final decision was left to the discretion of local officials. See GARF, f. A-353, op. 3, d. 731, ll. 35–35ob. (memo of 23 April 1919). These additions were published as a special circular addressed to all provincial Cheka officers in *Vlast' sovetov*, no. 6–7 (1919): 27.

113. Kurskii, "Tsirkuliar NKIu ot 25 avgusta 1920 g.," 69. The earliest drafts of the August decree allowed local officials the option of burying exhumed relics in lieu of placing them on display. Hardliners like VIII Section consultant I. A. Shpitsberg argued that burial was unacceptable: "The interment of the curiosities in question—this is the very method of liquidation that the cult servitors will jump at, and which will once again give [them] the opportunity to exploit the backwards masses out in the sticks [*v glukikh mestakh*] with tales of miracles being performed underground." See GARF, f. A-353, op. 4, d. 379, l. 5 (Shpitsberg to VIII Section, 3 August 1920).

114. GARF, f. A-353, op. 4, d. 379, l. 5.

115. Ibid., d. 381, ll. 4–4ob. (medical examination of Saint Ioasaf's relics by Narkomzdrav personnel with Red Army and Cheka witnesses, 30 December 1920).

116. Ibid., l. 9 (secret telegram from Belgorod administrative department, Kursk Province, to VIII Section, 30 December 1921). See also "Likvidatsiia moshchei Ioasafa Belgorodskogo," *Revoliutsiia i tserkov'*, no. 9–12 (1920): 106.

117. N. Semashko, "Nauka i sharlatanstvo (O vystavke 'moshchei')," *Revoliutsiia i tserkov'*, no. 1–3 (1922): 31. On the exhibit, see René Fülöp-Miller, *The Mind and Face of Bolshevism: An Examination of Cultural Life in Soviet Russia*, rev. ed. (New York, 1965), 186–88.

118. For a brief history of the Narkomzdrav museum, see A. V. Mol'kov, "Gosudarstvennyi Institut sotsial'noi gigieny Narodnogo komissariata zdravookhraneniia," in *Piat' let sovetskoi meditsiny, 1918–1923* (Moscow, 1923), 69–78. The comparison in attendance figures is based on 1924–1925 statistics from the Museum of Antireligious Propaganda in Leningrad. See I. Eliashevich, "Antireligioznaia propaganda v Leningrade (1924–1925 gg.)," *Antireligioznik*, no. 6 (June 1926): 52.

119. Semashko, "Nauka i sharlatanstvo," 32.

120. Ibid.

121. For a thoughtful discussion of the way in which design and structure can shape the museum-goer's experience, see Carol Duncan, *Civilizing Rituals: Inside Public Art Museums* (London, 1995).

122. *Pravoslavnye chudesa v XX veke: Svidetel'stva ochevidtsev* (Moscow, 1993), 95; Rogozianskii, *Strasti po moshcham*, 36–39.

123. Prof. N. A. Flerov, "Netlennye moshchi," *Bezbozhnik*, no. 3 (December 1925): 4–5. Elsewhere in Moscow, museum organizers placed photographs from the exhumation of Saint Feodosii Totemskii alongside the "relics" of a mummified frog. See Fedor Popov, "Razoblachennye chudesa," *Derevenskii bezbozhnik*, no. 11 (10 July 1929): 9. Later, in the 1930s, a more elaborate museum exhibit was designed to debunk holy relics: "A model of a shrine on a pedestal. When a mechanism is activated, the shrine lifts up. Model relics (a dummy) are visible; when a second mechanism is activated, the vestments on the dummy also lift up, revealing the contents, e.g., cotton wool, sawdust, etc." The model, intended for an antireligious exhibit at the Aleksandro-Nevskaia Lavra, appears never to have been constructed. See GARF, f. R-5263, op. 1, d. 1026, l. 24 (Leningrad oblast ispolkom to the VTsIK Standing Commission on Cult Questions, 26 October 1933).

124. Semashko, "Nauka i sharlatanstvo," 31, 30. See also Semashko, "Vopros o 'moshchakh'," 16–17; and Semenovskii, "Dannye nauki," 36–44. These arguments were subsequently incorporated into discussion sections for workers' groups and village reading clubs. See, for example, the course outline and sample discussion questions in I. A. Chikin, *Mogut li byt' netlennye moshchi?* (Briansk, 1926).

125. Semashko, "Nauka i sharlatanstvo," 32.

126. Popov, "Razoblachennye chudesa," 9.

127. F. Kovalev, "Piat' let Tsentral'nogo Antireligioznogo Muzeiia." *Bezbozhnik*, no. 6 (June 1934): 13.

128. A. D., "'Netlennye moshchi' Evfrosinii Polotskoi," *Bezbozhnik*, no. 9 (May 1928): 15. The official protokols from Evfrosiniia's exhumation appeared in *Revoliutsiia i tserkov'*, no. 1–2 (1924): 94–95.

129. "Antireligioznaia vystavka v Vologde," *Antireligioznik*, no. 1 (1928): 80–81.

130. P. K. Lobazov, "Bor'ba partii za ateisticheskoe vospitanie trudiashchikhsia mass v 1917–1925 gg.," in *Obshchestvennye nauki: Materialy konferentsii* (Vladivostok, 1971), 19; V. Listov, "'Sviatye moshchi' na ekrane," *Nauka i zhizn'*, no. 10 (1965): 46.

131. E. S. Gromov, *Lev Vladimirovich Kuleshov* (Moscow, 1984), 68–69; Lev Kuleshov, "50 let v kino," in his *Sobranie sochinenii*, 3 vols. (Moscow, 1988), 2:49–50; and Listov, "Sviatye moshchi," 47–48.

132. A. S. Khoroshev, *Politicheskaia istoriia russkoi kanonizatsii, XI–XVI vv.* (Moscow, 1986), 5 (emphasis in original).

133. V. D. Bonch-Bruevich, "Vladimir Il'ich v pervye gody posle Oktiabria," in *Vospominaniia o Lenine* (Moscow, 1955), 122.

134. GARF, f. A-353, op. 3, d. 732, ll. 21–21ob. (Vladimir Province department of justice to VIII Section, 14 May 1920); ibid., ll. 27–28 (Vladimir Province department of justice to VIII Section, 26 August 1920).

135. Ibid., d. 754, l. 55 (VIII Section to Narkompros Cinematography Commission, 2 June 1919); ibid., d. 736, l. 20.

136. See the expenditure receipts in ibid., d. 736, ll. 20, 35, 37–39, 46–48.

137. In May and June 1919, Narkomiust ordered copies of Tikhon's exhumation film for lectures in Klin and Serpukhov (Moscow Province), the Sokol'niki district of Moscow city, and Tver. See ibid., ll. 18–22, 25–32.

138. Ibid., op. 4, d. 377, l. 80 (Krasikov to Eniseisk gubrevkom department of justice, 11 September 1920).

139. M. Veremienko, "Kakie kartiny dalo Sovkino dlia derevni? (Material na

noiabr' 1925 g.)," in *Kino-iazva: Ob uprazhdeniiakh Sovkino nad derevnei*, ed. V. Meshcheriakov, M. Veremienko, and A. Katsigras (Leningrad, 1926), 20.

140. Mikh[ail] Gorev, "'Moshchi' Sergiia Radonezhskogo," *Krasnaia gazeta*, no. 83 (15 April 1919): 2; Mikh[ail] Gorev, "Vskrytie moshchei Sergiia Radonezhskogo," *Trudovaia nedelia*, no. 17/40 (21 April 1919): 4. The official protocol of Sergii's exhumation notes that the cameras were filming nonstop for one hour and forty minutes, thus shooting not only the actual inspection of the relics but also the preliminary medical examination and the signing of the protocol. But a *samizdat*' memoir written by a former student of the Moscow Theological Academy described the version screened in Sergiev Posad as "unsuccessful" and "very short, show[ing] only those moments prior to the actual exhumation. The rest of the film was not used, as the authorities explained, 'because of the film's poor quality.'" See "Protokol vskrytiia moshchei Sergiia Radonezhskogo 11 aprelia 1919 g.," *Trudovaia nedelia*, no. 18/41 (28 April 1919): 4; and Sergei Volkov, *Poslednie u Troitsy: Vospominaniia o Moskovskoi dukhovnoi akademii (1917–1920)* (Moscow, 1995), 213.

141. "Vystavka snimkov," *Sovetskaia gazeta*, no. 11/107 (2 February 1919): 2. See also R. Rein, "Bolee 200 let obmana," *Voronezhskaia bednota*, no. 23 (31 January 1919): 2.

142. GARF, f. A-353, op. 3, d. 731, l. 47 (VIII Section to Narkompros Cinematography Commission, 2 June 1919).

143. P. A. Krasikov, "Religioznaia khitrost' (Pis'mo v redaktsiiu)," *Revoliutsiia i tserkov'*, no. 2 (1919): 23; A. B., "Religiia i 'netlennye' moshchi," *Krasnaia gazeta*, no. 196 (2 September 1919): 4; and GARF, f. A-353, op. 3, d. 763, l. 19 (Krasikov to Petrograd department of justice, 27 August 1919).

144. P. A. Krasikov, "Zhenshchina, religiia i kommunizm" (1919), in *Izbrannye ateisticheskie proizvedeniia*, 32.

145. Krasikov, "Otchet," 113–14. The Sergiev Posad press also stressed that it was the "old middle-classers, shopkeepers, and kulaks" who were still indignant nearly one full year after the exhumation of Saint Sergii. See A. Mil'rud, "Lavra i Sovetskaia vlast'," *Trudovaia nedelia*, no. 13/88 (30 March 1920): 5–6.

146. Plaksin, *Krakh tserkovnoi kontrrevoliutsii*, 172. Privately, however, Bonch-Bruevich was less sanguine in his assessment of the campaign's merits. His reservations are discussed more fully in the epilogue.

147. Krasikov, "Otchet," 114. On the religious convictions of Red Army soldiers in the 1920s, see Evg. Boltin, "Antireligioznoe vospitanie krasnoarmeitsev," *Antireligioznik*, no. 1 (1928): 60–68.

148. "Krasn-tsy o religii," *Izvestiia* (Tver), no. 68 (28 March 1919): 3; republished as "Krasnoarmeitsy o moshchakh," *Revoliutsiia i tserkov'*, no. 2 (1919): 36. For a sociological analysis of religious belief among Red Cavalry soldiers in the 1920s, see Pastukhov, "Itogi ankety po religioznomu voprosu sredi molodykh krasnoarmeitsev (21-i kavaleriiskii polk 4-i divizii)," *Antireligioznik*, no. 6 (June 1926): 58-59.

149. "K voprosu ob otkrytii moshchei," *Izvestiia* (Tver), no. 84 (17 April 1919): 4; republished as "Pozharnye o moshchakh," *Revoliutsiia i tserkov'*, no. 2 (1919): 36.

150. Krasikov, "Otchet," 113–14.

151. Tovarishch Lelia, "Rezul'taty bespartiinoi gubernskoi konferentsii zhenshchin-rabotnits gor. Vladimira," *Kommunistka*, no. 3–4 (August–September 1920): 32–33. Early Soviet antireligious propaganda imagined women (and peasant women, particularly) to be especially susceptible to religious stupefaction. See Mikhail Gorev, "O zhenshchine i o religioznoi chertovshchine," *Kommunistka*, no. 3-4 (March–April 1923): 6-8; and Vl. Sarab'ianov, "Zhenshchina i religiia," *Bezbozhnik u stanka*, no. 8 (1923): 2.

152. On the working out of Soviet subjectivities on the written page, see Igal Halfin, *From Darkness to Light: Class, Consciousness, and Salvation in Revolutionary Russia* (Pittsburgh, 2000); and Jochen Hellbeck, *Revolution on My Mind: Writing a Diary under*

Stalin (Cambridge, MA, 2006).

153. Iakov Maksimovich Morozov, "Kak teper' postupiat s moshchami Sergiia Radonezhskogo?" *Pravda*, no. 82 (16 April 1919): 2. For the protocols of Sergii's exhumation, see GARF, f. A-353, op. 3, d. 736, ll. 13–16, subsequently republished as "Akt vskrytie t.-n. moshchei Sergiia Radonezhskogo, 11 apr. 1919 g.," in Rozhitsyn, *Moshchi*, 54–56; and "Sviatye chuchela," *Pravda*, no. 82 (16 April 1919): 2.

154. *Revoliutsiia i tserkov'*, no. 9–12 (1920): 74.

155. Bliakhin, *Kak popy durmaniat narod!* 37.

156. On the poetics of antireligious autobiographies, see I. N. Donina, "'Avtobiografii bezbozhnikov' kak vid massovogo istochnika po sotsial'noi psikhologii rubezha 1920–1930-x godov (po materialam rukopisnogo otdela Gosudarstvennogo muzeia istorii religii)," *Klio*, no. 3/6 (1998): 58–66.

157. Zavadskii, "Velikii sharlatan," 3.

158. Gorev, "Vskrytie moshchei Tikhona Zadonskogo," 59.

159. Bliakhin, *Kak popy durmaniat narod!* 29, 39.

CHAPTER SIX: RELICS IN RED RUSSIA

1. Marguerite E. Harrison, *Marooned in Moscow: The Story of an American Woman Imprisoned in Russia* (New York, 1921), 134.

2. Maksim Gor'kii, *O russkom krest'ianstve* (Berlin, 1922), 30.

3. Harrison, *Marooned in Moscow*, 134.

4. Gor'kii, *O russkom krest'ianstve*, 30–31.

5. Keith Thomas, *Religion and the Decline of Magic. Studies in Popular Beliefs in Sixteenth- and Seventeenth-Century England* (New York, 1971), 641.

6. N. Rybakov, "Tolki naroda o Tikhone," *Sovetskaia gazeta*, no. 11/107 (2 February 1919): 2; Gorev, "Vskrytie moshchei Tikhona Zadonskogo," 93; Liukov, *Taina serebrianoi grobnitsy*, 25; and V. F. Martsinkovskii, *Zapiski veruiushchego: Iz istorii religioznogo dvizheniia v Sovetskoi Rossii (1917–1923)* (Prague, 1929), 94.

7. Prisutstvovavshii, "Fanatik," *Belevskii proletarii*, no. 24/50 (26 March 1919): 3. On similar rumors in Vladimir, see Bogatov, *Vladimirskie sviatye*, 43.

8. A. Sh., "Chudo," *Golos pravdy*, no. 19 (15 February 1919): 3.

9. A. Sheenkov, "Monastyri ili fabriki kukol'nykh moshchei?" *Golos pravdy*, no. 20 (18 February 1919): 1.

10. GARF, f. A-353, op. 3, d. 731, l. 37 (petition from residents of Malaia Alekseevskaia Street, Moscow, 26 March 1919).

11. William B. Husband, "Soviet Atheism and Russian Orthodox Strategies of Resistance, 1917–1932," *Journal of Modern History* 70 (1998): 74–107; and William B. Husband, *"Godless Communists": Atheism and Society in Soviet Russia, 1917–1932* (DeKalb, 2000). My own reading of resistance tactics is influenced by James C. Scott, *Domination and the Arts of Resistance: Hidden Transcripts* (New Haven, 1990).

12. Lynne Viola, "Introduction," in *Contending with Stalinism: Soviet Power and Popular Resistance in the 1930s*, ed. Lynne Viola (Ithaca, 2002), 1. See also the thoughtful discussion on the contours of resistance to Soviet policy among non-Orthodox populations in Douglas Northrop, *Veiled Empire: Gender and Power in Stalinist Central Asia* (Ithaca, 2004), 164–208.

13. The unique "language of resistance" exhibited by peasant women protestors in the imperial and Soviet periods is treated in Barbara Alpern Engel, "Women, Men, and the Languages of Peasant Resistance, 1870–1907," in Frank and Steinberg, *Cultures in Flux*, 34–53; and Lynne Viola, "*Bab'i bunty* and Peasant Women's Protest during Collectivization," *Russian Review* 45 (1986): 23–42. See also the prominent—

often violent—role played by rural female Catholics during the French Revolution in Suzanne Desan, *Reclaiming the Sacred: Lay Religion and Popular Politics in Revolutionary France* (Ithaca, 1990), 169–200.

14. Mikhail Gorev, *Troitskaia lavra i Sergii Radonezhskii: Opyt istoriko-kriticheskogo issledovaniia* (Moscow, 1920), 45. Gorev's brochure appeared in a print run of 10,000 copies. See the correspondence between I. A. Shpitsberg and Gosizdat in GARF, f. A-353, op. 5, d. 720, l. 47 (28 January 1920).

15. Volkov, *Poslednie u Troitsy*, 213.

16. GARF, f. A-353, op. 5, d. 252, ll. 5–6ob.

17. V. N. Andreev, "Kak provodilas' podgotovka i vskrytie moshchei v Novgorode," in V. N. Andreev, N. G. Porfiridov, and A. I. Semenov, *Moshchi Sofiiskogo sobora* (Novgorod, 1931), 11.

18. GARF, f. A-353, op. 6, d. 22, l. 163 (report forwarded to the V Section by the Tiumen-Tobol'sk gubotdel upravleniia, 14 November 1922). Despite the clerics' precautions, Ioann's relics were exhumed on 9 October 1922. See the exhumation protocol in ibid., l. 160.

19. M. Iu. Nechaeva, "Verkhoturskie monastyri v XX v.," in *Ezhegodno Bogoslovskaia Konferentsiia Pravoslavnogo Sviato-Tikhonovskogo bogoslovskogo instituta: Materialy, 1999 g.* (Moscow, 1999), 334. Concealing relics to protect them from invaders was a common technique in late antiquity. See John McCulloh, "The Cult of Relics in the Letters and 'Dialogues' of Pope Gregory the Great: A Lexicographical Study," *Traditio* 32 (1976): 151.

20. GARF, f. A-353, op. 4, d. 379, l. 37 (Cheka plenipotentiary Fortunatov to Romanovskii, deputy director of the Secret Section of the Cheka, undated, no earlier than 5 August 1920).

21. GARF, f. A-353, op. 7, d. 17, l. 20 (excerpts from the protocols of the presidium of the Verkhoturskii city ispolkom, 3 September 1924).

22. A. Il'ich, "Okolo 'moshchei,'" *Izvestiia* (Tver), no. 111 (24 May 1919): 1. Fearful of what the crowds might do to them, members of the ispolkom and at least one Jewish woman on the square removed their hats, as well.

23. Gorev, *Troitskaia lavra i Sergii Radonezhskii*, 43.

24. M. Sluchainyi, "Sovershilos'," *Trudovaia nedelia*, no. 19/42 (5 May 1919): 1–2.

25. *Golos pravdy*, no. 19 (15 February 1919): 2.

26. N. M. Georgievskii, "K osmotru 'moshchei,'" *Izvestiia* (Vladimir), no. 37/197 (18 February 1919): 2. Georgievskii wrote another letter to the editor the following week, complaining that his name had been included as one of the signatories to the exhumation protocols of Saints Gleb, Georgii, and Andrei, as published in the Vladimir *Izvestiia* on 23 February. Insofar as he was not at the cathedral on the days in question and thus could not have signed the protocols, Georgievskii asked the newspaper to correct this "probably accidental inaccuracy." See "Pis'mo v redaktsiiu," in ibid., no. 43/203 (25 February 1919): 3.

27. Gorev, "Pod spudom," 98.

28. Salat, "Kukla Tikhona v monastyre," 2.

29. "Osmotr moshchei," *Izvestiia* (Vladimir), no. 46/206 (1 March 1919): 4.

30. "Vskrytie moshchei Evrosinii Polotskoi," 94–95.

31. Andreev, "Kak provodilas' podgotovka i vskrytie moshchei v Novgorode," 5–11. On the life and miracles of Saint Nikita, see Priest An. Konkordin, *Zhitiia sviatykh ugodnikov Bozhiikh, pochivaiushchikh v Sofiiskom sobore v Novgorod*, 2nd ed. (Novgorod, 1902), 9–15.

32. V. Klishko, *Karel'skie "chudotvortsy"* (Petrozavodsk, 1932), 102.

33. Ivan Safonov, "Veriat odni starukhi," *Voronezhskaia bednota* (27 March 1919): 2. An almost identical incident took place two years later in Zadonsk, where

an eleven-year-old blind boy named Pankov was cured by touching the relics of Saint Tikhon Zadonskii. In this instance, however, the boy's neighbors exposed the miracle as a scam. The case went to court, where the boy confessed that he had been induced to feign blindness by a monk who was on friendly terms with the Pankov family. See Iu. Sarkis, *O sviatykh moshchakh, chudotvornykh ikonakh i prochikh popovskikh chudesakh* (Sverdlovsk, 1926), 57.

34. Terence Emmons, ed. and trans., *Time of Troubles: The Diary of Iurii Vladimirovich Got'e. Moscow, July 8, 1917 to July 23, 1922* (Princeton, 1988), 258.

35. Pospielovsky, *Soviet Antireligious Campaigns*, 20.

36. GARF, f. A-353, op. 8, d. 6, ll. 6–6ob. (protocols of the exhumation of Simeon Verkhoturskii, 30 May 1924).

37. A. D. Sirin, "Sviatotattsy. Iz istorii moshchei sviatitelia Innokentiia (Kul'chitskogo)," in *Istoricheskie sud'by pravoslaviia v Sibiri* (Irkutsk, 1997), 98–99. Clerics in Sarov also took issue with the "tendentious protocol" drawn up by the commission to exhume Serafim Sarovskii. GARF, f. A-353, op. 3, d. 766, ll. 28–29ob. (copy of a report from the Dukhovnyi Cathedral to Bishop Pavel, 14/27 December 1920).

38. GARF, f. A-353, op. 3, d. 757, l. 303ob. The bishop's remarks were published in *Novgorodskiia eparkhial'nyia vedomosti*, 1919, no. 3; and in the Novgorod party organ, *Zvezda*. Aleksii's exegesis on the definition of *moshchi* was shouted down by a commission member: "Don't read us a lecture on relics." Patriarch Tikhon made a similar argument that "bones unclad in flesh" were also genuine moshchi in a March 1919 protest to Sovnarkom. See RGIA, f. 831, op. 1, d. 185, ll. 2–2ob.

39. Kuznetsov reiterated his arguments that same year in a letter to Sovnarkom protesting the relic campaign: "Hardly anyone among the faithful adhered to such a ridiculous position [that is, that moshchi must necessarily be uncorrupted bodies]. It is possible only through a complete lack of understanding of the subject and usually by people who are hostile to the Church." GARF, f. A-353, op. 3, d. 744, l. 59ob.

40. "Popy i kosty," *Voronezhskaia bednota*, no. 82 (15 April 1919): 3.

41. GARF, f. A-353, op. 3, d. 789, ll. 40–40ob. (Narkomiust Circular No. 17572/291, 18 May 1920).

42. Ibid., d. 757, ll. 101–101ob. (Novgorod department of justice to VIII Section, 3 January 1920); and Andreev, "Kak provodilas' podgotovka i vskrytie moshchei v Novgorode," 8–9. The Novgorod diocesan paper was shut down by Soviet authorities in 1919, but illegal underground copies continued to appear for a year thereafter. See A. Bovkalo, "Novgorodskaia eparkhiia v 1917–1919 godakh," in *Gde Sviataia Sofiia, tam i Novgorod* (Novgorod, 1997), 152.

43. Semashko, "Nauka i sharlatanstvo," 32.

44. *Pravoslavnye chudesa*, 96.

45. Semashko, "Nauka i sharlatanstvo," 32; *Pravoslavnye chudesa*, 95. The display of the relics of Saint Mitrofan Voronezhskii in the Mitrofanskii monastery in Voronezh elicited a similar show of crossing and pious adoration on the part of old women. See Ivan Safonov, "Veriat odni starukhi," *Voronezhskaia bednota* (27 March 1919): 2.

46. GARF, f. A-353, op. 3, d. 768, l. 6ob. (Vologda Province department of justice to VIII Section, undated, but no earlier than 2 April 1920). See also the petitions submitted by priests and believers in protest of Feodosii's museum display in ibid., ll. 8–9, 11–12ob., 14–15, 19–147.

47. W. P. Coates, *Religion in Tsarist and Soviet Russia* (London, 1930), 27. See also G. P. Fedotov, *The Russian Church since the Revolution* (London, 1928), 44.

48. "Otchet o deiatel'nosti V (likvidatsionnogo) Otdela Narodnogo Komissariata Iustitsii," *Revoliutsiia i tserkov'*, no. 1–3 (1922): 68–69. On the difficulties faced by antireligious lecturers in Moscow during the Civil War years, see Vl. Sarab'ianov, "Beglye vospominaniia," *Antireligioznik*, no. 10 (October 1927): 34–37.

49. *Piat' let Voronezhskogo antireligioznogo muzeia* (Voronezh, 1935), 8.
50. Semashko, "Nauka i sharlatanstvo," 32.
51. On the difficulties of staging antireligious displays, see B. P. Kandidov, *Monastyri-muzei i antireligioznaia propaganda* (Moscow, 1929), 128–48; and M. E. Kaulen, *Muzei-khramy i muzei-monastyri v pervoe desiatiletie Sovetskoi vlasti* (Moscow, 2001).
52. Husband, "Soviet Atheism and Strategies of Resistance," 77, 81, 87–91.
53. Angelica Balabanoff, *Impressions of Lenin*, trans. Isotta Cesari (Ann Arbor, 1968), 54–55.
54. Burbank, *Russian Peasants Go to Court*; Cathy A. Frierson, *Peasant Icons: Representations of Rural People in Late Nineteenth-Century Russia* (Oxford, 1993), 54–75.
55. See, for instance, the petition of the Nikolaevskaia Religious Society (Verkhotur'e, Urals oblast) to Kalinin, in GARF, f. A-353, op. 8, d. 6, ll. 3–4. On Kalinin's popularity with Soviet letter-writers, see Lewis Siegelbaum and Andrei Sokolov, *Stalinism as a Way of Life: A Narrative in Documents* (New Haven, 2000), 8; and Terry Martin, "Interpreting the New Archival Signals: Nationalities Policy and the Nature of the Soviet Bureaucracy," *Cahiers du Monde Russe* 40 (1999): 114. On the performative aspects of petitioning and petitioners' attempts to win the sympathy of their readers in the state apparatus, see Golfo Alexopoulos, "The Ritual Lament: A Narrative of Appeal in the 1920s and 1930s," *Russian History/Histoire Russe* 24 (1997): 117–29.
56. Liubimov's report is included in the documentation attached to Resolution No. 276 of the Patriarch, Synod, and Supreme Church Council, dated 22 November/5 December 1919, in RGIA, f. 831, op. 1, d. 25, ll. 93–95ob.
57. See, for example, Chris J. Chulos, comp. and ed., "Peasants' Attempts to Reopen Their Church, 1929–1936," *Russian History/Histoire Russe* 24 (1997): 203–13. Chulos notes both the predominantly lay makeup of the petitioners and the strong representation of women among the signatories.
58. RGIA, f. 831, op. 1, d. 185, l. 2ob.
59. Quoted in Lev Regel'son, *Tragediia Russkoi Tserkvi, 1917–1945* (Paris, 1977), 265.
60. Tikhon's letter to Kalinin is reprinted in M. I. Odintsov, comp. and ed., "... 'My dolzhny byt' iskrennimi po otnosheniiu k sovetskoi vlasti,'" *Voprosy nauchnogo ateizma* 39 (1989): 309.
61. Ibid., 309–10.
62. Kashevarov, *Gosudarstvo i tserkov'*, 74; Archpriest Vladislav Tsypin, *Russkaia tserkov', 1917–1925* (Moscow, 1996), 145–50.
63. "Popovskie litsemerie," *Krasnaia gazeta*, no. 210 (18 September 1919): 2.
64. Excerpts from Veniamin's appeals and Krasikov's rebuttal were published in P. A. Krasikov, "Religioznaia khitrost' (Pis'mo v redaktsiiu)," *Revoliutsiia i tserkov'*, no. 2 (1919): 23–25. In the end, the exhumation of Aleksandr Nevskii was delayed and not carried out until 12 May 1922, in conjunction with the state's campaign to requisition church valuables for the ostensible purpose of relief for the victims of the Volga famine. Aleksandr Nevskii's silver shrine was subsequently transferred to the Hermitage and his relics placed on display in a Petrograd antireligious museum. See Kashevarov, *Gosudarstvo i tserkov'*, 78.
65. GARF, f. A-353, op. 3, d. 731, ll. 53–54 (N. A. Liubimov to VIII Section, 25 August 1919).
66. On 9 December 1917, Lenin had instructed Lunacharskii to transfer the so-called Osman Koran from the State Public Library in Petrograd to the Muslim Congress of the Petrograd National Okrug. See A. V. Lunacharskii, *Ob ateizme i religii: Sbornik statei, pisem, i drugikh materialov* (Moscow, 1972), 448.
67. GARF, f. A-353, op. 3, d. 731, ll. 55–56 (Krasikov to Liubimov, 16 September 1919).

68. On Soviet newspaper letter-writing as an interactive, mediated process between state and subject, see Matthew E. Lenoe, "Letter-Writing and the State: Reader Correspondence with Newspapers as a Source for Early Soviet History," *Cahiers du Monde Russe* 40 (1999): 136–69. Contrast with the relative candor of private correspondence from the NEP period, as presented in Vladlen S. Izmozik, "Voices from the Twenties: Private Correspondence Intercepted by the OGPU," trans. William K. Wolf, *Russian Review* 55 (1996): 287–308.

69. GARF, f. A-353, op. 3, d. 731, l. 14 (petition received 15 March 1919). The petition was discussed by the Narkomiust collegium, which instructed Krasikov to respond to Svet and inquire whether she possessed the requisite credentials to present a petition on behalf of the entire brotherhood. See the protocols of the collegium meeting of 17 March 1919 in ibid., d. 841, l. 44.

70. *Russkaia pravoslavnaia tserkov' i kommunisticheskoe gosudarstvo*, 36.

71. Gorev, *Troitskaia lavra i Sergii Radonezhskii*, 41–43.

72. GARF, f. A-353, op. 3, d. 767, ll. 14–46.

73. Ibid., op. 4, d. 372, ll. 39–40ob.

74. Ibid., op. 3, d. 766, l. 13 (petition dated 4 June 1920).

75. Ibid., op. 4, d. 372, ll. 41–42 (petition from Petrovskaia Street, dom 1). The signatories included workers from the I. T. Volkov factory, the factory of G. Gordon and Company, and delegates from the Moscow section of the All-Union League of Metalworkers.

76. GARF, f. A-353, op. 4, d. 372, ll. 51–52 (petition of forty-nine residents from Izmailovskoe Shosse, dom 16, Moscow).

77. Ibid., ll. 43–44 (petition of thirty residents from Vtoraia Khapinovskaia Street, dom 7, Moscow). Other petitions concerning Sergii's relics may be found throughout this *delo* (which runs to some 180 pages) and also in ibid., op. 3, d. 731, ll. 23–28ob., 37–44, and d. 766, ll. 10, 13, 14.

78. Ibid., op. 3, d. 731, ll. 3–3ob. (petition dated 13 March 1919).

79. Ibid., ll. 8–8ob. (Voronezh gubispolkom to NKVD, 2 May 1919), and ll. 9–9ob. (VIII Section NKVD, 20 May 1919).

80. Ibid., op. 2, d. 692, ll. 280–280ob. (relics of Nil Stolobenskii, Tver), and op. 8, d. 6, ll. 2–2ob. (relics of Simeon Verkhoturskii, Urals oblast). The exception to the rule concerns the case of Saint Andrei Bobola, a Roman Catholic martyr exhumed at Polotsk in June 1922. Saint Andrei's body was relocated to Moscow for exhibition at the Narkomzdrav museum, but under pressure from the Polish government and the Vatican, Moscow rescinded the decision and allowed a Catholic delegation to remove the relics to Rome. The file on Saint Andrei's relics is housed in GARF, f. A-353, op. 6, d. 17.

81. Ivan Ul'ianov, *Kazaki, tserkov' i Sovetskaia vlast'* (Moscow, 1920), 14.

82. GARF, f. A-353, op. 3, d. 731, ll. 55ob.–56 (Krasikov to Liubimov, 16 September 1919). On the boundaries that Soviet legality placed on freedom of conscience, see P. Stuchka, *Uchenie o gosudarstve i o konstitutsii R.S.F.S.R.* 3rd rev. ed. (Moscow, 1923), 157–64. Concerns that relic veneration may be a threat to public hygiene surfaced in debates over what to do with the exhumed relics of Saint Simeon Verkhoturskii in 1924. See "Eshche udar po popovskoi lavochke: Moshchi—istochnik zarazy," *Ural'skii rabochii*, no. 138 (22 June 1924), in ibid., op. 8, d. 6, l. 7.

83. Ibid., op. 3, d. 768, ll. 35–38.

84. See, for example, Krivova, *Vlast' i tserkov'*; Kashevarov, *Gosurdarstvo i tserkov'*, 69–89; and Stepanov (Rusak), *Svidetel'stvo obvineniia*, 1:126–28.

85. Krasikov, "Otchet," 113.

86. "Praktika antireligioznoi bor'by," *Revoliutsiia i tserkov'*, no. 1 (1919): 11.

87. Lenin's remarks to the I All-Russian Congress of Women Workers on 19 November 1918 are reprinted in A. V. Belov, ed., *O religii i tserkvi: Sbornik vyskazyvan-*

nii klassikov marksizma-leninizma, dokumentov KPSS i sovetskogo gosudarstva, 2nd ed. (Moscow, 1981), 46.

88. GARF, f. A-353, op. 3, d. 692, ll. 92–93ob. (Aleksandr Povedskii to D. I. Kurskii, received 24 February 1919), and ll. 97–97ob. (VIII Section to Povedskii, 27 February 1919).

89. The document in question, outlining the procedural basis for dismissing complaints due to lack of evidence, is VIII Section Protocol No. 507 (13 March 1919), in *Revoliutsiia i tserkov'*, no. 2 (1919): 44 (emphasis in original). For the text of Znamenskii's complaint to Sovnarkom and Krasikov's response, see GARF, f. A-353, op. 2, d. 705, ll. 17–17a (20 March 1919), 18–18ob.

90. GARF, f. A-353, op. 3, d. 741, l. 1.

91. Ibid., d. 731, l. 45.

92. Ibid., d. 741, l. 2 (emphasis in original).

93. Born into a prominent Petersburg naval family, Ivan Anatol'evich Shpitsberg (1883–1933) was trained as a jurist and a lawyer. From 1918 to 1922, Shpitsberg served as legal consultant and "religious expert" for the VIII Section, where he participated in the drafting of legislation on the relic campaign. Shpitsberg served also as a plenipotentiary member of the Secret Section of the Cheka; as a juridical consultant to the Cheka, he played a leading role in the public show trials of prominent Orthodox clergymen and sectarians. Shpitsberg was expelled from the party as an "alien element" in 1921 but continued to work in the antireligious apparatus, editing the journal *Ateist* until his death in 1933. For biographical information on Shpitsberg, see M. Iu. Krapivin, "Religioznyi faktor v sotsial'no-politicheskoi zhizni sovetskogo obshchestva (oktiabr' 1917-go–konets 1920-x godov)" (Doktor ist. nauk. diss., Sankt-Peterburgskii gosudarstvennyi universitet, 1999), 268–70n249.

94. GARF, f. A-353, op. 3, d. 841, ll. 94–94ob. (protocols of the 15 July 1919 session of the Narkomiust Collegium). Shpitsberg's detailed report on the investigation is found in ibid., d. 741, ll. 1–21. See also "Istoriia zakrytiia Savvina Storozhevskogo monastyria: Po materialam Gosudarstvennogo arkhiva Russkoi Federatsii," *Zhurnal Moskovskoi Patriarkhii*, no. 2 (1998): 57–66; and Sergei Golubtsov, *Moskovskoe dukhovenstvo v preddverii i nachale gonenii, 1917–1922 gg.* (Moscow, 1999), 62n26.

95. The case was heard by the Moscow Province Revolutionary Tribunal, 11–16 January 1920. Among Kuznetsov's fellow defendants were A. D. Samarin, former overprocurator of the Holy Synod; two archpriests from Moscow; Hegumen Iona of the Storozhevskii monastery, along with two of his monks; three Zvenigorod schoolteachers; and a priest and deacon, both from Zvenigorod. The clergymen and lay defendants were given relatively light prison sentences, while Kuznetsov and Samarin received the death penalty. However, in light of "the victorious conclusion of the war against the Interventionists," the court commuted both men's sentences to "internment in a concentration camp until such time as the victory of the world proletariat over international imperialism." See "Delo ob"edinennogo Soveta prikhodov Moskvy," 89–91; N. V. Krylenko, *Za piat' let, 1918–1922 gg. Obvinitel'nye rechi po naibolee krupnym protsessam, zaslushannym v Moskovskom i verkhovnom revoliutsionnykh tribunalakh* (Moscow, 1923), 57–87. Kuznetsov eventually served some two years of his sentence and was fully amnestied by order of VTsIK on 21 December 1921. See Golubtsov, *Moskovskoe dukhovenstvo*, 169.

96. On the political and social context of nineteenth-century religious revivals and miracles in Western Europe, see David Blackbourn, *Marpingen: Apparitions of the Virgin Mary in Nineteenth-Century Germany* (New York, 1995); Harris, *Lourdes*, 320–56; and Kselman, *Miracles and Prophecies*, 113–40.

97. "Vskrytie moshchei sv. kniaza Mikhaila Blagovernogo," *Izvestiia* (Tver), no. 107 (20 May 1919): 3. See also Krivova, *Vlast' i tserkov'*, 15.

98. A. B. Chertkov, *Krakh* (Moscow, 1968), 79.
99. Klishko, *Karel'skie "chudotvortsy,"* 15.
100. GARF, f. A-353, op. 3, d. 763, l. 12 (A. A. Miliaev to D. I. Kurskii, 11 July 1919).
101. "Tikhon khochet uiti . . . ," *Sovetskaia gazeta*, no. 5/101 (19 January 1919): 6.
102. Klishko, *Karel'skie "chudotvortsy,"* 15.
103. "Sv. Simeon na sluzhbe u kontr-revoliutsii," *Krasnyi Ves'egonsk*, no. 6/19 (20 February 1919): 4.
104. Gorev, *Troitskaia lavra i Sergii Radonezhskii*, 44. On the wearing of caps in church as a symbolic gesture of Soviet resistance to Orthodox traditions of reverence and piety, see Young, *Power and the Sacred*, 77.
105. Alekseev, *Illiuzii i dogmy*, 80.
106. Bekannt, "Mestnaia zhizn'," *Trudovaia nedelia*, no. 15/38 (7 April 1919): 6. See also Lynne Viola, "The Peasant Nightmare: Visions of the Apocalypse in the Soviet Countryside," *Journal of Modern History* 62 (1990): 747–70; Leonid Heretz, *Russia on the Eve of Modernity: Popular Religion and Traditional Culture under the Last Tsars* (Cambridge, England, 2008); and Iu. A. Ivanov, *Mestnye vlasti, tserkov' i obshchestvo vo vtoroi polovine XIX–nachale XX v.* (Ivanovo, 2003), 229–39.
107. "Tikhon khochet uiti," 6.
108. V. L., "Vekovoi obman," *Izvestiia* (Murom), no. 15/112 (11 February 1919): 1. The exhumation of Saints Konstantin, Mikhail, and Feodor and the findings of the medical commission that examined the saints' bodies are reported in "Osmotr 'moshchei' v gor. Murome," *Izvestiia* (Vladimir), no. 34/194 (14 February 1919): 1. Photographs from the exhumation are found in GARF, f. A-353, op. 3, d. 734, ll. 7, 15–18.
109. "Novyi obman s 'moshchami,'" *Zvezda*, no. 50 (16 February 1919): 4. Similar satirical sentiments were expressed by the chairman of the exhumation commission of Suzdal: "The miraculous transformation of the incorruptible relics of Feodor and Ioann into rotten bones, wood shavings, rags, and cotton wool is most difficult for our sinful minds to grasp." See A. Sh., "Chudo," *Golos pravdy*, no. 19 (15 February 1919): 3.
110. G. Turkin, "Pis'mo Vladimirskomu dukhovenstvu," *Izvestiia* (Vladimir), no. 38/198 (19 February 1919): 2.
111. GARF, f. A-353, op. 3, d. 731, ll. 8–8ob. (communiqué of 2 May 1919).
112. Ibid., d. 763, l. 12 (A. A. Miliaev to D. I. Kurskii, 11 July 1919).
113. V. A. Shishakov, *Pogovorim o religii* (Moscow, 1960), 80. On religious rumors reported in the provincial Soviet press, see Ia. Shafir, *Gazety i derevnia*, 2nd ed. (Moscow, 1924), 99–128.
114. Miraculous healings had been reported at Prokopii's shrine since the discovery of his uncorrupted body in the seventeenth century. See Mordvinov, *Zhitiia sviatykh ugodnikov Bozhiikh*, 59–66.
115. "I-ia Vel'skaia Konferentsiia kommunistov i sochuvstvuiushchikh," *Krasnyi nabat*, no. 26/72 (19 March 1919): 2–3. The party conference's resolution calling for immediate exhumation was approved that same day by the Vel'skii district ispolkom, despite the prescient objections of one member, a certain Dmitriev, who maintained that exhumation without preliminary propaganda and agitation work among the populace was "a dangerous experiment." See the excerpts from the protocols of the 3 March 1919 session of the Vel'skii ispolkom in GARF, f. A-353, op. 4, d. 380, l. 138.
116. Ibid., l. 70. The official protocols and photographs of Prokopii's exhumation are found in ibid., ll. 71–72ob., 73, 144–46.
117. A. Verganovskii, "Chernaia lozh' (k vskrytiiu moshchei 'ugodnika' Prokopiia 'pravednogo')," *Krasnyi nabat*, no. 25/71 (16 March 1919): 1–2. The doctors who examined Prokopii's relics concluded that the mystery saint was likely "an ordinary drowned man" whose body had sunk to the river bottom, where it had naturally

mummified beneath a layer of silt before subsequently resurfacing as an allegedly uncorrupted holy body. See the report by the attending physician Grigor'ev, published as "O moshchakh 'pravednogo' Prokopiia Ust'ianskogo," *Krasnyi nabat*, no. 29/75 (26 March 1919): 1–2.

118. *Sledstvennoe delo Patriarkha Tikhona: Sbornik dokumentov po materialam Tsentral'nogo arkhiva FSB RF* (Moscow, 2000), 511–13.

119. See the report of Bishop Aleksandr of Vologda to Patriarch Tikhon (27 May 1919), in ibid., 524.

120. GARF, f. A-353, op. 4, d. 380, ll. 147–147ob. (excerpts from the protocols of an extraordinary session of the Vel'skii district ispolkom, 9 April 1919).

121. Sergei Vladimirovich Mikhailov, "Gosudarstvo i tserkov': Otnosheniia organov vlasti, religioznykh organizatsii i veruiushchikh na Arkhangel'skom Severe v 1918–1929 gg. " (Kand. diss., Pomorskii gosudarstvennyi universitet im. M. V. Lomonosova [Arkhangel'sk], 1998), 94.

122. Ibid., 94–95. For the perspective of the local officials involved, see the excerpts from emergency sessions of the Vel'skii district ispolkom in GARF, f. A-353, op. 4, d. 380, ll. 143–143ob., 147–147ob.

123. Mikhailov, "Gosudarstvo i tserkov'," 94.

124. GARF, f. A-353, op. 4, d. 380, l. 138.

125. Dal', "Vskrytie moshchei i Tverskoi gubispolkom," *Vlast' sovetov*, no. 6–7 (May 1919): 8–9. On the exhumation of Saint Efrem's relics, see "Dovol'no obmana—pravda otkryta," *Izvestiia* (Novotorzhok), no. 15 (9 February 1919): 2.

126. G. Baklaev, "O moshchakh (otvet na zapiski)," *Izvestiia* (Tver), no. 49 (4 March 1919): 2.

127. G. Baklaev, "Sharlatany," *Izvestiia* (Tver), no. 74 (4 April 1919): 2.

128. "K otkrytiiu moshchei," *Izvestiia* (Tver), no. 74 (4 April 1919): 3; and "K vskrytiiu moshchei," ibid., no. 75 (5 April 1919): 3.

129. "Rezoliutsiia o vskrytii moshchei," ibid, no. 63 (25 March 1919): 3.

130. "Rabochii o moshchakh," ibid., no. 82 (15 April 1919): 3.

131. "K vskrytiiu moshchei," ibid., no. 97 (8 May 1919): 2–3.

132. Ibid., 3.

133. "Kommunisty venchaiutsia," *Revoliutsiia i tserkov'*, no. 9–12 (1920): 65; and GARF, f. A-353, op. 4, d. 383, ll. 205–205ob. (Tver gubispolkom department of justice to VIII Section, 6 July 1920). Beginning in 1756, the festivities drew between 20,000 and 30,000 visitors to the monastery every year and were marked by a ceremonial procession in which the saint's relics were borne aloft and marched around the monastery grounds. See "Obnesenie sv. moshchei v Tverskoi eparkhii," *TEV*, no. 18 (15 September 1886): 514–20.

134. Throughout the 1920s and 1930s many provincial communists continued to participate in Orthodox religious ceremonies and rites of passage, much to the consternation of their superiors in Moscow and the regional centers. See Evgenii Sokol, "Chistite partiiu i ot sviatosh," *Bezbozhnyi byt* (Samara), no. 1 (1 May 1929): 3; M. V. Popov, *Kul'tura i byt krest'ian Urala v 1920–1941 godakh* (Ekaterinburg, 1997), 107–9; and Iu. A. Ivanov, "Mestnye vlasti i tserkov' v 1922–1941 gg. (po materialam arkhivov Ivanovskoi oblasti)," *Otechestvennye arkhivy*, no. 4 (1996): 90–94. For an instructive parallel with the People's Republic of China and the persistence of traditional beliefs among low-level cadres and rural officials, see Steve A. Smith, "Local Cadres Confront the Supernatural: The Politics of Holy Water (*Shenshui*) in the PRC, 1949–1966," *China Quarterly* 188 (2006): 999–1022.

135. "'Moshchi netlennye,'" *Golos pravdy*, no. 19 (15 February 1919): 2–3.

136. GARF, f. A-353, op. 5, d. 251, l. 103 (Krasikov to Smidovich, 16 July 1921).

Epilogue and Conclusion

1. Mikh. Gorev, *Sviatye ugodniki* (Moscow, 1925), 22.
2. Gorev, "Pod spudom," 100–101.
3. GARF, f. A-353, op. 3, d. 731, ll. 32–33ob. (Mitskevich to Lenin, 22 April 1919). See also S. I. Mitskevich, *Zapiski vracha-obshchestvennika (1888–1918)*, 2nd ed. (Moscow, 1969).
4. *Russkaia pravoslavnaia tserkov' i kommunisticheskoe gosudarstvo*, 41.
5. GARF, f. A-353, op. 4, d. 383, ll. 97–98 (VIII Section to the presidium of the ispolkom of the Union of Petrograd Communes, 25 January 1919).
6. Alekseev, *Illiuzii i dogmy*, 80–81.
7. RGIA, f. 831, op. 1, d. 25, ll. 93–95ob.
8. GARF, f. A-353, op. 5, d. 251, l. 19 (secret communiqué from Lunacharskii to Krasikov, 23 February 1921).
9. Ibid., l. 5ob. (copy of 20 January 1921 telegram from S. S. Said-Galeev, chair of the Tatar Republic Sovnarkom, to VTsIK, forwarded by Enukidze to Krasikov, 24 January 1921); and l. 6 (VIII Section to Said-Galeev, undated [February 1921]).
10. Alekseev, *Illiuzii i dogmy*, 79. The Kashin press had printed several articles in support of plans to exhume Anna's relics, but the ispolkom remained unconvinced. See, for example, Khrenov, "Snova pro moshchi," *Izvestiia* (Kashin), no. 72 (1 May 1919): 3.
11. Alekseev, *Illiuzii i dogmy*, 80–81.
12. GARF, f. A-353, op. 4, d. 380, ll. 7–7ob. (Viatka department of justice to VIII Section, 17 January 1920).
13. Ibid., l. 9ob. (Pskov department of justice to VIII Section, 8 July 1920).
14. Ibid., op. 5, d. 251, l. 23 (Tiumen-Tobol'sk provincial administration to VIII Section, 15 February 1921).
15. Ibid., l. 22 (Krasikov to the Omsk administrative bureau, 24 February 1921).
16. On the Tambov uprisings, see Delano DuGarm, "Peasant Wars in Tambov Province," in *The Bolsheviks in Russian Society: The Revolution and the Civil Wars*, ed. Vladimir Brovkin (New Haven, 1997), 177–98; and V. V. Sazonov, "U istokov krest'ianskogo vosstaniia na Tambovshchine," *Voprosy istorii*, no. 4 (2001): 75–83.
17. GARF, f. A-353, op. 4, d. 378, ll. 8–8ob.
18. Ibid., d. 380, l. 9ob.
19. The Petrograd city soviet was lukewarm on the question of exhumation in general, which led to clashes with provincial justice officials. In the spring of 1919, the presidium had voted down a motion to exhume the relics housed in the Aleksandro-Nevskaia Lavra in order to avoid any "popular grumblings of discontent." See ibid., op. 2, d. 734, l. 80 (Petrograd department of justice to VIII Section, 9 March 1921).
20. Ibid., op. 4, d. 379, l. 10 (protocol from the 10 August 1920 session of the presidium of the Petrograd city soviet).
21. Ibid., d. 377, ll. 119–119ob. (Eniseisk Province department of justice to VIII Section, 8 July 1921). Saint Innokentii's finger was spared the journey to Moscow by special resolution of the II Congress of Soviets in Eniseisk Province, whose delegates decided that it would be more prudent to keep the relic in the Krasnoiarsk cathedral rather than run the risk of inciting the Orthodox populace to revolt. Ibid., l. 126ob. (Eniseisk Province ispolkom to Eniseisk Province department of justice, 25 July 1921, copy forwarded to VIII Section).
22. GARF, f. A-353, op. 4, d. 380, ll. 35–35ob. (Arkhangel'sk Province department of justice to VIII Section, 29 January 1920).
23. Ibid., op. 3, d. 757, ll. 101–101ob.
24. *Russkaia pravoslavnaia tserkov' i kommunisticheskoe gosudarstvo*, 61.

25. Plaksin, *Krakh tserkovnoi kontrrevoliutsii*, 173; "Otchet o deiatel'nosti V (likvidatsionnogo) Otdela," 68. Regarding these final exhumations, see "Vskrytie 'moshchei' v Solovkakh," *Bezbozhnik*, no. 2 (1925): 8–9; A. Meshkov, "Vskrytie mogily skhimonakha Alekseia," *Bezbozhnik*, no. 23 (1928): 12; B. F—n, "Moshchi 'sviatogo' Pitirima," *Bezbozhnik*, no. 5 (March 1930): 12; and Bogatov, *Vladimirskie sviatye*, 59–61.

26. Pipes, *Russia under the Bolshevik Regime*, 338. On the evolution of a "middle line" in Soviet antireligious policy of the mid-1920s, see Joan Delaney, "The Origins of Soviet Antireligious Organizations," in *Aspects of Religion in the Soviet Union, 1917–1967*, ed. Richard H. Marshall, Jr. (Chicago, 1971), 103–29; and F. Putintsev, "Grazhdanskaia voina, NEP, i religiia," *Antireligioznik*, no. 11 (November 1926): 3–8.

27. Helmut Altrichter, "Insoluble Conflicts: Village Life between Revolution and Collectivization," in *Russia in the Era of NEP: Explorations in Soviet Society and Culture*, ed. Sheila Fitzpatrick, Alexander Rabinowitch, and Richard Stites (Bloomington, 1991), 192. See also Gregory L. Freeze, "Subversive Atheism: From Dechristianization to Religious Revival in the Soviet Ukraine in the 1920s" (paper presented to the conference "Modern History of Eastern Christianity: Transitions and Problems," Harvard University, 26–27 March 2004).

28. I. Skvortsov-Stepanov, "Itogi nashei antireligioznoi bor'by i ee sovremennye zadachi," *Kommunisticheskaia revoliutsiia*, no. 4 (1923): 23.

29. K. Troitskii, *Tserkov' i gosudarstvo v Rossii* (Moscow, 1923), 21.

30. GARF, f. R-5263, op. 1, d. 1077, ll. 22–24 (report of the chair of the Novgorod raion ispolkom to V. S. Ageev, secretary of the VTsIK's Commission for the Affairs of Religious Cults, 26 February 1936).

31. V. Shishakov, "Moshchi, chudesa i antireligioznaia propaganda," *Bezbozhnik*, no. 11 (June 1930): 9. A second, more decisive, exhumation in 1930 resulted in Saint Mitrofan's relics being deposited in the Voronezh antireligious museum. See "Vskrytie 'moshchei' Mitrofaniia Voronezhskogo," *Izvestiia*, no. 8 (8 January 1930): 3.

32. RGIA, f. 831, op. 1, d. 23, ll. 102–102ob. (report from the archbishop of Vologda to the Patriarch, Synod, and Supreme Church Council, 24 May/6 June 1919). For his efforts the chief organizer of the march, Hegumen Kirill of the Spaso-Sumorin monastery, was arrested, tried, and found guilty by the Vologda Province Revolutionary Tribunal.

33. GARF, f. A-353, op. 4, d. 380, l. 33 (Belevskii district militia to Tula Province department of justice, 11 February 1920, forwarded to VIII Section on 20 August 1920). The previous year local officials had claimed that the number of pilgrims to Makarii's shrine "diminished" in the two months immediately following his exhumation. Ibid., op. 2, d. 700, ll. 100–101 (Belevskii district ispolkom to VIII Section, 21 May 1919).

34. "'Chudesa' s moshchami," *Zvezda*, no. 69 (11 March 1919): 4.

35. Em. Iaroslavskii, "Postanovka antireligioznoi propagandy," in *Anti-religioznaia propaganda: Sbornik materialov* (Khar'kov, 1922), 178.

36. M. Boldyrev, "Ne uspeli sfabrikovat' ugodnika," *Voronezhskaia bednota*, no. 44 (25 February 1919): 4. Two years later, Cheka officers in Tula Province foiled a similar plot by local clergymen and lay activists to glorify a new saint and open his relics for veneration. The successful operation prompted the Cheka plenipotentiary in the province to submit a story to *Revoliutsiia i tserkov'*, recounting his office's role in uncovering the plot. The author proved a better Chekist than a stylist, and the editorial board never published the submission. See Aleshin, "Tozhe moshchi (iz deiatel'nosti Tul'skoi dukhovenstva)," in GARF, f. A-353, op. 5, d. 259. ll. 111–12.

37. *Sledstvennoe delo Patriarkha Tikhona*, 509–11.

38. Gorev, "Tserkovniki i ikh agenty pered narodnym revoliutsionnym sudom," 124–29. Hieromonk Dosifei and Serafima were tried and found guilty of "relic fraud" by the Moscow City People's Court on 21–22 July 1920. While finding Serafima guilty for "her decades of parasitical [activity] at the expense of the laborers," the court was

lenient and sentenced the abbess to an old-age home run by the Commissariat of Social Welfare, even granting her a stipend from the state. Dosifei received five years in a labor camp, but the court commuted his sentence. For the sentence, see GARF, f. A-1571, op. 1, d. 2, ll. 211–15.

39. *Sledstvennoe delo Patriarkha Tikhona*, 502–4.

40. A. Salomatin, "Kul'turno-istoricheskie tsennosti i religioznaia propaganda," *Antireligioznik*, no. 7 (July 1928): 71. The body may have been Sergii's but the head, reportedly, had been swapped surreptitiously by Archimandrite Kronid and a cabal of clerics prior to the April 1919 exhumation; on the whereabouts of Sergii's head after 1920 and its return to the Lavra after the Second World War, see Andronik (Trubachev), *Zakrytie Troitse-Sergievoi Lavry i sud'ba moshchei Prepodobnogo Sergiia Radonezhskogo v 1918–1946 gg.* (Moscow, 2008), 198–226.

41. Mikhail Gorev, "Delo 'Vilenskikh ugodnikov,'" in Rozhitsyn, *Moshchi*, 134.

42. V. V. Dubrovskii, *Zhizn' i dela Feodosiia Uglitskago (Polonitskago)* (Ekaterinoslav, 1925), 57. On the connection between psychosomatic suggestion, "hysteria," and miracle stories, see V. Nikol'skii, *Sueveriia, znakharstvo, religioznye predrassudki i sovetskaia meditsina* (Moscow, 1926), 22–23.

43. GARF, f. R-5263, op. 1, d. 1077, ll. 7–8, 48–53, 61–64 (protocols and photographs of the exhumation of Moisei Skovorodskii, 24 February 1936). Coverage of the exhumation of Ioasaf Belgorodskii mentioned, too, that coins and paper money issued by the Provisional Government and the White governments of the Don region were found inside the saint's shrine—a discovery intended to highlight the counterrevolutionary dimension of the saint's cult. See "Vskrytie moshchei Ioasafa Belgorodskogo," 2.

44. Kandidov, *Monastyri-muzei*, 148.

45. Gregory L. Freeze, "The Stalinist Assault on the Parish, 1929–1941," in *Stalinismus vor dem Zweiten Weltkrieg. Neue Wege der Forschung*, ed. Manfred Hildermeier (Munich, 1998), 209–32; Sheila Fitzpatrick, "Cultural Revolution Revisited," *Russian Review* 58 (1999): 202–9.

46. F—n, "Moshchi 'sviatogo' Pitirima," 12; and Bogatov, *Vladimirskie sviatye*, 59–61.

47. Shishakov, "Moshchi, chudesa i antireligioznaia propaganda," 9.

48. "Vskrytie moshchei Anny Kashinskoi," *Bezbozhnik*, no. 4 (February 1930): 14–15.

49. Bogatov, *Vladimirskie sviatye*, 9. The class origins of the saints had been a peripheral component of Soviet antireligious propaganda since the very earliest days of the Revolution. By the late 1920s, however, it had become a central aspect thereof. See V. V. Nesterenko, *Rabotnitsa i religiia* (Moscow, 1926), 37–43; Anton Loginov, *Zhitiia sviatykh* (Moscow, 1930).

50. Mikh. Artamaonov, "Sredi umershikh bogov (progulka po antireligioznomu muzeiu)," *Derevenskii bezbozhnik*, no. 9 (1930): 8–9.

51. F. Pisarev-Bogoliubskii, *Rostov s tochki zreniia bezbozhnika* (Rostov, 1929), 10–14.

52. Taradin, *Zadonskii Bogoroditskii monastyr'*, 86–87.

53. I. A. Chikin, *Chem vredna religiia i znakharstvo dlia krest'ianskogo zdorov'ia i skota?* (Briansk, 1927), 8–9.

54. Soviet literature on the saints' pernicious influence on agriculture is enormous. See, for instance, I. Ia. Eliashevich, *Letnie religioznye prazdniki* (Leningrad, 1929); V. G., "Doloi vesennie popovskie prazdniki," *Derevenskii bezbozhnik*, no. 9 (1930): 3; and N. Amosov, *Kolkhoznyi stroi i religiia* (Moscow, 1934). On Soviet efforts to establish new holidays to supplant the old feast days, see Mal'te Rol'f, *Sovetskii massovyi prazdnik v Voronezhe i Tsentral'no-Chernozemnoi oblasti Rossii (1927–1932)* (Voronezh, 2000), 23–27, 54–60.

55. Belov, *Pravda o pravoslavnykh "sviatykh"*, 79. See also *Vesennie i letnie religioznye prazdniki, ikh sushchnost' i vred* (Stalingrad, 1938), 45-55.

56. "Nepobedimye soprotivnymi silami," 36–37.

57. Z. Gurskaia, "Istoriia kanonizatsii 'startsa' Serafima Sarovskogo," *Antireligioznik*, no. 4 (July–August 1935): 34–36.

58. Novgorod officials, for example, incinerated the bones uncovered during the 1936 exhumation of Moisei Skovorodskii. See GARF, f. R-5263, op. 1, d. 1077, ll. 14–14ob. (report from the Novgorod raion ispolkom to V. S. Ageev, 3 July 1936).

59. With the rapprochement between the Orthodox Church and the Soviet state, several parishes and prelates petitioned successfully for the return of holy relics to their churches after 1945. See M. V. Shkarovskii, *Russkaia pravoslavnaia tserkov' i Sovetskoe gosudarstvo v 1943–1964 godakh: Ot "peremiriia" k novoi voine* (St. Petersburg, 1995), 29, 130–31. On the return of holy relics during perestroika, see Archpriest Igor' Ekonomtsev, "Peredacha sviatyn' Russkoi Pravoslavnoi Tserkvi," *Zhurnal Moskovskoi Patriarkhii*, no. 9 (1988): 46.

60. G. V. Vorontsov, *Leninskaia programma ateisticheskogo vospitaniia v deistvii (1917–1937 gg.)* (Leningrad, 1973), 139–42. The 1932 figure includes antireligious wings of local history museums. On the "new phase" in antireligious museum work, see N. Matorin, "Vserossiiskii muzeinii s"ezd i antireligioznaia rabota," *Antireligioznik*, no. 2 (1931): 62–64.

61. Eliashevich, "Antireligioznaia propaganda v Leningrade," 52. For provincial statistics, see "Antireligioznye muzei," *Antireligioznik*, no. 7 (1927): 65–66.

62. L. Finn, L. Lebedianskii, N. Troshin, A. Rostovtsev, and N. Kamen'shchikov, *Iz ochaga mrakobesiia—v ochag kul'tury* (Leningrad, 1931), 9.

63. Jean Bernard Louis Foucault (1819–1868) first demonstrated his pendulum at the Paris Pantheon in 1851. To the naked eye, the pendulum's swing appears to shift over time, though in fact it is always swinging in the same plane. It is not the pendulum's arc that is rotating, but rather the earth beneath it. See Brian L. Silver, *The Ascent of Science* (Oxford, 2000), 420. Foucault's pendulum was first demonstrated in Russia in Vologda in 1929, in conjunction with an anti-Easter agitprop campaign. See G. P. Butikov and G. A. Khvostova, *Isaakievskii sobor* (Leningrad, 1979), 162–64; T. V. Iakirina and I. D. Karpovich, *Isaakievskii sobor* (Leningrad, 1965), 85–86.

64. Ivanych, "Kak perevilis' chudotvortsy na Sov. Rusi," in *Antireligioznyi sbornik*, no. 2 (Saratov, 1924), 47–48.

65. I. Ia. Elizarov, *Prazdniki nastoiashchego i prazdniki proshlogo (Religioznye i obshchestvennye prazdniki)* (Leningrad, 1926), 29.

66. On the embalming of Lenin, see A. A. Panchenko and A. M. Panchenko, "Os'moe chudo sveta," in *Kanun: Al'manakh*, vyp. 16, *Poliarnost' v kul'ture*, ed. V. E. Bagno and T. A. Novichkova (St. Petersburg, 1996), 166–202; Zh. F. Konovalova, *Mif v Sovetskoi istorii i kul'ture* (St. Petersburg, 1998); Ilya Zbarsky and Samuel Hutchinson, *Lenin's Embalmers*, trans. Barbara Bray (London, 1998); Nina Tumarkin, *Lenin Lives! The Lenin Cult in Soviet Russia*, 2nd ed. (Cambridge, MA, 1997).

67. Olga Tian-Shanskaia, *Village Life in Late Tsarist Russia*, ed. David L. Ransel (Bloomington, 1993), 136.

68. E. Yaroslavsky, *Religion in the U.S.S.R.*, 2nd rev. ed. (London, 1932), 28.

69. Shevzov, *Russian Orthodoxy*, esp. ch. 5.

Selected Bibliography

ARCHIVAL SOURCES

Gosudarstvennyi Arkhiv Rossiisskoi Federatsii (GARF)
    fond A-353 (People's Commissariat of Justice)
    fond A-1571 (Museum of Social Hygiene of the People's Commissariat of Public Health)
    fond A-2306 (People's Commissariat of Enlightenment)
    fond R-3431 (All-Russian Church Sobor and Holy Synod)
    fond R-4652 (Chancellery of Patriarch Tikhon)
    fond R-5263 (Central Standing Commission on Religious Cults, VTsIK)
Rossiiskii Gosudarstvennyi Istoricheskii Arkhiv (RGIA)
    fond 776 (Chief Administration for Press Affairs, Ministry of Internal Affairs)
    fond 796 (Chancellery of the Holy Synod)
    fond 797 (Chancellery of the Over-Procurator of the Holy Synod)
    fond 815 (Aleksandro-Nevskaia Lavra, St. Petersburg)
    fond 831 (Chancellery of Patriarch Tikhon and the Holy Synod)
    fond 1282 (Chancellery of the Ministry of Internal Affairs)

PREREVOLUTIONARY NEWSPAPERS AND JOURNALS

Arkhangel'skiia eparkhial'nyia vedomosti
Astrakhanskiia eparkhial'nyia vedomosti
Bogoslovskii vestnik
Chernigovskiia eparkhial'nyia izvestiia
Chernigovskiia gubernskiia vedomosti
Donskiia eparkhial'nyia vedomosti
Dukhovnaia beseda
Golos Iakutskoi tserkvi
Iakutskiia eparkhial'nyia vedomosti
Iaroslavskiia eparkhial'nyia vedomosti
Irkutskiia eparkhial'nyia vedomosti
Kaluzhskiia eparkhial'nyia vedomosti
Kavkazkiia eparkhial'nyia vedomosti
Kievskiia eparkhial'nyia vedomosti
Kormchii
Novgorodskiia eparkhial'nyia vedomosti
Olonetskiia eparkhial'nyia vedomosti
Pastyrskii sobesednik
Permskiia eparkhial'nyia vedomosti
Pochaevskii listok
Poslednyia Tverskiia novosti
Pravoslavno-missionerskii listok
Pravoslavnyi putevoditel'
Pravoslavnyi sobesednik
Pribavleniia k Tserkovnym vedomostiam
Rukovodstvo dlia sel'skikh pastyrei
Russkii palomnik

Russkoe obozrenie
Stavropol'skiia eparkhial'nyia vedomosti
Strannik
Tobol'skiia eparkhial'nyia vedomosti
Tomskiia eparkhial'nyia vedomosti
Tserkovnyia vedomosti
Tverskiia eparkhial'nyia vedomosti
Vestnik tserkovnago edineniia (Voronezh)
Viatskiia eparkhial'nyia vedomosti
Volynskiia eparkhial'nyia vedomosti
Voronezhskiia eparkhial'nyia vedomosti
Voskresnoe chtenie

Soviet Newspapers and Journals

Antireligioznik
Ateist
Belevskii proletarii
Bezbozhnik
Bezbozhnik u stanka
Bezbozhnyi byt (Samara)
Derevenskii bezbozhnik
Golos pravdy (Suzdal)
Golos trudovogo krest'ianstva
Izvestiia
Izvestiia Iaroslavskogo gubernskogo ispolnitel'nogo komiteta sovetov rabochikh, krest'ianskikh i krasnoarmeiskikh deputatov
Izvestiia Kashinskogo soveta rabochikh, krest'ianskikh i krasnoarmeiskikh deputatov
Izvestiia Muromskogo soveta rabochikh i krest'ianskikh deputatov
Izvestiia Novotorzheskogo uezdnogo soveta rabochikh i krest'ianskikh deputatov
Izvestiia Tverskogo gubernskogo ispolnitel'nogo komiteta soveta rabochikh, krest'ianskikh i krasnoarmeiskikh deputatov
Izvestiia Vladimirskogo gubernskogo i uezdnogo ispolnitel'nykh komitetov sovetov rabochikh, krasnoarmeitskikh i krest'ianskikh deputatov
Izvestiia Vologodskogo gubernskogo ispolnitel'nogo komiteta sovetov rabochikh, kresti'ianskikh i krasnoarmeiskikh deputatov
Izvestiia VTsIK
Krasnaia gazeta
Krasnyi nabat (Vel'sk)
Krasnyi Ves'egonsk
Kurskaia pravda
Nash bezbozhnik (Tambov)
Pravda
Revoliutsiia i tserkov'
Sovetskaia gazeta (Zadonsk)
Trudovaia nedelia (Sergiev Posad)
Vlast' sovetov
Voronezhskaia bednota
Voronezhskie izvestiia
Voronezhskii bezbozhnik
Zvezda (Novgorod)

Published Sources

A. D. "'Netlennye moshchi' Evfrosinii Polotskoi." *Bezbozhnik*, no. 9 (May 1928): 15.
Abramov, Nikolai. "O pochitanii sv. Ugodnikov i chestnykh moshchei." *Volynskiia eparkhial'nyia vedomosti*, no. 35 (11 December 1904): 1119–30.
"Akty o vskrytii t.-n. moshchei katolicheskogo sviatogo Andreia Boboli." *Revoliutsiia i tserkov'*, no. 1–2 (1924): 90–94.
Alekseev, V. A. *Illiuzii i dogmy*. Moscow, 1991.
———. "Shturm nebes" otmeniaetsia? *Kriticheskie ocherki po istorii bor'by s religiei v SSSR*. Moscow, 1992.
Alexopoulos, Golfo. "The Ritual Lament: A Narrative of Appeal in the 1920s and 1930s." *Russian History/Histoire Russe* 24 (1997): 117–29.
Altrichter, Helmut. "Insoluble Conflicts: Village Life between Revolution and Collectivization." In *Russia in the Era of NEP: Explorations in Soviet Society and Culture*, ed. Sheila Fitzpatrick, Alexander Rabinowitch and Richard Stites, 192–209. Bloomington, 1991.
Amosov, N. *Kolkhoznyi stroi i religiia*. Moscow, 1934.
Andreev, V. N. "Kak provodilas' podgotovka i vskrytie moshchei v Novgorode." In *Moshchi Sofiiskogo sobora*, ed. V. N. Andreev, N. G. Porfiridov, and A. I. Semenov, 5–11. Novgorod, 1931.
Andronik (Trubachev). *Zakrytie Troitse-Sergievoi Lavry i sud'ba moshchei Prepodobnogo Sergiia Radonezhskogo v 1918–1946 gg*. Moscow, 2008.
"Antireligioznaia vystavka v Vologde." *Antireligioznik*, no. 1 (1928): 80–81.
"Antireligioznye muzei." *Antireligioznik*, no. 7 (1927): 65–66.
Antonii, Archimandrite. *Dogmaticheskoe bogoslovie pravoslavnoi kafolicheskoi vostochnoi tserkvi, s prisovokupleniem obshchago vvedeniia v kurs bogoslovskikh nauk*. St. Petersburg, 1862.
Antoninov, Priest Ioann. *Palomnichestvo iz Ekaterinburga v Verkhotur'e, 6–24 maia 1914 g*. Ekaterinburg, 1914.
Arkhangelov, G. A. *Kholernyia epidemii v Evropeiskoi Rossii v 50-ti-letnii period 1823–1872 gg*. St. Petersburg, 1874.
Arkhangelov, Priest S. A. "Opredelenie Moskovskago Sobora 1678 goda o zhitii i podviga Blagovernoi Velikoi Kniagini Anny Kashinskoi." *Strannik*, t. 1, otd. 1 (April 1909): 534–54.
———. *Sviataia blagovernaia velikaia kniaginia Anna Kashinskaia k dniu—12 iiunia 1909 g.—vozstanovleniia Eia proslavleniia*. St. Petersburg, 1909.
———. *Zhitie i chudesa sviatoi blagovernoi kniagini Anny Kashinskoi*. St. Petersburg, 1909.
Arkhangel'skii, Archpriest Mikhail. *O taine sv. eleia*. St. Petersburg, 1895.
Arrignon, Jean-Pierre. "Le rôle des reliques dans la Rus' de Kiev." In *Les reliques: Objets, cultes, symboles*, ed. Edina Bozóky and Anne-Marie Helvétius, 57–63. Tournhout, 1999.
Artamaonov, Mikh. "Sredi umershikh bogov (progulka po antireligioznomu muzeiu)." *Derevenskii bezbozhnik*, no. 9 (1930): 8–9.
Averintsev, S. S., ed. *Khristianstvo: Entsiklopedicheskii slovar'*. 3 vols. Moscow, 1995.
Babanin, Iv. *Sbornik razskazov religiozno-nravstvennykh, istoricheskikh i bytovykh*. Moscow, 1908.
Balabanoff, Angelica. *Impressions of Lenin*, trans. Isotta Cesari. Ann Arbor, 1968.
Bantjes, Adrian A. "Idolatry and Iconoclasm in Revolutionary Mexico: The De-Christianization Campaigns, 1929–1940." *Mexican Studies/Estudios Mexicanos* 13 (1997): 87–120.
Bantysh-Kamenskii, D. N. *Rossianin pri grobe Patriarkha Germogena*. 2nd ed. Moscow, 1806.

Baron, Samuel H., and Nancy Shields Kollmann, eds. *Religion and Culture in Early Modern Russia and Ukraine*. DeKalb, 1997.
Barsukov, N. P. *Istochniki russkoi agiografii*. St. Petersburg, 1882.
Batalden, Stephen K., ed. *Seeking God: The Recovery of Religious Identity in Orthodox Russia, Ukraine, and Georgia*. DeKalb, 1993.
Bazhanov, Archpriest V. G. *Primery blagochestiia iz zhitii sviatykh*. 11th ed. St. Petersburg, 1914.
Bazhenov, I. V. *Sv. blagovernaia kniaginia Anna Kashinskaia*. St. Petersburg, 1891.
Becker, Seymour. *Nobility and Privilege in Late Imperial Russia*. DeKalb, 1985.
Belov, A. V. *Pravda o pravoslavnykh "sviatykh."* Moscow, 1968.
———, ed. *O religii i tserkvi: Sbornik vyskazyvannii klassikov marksizma-leninizma, dokumentov KPSS i sovetskogo gosudarstva*. 2nd ed. Moscow, 1981.
Bergman, Jay. "The Image of Jesus in the Russian Revolutionary Movement: The Case of Russian Marxism." *International Review of Social History* 35 (1990): 220–48.
Biriukov, Priest Evlampii. *Katikhizicheskiia besedy k sel'skim prikhozhanam*. Kamyshlov, 1900.
Blackbourn, David. *Marpingen: Apparitions of the Virgin Mary in Nineteenth-Century Germany*. New York, 1995.
Blazhennyi Sviatitel' Feodosii Uglitskii, Arkhiepiskop Chernigovskii, i chudesa ot moshchei ego. St. Petersburg, 1896.
Bliakhin, P. *Doloi chertei, doloi bogov, doloi monakhov i popov!* 2nd ed. Odessa, 1920.
———. *Kak popy durmaniat narod!* Petrograd, 1920.
Blinov, N. *Popy i interventsiia na severe*. Arkhangel'sk, 1930.
Bogatov, I. P. *Vladimirskie sviatye i ikh chudesa*. Vladimir, 1929.
Bogdanov, A. P. *Russkie patriarkhi, 1589–1700*. 2 vols. Moscow, 1999.
Bogdanovich, Priest Savva. *Beseda so shtundistom o tom, chto dolzhno pochitat' sviatykh i molit'sia im*. 4th ed. Kiev, 1907.
Bogoraz-Tan, V. G. *Khristianstvo v svete etnografii*. Moscow, 1928.
Boltin, Evg. "Antireligioznoe vospitanie krasnoarmeitsev." *Antireligioznik*, no. 1 (1928): 60–68.
Bonch-Bruevich, V. D. *Izbrannye ateisticheskie proizvedeniia*. Moscow, 1971.
Borisov, V. A. *Sviatitel' Iosaf Gorlenko, episkop Belgorodskii i Oboianskii: Ego zhizn' i deiatel'nost'*. Sergiev Posad, 1911.
Bosley, Richard. "The Changing Profile of the Liturgical Calendar in Muscovy's Formative Years." In *Culture and Identity in Muscovy, 1359–1584*, ed. A. M. Kleimola and G. D. Lenhoff, 26–38. Moscow, 1997.
Bovkalo, A. "Novgorodskaia eparkhiia v 1917–1919 godakh." In *Gde Sviataia Sofiia, tam i Novgorod*. Novgorod, 1997.
Brennan, Brian. "Piety and Politics in Nineteenth-Century Poitiers: The Cult of St. Radegund." *Journal of Ecclesiastical History* 47 (1996): 65–81.
Brooks, Jeffrey. *When Russia Learned to Read: Literacy and Popular Literature, 1861–1917*. Princeton, 1987.
Brower, Daniel R. "'The City in Danger': The Civil War and the Russian Urban Population." In *Party, State, and Society in the Russian Civil War: Explorations in Social History*, ed. Diane P. Koenker, William G. Rosenberg, and Ronald Grigor Suny, 58–80. Bloomington, 1989.
Brown, Peter. *The Cult of the Saints: Its Rise and Function in Latin Christianity*. Chicago, 1982.
Bukharin, N., and E. Preobrazhensky. *The ABC of Communism: A Popular Explanation of the Program of the Communist Party of Russia*. Ann Arbor, 1988.
Bulgakov, S. D. *O pochitanii netlennykh moshchei sv. ugodnikov Bozhiikh: K predstoiashchemu torzhestvu proslavleniia Sviatitelia Iosafa, Episkopa Belgorodskago, v 4-i den' mesiatsa sentiabria 1911 goda*. Kursk, 1911.
Burbank, Jane. *Russian Peasants Go to Court: Legal Culture in the Countryside, 1905–1917*. Bloomington, 2004.

Burds, Jeffrey. *Peasant Dreams and Market Politics: Labor Migration and the Russian Village, 1861–1905*. Pittsburgh, 1998.
Burke, Peter. "How to Be a Counter-Reformation Saint." In *Religion and Society in Early Modern Europe*, ed. Kaspar von Greyerz, 45–55. London, 1984.
Burov, Ia. M. *Chto oznachaet zakon o svobode sovesti i otdelenii tserkvi ot gosudarstva? (Podrobnoe, postateinoe rasmotrenie dekreta o svobode sovesti s prilozheniem samogo dekreta)*. Moscow, 1918.
Bushkovitch, Paul. *Religion and Society in Russia: The Sixteenth and Seventeenth Centuries*. Oxford, 1992.
Butikov, G. P., and G. A. Khvostova. *Isaakievskii sobor*. Leningrad, 1979.
Bynum, Caroline Walker. *The Resurrection of the Body in Western Christendom, 200–1336*. New York, 1995.
Caseau, Béatrice. "Sacred Landscapes." In *Intepreting Late Antiquity: Essays on the Postclassical World*, ed. G. W. Bowersock, Peter Brown, and Oleg Grabar, 21–59. Cambridge, MA, 2001.
Cassiday, Julie A. *The Enemy on Trial: Early Soviet Courts on Stage and Screen*. DeKalb, 2000.
Chefranov, Archpriest Milii. *Blazhennyi Sofronii, 3-i episkop irkutskii*. Moscow, 1907.
Chernigovskaia pamiatka. Karmannaia spravochnaia knizhka na 1896/7 god. Chernigov, 1896.
Chernigovskaia pamiatka. Spravochnaia knizhka na 1898/9 god. Chernigov, 1898.
Chertkov, A. B. *Krakh*. Moscow, 1968.
Chikin, I. A. *Chem vredna religiia i znakharstvo dlia krest'ianskogo zdorov'ia i skota?* Briansk, 1927.
———. *Mogut li byt' netlennye moshchi?* Briansk, 1926.
Christian, William A., Jr. *Person and God in a Spanish Valley*. New York, 1972.
Chulos, Chris J. *Converging Worlds: Religion and Community in Peasant Russia, 1861–1917*. DeKalb, 2003.
———. "Orthodox Identity at Russian Holy Places." In *The Fall of the Empire, the Birth of a Nation: National Identities in Russia*, ed. Chris J. Chulos and Timo Piirainen, 28–50. Aldershot, 2000.
———. "Peasant Perspectives of Clerical Debauchery in Post-Emancipation Russia." *Studia Slavica Finlandensia* 12 (1995): 33–53.
———. "Revolution and Grassroots Re-evaluations of Russian Orthodoxy: Parish Clergy and Peasants of Voronezh Province, 1905–17." In *Transforming Peasants: Society, State and the Peasantry, 1861–1930*, ed. Judith Pallot, 90–112. New York, 1998.
———, comp. and ed. "Peasants' Attempts to Reopen Their Church, 1929–1936." *Russian History/Histoire Russe* 24 (1997): 203–13.
Chumachenko, Tatiana A. *Gosudarstvo, pravoslavnaia tserkov', veruiushchie, 1941–1961 gg.* Moscow, 1999.
Coates, W. P. *Religion in Tsarist and Soviet Russia*. London, 1930.
Coleman, Heather J. *Russian Baptists and Spiritual Revolution, 1905–1929*. Bloomington, 2005.
Connolly, S. J. *Priests and People in Pre-Famine Ireland, 1780–1845*. New York, 1982.
Cormack, Margaret. *The Saints in Iceland: Their Veneration from the Conversion to 1400*. Subsidia Hagiographica 78. Brussels, 1994.
Coulter, Debra. "Ukrainian Pilgrimage to the Holy Land, 988–1914." *Ukrainian Review* 43 (1996): 62–77
Crook, John. *The Architectural Setting of the Cult of the Saints in the Early Christian West, c. 300–1200*. Oxford, 2000.
Cueva, Julio de la. "Religious Persecution, Anticlerical Tradition and Revolution: On Atrocities against the Clergy during the Spanish Civil War." *Journal of Contemporary History* 33 (1998): 355–69.

Curtiss, John Shelton. *Church and State in Russia: The Last Years of the Empire, 1900–1917.* New York, 1940.

———. *The Russian Church and the Soviet State, 1917–1950.* Boston, 1953.

Dal'. "Vskrytie moshchei i Tverskoi gubispolkom." *Vlast' sovetov,* no. 6–7 (May 1919): 8–9.

Dal', Vladimir. *O pover'iakh, sueveriiakh i predrassudkakh russkago naroda.* 2nd ed. St. Petersburg, 1880.

Dashkevich, V. *Pereselenie v Sibir'.* St. Petersburg, 1912.

Davis, Natalie Zemon. "The Rites of Violence." In *Society and Culture in Early Modern France,* ed. Natalie Zemon Davis, 124–51. Stanford, 1975.

———. "The Sacred and the Body Social in Sixteenth-Century Lyon." *Past and Present,* no. 90 (1981): 40–70.

Delaney, Joan. "The Origins of Soviet Antireligious Organizations." In *Aspects of Religion in the Soviet Union, 1917–1967,* ed. Richard H. Marshall, Jr., 103–29. Chicago, 1971.

"Delo ob"edinennogo Soveta prikhodov Moskvy." *Revoliutsiia i tserkov',* no. 9–12 (1920): 89–91.

Delooz, Pierre, "Towards a Sociological Study of Canonized Sainthood in the Catholic Church." In *Saints and Their Cults: Studies in Religious Sociology, Folklore and History,* ed. Stephen Wilson, 189–216. Cambridge, 1983.

Dement'eva, N. M. *Patriarkh Germogen. Razskaz iz istorii Russkoi tserkvi.* Moscow, 1914.

Denisov, Leonid I. *Chudesa Bozhii. Sovremennyia nam znameniia milosti Bozhiei, iavlennyia za posledniia gody chrez sv. moshchei i ikony.* 2nd ed. Moscow, 1904.

———. *Novoiavlennyi ugodnik Bozhii, Sv. Feodosii Uglitskii, arkhiepiskop i chudotvorets Chernigovskii.* Moscow, 1897.

Desan, Suzanne. *Reclaiming the Sacred: Lay Religion and Popular Politics in Revolutionary France.* Ithaca, 1990.

Diakonov, Priest Olimp. *O sv. moshchakh.* Saratov, 1914.

Dixon, Simon. "The Orthodox Church and the Workers of St. Petersburg, 1880–1914." In *European Religion in the Age of Great Cities, 1830–1930,* ed. Hugh McLeod, 119–41. New York, 1995.

———. "Superstition in Imperial Russia." *Past and Present,* no. 199, supplement 3 (2008): 207–28.

"Dlia chego chestvuetsia sv. Anna Kashinskaia? (K voprosu o znachenii zhenshchiny sovremennom khristianskom obshchestve)." *Tverskie eparkhial'nye vedomosti,* no. 22 (8 June 1909): 438–39.

Dmitriev, D. S. *Patriarkh Germogen (ocherk).* Moscow, 1906.

Dmitriev, Mikhail E. "Riazan Diocese in 1917." *Russian Studies in History* 38 (1999): 66–82.

Dobrogaev, M. A. *Russkomu palomniku na pamiat' o poseshchenie Chernigova, po sluchaiu otkrytiia chestnykh moshchei Ugodnika Bozhiia Sviatitelia Feodosiia, 1896 goda 9-sentiabria.* Chernigov, 1896.

Dolginov, M. "'Sviatye' moshchi i blagochestivaia spekuliatsiia." In *O sviatykh moshchakh: Sbornik materialov,* ed. M. Dolginov, 3–46. Moscow, 1961.

Donina, I. N. "'Avtobiografii bezbozhnikov' kak vid massovogo istochnika po sotsial'noi psikhologii rubezha 1920–1930-x godov (po materialam rukopisnogo otdela Gosudarstvennogo muzeia istorii religii)." *Klio,* no. 3/6 (1998): 58–66.

Dubrovskii, V. V. *Zhizn' i dela Feodosiia Uglitskago (Polonitskago).* Ekaterinoslav, 1925.

DuGarm, Delano. "Peasant Wars in Tambov Province." In *The Bolsheviks in Russian Society: The Revolution and the Civil Wars,* ed. Vladimir Brovkin, 177–98. New Haven, 1997.

Duncan, Carol. *Civilizing Rituals: Inside Public Art Museums.* London, 1995.

Efimov, Priest A. N. *Novoiavlennyi ugodnik Bozhii, Sviatitel' i Chudotvorets Vserossiiskii Feodosii Uglitskii, arkhiepiskop Chernigovskii.* Chernigov, 1902.

———. *Razmyshlenie o torzhestvennom otkrytii sviatykh moshchei Sviatitelia i Chudotvortsa*

Chernigovskago Feodosiia Uglitskago. Chernigov, 1897.
Eire, Carlos M. N. *The War against the Idols: The Reformation of Worship from Erasmus to Calvin*. Cambridge, 1986.
Ekonomtsev, Archpriest Igor'. "Peredacha sviatyn' Russkoi Pravoslavnoi Tserkvi." *Zhurnal Moskovskoi Patriarkhii*, no. 9 (1988): 46.
Eliashevich, I. "Antireligioznaia propaganda v Leningrade (1924–1925 gg.)." *Antireligioznik*, no. 6 (June 1926): 48–55.
——. *Letnie religioznye prazdniki*. Leningrad, 1929.
Elizarov, I. Ia. *Prazdniki nastoiashchego i prazdniki proshlogo (Religioznye i obshchestvennye prazdniki)*. Leningrad, 1926.
Emeliakh, L. I. "Antiklerikalizm i ateizm russkikh krest'ian nakanune Velikoi Oktiabr'skoi sotsialisticheskoi revoliutsii." In *Po etapam razvitiia ateizma v SSSR*. Leningrad, 1967.
——. *Antiklerikal'noe dvizhenie krest'ian v period pervoi russkoi revoliutsii*. Moscow, 1965.
Emel'ianov, S. N. *Vlast' i tserkov': Evoliutsiia gosudarstvennoi religioznoi politiki i institutov tserkovnogo upravleniia v guberniiakh Tsentral'nogo Chernozem'ia: 1917–1922*. Kursk, 2001.
Emmons, Terence, trans. and ed. *Time of Troubles: The Diary of Iurii Vladimirovich Got'e. Moscow, July 8, 1917 to July 23, 1922*. Princeton, 1988.
Engel, Barbara Alpern. "Women, Men, and the Languages of Peasant Resistance, 1870–1907." In Frank and Steinberg, *Cultures in Flux*, 34–53.
Engelstein, Laura. "Old and New, High and Low: Straw Horsemen of Russian Orthodoxy." In Kivelson and Greene, *Orthodox Russia*, 23–32.
Ermilov, V. *Ugodnik Bozhii Sviatitel' Tikhon Zadonskii*. 2nd ed. Moscow, 1899.
Eshenbakh, A. I. *Velikii pechal'nik zemli Russkoi, Sviateishii Patriarkh Germogen*. Moscow, 1913.
Esipov, N. N. *Sviatitel' i Chudotvorets arkhiepiskop Chernigovskii Feodosii Uglitskii*. St. Petersburg, 1897.
Evdokim, Bishop. *Sviatye minuty: Primery blagochestiia i dobrodetelei izvlechennye iz zhitii sviatykh*. Sergiev Posad, 1909.
Evstratova, A. N., and G. G. Bril'. "Sovetskaia vlast' i dukhovenstvo: K voprosu o vzaimootnosheniiakh v 1917 — nachale 20-x godov (Na materialakh Verkhnego Povolzh'ia)." In *Intelligentsiia, provintsiia, otechestvo: Problemy istorii, kul'tury, politiki*. Ivanovo, 1996.
Faragó, Tamás. "Seasonality of Marriages in Hungary from the Eighteenth to the Twentieth Century." *Journal of Family History* 19 (1994): 333–50.
Fedotov, G. P. *The Russian Church since the Revolution*. London, 1928.
——. *Sviatye drevnei Rusi*. Paris, 1931.
Feodosii (Almazov), Archimandrite. *Moi vospominaniia (Zapiski Solovetskogo uznika)*. Edited by M. I. Odintsov. Moscow, 1997.
Finn, L., L. Lebedianskii, N. Troshin, A. Rostovtsev, and N. Kamen'shchikov. *Iz ochaga mrakobesiia—v ochag kul'tury*. Leningrad, 1931.
Finucane, Ronald C. *Miracles and Pilgrims: Popular Beliefs in Medieval England*. London, 1977.
Fitzpatrick, Sheila. "Cultural Revolution Revisited." *Russian Review* 58 (1999): 202–9.
——. "Supplicants and Citizens: Public Letter-Writing in Soviet Russia in the 1930s." *Slavic Review* 55 (1996): 78–105.
Flerov, Prof. N. A. "Netlennye moshchi." *Bezbozhnik*, no. 3 (December 1925): 4–5.
F—n, B. "Moshchi 'sviatogo' Pitirima." *Bezbozhnik*, no. 5 (March 1930): 12.
Fomenko, Archpriest K. I. *O russkom palomnichestve k mirotochivym moshcham Sviatitelia Nikolaia*. Kiev, 1901.
Ford, Caroline. "Religion and Popular Culture in Modern Europe." *Journal of Modern History* 65 (1993): 152–75.

Frank, Stephen P., and Mark D. Steinberg, eds. *Cultures in Flux: Lower-Class Values, Practices, and Resistance in Late Imperial Russia.* Princeton, 1994.
Freeze, Gregory L. "A Case of Stunted Anticlericalism: Clergy and Society in Imperial Russia." *European Studies Review* 13 (1983): 177–200.
———. "Handmaiden of the State? The Orthodox Church in Imperial Russia Reconsidered." *Journal of Ecclesiastical History* 36 (1985): 82–102.
———. "Institutionalizing Piety: The Church and Popular Religion, 1750–1850." In *Imperial Russia: New Histories for the Empire*, ed. Jane Burbank and David L. Ransel, 210–49. Bloomington, 1998.
———. "The Orthodox Church and Serfdom in Prereform Russia." *Slavic Review* 48 (1989): 361–87.
———. *The Parish Clergy in Nineteenth-Century Russia: Crisis, Reform, Counter-reform.* Princeton, 1983.
———. "Recent Scholarship on Russian Orthodoxy: A Critique." *Kritika* 2 (2001): 269–78.
———. "The Rechristianization of Russia: The Church and Popular Religion, 1750–1850." *Studia Slavica Finlandensia* 7 (1990): 101–36.
———. "The Stalinist Assault on the Parish, 1929–1941." In *Stalinismus vor dem Zweiten Weltkrieg. Neue Wege der Forschung*, ed. Manfred Hildermeier, 209–32. Munich, 1998.
———. "Subversive Atheism: From Dechristianization to Religious Revival in the Soviet Ukraine in the 1920s." Paper presented to the conference "Modern History of Eastern Christianity: Transitions and Problems," Harvard University, 26–27 March 2004.
———. "Subversive Piety: Religion and the Political Crisis in Late Imperial Russia." *Journal of Modern History* 68 (1996): 308–50.
Frierson, Cathy A. *Peasant Icons: Representations of Rural People in Late Nineteenth-Century Russia.* Oxford, 1993.
Froese, Paul. *The Plot to Kill God: Findings from the Soviet Experiment in Secularization.* Berkeley and Los Angeles, 2008.
Fülöp-Miller, René. *The Mind and Face of Bolshevism: An Examination of Cultural Life in Soviet Russia.* Rev. ed. New York, 1965.
Gadalova, G. S. "Zhenshchiny Tverskogo kniazheskogo dvora (Velikie Kniagini Kseniia i Anna—mat' i zhena Mikhaila Tverskogo)." In *Velikii Kniaz' Tverskoi i Vladimirskii Mikhail Iaroslavich: Lichnost', epokha, nasledie.* Tver, 1996.
Geary, Patrick J. *Furta Sacra: Thefts of Relics in the Central Middle Ages.* Princeton, 1978.
Georgievskii, Georgii. *Prazdnichnye sluzhby i tserkovnye torzhestva v staroi Moskve.* St. Petersburg, 1899.
Georgievskii, V. T. *Raka i oblachenie dlia moshchei Sviatitelia Germogena.* Moscow, 1914.
Gidulianov, P. V., ed. *Otdelenie tserkvi ot gosudarstva: Sistematizirovannyi sbornik deistvuiushchego v SSSR zakonodatel'stva.* 3rd ed. Moscow, 1926.
———. *Tserkov' i gosudarstvo po zakonodatel'stvu R.S.F.S.R.: Sbornik uzakonenii i rasporiazhenii s raz"iasneniiami V Otdela NKIu.* Moscow, 1923.
Gimpel'son, E. G. "Sovetskie upravlentsy: Politicheskii i nravstvennyi oblik (1917–1920 gg.)." *Otechestvennaia istoriia*, no. 5 (1997): 44–54.
Gindin, A. M., and G. M. Gindin. *Petr Krasikov: Zhizn' i revoliutsionnaia deiatel'nost'* Krasnoiarsk, 1972.
———. *S Leninym v serdtse: Zhizn' Petra Krasikova.* Moscow, 1968.
Ginzburg, V. "Chto predstavliaiut soboiu 'moshchei' byvshei Kievo-Pecherskoi lavry." *Antireligioznik*, no. 7 (1939): 48–50.
Golosov, Aleksandr. *Osnovy pravoslaviia (Kurs VIII-go kl. zhenskikh gimnazii Ministerstva narodnago prosveshcheniia).* 5th ed. Moscow, 1912.
Golubinskii, E. E. *Istoriia kanonizatsii sviatykh v Russkoi tserkvi.* 2nd ed. Moscow, 1903.
———. "Zametka o slove 'kanonizatsiia.'" *Bogoslovskii vestnik*, t. 1, no. 1 (January 1895): 166–67.

Golubtsov, Sergei. *Moskovskoe dukhovenstvo v preddverii i nachale gonenii, 1917–1922 gg.* Moscow, 1999.
Gorev, Mikhail. "Delo 'Vilenskikh ugodnikov.'" In Rozhitsyn, *Moshchi*, 124–36.
———. "'Moshchi' Sergiia Radonezhskogo." *Krasnaia gazeta*, no. 83 (15 April 1919): 2.
——— "O zhenshchine i o religioznoi chertovshchine." *Kommunistka*, no. 3-4 (March–April 1923): 6-8.
———. "Pod spudom." *Revoliutsiia i tserkov'*, no. 3–5 (1919): 28–32.
———. *Poslednii sviatoi: Poslednie dni Romanovskoi tserkvi*. Moscow, 1928.
———. *Sviatye ugodniki*. Moscow, 1925.
———. *Troitskaia lavra i Sergii Radonezhskii: Opyt istoriko-kriticheskogo issledovaniia.* Moscow, 1920.
———. "Tserkovniki i ikh agenty pered narodnym revoliutsionnym sudom." *Revoliutsiia i tserkov'*, no. 9–12 (1920): 45–53.
———. "Vskrytie moshchei Sergiia Radonezhskogo." *Trudovaia nedelia*, no. 17/40 (21 April 1919): 4.
———. "Vskrytie moshchei Tikhona Zadonskogo i Mitrofana Voronezhskogo." In Rozhitsyn, *Moshchi*, 59–95.
Gor'kii, Maksim. *O russkom krest'ianstve*. Berlin, 1922.
Gromov, E. S. *Lev Vladimirovich Kuleshov*. Moscow, 1984.
Gromov, Archpriest P. V. *Nachalo khristianstvo v Irkutske, i Sviatyi Innokentii, pervyi episkop Irkutskii, ego sluzhenie, upravlenie, konchina, chudesa i proslavlenie*. Irkutsk, 1868.
Gromyko, M. M. *Mir russkoi derevni*. Moscow, 1991.
Gromyko, M. M., and A. V. Buganov. *O vozzreniiakh russkogo naroda*. Moscow, 2000.
Gurskaia, Z. "Istoriia kanonizatsii 'startsa' Serafima Sarovskogo." *Antireligioznik*, no. 4 (July–August 1935): 34–36.
Halfin, Igal. *From Darkness to Light: Class, Consciousness, and Salvation in Revolutionary Russia*. Pittsburgh, 2000.
Harris, Ruth. *Lourdes: Body and Spirit in the Secular Age*. London, 1999.
Harrison, Marguerite E. *Marooned in Moscow: The Story of an American Woman Imprisoned in Russia*. New York, 1921.
Hart, Laurie Kain. *Time, Religion, and Social Experience in Rural Greece*. Lanham, 1992.
Hayward, Paul Antony. "Demystifying the Role of Sanctity in Western Christendom." In *The Cult of Saints in Late Antiquity and the Middle Ages: Essays on the Contribution of Peter Brown*, ed. James Howard-Johnston and Paul Antony Hayward, 115–42. Oxford, 1999.
Hecker, Julius F. *Religion under the Soviets*. New York, 1927.
Hedda, Jennifer. *His Kingdom Come: Orthodox Pastorship and Social Activism in Revolutionary Russia*. DeKalb, 2008.
Hellbeck, Jochen. *Revolution on My Mind: Writing a Diary under Stalin*. Cambridge, MA, 2006.
Heretz, Leonid. *Russia on the Eve of Modernity: Popular Religion and Traditional Culture under the Last Tsars*. Cambridge, England, 2008.
Herrlinger, Page. "Orthodoxy and the Experience of Factory Life in St. Petersburg, 1881–1905." In *New Labor History: Worker Identity and Experience in Russia, 1840–1918*, ed. Michael Melancon and Alice K. Pate, 35–63. Bloomington, 2002.
Hollander, Paul d'. "Les ostensions en Limousin au XIXe siècle." *Revue de l'Histoire des Religions* 217 (2000): 503–16.
Husband, William B. *"Godless Communists": Atheism and Society in Soviet Russia, 1917–1932*. DeKalb, 2000.
———. "Soviet Atheism and Russian Orthodox Strategies of Resistance, 1917–1932." *Journal of Modern History* 70 (1998): 74–107.
Hussey, J. M. *The Orthodox Church in the Byzantine Empire*. Oxford, 1986.
Iakimov, Priest Ioann. *Besedy iz zhizni sviatykh. Posobie pri vedenie pastyrskikh vnebogoslu-*

zhebnykh sobesedovanii s sel'skimi prikhozhanami. Moscow, 1895.
Iakirina, T. V., and I. D. Karpovich. *Isaakievskii sobor*. Leningrad, 1965.
Jaroslavskii, E. M. "12 funtov sibirskikh moshchei." In E. M. Iaroslavskii, *O religii*. Moscow, 1957.
———. *Na antireligioznom fronte. Sbornik statei, dokladov, lektsii i tsirkuliarov za shest' let, 1919–1925*. Moscow, 1925.
———. *O religii*. Moscow, 1957.
———. "Postanovka antireligioznoi propagandy." In *Anti-religioznaia propaganda: Sbornik materialov*. Khar'kov, 1922.
Iarygin, A. *Putevoditel' po gorodu Chernigovu*. Chernigov, 1900.
Iavlenie blagodatnoi pomoshchi Sviatitelia Sofroniia, 3-go episkopa irkutskago. Irkutsk, 1915.
Il'igorskii, Priest Ioann. "Po povodu Kashinskikh torzhestv." *Tverskiia eparkhial'nyia vedomosti*, no. 37 (21 September 1909): 761–68.
Iosif, Archimandrite. *O sviatykh ugodnikakh Bozhiikh, Moskovskikh chudotvortsakh*. Moscow, 1877.
Iraklii, Hieromonk. *S bogomol'ia ot "Troitsy-Sergiia."* Sergiev Posad, 1916.
Irkutskii missionerskii s"ezd. 24 iiulia—5 avgusta 1910 goda. (Dnevnik uchastnika s"ezda). Tomsk, 1910.
"Istoriia zakrytiia Savvina Storozhevskogo monastyria: Po materialam Gosudarstvennogo arkhiva Russkoi Federatsii." *Zhurnal Moskovskoi Patriarkhii*, no. 2 (1998): 57–66.
Iurasov, I. N. "Proverka very." In *O Emel'iane Iaroslavskom: Vospominaniia, ocherki, stat'i*, ed. P. S. Fateev and V. V. Korolev, 207–12. Moscow, 1988.
Iurchenkov, V. A. "Likvidatsiia moshchei sviatykh kak faktor obshchestvenno-politicheskoi zhizni 20-х godov." In *Obshchestvenno-politicheskaia zhizn' rossiiskoi provintsii, XX vek*. Vyp. 1. Tambov, 1993.
Ivanchenko, D. D. *K sviatym mestam. Zapiski palomnika*. Saratov, 1911.
———. *Zapiski pri poezdke v Sarovskuiu pustyn'*. Saratov, 1908.
Ivanov, Iu. A. "Mestnye vlasti i tserkov' v 1922–1941 gg. (po materialam arkhivov Ivanovskoi oblasti)." *Otechestvennye arkhivy*, no. 4 (1996): 90–94.
———. *Mestnye vlasti, tserkov' i obshchestvo vo vtoroi polovine XIX–nachale XX v.* Ivanovo, 2003.
Ivanych. "Kak perevilis' chudotvortsy na Sov. Rusi." In *Antireligioznyi sbornik*, no. 2. Saratov, 1924.
Ivin, Iv. "O narodno-lubochnoi literature. K voprosu o tom, chto chitaet narod (Iz nabliudenii krest'ianina nad chteniem v derevne)." *Russkoe obozrenie*, t. 22, no. 9 (September 1893): 242–60; t. 23, no. 10 (October 1893): 768–85.
Izmozik, Vladlen S. "Voices from the Twenties: Private Correspondence Intercepted by the OGPU," trans. William K. Wolf. *Russian Review* 55 (1996): 287–308.
Izrailev, Archpriest Aristarkh. *Netlennyia moshchi sviatykh blagovernykh kniazei Feodora i chad ego Davida i Konstantina, v Iaroslavskom Spaso-Preobrazhenskom monastyre, nyne Arkhiereiskom dome*. 2nd ed. Moscow, 1899.
James, William. *The Varieties of Religious Experience: A Study in Human Nature*. New York, 1902.
Kabuzan, V. M. *Emigratsiia i reemigratsiia v Rossii v XVIII–nachale XX veka*. Moscow, 1998.
Kafedral'nye Chernigovskie monastyri: Il'inskii, Eletskii i Borisoglebskii. Kiev, 1860.
Kaiander, E. G. *Russkie sviatye*. Moscow, 1930.
Kaiser, Daniel H. "Naming Cultures in Early Modern Russia." *Harvard Ukrainian Studies* 19 (1995): 271–91.
Kak ia ubedilsia v netlenii sviatykh moshchei. Moscow, 1913.
Kalendar'-spravochnik po g. Irkutsku i Irkutskoi gubernii na 1914 god. Irkutsk, 1914.
Kalinskii, I. P. *Tserkovno-narodnyi mesiatseslov na Rusi*. St. Petersburg, 1877.
Kal'nev, M. A. *O pochitanii sv. moshchei i drugikh ostankov ugodnikov Bozhiikh*. Odessa, 1912.

Kandidov, B. P. "Antireligioznaia agitatsiia v gody grazhdanskoi voiny." *Bezbozhnik*, no. 19–20 (October 1932), n.p.
———. "Antireligioznaia rabota NKIu v gody grazhdanskoi voiny." *Bezbozhnik*, no. 1 (January 1933), n.p.
———. *Monastyri-muzei i antireligioznaia propaganda*. Moscow, 1929.
Kanonizatsiia sviatykh v XX veke. Moscow, 1999.
Kartiny tserkovnoi zhizni Chernigovskoi eparkhii iz IX vekovoi eia istorii. Kiev, 1911.
Kashevarov, A. V. *Gosudarstvo i tserkov': Iz istorii vzaimootnoshenii sovetskoi vlasti i russkoi pravoslavnoi tserkvi, 1917–1945 gg.* St. Petersburg, 1995.
———. "Kampaniia sovetskoi vlasti po vskrytiiu sviatykh moshchei v 1918–1920 gg." In *Tserkov' i gosudarstvo v russkoi pravoslavnoi i zapadnoi latinskoi traditsiiakh*. St. Petersburg, 1996.
Kashin, pravoslavnyi russkii gorod. St. Petersburg, 1998.
Kaufman, Suzanne K. "Selling Lourdes: Pilgrimage, Tourism, and the Mass-Marketing of the Sacred in Nineteenth-Century France." In *Being Elsewhere: Tourism, Consumer Culture, and Identity in Modern Europe and North America*, ed. Shelley Baranowski and Ellen Furlough, 63–88. Ann Arbor, 2001.
Kaulen, M. E. *Muzei-khramy i muzei-monastyri v pervoe desiatiletie Sovetskoi vlasti*. Moscow, 2001.
Kenez, Peter. *Civil War in South Russia, 1919–1920*. Berkeley and Los Angeles, 1977.
Kenworthy, Scott M. "The Revival of Monasticism in Modern Russia: The Trinity–Sergius Lavra, 1825–1921." Ph.D. diss., Brandeis University, 2002.
Kharlamova, S. S. "Tserkovnye periodicheskie izdaniia kak istochnik izuheniia etnograficheskikh aspektov pravoslaviia." In *Biblioteka i istoriia. Sbornik nauchnykh trudov*. Vyp. 2. Moscow, 1994.
Khitrov, Archpriest M. *Svetochi khristianstva*. St. Petersburg, 1898.
Khoroshev, A. S. *Politicheskaia istoriia russkoi kanonizatsii, XI–XVI vv*. Moscow, 1986.
Kivelson, Valerie A., and Robert H. Greene, eds. *Orthodox Russia: Belief and Practice under the Tsars*. University Park, 2003.
Kizenko, Nadieszda. *A Prodigal Saint: Father John of Kronstadt and the Russian People*. University Park, 2000.
———. "Protectors of Women and the Lower Orders: Constructing Sainthood in Modern Russia." In Kivelson and Greene, *Orthodox Russia*, 106–24.
Klimiuk, I. "Slovo o pochitanii sviatykh." *IEV*, no. 9 (1 May 1913): 289–95.
Klishko, V. *Karel'skie "chudotvortsy."* Petrozavodsk, 1932.
Kliucharev, Priest G. "V zashchitu pochitaniia netlennykh moshchei sv. ugodnikov Bozhiikh." *Pravoslavnyi putevoditel'*, no. 7 (July 1903): 9–27.
Kliuchevskii, V. O. *Drevnereusskiia zhitiia sviatykh kak istoricheskii istochnik*. Moscow, 1871.
Koenker, Diane P. "Urbanization and Deurbanization in the Russian Revolution and Civil War." In *Party, State, and Society in the Russian Civil War: Explorations in Social History*, ed. Diane P. Koenker, William G. Rosenberg, and Ronald Grigor Suny, 81–104. Bloomington, 1989.
Kogol', T. N. *Vzaimootnosheniia Russkoi Pravoslavnoi Tserkvi i gosudarstva v pervoe desiatiletie Sovetskoi vlasti (Istoricheskii analiz na materialakh Zapadnoi Sibiri)*. Tomsk, 2005.
Kohl, J. G. *Russia: St. Petersburg, Moscow, Kharkoff, Riga, Odessa, the German Provinces on the Baltic, the Steppes, the Crimea, and the Interior of the Empire*. London, 1844; reprint, New York, 1970.
Kollmann, Nancy Shields. "Pilgrimage, Procession and Symbolic Space in Sixteenth-Century Russian Politics." In *Medieval Russian Culture*, vol. 2, ed. Michael S. Flier and Daniel Rowland, 163–81. Berkeley and Los Angeles, 1994.
Kolonitskii, Boris I. "Antibourgeois Propaganda and Anti-'*Burzhui*' Consciousness in 1917." *Russian Review* 53 (1994): 183–96.

———. *Simvoly vlasti i bor'ba za vlast': K izucheniiu politicheskoi kul'tury rossiiskoi revoliutsii 1917 goda.* St. Petersburg, 2001.
Kolosov, V. I. *Blagovernaia kniaginia Anna Kashinskaia.* Tver, 1905.
Koltypin, P. *Svedeniia o zhizni blagovernoi velikoi kniagini Anny Kashinskoi, suprugi sv. velikago kniazia Mikhaila Tverskogo.* St. Petersburg, 1872.
"Kommunisty venchaiutsia." *Revoliutsiia i tserkov'*, no. 9–12 (1920): 65.
Konkordin, Priest An. *Zhitiia sviatykh ugodnikov Bozhiikh, pochivaiushchikh v Sofiiskom sobore v Novgorode.* 2nd ed. Novgorod, 1902.
Konovalova, Zh. F. *Mif v Sovetskoi istorii i kul'ture.* St. Petersburg, 1998.
"'Kosti, kotorye dorozhe dragotsennykh kamnei i blagorodnee zolota . . .': O pochitanii sviatykh moshchei v drevnei tserkvi." *Danilovskii blagovestnik*, no. 10 (1999): 19–23.
Kovalev, F. "Piat' let Tsentral'nogo Antireligioznogo Muzeiia." *Bezbozhnik*, no. 6 (June 1934): 12–13.
Kovalevskii, A. *Vospominanie ochevidtsa torzhestva otkrytiia sviatykh i mnogotselebnykh moshchei Sviatitelia Feodosiia Uglitskago, Arkhiepiskopa Chernigovskago, Chudotvortsa.* 4th ed. Moscow, 1908.
Kovrigina, V. A. "Zemstvo i zdravookhranenie v Rossii vtoroi poloviny XIX v. (k voprosu o zemskoi meditsine)." In *Rossiiskaia provintsiia XVIII–XX vekov: Realii kul'turnoi zhizni.* Penza, 1996.
Kozlov, Priest I. *V pomoshch' missioneru, pastyriu i revniteliu pravoslaviia. Posobie po noveishei polemike s raskolom, izlozhennoe po predmetam v alfavitnom poriadke.* Petrograd, 1915.
Krapivin, M. Iu. *Nepridumannaia tserkovnaia istoriia: Vlast' i tserkov' v Sovetskoi Rossii (oktiabr' 1917-go–konets 1930-x godov).* Volgograd, 1997.
———. "Religioznyi faktor v sotsial'no-politicheskoi zhizni sovetskogo obshchestva (oktiabr' 1917-go konets 1920-x godov)." Doktor ist. nauk. diss., Sankt-Peterburgskii gosudarstvennyi universitet, 1999.
Krasikov, P. A. *Izbrannye ateisticheskie proizvedeniia.* Moscow, 1970.
———. "Otchet VIII-go (Likvidatsionnogo) otdela Narodnogo Komissariata Iustitsii VIII-mu Vserossiiskomu s"ezdu Sovetov." In Rozhitsyn, *Moshchi*, 105–14.
———. "Religioznaia khitrost' (Pis'mo v redaktsiiu)." *Revoliutsiia i tserkov'*, no. 2 (1919): 23–25.
Krasnikov, N. P. "Velikaia Oktiabr'skaia sotsialisticheskaia revoliutsiia i provozglashenie svobody sovesti." In *Po etapam razvitiia ateizma v SSSR.* Leningrad, 1967.
"Krasnoarmeitsy o moshchakh." *Revoliutsiia i tserkov'*, no. 2 (1919): 36.
Kremleva, I. A. "Obet v religioznoi zhizni russkogo naroda." In *Pravoslavie i russkaia narodnaia kul'tura*, vol. 2, 127–57. Moscow, 1993.
Krivova, N. A. *Vlast' i tserkov' v 1922–1925 gg.: Politbiuro i GPU v bor'be za tserkovnye tsennosti i politicheskoe podchinenie dukhovenstva.* Moscow, 1997.
Krupskaia, N. K. "Zadachi antireligioznoi propagandy." In *Deiateli Oktiabria o religii i tserkvi: Stat'i, rechi, besedy, vospominaniia*, ed. M. M. Persits, 121–25. Moscow, 1968.
Krylenko, N. V. *Za piat' let, 1918–1922 gg. Obvinitel'nye rechi po naibolee krupnym protsessam, zaslushannym v Moskovskom i verkhovnom revoliutsionnykh tribunalakh.* Moscow, 1923.
Kselman, Thomas A. *Miracles and Prophecies in Nineteenth-Century France.* New Brunswick, 1983.
Kukla Tikhona v Zadonskom monastyre. Zadonsk, n. d.
Kuleshov, Lev. *Sobranie sochinenii.* 3 vols. Moscow, 1988.
Kunkin, I. Ia. *Gorod Kashin: Materialy dlia ego istoriia.* Vyp. 2. Moscow, 1905.
Kurskii, D. I. "Tsirkuliar NKIu ot 25 avgusta 1920 g." In *Otdelenie tserkvi ot gosudarstva: Sistematizirovannyi sbornik deistvuiushchego v SSSR zakonodatel'stva*, ed. P. V. Gidulianov, 66–69. 3rd ed. Moscow, 1926.

Kurtsev, A. N. "Kul'tovye migratsii naseleniia Tsentral'nogo Chernozem'ia v 1861–1917 gg." In *Iz istorii monastyrei i khramov Kurskogo kraia*, 92–96. Kursk, 1998.

———. "Palomnichestvo v Tsentral'nom Chernozem'e (1861–1917 gg.)." In *Materialy dlia izucheniia selenii Rossii*. Vol. 1, 142–46. Moscow, 1997.

Kutepov, Priest I. "Beseda o podrazhanii Sviatym." *Pastyrskii sobesednik*, no. 28–29 (13–20 July 1896): 467–69.

Larkin, Brian R. "Liturgy, Devotion, and Religious Reform in Eighteenth-Century Mexico City." *Americas* 60 (2004): 493–518.

Latsis, M. Ia. *Dva goda bor'by na vnutrennem fronte*. Moscow, 1920.

Lavrovskii, L. Ia. *Sv. Blagovernyi Rostislavich Smolenskii i Iaroslavskii*. Smolensk, 1899.

Lebedev, A. *V kakoi den' naibolee prilichno chestvovat' pamiat' Patriarkha Germogena*. Saratov, 1910.

Lenhoff, Gail. "The Notion of 'Uncorrupted Relics' in Early Russian Culture." In *Slavic Cultures in the Middle Ages*, ed. Boris Gasparov and Olga Raevsky-Hughes, 252–75. Berkeley and Los Angeles, 1993.

Lenin, V. I. *Collected Works*. 4th ed. 45 vols. Moscow, 1974.

Lenoe, Matthew E. "Letter-Writing and the State: Reader Correspondence with Newspapers as a Source for Early Soviet History." *Cahiers du Monde Russe* 40 (1999): 136–69.

Leont'ev, P. A. "Revoliutsiia v tserkvi: S"ezdy dukhovenstva i mirian v 1917 godu." In *Tserkov' v istorii Rossii*. Vyp. 2. Moscow, 1998.

Leshchenko, V. Iu. *Sem'ia i russkoe pravoslavie (XI–XIX vv.)*. St. Petersburg, 1999.

Levin, Eve. "*Dvoeverie* and Popular Religion." In *Seeking God: The Recovery of Religious Identity in Orthodox Russia*, ed. Stephen K. Batalden, 29–52. DeKalb, 1993.

———. "False Miracles and Unattested Dead Bodies: Investigations into Popular Cults in Early Modern Russia." In *Religion and the Early Modern State: Views from China, Russia, and the West*, ed. James D. Tracy and Marguerite Ragnow, 253–83. Cambridge, 2004.

———. "From Corpse to Cult in Early Modern Russia." In Kivelson and Greene, *Orthodox Russia*, 81–103.

———. *Sex and Society in the World of the Orthodox Slavs, 900–1700*. Ithaca, 1989.

———. "Supplicatory Prayers as a Source for Popular Religious Culture in Muscovite Russia." In Baron and Kollman, *Religion and Culture*, 96–114.

Lewin, Moshe. "Popular Religion in Twentieth-Century Russia." In Moshe Lewin, *The Making of the Soviet System: Essays in the Social History of Interwar Russia*, 57–71. New York, 1994.

"Likvidatsiia moshchei Ioasafa Belgorodskogo." *Revoliutsiia i tserkov'*, no. 9–12 (1920): 106.

Lincoln, Bruce. "Revolutionary Exhumations in Spain, July 1936." *Contemporary Studies in Society and History* 27 (1985): 241–60.

Listov, V. "'Sviatye moshchi' na ekrane." *Nauka i zhizn'*, no. 10 (1965): 46–48.

Liukov, I. V. *Taina serebrianoi grobnitsy*. Lipetsk, 1963.

Lobazov, P. K. "Bor'ba partii za ateisticheskoe vospitanie trudiashchikhsia mass v 1917–1925 gg." In *Obshchestvennye nauki: Materialy konferentsii*. Vladivostok, 1971.

Loginov, Anton. *Zhitiia sviatykh*. Moscow, 1930.

Lomakin, I. *Moshchi*. Moscow, 1919.

Lunacharskii, A. V. *Ob ateizme i religii: Sbornik statei, pisem, i drugikh materialov*. Moscow, 1972.

———. *Pochemu nel'zia verit' v boga? Izbrannye ateisticheskie proizvedeniia*. Moscow, 1965.

Luukkanen, Arto. *The Party of Unbelief: The Religious Policy of the Bolshevik Party, 1917–1929*. Helsinki, 1994.

———. *The Religious Policy of the Stalinist State. A Case Study: The Central Standing Commission, 1929–1938*. Helsinki, 1997.

MacCormack, Sabine. "Loca Sancta: The Organization of Sacred Topography in Late Antiquity." In *The Blessings of Pilgrimage*, ed. Robert Ousterhout, 7–40. Urbana, 1990.
Mackenney, Richard. "Public and Private in Renaissance Venice." *Renaissance Studies* 12 (1998): 109–30.
Manukhina, T. *Sviataia blagovernaia kniaginia Anna Kashinskaia*. Paris, 1954.
Marasanova, V. M. "Izmenenie otnoshenii tserkvi i gosudarstva ot grazhdanskoi k Velikoi Otechestvennoi Voine (na materialakh Volgo-Viatskogo i Iaroslavskogo kraia)." In *Religiia i tserkov' v kul'turno-istoricheskom razvitii Russkogo Severa (k 450-letiiu prepodobnogo Trifona, Viatskogo chudotvortsa)*. 2 vols. Kirov, 1996.
Marchadier, Bernard. "L'exhumation des reliques dans les premières années du pouvoir soviétique." *Cahiers du Monde Russe et Soviétique* 22 (1981): 67–88.
Marker, Gary. "God of Our Mothers: Reflections on Lay Female Spirituality in Late Eighteenth- and Early Nineteenth-Century Russia." In Kivelson and Greene, *Orthodox Russia*, 193–209.
———. *Publishing, Printing, and the Origins of Intellectual Life in Russia, 1700–1800*. Princeton, 1985.
Martin, Terry. "Interpreting the New Archival Signals: Nationalities Policy and the Nature of the Soviet Bureaucracy." *Cahiers du Monde Russe* 40 (1999): 113–24.
Martsinkovskii, V. F. *Zapiski veruiushchego: Iz istorii religioznogo dvizheniia v Sovetskoi Rossii (1917–1923)*. Prague, 1929.
Marx, Karl, *The Eighteenth Brumaire of Louis Bonaparte*. In *The Marx-Engels Reader*, ed. Robert C. Tucker, 594–617. 2nd ed. London and New York, 1978.
Materialy dlia istorii Tverskoi eparkhii. Tver, 1898.
Matorin, N. "Vserossiiskii muzeinii s"ezd i antireligioznaia rabota." *Antireligioznik*, no. 2 (1931): 62–64.
McCulloh, John. "The Cult of Relics in the Letters and 'Dialogues' of Pope Gregory the Great: A Lexicographical Study." *Traditio* 32 (1976): 145–84.
McDannell, Colleen. *Material Christianity: Religion and Popular Culture in America*. New Haven, 1995.
McReynolds, Louise. *The News under Russia's Old Regime: The Development of a Mass-Circulation Press*. Princeton, 1991.
Mechev, Archpriest Aleksii. "O moshchakh ugodnikov Bozhiikh." *Zhurnal Moskovskoi Patriarkhii*, no. 12 (1993): 68–71.
Meehan, Brenda. "The Authority of Holiness: Women Ascetics and Spiritual Elders in Nineteenth-Century Russia." In *Church, Nation, and State in Russia and Ukraine*, ed. Geoffrey A. Hosking, 38–51. London, 1991.
———. "Popular Piety, Local Initiative and the Founding of Women's Religious Communities in Russia, 1764–1907." In *Seeking God: The Recovery of Religious Identity in Orthodox Russia, Ukraine, and Georgia*, ed. Stephen K. Batalden, 83–105. DeKalb, 1993.
———. "To Save Oneself: Russian Peasant Women and the Development of Women's Religious Communities in Pre-Revolutionary Russia." In *Russian Peasant Women*, ed. Beatrice Farnsworth and Lynne Viola, 121–33. Oxford, 1992.
Meinardus, Otto. "A Study of the Relics of Saints of the Greek Orthodox Church." *Oriens Christianus* 54 (1970): 130–278.
Mel'nikov, A. *Putevoditel' dlia palomnikov v Serafimo-Sarovskuiu pustyn'*. Nizhnii Novgorod, 1903.
Mertsalov, Archimandrite Evgenii. *Kak sovershalas' kanonizatsiia sviatykh v pervoe vremia sushchestvovaniia russkoi tserkvi?* 2nd ed. Murom, 1910.
Meshcheriakov, N. *Popovskie prodelki*. Samara, 1919.
Meshcheriakov, V., M. Veremienko, and A. Katsigras, eds. *Kino-iazva: Ob uprazhdeniiakh Sovkino nad derevnei*. Leningrad, 1926.

Meshkov, A. "Vskrytie mogily skhimonakha Alekseia." *Bezbozhnik*, no. 23 (1928): 12.
Miasnikova, L. N. "Dokumenty svidetel'stvuiut . . . (Materialy GAVO o vskrytii moshchei prepodobnogo Feodosiia)." In *Tot'ma: Kraevedcheskii al'manakh*. Vyp. 2. Vologda, 1997.
Michels, Georg. "Rescuing the Orthodox: The Church Policies of Archbishop Afanasii of Kholmogory, 1682–1702." In *Of Religion and Empire: Missions, Conversion, and Tolerance in Tsarist Russia*, ed. Robert P. Geraci and Michael Khodarkovsky, 19–37. Ithaca, 2001.
———. "Ruling without Mercy: Seventeenth-Century Russian Bishops and Their Officials." *Kritika* 4 (2003): 515–42.
Mikhailov, Sergei Vladimirovich. "Gosudarstvo i tserkov': Otnosheniia organov vlasti, religioznykh organizatsii i veruiushchikh na Arkhangel'skom Severe v 1918–1929 gg.." Kand. diss., Pomorskii gosudarstvennyi universitet im. M. V. Lomonosova (Arkhangel'sk), 1998.
Mitrokhin, L. N., ed. *Khristianstvo: Slovar'*. Moscow, 1994.
Mitskevich, S. I. *Zapiski vracha-obshchestvennika (1888–1918)*. 2nd ed. Moscow, 1969.
Mokeev, G. Ia., and I. Iu. Merkulova. "Kashin XVI–XVII vv. i goroda skhodnogo tipa." *Arkhitekturnoe nasledstvo* 36 (1988): 165–74.
Mol'kov, A. V. "Gosudarstvennyi Institut sotsial'noi gigieny Narodnogo komissariata zdravookhraneniia." In *Piat' let sovetskoi meditsiny, 1918–1923*. Moscow, 1923.
Moore, R. Laurence. *Selling God: American Religion in the Marketplace of Culture*. Oxford, 1994.
Mordvinov, Vladimir. *Zhitiia sviatykh ugodnikov Bozhiikh v predelakh Vologodskoi eparkhii, proslavlennykh Tserkov'iu i mestno chtimykh*. Moscow, 1879.
Morozov, Iakov Maksimovich. "Kak teper' postupiat s moshchami Sergiia Radonezhskogo?" *Pravda*, no. 82 (16 April 1919): 2.
"Moshchi istseleli." *Revoliutsiia i tserkov'*, no. 2 (1919): 36.
Motorin, I. *Netlennye moshchi i revoliutsiia (Istoricheskii ocherk)*. Khar'kov, 1927.
Muller, Alexander V., trans. and ed. *The Spiritual Regulation of Peter the Great*. Seattle, 1972.
Naiman, Eric. *Sex in Public: The Incarnation of Early Soviet Ideology*. Princeton, 1999.
Narodnaia vera v sviatost' Patriarkha Ermogena i plody etoi very—chudesa sovershaiushchiiasia po Ego molitvam. Moscow, n.d.
Naumova, O. E. *Irkutskaia eparkhiia XVIII—pervaia polovina XIX veka*. Irkutsk, 1996.
Nazarevskii, K. K. *Novoproslavlennyi sviatitel' Sviateishii Ermogen, Patriarkh vseia Rossii*. Moscow, 1912.
Nechaev, P. I. *Prakticheskoe rukovodstvo dlia sviashchennosluzhitelei, ili sistematicheskoe izlozhenie polnago kruga ikh obiazannostei i prav*. 12th ed. Petrograd, 1915.
Nechaeva, M. Iu. "Verkhoturskie monastyri v XX v." In *Ezhegodno Bogoslovskaia Konferentsiia Pravoslavnogo Sviato-Tikhonovskogo bogoslovskogo instituta: Materialy, 1999 g*. Moscow, 1999.
Neitman, M. L. "Iz istorii provedeniia v zhizn' Leninskogo dekreta ob otdelenii tserkvi ot gosudarstva i shkoly ot tserkvi (1918–1920 gg.)." In *Zabaikal'skii kraevedcheskii ezhegodnik*, no. 2. Chita, 1968.
"Neobychainoe religioznoe voodushevlenie v g. Kashine." *TEV*, no. 30 (21 July 1908): 670–73.
"'Nepobedimye soprotivnymi silami': Sud'ba sviatykh moshchei russkikh ugodnikov Bozhiikh v XX veke." *Danilovskii blagovestnik*, no. 10 (1999): 31–39.
Nesterenko, V. V. *Rabotnitsa i religiia*. Moscow, 1926.
Nevskii, A. A. *Russkaia dukhovno-nravstvennaia khristomatiia*. 3rd ed. Moscow, 1874.
Nezhnyi, A. I. *Komissar d'iavola*. Moscow, 1993.
Nichols, Robert L. "The Friends of God: Nicholas II and Alexandra at the Canonization of Serafim of Sarov, July 1903." In *Religious and Secular Forces in Late Tsarist Russia: Essays*

in Honor of Donald W. Treadgold, ed. Charles E. Timberlake, 206–30. Seattle, 1992.
Nichols, Robert L., and Theofanis George Stavrou, eds. *Russian Orthodoxy Under the Old Regime*. Minneapolis, 1978.
Nikanor, Archimandrite. *Sv. German, vtoroi arkhiepiskop Kazanskii*. Kazan, 1890.
Nikol'skii, N., and M. Izvol'skii. *Sistematicheskii sbornik nedoumennykh voprosov i otvetov na nikh vstrechaiushchikhsia v tserkovno-prikhodskoi praktike, pomeshchennyia v izdavaemom pri S.-Peterburgskoi Dukhovnoi akademii "Tserkovnom vestnike" za posledniia (1875–1895) dvadtsat' let*. St. Petersburg, 1896.
Nikol'skii, V. *Sueveriia, znakharstvo, religioznye predrassudki i sovetskaia meditsina*. Moscow, 1926.
Nilson, Ben. *Cathedral Shrines of Medieval England*. Woodbridge, 2001.
Northrop, Douglas. *Veiled Empire: Gender and Power in Stalinist Central Asia*. Ithaca, 2004.
Novye chudesa ot moshchei Sviatitelia Feodosiia Uglitskago, arkhiepiskopa Chernigovskago. Chernigov, 1890.
"Novyi molitvennik za zemliu Russkuiu pred Gospodom, sviatitel' Feodosii Uglitskii, arkhiepiskop Chernigovskii." *Rukovodstvo dlia sel'skikh pastyrei*, t. 3, no. 41 (13 October 1896): 161–68.
O krestnykh khodakh sovershaemykh iz Moskovskago Uspenskago sobora. Moscow, 1893.
O netlenii sviatykh moshchei i chudesa ot nikh. Moscow, 1902.
O pochitanii moshchei sv. ugodnikov Bozhiikh. St. Petersburg, 1912.
O sviatykh Ugodnikakh Bozhiikh, koikh netlennyia moshchi pochivaiut v Uspenskom sobore. Moscow, 1893.
"Ob obychae sovershat' liturgiiu na moshchakh sviatykh." *Danilovskii blagovestnik*, no. 10 (1999): 23–25.
Ocherk istorii goroda Chernigova, 907–1907. Chernigov, 1908.
Odintsov, M. I. *Gosudarstvo i tserkov' (Istoriia vzaimootnoshenii. 1917–1938 gg.)* Moscow, 1991.
———, comp. and ed. ". . . 'My dolzhny byt' iskrennimi po otnosheniiu k sovetskoi vlasti.'" *Voprosy nauchnogo ateizma* 39 (1989): 292–331.
Oglezneva, G. V. "Usloviia deiatel'nosti pravoslavnoi tserkvi v vostochnoi Sibiri vo vtoroi polovine XIX–nachale XX vekov: Regional'nye osobennosti." In *Konfessii narodov Sibiri v XVII–nachale XX vv.: Razvitie i vzaimodeistvie*. Irkutsk, 2005.
Orlov, Vasilii. *Rukovoditel' Vladimirskikh bogomol'tsev*. Vladimir, 1880.
Orlova, V. D. "Massovye politicheskie prazdnestva 1917–1918 godov v guberniiakh chernozemnogo tsentra." In *Obshchestvenno-politicheskaia zhizn' rossiiskoi provintsii, XX vek*. Vyp. 1. Tambov, 1993.
Orsi, Robert A. *The Madonna of 115th Street: Faith and Community in Italian Harlem, 1880–1950*. New Haven, 2002.
———. *Thank You, Saint Jude: Women's Devotion to the Patron Saint of Hopeless Causes*. New Haven, 1996.
Ostroumov, Archpriest Stefan. *Pis'ma o pravoslavnom blagochestii*. 2nd ed. St. Petersburg, 1907.
Ostrov, Pavel, *O pochitanii sviatykh moshchei*. Moscow, 1847.
"Ot chego chasto ne ispolniaiutsia molitvy nashi?" *Tverskia eparkhial'nyia vedomosti*, no. 18 (15 September 1880): 330–40.
"Otchet o deiatel'nosti V (likvidatsionnogo) Otdela Narodnogo Komissariata Iustitsii." *Revoliutsiia i tserkov'*, no. 1–3 (1922): 66–80.
Ot Komiteta po delu otkrytiia i proslavleniia chestnykh ostankov Mitropolita Iosif Ubiennago. Astrakhan, 1911.
P. "Torgovlia moshchami." *Bezbozhnik*, no. 3 (15 February 1932): 16.
P. L. *Kievo-Pecherskaia Lavra v eia proshedshem i nyneishnem sostoianii, s fasadami velikoi Lavrskoi tserkvi, planom eia i planom peshcher*. Kiev, 1894.
Palomnichestvo. Putevyia vpechatleniia. Tula, 1902.
Pamiat' o Chernigove, 6–9 sentiabria 1896 goda. Sviatitel' Feodosii Uglitskii, arkhiepiskop

Chernigovskii i Novgorodseverskii. Kiev, 1897.
Pamiati novoproslavlennago sviatitelia Feodosiia Uglitskago, arkhiepiskopa Chernigovskago. Tobol'sk, 1899.
Pamiati sv. blagovernoi kniagini Anny Kashinskoi. Moscow, 1909.
Panchenko, A. A., and A. M. Panchenko. "Os'moe chudo sveta." In *Kanun: Al'manakh.* Vyp. 16: *Poliarnost' v kul'ture*, ed. V. E. Bagno and T. A. Novichkova. St. Petersburg, 1996.
Pankeev, Ivan. *Obychai i traditsii russkogo naroda.* Moscow, 1999.
Paozerskii, M. F. *Prepodobnyi Serafim Sarovskii.* Moscow, 1924.
———. *Russkie sviatye pred sudom istorii.* Moscow, 1923.
Pastukhov. "Itogi ankety po religioznomu voprosu sredi molodykh krasnoarmeitsev (21-i kavaleriiskii polk 4-i divizii)." *Antireligioznik*, no. 6 (June 1926): 58-59.
Peeters, P. "La canonisation des saints dans l'Eglise russe." *Analecta Bollandiana* 33 (1914): 380–420; 38 (1920): 172–76.
Pereira, N. G. O. *White Siberia: The Politics of Civil War.* Montreal, 1996.
Peris, Daniel. "Commissars in Red Cassocks: Former Priests in the League of the Militant Godless." *Slavic Review* 54 (1995): 340–64.
———. *Storming the Heavens: The Soviet League of the Militant Godless.* Ithaca, 1998.
Persits, M. M., ed. *Deiateli Oktiabria o religii i tserkvi: Stat'i, rechi, besedy, vospominaniia.* Moscow, 1968.
———. *Otdelenie tserkvi ot gosudarstva i shkoly ot tserkvi v SSSR (1917–1919 gg.)* Moscow, 1958.
Petrenko, M. Z. *Pravda pro pechery i moshchi Kyïvs'koï lavry.* Kiev, 1957.
Petrovskii, I. E. *Chernigovskaia guberniia v etnograficheskom, administrativnom, ekonomicheskom, promyshlennom, uchebnom i drugikh otnosheniiakh. 1915 god.* Chernigov, 1915.
Piat' let Voronezhskogo antireligioznogo muzeia. Voronezh, 1935.
Pilnyak, Boris. *The Naked Year.* Translated by Alexander R. Tulloch. Ann Arbor, 1975.
Pina-Cabral, João de. *Sons of Adam, Daughters of Eve: The Peasant Worldview of the Alto Minho.* Oxford, 1986.
Pipes, Richard. *Russia under the Bolshevik Regime.* New York, 1993.
Pisarev-Bogoliubskii, F. *Rostov s tochki zreniia bezbozhnika.* Rostov, 1929.
Plaksin, R. Iu. *Krakh tserkovnoi kontrrevoliutsii, 1917–1923 gg.* Moscow, 1968.
Platonov, Archpriest I. A. *Novye chudesa ot moshchei Sviatitelia Feodosiia Uglitskago, arkhiepiskopa Chernigovskago.* Chernigov, 1890.
Platonov, Archpriest Ioann. "Slovo v nedeliu Syropustnuiu i den' 200-letiia so vremeni blazhennoi konchiny Sviatitelia Feodosiia Uglitskago, Arkhiepiskopa Chernigovskago, 4 fevralia 1896 goda." *Chernigovskiia eparkhial'nyia izvestiia*, no. 4 (15 February 1896): 119–23.
Pletnev, M. D. *U moshchei sviatitelia Iosafa. Vpechatleniia palomnika.* Moscow, 1911.
"Pod flagam religii." *Revoliutsiia i tserkov'.* no. 1 (1919): 23.
Pokrovskii, N. N., and S. G. Petrov, eds. *Arkhivy Kremlia: Politbiuro i tserkov', 1922–1925 gg.* 2 vols. Moscow, 1997.
Pokrovskii, Priest. *Sv. blagovernaia kniaginia Anna Kashinskaia. Zhizn', chudesa i molitvennoe pochitanie blagovernoi kniagini Anny Kashinskoi pravoslavnym russkim narodom.* Moscow, 1909.
Polunov, A. Iu. "The State and Religious Heterodoxy in Russia (from 1880 to the beginning of the 1890s)." *Russian Studies in History* 39 (2001): 54–65.
Ponomarev, K. *Netlenie sv. moshchei i znachenie ikh dlia khristianina.* Chernigov, 1915.
Popov, Priest Ioann. *V Kashin i Poltavu, na vserossiiskiia torzhestva i "mimoezdy moi" (Nabliudeniia, vpechatleniia i zametki palomnika-turista).* Vladikavkaz, 1909.
Popov, M. V. *Kul'tura i byt krest'ian Urala v 1920–1941 godakh.* Ekaterinburg, 1997.
Popovic, Danila. "The Political Role of Relics in Medieval Serbia." In *Relikvii v iskusstve i kul'ture vostochnokhristianskogo mira*, ed. A. M. Lidov, 58–61. Moscow, 2000.

Porterfield, Amanda. *Healing in the History of Christianity*. Oxford, 2005.
Poselianin, E. *Vpechatlenie bogomol'tsa u moshchei Sviatitelia Feodosiia, novoiavlennago chudotvortsa Chernigovskago*. Moscow, 1897.
"Poslanie Sviateishago Sinoda vozliublennym o Gospode chadam Pravoslavnoi Russkoi Tserkvi o vozstanovlenii tserkovnago pochitaniia blagovernoi velikoi kniagini Anny Kashinskoi." Published as a special supplement to *Tserkovnyia vedomosti*, no. 21 (23 May 1909).
Pospielovsky, Dimitry V. *Soviet Antireligious Campaigns and Persecutions*. New York, 1988.
Postnov, O. G. "Netlennye moshchi i mertvye dushi: smert' v Rossii." In *Traditsiia i literaturnyi protsess*. Novosibirsk, 1999.
"Pozharnye o moshchakh." *Revoliutsiia i tserkov'*, no. 2 (1919): 36.
"Praktika antireligioznoi bor'by." *Revoliutsiia i tserkov'*, no. 1 (1919): 6–12.
Pravoslavnye chudesa v XX veke: Svidetel'stva ochevidtsev. Moscow, 1993.
Programma torzhestvennago sobraniia v pamiat' Sviateishago Germogena, Patriarkha Vserossiiskago, 19 fevralia 1912 goda. Moscow, 1912.
Prokopovich, Archbishop Feofan. *Razsuzhdenie o netlenii moshchei sviatykh ugodnikov Bozhiikh, v Kievskikh peshcherakh, netlenno pochivaiushchikh*. Moscow, 1786.
Prudnikov. *Istoricheskiia svideniia o blagovernoi kniagine Anne Kashinskoi, supruge sv. Mikhaila Tverskago*. 2nd ed. St. Petersburg, 1859.
Puteshestvie Irkutianina v Bargrad dlia pokloneniia moshcham Sviatitelia Nikolaia Chudotvortsa. St. Petersburg, 1861.
Putintsev, F. "Grazhdanskaia voina, NEP, i religiia." *Antireligioznik*, no. 11 (November 1926): 3–8.
Raleigh, Donald J. *Experiencing Russia's Civil War: Politics, Society, and Revolutionary Culture in Saratov, 1917–1922*. Princeton, 2002.
Ramer, Samuel C. "Feldshers and Rural Health Care in the Early Soviet Period." In Solomon and Hutchinson, *Health and Society in Revolutionary Russia*, 121–45.
Ranovich, A. *Proiskhozhednie khristianskogo kul'ta sviatykh*. Moscow, 1931.
Ratcliffe, Barrie M. "Workers and Religion in Mid-Nineteenth-Century Paris: The Evidence from the Timing of Weddings and Baptisms." *Historical Reflections/Réflexions Historique* 24 (1998): 283–327.
Redfield, Robert. *Peasant Society and Culture: An Anthropological Approach to Civilization*. Chicago, 1956.
Regel'son, Lev. *Tragediia Russkoi Tserkvi, 1917–1945*. Paris, 1977.
Reinburg, Virginia. "Praying to Saints in the Late Middle Ages." In *Saints: Studies in Hagiography*, ed. Sandro Sticca, 269–82. Binghamton, 1996.
Rey, Terry. *Our Lady of Class Struggle: The Cult of the Virgin Mary in Haiti*. Trenton, 1999.
Robson, Roy R. *Solovki: The Story of Russia Told through Its Most Remarkable Islands*. New Haven, 2004.
———. "Transforming Solovki: Pilgrim Narratives, Modernization, and Late Imperial Monastic Life." In Steinberg and Coleman, *Sacred Stories*, 44–60.
Rock, Stella. *Popular Religion in Russia: "Double Belief" and the Making of an Academic Myth*. New York, 2007.
Rogozianskii, A. *Strasti po moshcham: Iz istorii gonenii na ostanki sviatykh v sovetskoe vremia*. St. Petersburg, 1998.
Rol'f, Mal'te [Malte Rolf]. *Sovetskii massovyi prazdnik v Voronezhe i Tsentral'no-Chernozemnoi oblasti Rossii (1927–1932)*. Voronezh, 2000.
Romanov, Priest V. *Kratkiia skazaniia o zhitii sviatykh ugodnikov Bozhiikh, koikh chastitsy moshchei pochivaiut v khrame Sviatyia Troitsy, s. Isache, Lubenskago uezda*. Poltava, 1901.
Romodanovskaia, E. K. "Rasskazy sibirskikh krest'ian o videniiakh (k voprosu o spetsifike zhanra videnii)." *Trudy Otdela drevnerusskoi literatury* 49 (1996): 141–56.

Rossiev, Pavel. *Velikii pechal'nik za rodinu, Patriarkh Germogen: Istoricheskii ocherk.* Moscow, 1912.
Rothkrug, Lionel. "The 'Odour of Sanctity' and the Hebrew Origins of Christian Relic Veneration." *Historical Reflections/Réflexions Historiques* 8 (1981): 95–142.
———. "Religious Practices and Collective Perceptions: Hidden Homologies in the Renaissance and Reformation." *Historical Reflections/Réflexions Historiques* 7 (1980): 1–264.
Rozhitsyn, Vladimir, "Kogda i pochemu poiavilas' vera v moshchi." In Rozhitsyn, *Moshchi*, 3–29.
———, ed. *Moshchi: Sbornik materialov, dokumentov i razoblachenii.* Kharkiv, 1922.
Rublev, Andrei. "O moshchakh i prochikh veshchakh." *Izvestiia Vladimirskogo gubernskogo i uezdnogo ispolnitel'nykh komitetov sovetov rabochikh, krasnoarmeitskikh i krest'ianskikh deputatov,* no. 38/198 (19 February 1919): 2.
The Russian Primary Chronicle: Laurentian Text, ed. Samuel Hazzard Cross and Olgerd P. Sherbowitz-Wetzor. Cambridge, MA, 1953.
Russkaia pravoslavnaia tserkov' i kommunisticheskoe gosudarstvo, 1917–1941 gg.: Dokumenty i fotomaterialy. Moscow, 1996.
Russkaia sviatynia. St. Petersburg, 1873.
R—v, N. *Ocherk Kashina.* n.p., 1867.
"S kakoiu tseliiu khranit Gospod' moshchi pravednykh." *Kormchi,* no. 40 (1896): 528–29.
Sadkov, Vitalii Nikolaevich. "Narkomat iustitsii RSFSR i sovetskoe zakonodatel'stvo (1917–1922 gody)." Doktor ist. nauk. diss., Rossiiskii gosudarstvennyi gumanitarnyi universitet, 1996.
Salat. "Kukla Tikhona v monastyre." *Sovetskaia gazeta,* no. 9/105 (31 January 1919): 1–2.
Salomatin, A. "Kul'turno-istoricheskie tsennosti i religioznaia propaganda." *Antireligioznik,* no. 7 (July 1928): 70–74.
Sarab'ianov, Vl. "Beglye vospominaniia." *Antireligioznik,* no. 10 (October 1927): 34–37.
———. *Ob antireligioznoi propagande.* 3rd ed. Moscow, 1926.
———. "Zhenshchina i religiia." *Bezbozhnik u stanka,* no. 8 (1923): 2.
Sarkis, Iu. *O sviatykh moshchakh, chudotvornykh ikonakh i prochikh popovskikh chudesakh.* Sverdlovsk, 1926.
Sazonov, V. V. "U istokov krest'ianskogo vosstaniia na Tambovshchine." *Voprosy istorii,* no. 4 (2001): 75–83.
Scott, James C. *Domination and the Arts of Resistance: Hidden Transcripts.* New Haven, 1990.
Semashko, N. "Nauka i sharlatanstvo (O vystavke 'moshchei')." *Revoliutsiia i tserkov',* no. 1–3 (1922): 30–32.
———. "Vopros o 'moshchakh' s nauchno-meditsinskoi tochki zreniia." *Revoliutsiia i tserkov',* no. 1 (1919): 16–17.
Semenov, N. "V byvshei Kievo-Pecherskoi lavre." *Bezbozhnik,* no. 12 (December 1937): 19.
Semenovskii, P. "Dannye nauki o mumifikatsii trupov." *Revoliutsiia i tserkov',* no. 9–12 (1920): 36–44.
Seredinskii, Priest Tarasii. "Opredelenie razlichiia mezhdu vostochnoiu i zapadnoiu tserkoviiu otnositel'no ucheniia o sostoianii dush sviatykh do vseobshchago voskreseniia." *Dukhovnaia beseda,* t. 11, no. 39 (24 September 1860): 98–105.
Shafir, Ia. *Gazety i derevnia.* 2nd ed. Moscow, 1924.
Shakhnovich, M. I. *Lenin i problemy ateizma: Kritika religii v trudakh V. I. Lenina.* Moscow, 1961.
Shangina, I. I. "Etnograficheskie muzei Leningrada v pervye gody sovetskoi vlasti (1918–1923 gg.)." *Sovetskaia etnografiia,* no. 5 (1987): 71–80.

---. "Etnograficheskie muzei Moskvy i Leningrada na rubezhe 20-x–30-x godov XX v." *Sovetskaia etnografiia*, no. 2 (1991): 71–80.
Sharf, Robert H. "The Idolization of Enlightenment: On the Mummification of Ch'an Masters in Medieval China." *History of Religions* 32 (1992): 1–31.
Shchukin, Priest V. *Patriarkh Germogen kak predstavitel' i pobornik natsional'noi religioznosti (1612–1912 g.)*. Riga, 1913.
Shervud, Boris. *Skazanie v stikakh o Patriarkhe Germogene*. Moscow, 1912.
Shevzov, Vera. "Chapels and the Ecclesial World of Pre-Revolutionary Russian Peasants." *Slavic Review* 55 (1996): 585–613.
---. "Letting the People into Church: Reflections on Orthodoxy and Community in Late Imperial Russia." In Kivelson and Greene, *Orthodox Russia*, 59–77.
---. "Miracle-Working Icons, Laity, and Authority in the Russian Orthodox Church, 1861–1917." *Russian Review* 58 (1999): 26–48.
---. *Russian Orthodoxy on the Eve of Revolution*. Oxford, 2004.
Shidenko, V. A. *Peshchery i moshchi Kievo-Pecherskoi Lavry*. Kiev, 1962.
Shishakov, V. "Moshchi, chudesa i antireligioznaia propaganda." *Bezbozhnik*, no. 11 (June 1930): 9.
Shishakov, V. A. *Pogovorim o religii*. Moscow, 1960.
Shkarovskii, Mikhail V. *Peterburgskaia eparkhiia v gody gonenii i utrat, 1917–1945*. St. Petersburg, 1995.
---. "The Russian Orthodox Church." In *Critical Companion to the Russian Revolution*, ed. Edward Acton, Vladimir Iu. Cherniaev, and William G. Rosenberg, 424–27. London, 1997.
---. *Russkaia pravoslavnaia tserkov' i Sovetskoe gosudarstvo v 1943–1964 godakh: Ot "peremiriia" k novoi voine*. St. Petersburg, 1995.
---. *Russkaia pravoslavnaia tserkov' pri Staline i Khrushcheve: Gosudarstvenno-tserkovnye otnosheniia v SSSR v 1939–1964 godakh*. Moscow, 1999.
Shkol'noe puteshestvie v Zadonsk na bogomol'e. Voronezh, 1890.
Siegelbaum, Lewis, and Andrei Sokolov. *Stalinism as a Way of Life: A Narrative in Documents*. New Haven, 2000.
Silant'ev, V. I. *Bol'sheviki i pravoslavnaia tserkov' na Ukraine v 20-e gody*. Khar'kov, 1998.
Silver, Brian L. *The Ascent of Science*. Oxford, 2000.
Simakov, A. V. *Zhitie i podvigi blagovernoi velikoi kniagini Anny Kashinskoi*. Ural'sk, 1909.
Simonov, F. "Chto chitaiut nashi sovremennye krest'iane?" *Permskiia eparkhial'nyia vedomosti*, no. 13 (May 1914): 231–35.
Sin'kevich, Feodor (priest). *Palomnichestvo v Chernigov*. Kiev, 1916.
Sirin, A. D. "Sviatotattsy. Iz istorii moshchei sviatitelia Innokentiia (Kul'chitskogo)." In *Istoricheskie sud'by pravoslaviia v Sibiri*. Irkutsk, 1997.
Skobnikov, Archpriest Aleksandr. *Na mogile kashinskoi pravednitsy v Uspenskom sobore*. Elets, 1909.
---. *Sviataia blagovernaia kniaginia Anna Kashinskaia*. Kashin, 1909.
Skvortsov, V. M. *Chudesa ot netlennykh moshchei novoiavlennago Ugodnika Bozhiia, Sviatitelia Feodosiia (Uglitskago)*. Kiev, 1896.
---. *O pochitanii moshchei sv. ugodnikov Bozhiikh*. St. Petersburg, 1910.
Skvortsov-Stepanov, I. I. "Itogi nashei antireligioznoi bor'by i ee sovremennye zadachi." *Kommunisticheskaia revoliutsiia*, no. 4 (1923).
---. *Izbrannye ateisticheskie proizvedeniia*. Moscow, 1959.
Slater, Candace. *City Steeple, City Streets: Saints' Tales from Granada and a Changing Spain*. Berkeley and Los Angeles, 1990.
Sledstvennoe delo Patriarkha Tikhona: Sbornik dokumentov po materialam Tsentral'nogo arkhiva FSB RF. Moscow, 2000.
Slovar' istoricheskii o sviatykh, proslavlennykh v Rossiiskoi Tserkvi, i o nekotoryia podvizhni-

kakh blagochestiia, mestno chtimykh. 2nd ed. St. Petersburg, 1862.
Sluhovsky, Moshe. *Patroness of Paris: Rituals of Devotion in Early Modern France*. Leiden, 1998.
"Slushka dlia moshchei." *Bezbozhnik*, no. 1 (January 1926): 14.
Smirnov, Archimandrite Misail. *Sviatyi blagovernyi kniaz' Konstantin, prosvitel' Muromskago kraia, i chada ego: Mikhail i Feodor*. Vladimir, 1896.
Smirnov, Priest N. I. *O prikhodskikh palomnichestvakh ko sviatyniam*. Moscow, 1911.
Smirnov, Archpriest Petr. *Chudesa v prezhnee i nashe vremia*. 2nd ed. Moscow, 1895.
———. *U moshchei Sviatitelia Feodosiia v Chernigove. Vpechatleniia i vospominaniia*. St. Petersburg, 1902.
Smith, Steve A. "Local Cadres Confront the Supernatural: The Politics of Holy Water (*Shenshui*) in the PRC, 1949–1966." *China Quarterly* 188 (2006): 999–1022.
S—n, N. *O netlenii sviatykh moshchei*. Kiev, 1896.
Sokol, Evgenii. "Chistite partiiu i ot sviatosh." *Bezbozhnyi byt*, no. 1 (1 May 1929): 3.
Sokolov, A. I. *Kul't, kak neobkhodimaia prinadlezhnost' religii. Polemiko-apologicheskoe bogoslovskoe izsledovanie*. Kazan, 1900.
Sokolov, Priest A. V. *Sviatyi blagovernoi velikii kniaz' Mikhail Iaroslavich Tverskii*. Tver, 1864.
Sokolov, Priest V. *Sviateishii Patriarkh Germogen*. Moscow, 1912.
Solomon, Susan Gross, and John F. Hutchinson, eds. *Health and Society in Revolutionary Russia*. Bloomington, 1990.
Solov'ev, Archpriest I. *Kakoi smysl' i znachenie imeet prichtenie Sviateishago Patriarkha Ermogena k liku Sviatykh? V otvet nedoumevaiushchim i voproshaiushchim o znachenii etogo torzhestva i prave na nego Sviateishchago Sinoda*. Sergiev Posad, 1913.
Sosnin, Dmitrii. *O netlenii sviatykh moshchei v Tserkvi Khristianskoi*. St. Petersburg, 1832.
Sperber, Jonathan. *Popular Catholicism in Nineteenth-Century Germany*. Princeton, 1984.
Stark, Laura. *Peasants, Pilgrims, and Sacred Promises: Ritual and the Supernatural in Orthodox Karelian Folk Religion*. Helsinki, 2002.
Steinberg, Mark D. *Proletarian Imagination: Self, Modernity, and the Sacred in Russia, 1910–1925*. Ithaca, 2002.
———. *Voices of Revolution, 1917*. New Haven, 2001.
Steinberg, Mark D., and Heather J. Coleman, eds. *Sacred Stories: Religion and Spirituality in Modern Russia*. Bloomington, 2007.
Stepanov (Rusak), Vladimir. *Svidetel'stvo obvineniia*. 3 vols. Moscow, 1993.
Stevenson, J., ed. *Creeds, Councils and Controversies: Documents Illustrative of the History of the Church, A.D. 337–461*. New York, 1966.
Stites, Richard. "Iconoclastic Currents in the Russian Revolution: Destroying and Preserving the Past." In *Bolshevik Culture: Experiment and Order in the Russian Revolution*, ed. Abbot Gleason, Peter Kenez, and Richard Stites, 1–24. Bloomington, 1989.
———. *Revolutionary Dreams: Utopian Vision and Experimental Life in the Russian Revolution*. Oxford, 1989.
Stradalitsa, istselennaia moliltvami ugodnika Bozhiia, sv. Mitrofana Voronezhskago. St. Petersburg, 1874.
Stuchka, P. *Uchenie o gosudarstve i o konstitutsii R.S.F.S.R.* 3rd rev. ed. Moscow, 1923.
"Sudebnye protsessy o poddelke moshchei." In Rozhitsyn, *Moshchi*, 124–67.
Sv. Feodosii Uglitskii. Znameniia milosti Bozhiei po molitvam Sviatitelia. Moscow, 1896.
"Svetlye dni v gorode Kashine." *TEV*, no. 15–16 (20–27 April 1909): 291–98.
Sviashchennomuchenik Ermogen, Patriarkh Moskovskii i vseia Rossii Chudotvorets. Moscow, 1913.
Sviataia blagovernaia velikaia kniaginia Anna Kashinskaia. Moscow, 1910.
Sviateishii Patriarkh Germogen i chudesa ot ego moshchei. 17 fevralia 1612–1912 g. Moscow, 1911.
Sviatitel' Feodosii, Chudotvorets Chernigovskii. Chernigov, n.d.

Sviatiteli-podvizhniki novago vremeni, proslavlennye v XVIII–XIX stoletiiakh. Moscow, 1903.
"Sviatye chuchela." *Pravda*, no. 82 (16 April 1919): 2.
Sviatyni Chernigova. St. Petersburg, 1900.
Szczesniak, Boleslaw, ed. and trans. *The Russian Revolution and Religion: A Collection of Documents concerning the Suppression of Religion by the Communists, 1917–1925.* Notre Dame, 1959.
Taradin, I. P. *"Sviatoi" Mitrofan, episkop Voronezhskii.* Voronezh, 1926.
———. *Zadonskii Bogoroditskii monastyr' i Sviatoi Tikhon: Istoriko-kriticheskoe issledovanie.* Voronezh, 1927.
Theissen, Gerd. *The Miracle Stories of the Early Christian Tradition*, trans. Francis McDonagh. Edinburgh, 1983.
Thomas, Keith. *Religion and the Decline of Magic. Studies in Popular Beliefs in Sixteenth- and Seventeenth-Century England.* New York, 1971.
Thyrêt, Isolde. "Accounts of the Transfer of Relics and Cults of Saints in Muscovite Russia: Saints Arsenii and Mikhail of Tver." Paper presented to the conference "Modern History of Eastern Christianity: Transitions and Problems," Harvard University, 26–27 March 2004.
———. "Muscovite Miracle Stories as Sources for Gender-Specific Religious Experience." In Baron and Kollman, *Religion and Culture*, 115–31.
———. "Women and the Orthodox Faith in Muscovite Russia: Spiritual Experience and Practice." In Kivelson and Greene, *Orthodox Russia*, 159–75.
Tian-Shanskaia, Olga. *Village Life in Late Tsarist Russia.* Edited by David L. Ransel. Bloomington, 1993.
"Tikhon khochet uiti . . . ," *Sovetskaia gazeta*, no. 5/101 (19 January 1919): 6.
Titlinov, B. V. *Tserkov' vo vremia revoliutsii.* Petrograd, 1924.
Titov, Priest F. I. *Pouchitel'noe chtenie o znachenii torzhestvennago otkrytiia chestnykh moshchei sviatitelia Feodosiia, Chernigovskago chudotvortsa.* Kiev, 1896.
Tovarishch Lelia. "Rezul'taty bespartiinoi gubernskoi konferentsii zhenshchin-rabotnits gor. Vladimira." *Kommunistka*, no. 3–4 (August–September 1920): 32–33.
Trainor, Kevin. *Relics, Ritual, and Representation in Buddhism: Rematerializing the Sri Lankan* Theravāda *Tradition.* Cambridge, England, 1997.
Treadgold, Donald W. *The Great Siberian Migration: Government and Peasant in Resettlement from Emancipation to the First World War.* Princeton, 1957.
Tresviatskii, Priest Aleksandr. *Kalendar' sviashchennika.* Samara, 1893.
Trexler, Richard. "Florentine Religious Experience: The Sacred Image." *Studies in the Renaissance* 19 (1972): 7–41.
Troitskii, Priest A. G. *Palomnichestvo ko Sv. Muromskim Chudotvortsam.* Nizhnii Novgorod, 1917.
Troitskii, K. *Tserkov' i gosudarstvo v Rossii.* Moscow, 1923.
Trotsky, Leon. "Vodka, the Church, and the Cinema" (1923). In *Bolshevik Visions: First Phase of the Cultural Revolution in Russia*, ed. William G. Rosenberg, vol. 2, 106–9. Ann Arbor, 1984.
"'Tserkov' otdeliaetsia ot gosudarstva': Doklady eksperta Narkomiusta M. V. Galkina, 1918 g." *Istoricheskii arkhiv*, no. 6 (1993): 162–70; no. 1 (1994): 136–47.
Tsypin, Archpriest Vladislav. *Istoriia Russkoi tserkvi, 1917–1997.* Moscow, 1997.
———. *Russkaia tserkov', 1917–1925.* Moscow, 1996.
Tumarkin, Nina. *Lenin Lives! The Lenin Cult in Soviet Russia.* 2nd ed. Cambridge, MA, 1997.
Ul'ianov, Ivan. *Kazaki, tserkov' i Sovetskaia vlast'.* Moscow, 1920.
Uspenskii, F. B. "Netlennost' moshchei. Grecheskaia, russkaia i skandinavskaia traditsii." In *Relikvii v iskusstve i kul'ture vostochnokhristianskogo mira*, ed. A. M. Lidov, 42–45. Moscow, 2000.
van Os, Henk. *The Way to Heaven: Relic Veneration in the Middle Ages.* Baarn, 2001.
van Poppel, Frans. "Seasonality of Work, Religion and Popular Customs: The Seasonality

of Marriage in the Nineteenth- and Twentieth-Century Netherlands." *Continuity and Change* 10 (1995): 215–56.
Varushkin, Archpriest Nikolai. *Istselenie bol'noi pri rake moshchei Sviatago Feodosiia Chernigovskago*. Kazan, 1901.
Vasil'ev, Vasilii. *Istoriia kanonizatsii russkikh sviatykh*. Moscow, 1893.
Vasiutinskii, Archpriest Feodor. *Chernigov, ego sviatye khramy, chudotvornyia ikony i mestnochtimyia sviatyni*. Chernigov, 1911.
Vauchez, André. *Sainthood in the Later Middle Ages*. Translated by Jean Birrell. Cambridge, England, 1997.
Veisensel, Piter R. [Peter R. Weisensel]. "Soobshcheniia russkikh krest'ian-palomnikov o Palestine kak otobrazhenie zhizni russkoi sel'skoi obshchiny." *Pravoslavnyi Palestinskii sbornik*, no. 31/94 (1992): 37–44.
Venediktov, G. "Tsarskaia okhrana i moshchi Serafima Sarovskogo." *Ateist*, no. 56–57 (1930): 1–35.
Vera, sueveriia i krest'ianskoe khoziastvo. Leningrad, 1925.
Veremienko, M. "Kakie kartiny dalo Sovkino dlia dereveni? (Material na noiabr' 1925 g.)." In *Kino-iazva: Ob uprazhdeniiakh Sovkino nad derevnei*, ed. V. Meshcheriakov, M. Veremienko, and A. Katsigras, 18–25. Leningrad, 1926.
Veriuzhskii, Priest Ioann. *Istoricheskiia skazaniia o zhizni sviatykh podvizavshikhsia v Vologodskoi eparkhii proslavliaemykh vseiu Tserkoviiu i mestno chtimykh*. Vologda, 1880.
Veselovskii, G. M. *Voronezh v istoricheskom i sovremenno-statisticheskom otnosheniiakh s podrobnym planom goroda i ego okrestnostei*. Voronezh, 1866.
Vesennie i letnie religioznye prazdniki, ikh sushchnost' i vred. Stalingrad, 1938.
Viola, Lynne. "*Bab'i bunty* and Peasant Women's Protest during Collectivization." *Russian Review* 45 (1986): 23–42.
———. "Introduction." In Lynne Viola, ed., *Contending with Stalinism: Soviet Power and Popular Resistance in the 1930s*, 1–16. Ithaca, 2002.
———. "The Peasant Nightmare: Visions of the Apocalypse in the Soviet Countryside." *Journal of Modern History* 62 (1990): 747–70.
Vissarion, Bishop. *O khristianskikh imenakh*. 2nd ed. Moscow, 1890.
Vlastov, P. M. *O netlenii sviatykh moshchei. Kratkoe istoricheskoe izsledovanie*. Moscow, 1890.
Volkov, Sergei. *Poslednie u Troitsy: Vospominaniia o Moskovskoi dukhovnoi akademii (1917–1920)*. Moscow, 1995.
Voronets, E. N. *Ob angelakh-khraniteliakh i o podrazhanii sviatym, imenami kotorykh my nazyvaemsia*. Khar'kov, 1877.
Voronina, T. A. *Russkii lubok 20–60-x godov XIX veka: Proizvodstvo, bytovanie, tematika*. Moscow, 1993.
———. "Russkii religioznyi lubok." *Zhivaia starina*, no. 3 (1994): 6–11.
Vorontsov, G. V. *Leninskaia programma ateisticheskogo vospitaniia v deistvii (1917–1937 gg.)*. Leningrad, 1973.
Vospominaniia o Lenine. Moscow, 1955.
Vostryshev, M. I. *Patriarkh Tikhon*. Moscow, 1995.
"Vskrytie moshchei Anny Kashinskoi." *Bezbozhnik*, no. 4 (February 1930): 14–15.
"Vskrytie moshchei Evrosinii Polotskoi." *Revoliutsiia i tserkov'*, no. 1–2 (1924): 94–95.
"Vskrytie moshchei Ioasafa Belgorodskogo." *Kurskaia pravda*, no. 270/304 (10 December 1920): 2.
"Vskrytie 'moshchei' v Solovkakh." *Bezbozhnik*, no. 2 (1925): 8–9.
Vvedenskii, A. I. *Tserkov' i gosudarstvo: Ocherk vzaimootnoshenii tserkvi i gosudarstva v Rossii, 1918–1922*. Moscow, 1923.
Waddy, Helena. "St. Anthony's Bread: The Modernized Religious Culture of German Catholics in the Early Twentieth Century." *Journal of Social History* 31 (1997): 347–70.

Wagner, William G. "Paradoxes of Piety: The Nizhegorod Convent of the Exaltation of the Cross, 1807–1935." In Kivelson and Greene, *Orthodox Russia*, 211–38.
Ware, Kallistos. "'My Helper and My Enemy': The Body in Greek Christianity." In *Religion and the Body*, ed. Sarah Coakley, 90–110. Cambridge, England, 1997.
Weinstein, Donald, and Rudolph Bell. *Saints and Society: The Two Worlds of Western Christendom, 1000–1700*. Chicago, 1982.
Weissman, Neil B. "Origins of Soviet Health Administration: Narkomzdrav, 1918–1928." In Solomon and Hutchinson, *Health and Society in Revolutionary Russia*, 97–120.
Williams, Sarah. "Urban Popular Religion and the Rites of Passage." In *European Religion in the Age of Great Cities, 1830–1930*, ed. Hugh McLeod, 216–36. New York, 1995.
Wilson, Stephen. *The Means of Naming: A Social and Cultural History of Naming in Western Europe*. London, 1998.
———, ed. *Saints and Their Cults: Studies in Religious Sociology, Folklore and History*. Cambridge, 1983.
Wood, Alan. "Russia's 'Wild East': Exile, Vagrancy and Crime in Nineteenth-Century Siberia." In Alan Wood, ed., *The History of Siberia: From Russian Conquest to Revolution*, 117–39. London, 1991.
Wood, Elizabeth A. *Performing Justice: Agitation Trials in Early Soviet Russia*. Ithaca, 2005.
Worobec, Christine D. "Death Ritual among Russian and Ukrainian Peasants: Linkages between the Living and the Dead." In Frank and Steinberg, *Cultures in Flux*, 11–33.
———. "Miraculous Healings." In Steinberg and Coleman, *Sacred Stories*, 22–43.
———. *Possessed: Women, Witches, and Demons in Imperial Russia*. DeKalb, 2001.
Wortman, Richard. *Scenarios of Power: Myth and Ceremony in Russian Monarchy*. Volume 2: *From Alexander II to the Abdication of Nicholas II*. Princeton, 2000.
Wynot, Jennifer J. *Keeping the Faith: Russian Orthodox Monasticism in the Soviet Union, 1917–1939*. College Station, 2004.
Yaroslavsky, E. *Religion in the U.S.S.R.* 2nd rev. ed. London, 1932.
Young, Glennys. *Power and the Sacred in Revolutionary Russia: Religious Activists in the Village*. University Park, 1997.
Zaitseva, L. Iu. "Prikhodskaia zhizn' v iuzhnom Zaural'e v pervye gody Sovetskoi vlasti." In *Kul'tura Zaural'ia: Proshloe i nastoiashchee*. Kurgan, 1998.
Zavadskii, I. "Velikii sharlatan." *Izvestiia Vladimirskogo gubernskogo i uezdnogo ispolnitel'nykh komitetov sovetov rabochikh, krasnoarmeitskikh i krest'ianskikh deputatov*, no. 42/202 (23 February 1919): 2–3.
Zav'ialov, Priest Ioann. *Gorod Kashin, ego istoriia, sviatyni i dostoprimechatel'nosti. S kratkim zhitiem blagovernoi kniagini Anny*. St. Petersburg, 1909.
Zbarsky, Ilya, and Samuel Hutchinson. *Lenin's Embalmers*. Translated by Barbara Bray. London, 1998.
Zhakov, M. "Dva Makariia." *Bezbozhnik u stanka*, no. 5 (May 1923): 15.
Zhekulin, V. "Kak tvoriat chudesa." In *Molodym bezbozhnikam: Materialy k komsomol'skomu rozhdestvu*. Moscow, 1924.
Zhitie i otkrytie netlennykh moshchei Sviatitelia Feodosiia Uglitskago, arkhiepiskopa Chernigovskago. Moscow, 1896.
Zhizn' i podvigi sviatitelei Moskovskikh: Petra, Aleksiia, Iony, Filippa i Germogena. Moscow, 1903.
Zhurnaly Irkutskago 49-go ekstrennago eparkhial'nago s"ezda dukhovenstva i mirian Irkutskoi eparkhii 29 maia–11 iiunia 1917 goda. Nizheudinsk, 1917.
Zybkovets, V. F. *Natsionalizatsiia monastyrskikh imushchestv v sovetskoi Rossii, 1917–1921 gg.* Moscow, 1975.
Zyrianov, P. N. *Russkie monastyri i monashestvo v XIX i nachale XX veka*. Moscow, 1999.

Index

Adrian Poshekhonskii (saint), 149
Aleksandr, bishop of Vologda, 17–19, 22
Aleksandr Nevskii (prince and saint), 25, 111, 112, 113, 118–19, 260n.64; icon of, 109; petitions concerning, 155, 175; rumors of exhumation, 183
Aleksandr Svirskii (saint), 25; exhumation of, 123–26, 127, 138, 140, 158, 197
Aleksandro-Nevskaia Lavra, 118–19, 255n.123, 265n.19
Aleksandro-Svirskii monastery, 123–26
Aleksei Mikhailovich, tsar, 77, 88
Aleksii (saint and prelate), 176–77
Aleksii the Man of God (saint), 25
Aleksii (Simanskii), bishop of Novgorod: trial of, 135–37; in defense of relics, 168, 170, 171
Alexander II, emperor, 86
Alexander III, emperor, 66, 82, 109
All-Union Central Executive Committee. *See* VTsIK
Altrichter, Helmut, 201
Amenitskii, Ioann, 83–84, 86
Andrei Bogoliubskii (prince and saint), 42, 154
Anna Kashinskaia (princess and saint), 15, 190, 210; canonizations of, 74–74, 76–79, 86–88; exhumation of, 198, 205; gifts offered to, 66, 88; icons of, 89; Orthodox devotion to, 78–88; relics of, 23, 82–83. *See also* Kashin
antireligious museums, 146–53; during First Five Year Plan, 206–7. *See also* Central Antireligious Museum; Museum of Social Hygiene
antireligious policy: during the Revolution and Civil War, 104–21, 141, 180; during NEP, 201–4; during First Five Year Plan, 204–7; resistance and response to, 163–64, 165–95. *See also* Bolshevik Party; exhumation of relics
antireligious propaganda: and cinema, 153–55; and clergy, 132–37; and satire, 114–15, 130–32, 207–8; and science, 144–46, 151–52. *See also* antireligious museums

Antonii (saint). *See* Vilnius Martyrs
Arkhangel'sk, 65, 118, 127, 129, 200, 247n.62, 249n.29
Arsenii the Miracle-Worker (saint), 182–83, 191, 192, 235n.11, 253n.103
Artemii Verkol'skii (saint), 25; exhumation of, 129–30
Avraamii the Martyr (saint), 42, 53–54; exhumation of, 131–32, 167, 185

Baba-Yaga, 208
Baptists, 35–36
Balabanoff, Angelica, 173
Bari, 39–41, 43
Basil the Great, 22
Besedy iz zhizni sviatykh, 27
Bestuzhevo, 186–88
Bezbozhnik, 205
Bezhetsk, 84
Blagoveshchenskii Cathedral (Kashin), 83
Blagoveshchenskii monastery (Vladimir), 43, 127–29
Bliakhin, P. A., 143, 159, 249n.28
Bogoiavlenskii Cathedral (Irkutsk), 93, 97, 98
Bolshevik Party, 15–16, 210–11; on canonization, 106–9, 113–15; and definition of relics, 17–20. *See also* antireligious policy; antireligious propaganda; exhumation of relics
Bonch-Bruevich, V. D., 105, 140, 153, 155, 197, 198
Borisoglebskii Cathedral (Chernigov), 20
Brooks, Jeffrey, 26
Brothers Karamazov, The, 136
Brown, Peter, 12, 32, 35, 47, 71
Bukharin, N. I., 105, 140, 142
Bulgakov, S. D., 33
Burke, Peter, 8

canonization, 8, 14, 86–88, 94, 99; Bolshevik position on, 106–9, 113–15; criteria for, 59, 95–97; Orthodox position on, 74–76. *See also* relics; saints; and individual saints
Cassiday, Julie A., 135

294 ~ Index

Cathedral of the Annunciation (Moscow), 3–4, 245n.35
Cathedral of the Archangel (Moscow), 3
Catholics, 29, 34–35, 57, 61
Central Antireligious Museum (Moscow), 152–53. *See also* antireligious museums
Central Black Earth Region, 44, 199, 201
Chernigov, 12, 13, 20, 23, 34, 43, 47, 53–55, 164, 203; diocesan press in, 17, 37, 44–45, 61–62; miracle stories in, 61–69. *See also* Feodosii Chernigovskii (saint)
Chita, 93
Christian, William, 13
Chudov monastery (Moscow), 140
Chulos, Chris, 44
Church Council of 1666–67, 20
Church Council of 1677–78, 74–5, 84, 86, 88
Church Sobor of 1917–18, 98, 99, 112–13, 117
Civil War: administrative difficulties during, 198–201; heroic ethos of, 143–44; and Orthodox Church, 113–21, 171; petitions during, 174; show trials during, 135. *See also* antireligious policy
clergy: attitudes toward the saints, 8–9, 24–25, 38, 71–72; opposition to antireligious policy by, 115–21, 166–71, 200–1; as recipients of miracles, 69–70; as recorders of miracle stories, 64–65, 83–84; sermons and services of, 26–27, 33–36, 71; Soviet stereotypes of, 19, 132–37; on trial after 1917, 135–37, 204
Constantine, Byzantine emperor, 111
Council of People's Commissars. *See* Sovnarkom
cult of the saints: adaptability of, 14, 16, 210; and local dimension, 73–102, 185–93, 211; physicality of, 10–11, 16, 41–42, 163; and reciprocity, 11–12, 41–42, 64–72, 76, 92–94, 163–64, 177–80, 189, 195, 211. *See also* miracles; pilgrimage; relics; Russian Orthodoxy; saints; shrines; women

Danilovskii monastery (Moscow), 86, 166
David Muromskii (prince and saint), 27

Delooz, Pierre, 17
Denikin, A. I., 113, 114, 208
Dimitrii Rostovskii (saint), 29–30, 50, 205
Dmitrii Ivanovich (saint and prince), 3–4
Donskoi monastery (Moscow), 204
Dostoevsky, F. M., 136
Dukhovnaia beseda, 33, 35, 73, 110

Eire, Carlos M. N., 106
Ekaterinburg, 10
Elisei Sumskii (saint); exhumation of, 168; rumors concerning, 183
Elizabeth Petrovna, empress, 90
Engelstein, Laura, 9
Eniseisk, 154, 200
Enukidze, Avel, 197–98, 199
Evfrosiniia Muromskaia (saint), 27
Evfrosiniia Polotskaia (saint): exhumation of, 167; relics on display, 153
Evstafii (saint). *See* Vilnius Martyrs
exhumation of relics, 15–19, 104–6, 122–59; Bolshevik reservations concerning, 196–204; Orthodox response and resistance to, 161–95, 200–201; as revolutionary tactic, 157–59, 207–9; rumors surrounding, 182–85. *See also* antireligious museums; antireligious policy; Krasikov, P. A.; Narkomiust; VIII Section; women; and individual saints

Feodor Iaroslavovich (saint), 27
Feodor Suzdal'skii (saint): exhumation of, 127, 162, 165–66, 263n.109
Feodosii Chernigovskii (saint), 12, 13, 15, 33–34, 39, 42; canonization of, 35, 43, 50, 65, 74; exhumation of, 146, 164–65; miracle stories concerning, 28–29, 46–47, 53–56, 57–59, 60–63, 64–65, 69–70; popularity of, 44–45, 66–67; as protector of Chernigov, 24, 71; relics and shrine of, 20, 37, 48, 49–50, 66–68, 172, 203. *See also* Chernigov
Feodosii Totemskii (saint): exhumation of, 17–19, 255n.123; petitions concerning relics, 179–80; veneration after exhumation, 202–3
Filaret (Drozdov), metropolitan of Moscow, 86
Filaret the Merciful (saint), 25
Filipp (saint and prelate), 31–32, 112

Finucane, Ronald, 45, 58
First Five Year Plan, 14, 204–7
Fomenko, K. I., 39–41
Freeze, Gregory L., 7, 9, 25, 75
Froese, Paul, 16

Galkin, M. V. *See* Gorev, Mikhail
Gavriil the Martyr (saint), 168–69
Geary, Patrick, 13
Georgii (prince of Vladimir and saint), 42, 154
Germogen (saint and patriarch), 15, 42, 111, 112, 117, 241n.109; miracles of, 45–46, 52–53, 55, 57–58, 68, 69
Germogen Kazanskii (saint), 198
Gleb (prince of Vladimir and saint), 24, 42; exhumation of, 154, 169
Golubinskii, E. E., 18, 22, 74, 97
Gorev, Mikhail (M. V. Galkin), 104, 172, 246n.48; on exhumations, 126–27, 135, 138, 159, 164, 177, 183, 196, 204; as editor of Revoliutsiia i tserkov', 146, 194; on separation of church and state, 115, 123–24, 125
Gorky, Maxim, 160–61
Got'e, Iu. V., 168–69
Great Reforms, 14, 61, 87, 173; and access to medical care, 56–57
Gregory the Theologian, 22
Gromyko, M. M., 11
Grozny, 101
Gurii Kazanskii (saint), 23

Halfin, Igal, 157
Harrison, Marguerite E., 160–61
Hellbeck, Jochen, 157
Helsinki, 62
holy oil, 11, 41, 52–53, 54, 57, 58, 59, 71, 163, 229n.56. *See also* icon lanterns; miracles; shrines
Holy Synod, 8, 13, 15, 74, 76, 90, 110–11, 182; and canonization of Anna Kashinskaia, 86–88; and canonization of Sofronii Irkutskii, 94–99
holy water, 11, 24, 73, 113, 163. *See also* miracles; shrines
Husband, William B., 163, 173

Iaroslavl, 42, 46, 57, 141, 149, 176, 178
Iaroslavskii, E. M., 90, 105, 140, 142, 146, 210

icon lanterns, 11, 32, 48, 52, 54, 58, 66, 67, 71, 98, 211. *See also* holy oil; icons; miracles; shrines
icons, 5, 11, 29, 48, 54, 59, 211; of Anna Kashinskaia, 78–79, 82, 84, 85, 89; Bolshevik rejection of, 136, 148, 172, 202; and iconoclasm after the Revolution, 108–10, 124; of Sofronii Irkutskii, 93, 98; as spiritual souvenirs, 43, 89, 90–91. *See also* holy oil; miracles; saints; shrines
incorruptibility, 15–16, 17, 210; Bolshevik rejection of, 144–53; disputes over definition, 17–20, 135–37; as grounds for canonization, 20; Orthodox definition of, 21–24; as product of climate conditions, 23; as proof of the truth of the teachings of Orthodoxy, 10, 21, 33–38, 71–72. *See also* cult of the saints; exhumation of relics; relics; saints
Innokentii Irkutskii (saint); 34, 91; confraternity of, 97; exhumation of, 140–169–70, 199, 200
Ioakim, patriarch, 77, 78, 84
Ioann (saint). *See* Vilnius Martyrs
Ioann the Holy Fool (saint), 25
Ioann Suzdal'skii (saint): exhumation of, 127, 162, 166–67
Ioann Tobol'skii (saint), 98, 165, 235n.6
Ioasaf Belgorodskii (saint), 31, 111; exhumation of, 146; miracles of, 68; relics on display, 150–53, 171–72
Iosif the Murdered (saint), 52, 53, 96–97, 113–14, 241n.110
Irkutsk, 69, 89, 92, 199; diocesan press in, 90–91, 96. *See also* Siberia; Sofronii Irkutskii (saint)
Irkutsk Missionary Congress, 89
Ivan IV, tsar, 3

James, William, 4
Jews, 36, 37
John of Kronstadt (saint), 61, 65, 226n.98
John Chrysostom, 22

Kalinin, M. I., 173–74, 175, 197
Kaluga, 59
Kamenskii convent, 53
Kashin, 73–74, 198, 205. *See also* Anna Kashinskaia (saint)
Kazan, 23

Kazanskii Cathedral (Irkutsk), 89, 98
Kenez, Peter, 113
Kharkov, 51, 57
Kherson, 5, 23
Kiev, 5, 101
Kiev Monastery of the Caves, 24, 110–11, 145
Kirill Belozerskii (saint): exhumation of, 184–85
Kirov, S. M., 206
Kizenko, Nadieszda, 46, 61, 64
Kohl, Johann, 3–4, 5, 11, 213n.4
Kolchak, A. V., 113, 114, 192, 197, 208
Kollontai, A. M., 119
Komsomol, 130, 207–8
Konstantin Muromskii (prince and saint), 43; exhumation of, 128–30, 133, 184
Kormchii, 27, 34, 47, 101
Kostroma, 117
Kovrigina, V. A., 56
Krasikov, P. A., 105, 138–42, 144, 146–49, 153–55, 162, 166, 175–79, 180–81, 194, 197–99, 200, 202, 211. *See also* Narkomiust; VIII Section
Kremleva, I. A., 68, 71
Kselman, Thomas A., 57
Kseniia (saint), 61
Kuleshov, Lev, 153
Kunkin, I. Ia., 87
Kursk, 31, 56, 62, 146
Kurskii, D. I., 105–6, 113–14, 123, 140, 149, 174, 185, 197. *See also* Narkomiust
Kuznetsov, N. D., 170, 181–82, 262n.95

lampady. *See* icon lanterns
League of the Militant Godless, 205
Lenhoff, Gail, 20
Lenin, V. I., 107, 122, 140, 153, 173, 176–77, 180, 181, 183, 196–97; embalmed body as "anti-miracle," 209
Lent: fasting, 29
Levendal', N. N., 135–37
Levin, Eve, 8
Liubimov, Nikolai, 118, 174, 175–76
Lunacharskii, A. V., 197, 201
Lutherans, 4, 29, 31, 32
L'vov, V. N., 110–11

Makarii Kaliazinskii (saint), 83; exhumation of, 130
Makarii Zhabynskii (saint): exhumation of, 130, 131, 135, 167, 196; rumors concerning, 162; veneration after exhumation, 203
Mariia of Egypt (saint), 26
Mariia Feodorovna, empress, 82, 232n.112, 237n.42
Marx, Karl, 126–27
Mikhail Chernigovskii (prince and saint), 44–45
Mikhail Tverskoi (prince and saint), 80; confraternities of, 87; exhumation of, 154, 156, 166, 190–93; icons of, 89. *See also* Anna Kashinskaia
miracles, 4–6, 9, 10, 14, 25, 41–42, 210; and medical science, 55–60; and modern problems, 14, 60–64, 91–94; on need to report, 84; publicity of, 45–47, 64–71. *See also* canonization; cult of the saints; relics; saints; shrines; women; and individual saints
Mitrofanskii monastery. *See* Mitrofan Voronezhskii (saint)
Mitrofan Voronezhskii (saint), 43, 44–45; exhumation of, 103–4, 132, 172, 259n.45; Orthodox efforts to defend relics of, 119–21; rumors concerning, 162, 168, 183, 185; veneration after exhumation, 202, 203
Mitskevitch, S. I., 196–97
Mogilev, 141
Moisei Skovorodskii (saint): exhumation of, 204
moleben (pl., molebny), 11, 51, 56, 65, 67, 73, 78, 79, 86, 186, 192
monasteries, 5, 47–48; profit from relics, 43–44; and separation of church and state, 118–21. *See also* pilgrimage
Morozov, Ia. M., 158, 159
Moscow, 3, 52–53, 56, 57, 69, 101, 127, 140, 144, 146, 154, 197, 203–4, 208; city soviet, 199; petitions from, 162–63, 177–78. *See also* Uspenskii Cathedral; Germogen (saint and patriarch)
Moscow Theological Academy, 22, 170, 173
moshchi. *See* relics
Murom, 43, 51; exhumations at, 127–30, 184, 205
Museum of Social Hygiene: relic displays, 150–53, 172–73, 199, 206. *See also* antireligious museums
Muslims, 36, 176

Naked Year, The, 122
Narkomiust (People's Commissariat of Justice), 104, 105, 123, 124; and diocesan councils, 171; and local officials, 109–10. *See also* exhumation of relics; Krasikov, P. A., Kurskii, D. I.; VIII Section
Narkomzdrav Museum. *See* Museum of Social Hygiene
netlenie; netlennye moshchi. *See* incorruptibility
New Economic Policy (NEP): and antireligious policy, 201–4
Nicholas II, emperor, 28, 35, 66, 74–75, 82, 107, 109
Nicholas the Wonder-Worker (saint), 33, 39–41, 70, 110, 113, 208–9
Nifont Novgorodskii (saint), 111
Nikita Novgorodskii (saint): exhumation of, 147, 168
Nikon, patriarch, 78
Nil Stolobenskii (saint): exhumation of, 130, 181, 190; relics as pilgrimage destination, 194
NKVD (People's Commissariat of Internal Affairs), 123, 141, 142, 148, 178, 185, 190
Novgorod, 116, 135; exhumations in, 127, 144, 171, 184–85, 199, 200, 202, 204; trials in, 135–37
Novitskii, P. K., 153

Old Believers, 28, 29–30, 36–37, 77–78, 100
Olonets, 123–26, 127
Omsk, 113, 199
Orel, 110

Paisii (saint), 111
panikhida (pl., panikhidy), 46, 58, 59, 67, 68, 77, 78, 91, 93, 97, 98
Paozerskii, M. F., 107, 145, 146
Paul the Apostle, 3, 26, 33, 206
People's Commissariat of Internal Affairs. *See* NKVD
People's Commissariat of Justice. *See* Narkomiust
Peter the Apostle, 3, 26, 206
Peter the Great, emperor, 8
Petrograd, 127, 148–49; city soviet, 175, 199. *See also* St. Petersburg
pilgrimage, 6, 8, 12; after the Revolution, 194–95, 200, 203–4; and modern technology, 14; overseas destinations, 39–41, 44; profit to local communities, 13, 43–44; publicity of, 42–44; and women, 68. *See also* miracles; relics; saints; shrines; women; individual saints
Pilnyak, Boris, 122, 123
Pitirim Tambovskii (saint), 35, 235n.6, 240n.94
Pokrovskii Cathedral (Tobol'sk), 165
Popov, I. V., 173–74
Poselianin, Evgenii, 22
Pravoslavno-missionerskii listok, 36
Pravoslavnyi sobesednik, 79
Preobrazhenskii, E. A., 140, 142
Primary Chronicle, The, 5
Prokopii Ust'ianskii (saint), 164, 211, 242n.125; exhumation of, 185–89, 193
proxy relics, 11, 52, 54, 217n.38, 229n.52. *See also* relics
Pskov, 198, 199

Ramer, Samuel C., 56
relics, 3–5, 13; definition of, 17–19; exuding holy oil, 24, 40–41; and proper attitude toward, 28–33; as proof of the teachings of the Orthodox Church, 10, 33–38; physical contact with, 51–55; and sweet-smelling fragrance, 24, 95. *See also* canonization; cult of the saints; exhumation of relics; incorruptibility; miracles; pilgrimage; proxy relics; saints; shrines; and individual saints
religious toleration, 36
Revoliutsiia i tserkov', 103, 141, 144, 146–47, 154, 155–56, 175. *See also* Gorev, M. V.; Krasikov, P. A.
Revolution of 1905, 35, 56, 80, 100–101, 110, 232n.102
Revolution of 1917, 6, 7, 15, 101–2. *See also* Bolshevik Party; exhumation of relics
revolutionary iconoclasm, 109–11. *See also* exhumation of relics
Rey, Terry, 61
Riazan, 116, 209
Robson, Roy R., 44
Roman Catholic Church. *See* Catholics
Rostov-na-Donu, 113

Rudchenko, M. A., 91
Russian Orthodoxy: as proactive faith, 4–5; and historiography, 7–9, 105; and popular religion, 8–9, 15; and modernity, 14; and efforts to catechize the laity, 15, 20–21, 24–28, 32–33; and "feminization of piety," 68; and counter-revolution, 104–21. *See also* clergy; cult of the saints; exhumation of relics; incorruptibility; miracles; pilgrimage; relics; saints; shrines; and individual saints
Russian Social Democratic Workers' Party (RSDRP). *See* Bolshevik Party
Russkii palomnik, 43

St. Petersburg, 61, 62, 76, 82, 86, 87, 89, 93, 98, 102, 138, 175, 182. *See also* Petrograd
saints: appearing in dreams, 28–33, 55–56, 59–60, 70, 83–84; as class enemies, 205–6; as exemplars to be emulated, 15, 21, 24–28; as intercessors, 10, 28, 40; lives of, 5, 8–9, 26–28; and local communities, 12, 15, 75–76, 99–102, 119–21; and naming practices, 5, 10, 28, 80; and Orthodox devotional practices, 6, 8; rejection by sectarians, 9, 21, 29; as symbols of counter-revolution, 106–21. *See also* cult of the saints; exhumation of relics; incorruptibility; miracles; pilgrimage; relics; saints; shrines; and individual saints
Samara, 109, 135
Savva Storozhevskii (saint): exhumation of, 181–82; rumors concerning, 162, 183–84
Semashko, N. A., 144–45, 150, 152, 171–72
Semenovskii, P. S., 145, 253n.95
separation of church and state, 115–21, 123–25, 175, 177
Serafim Sarovskii (saint), 22, 24, 51, 75, 107; exhumation of, 195; display of relics, 206
Sergiev Posad: response to exhumation in, 161, 183–84, 198. *See also* Sergii Radonezhskii (saint); Troitskaia Lavra
Sergii Radonezhskii (saint), 53, 112, 133; exhumation of, 153, 158, 164, 168, 196–97, 198; film of exhumation, 154; petitions in support of, 162, 173–75, 177–78, 197; rumors concerning, 183–84; relic fragments of, 198; veneration after exhumation, 204. *See also* Sergiev Posad; Troitskaia Lavra
Shevzov, Vera, 211
Shishakov, V., 202
Shkarovskii, M. V., 110
Shpitsberg, I. A., 149–50, 181–82, 262n.93
shrines, 3–4; architecture of, 47–48; and Orthodox devotional practices, 5–6, 47–55, 71–72; and votive gifts, 64–71. *See also* cult of the saints; exhumation of relics; incorruptibility; miracles; pilgrimage; relics; saints; and individual saints
Siberia: and piety, 89–90, 95; migration to, 91–94. *See also* Sofronii Irkutskii (saint)
Sil'vestr Obnorskii (saint), 46
Simeon the Stylite (saint), 27
Simeon Verkhoturskii (saint): shrine and relics of, 48–49, 165–66, 225n.95, 232n.112; exhumation of, 169; rumors concerning, 183
Skvortsov-Stepanov, I. I., 201
Sluhovsky, Moshe, 13
Smidovich, P. G., 195
Sofiiskii Cathedral (Novgorod), 136–37, 147, 165, 167–68, 200
Sofronii Irkutskii (saint), 15, 24, 76, 90, 210; canonization of, 94–99; images and icons of, 90–91, 93, 94; miracles of, 53, 59–60, 91–94; Orthodox devotion to, 90–102; relics of, 90, 97–98
Solovetskii monastery, 44
Sovnarkom (Council of People's Commissars), 115, 149, 162; petitions to, 173–74, 174–80, 181–82, 197
Spiritual Regulation, The (1721), 8
Stites, Richard, 109
Suzdal: exhumations at, 127–29, 132, 162, 166–69
Sviazhsk, 198

Tambov, 116, 195; peasant rebellion in, 199
Tereshchenko, N. A., 66
Thomas, Keith, 161
Tian-Shanskaia, O. S., 209–10
Tikhon (Bellavin), patriarch, 98, 113, 117, 119, 170, 173–75

Tikhon Zadonskii (saint): as class enemy, 205–6; as exemplar for Orthodox youth, 27; exhumation of, 130, 132, 133, 143, 144, 153, 167; film of exhumation, 154–55; miracles of, 53, 203; popularity of, 44, 68; rumors concerning, 162, 183, 184
Time of Troubles, 45, 76, 80
Tisse, Eduard, 153
Titlinov, B. V., 137
Titus the Warrior (saint), 111
Tobol'sk, 165, 198–99
Tolstoi, A. P., 86
Tomsk, 89, 92, 93, 94
Tot'ma, 17, 179
Troitskaia Lavra, 44, 83, 158, 164, 168, 184, 197, 204. *See also* Sergiev Posad; Sergii Radonezhskii (saint)
Trotsky, L. D., 109
Trubetskoi, E. N., 112, 119
Tula, 110, 114, 148, 167, 196, 203, 266n.36
Tver, 73–74, 76, 81, 82, 87; diocesan press, 84, 88, 101; exhumations in, 127, 156, 166, 180–83, 189–93; local saints, 42. *See also* Anna Kashinskaia (saint); Kashin
Tver Scholarly Archival Commission, 87

Union of Orthodox Christians (Irkutsk), 98, 101
Uspenskii Cathedral (Kashin), 76, 77
Uspenskii Cathedral (Moscow), 31–32, 45–46, 52, 55, 57–58, 69, 111, 112, 117–18, 174. *See also* Germogen (saint and patriarch)

Varieties of Religious Experience, The, 4
Varsonofii Kazanskii (saint), 23
Vel'sk, 164, 185–89, 193, 211
Veniamin, metropolitan of St. Petersburg, 112, 175
Verkholensk, 93
Vertov, Dziga, 153

Vetoshkin, M. K., 17–19
Viatka, 198
VIII Section, 104; correspondence with local officials, 115–16, 140–44, 148–49, 153–55, 166; endorsement of exhumation policy, 138–40, 200–201; petitions and complaints received by, 162–63, 178–80, 180–82, 197–99. *See also* exhumation of relics; Krasikov, P. A.; Narkomiust
Vilnius Martyrs (Antonii, Ioann, Evstafii): petitions in support of, 175; relics on display, 150, 171–72, 203–4
Viola, Lynne, 163
Vladimir, 24, 37, 42, 43, 205; exhumations in, 127–28, 131–32, 149, 156–57, 159, 167, 169, 178, 184, 185
Vladimir (prince and saint), 5, 109
Vlastov, P. M., 21
Vologda, 17–19, 38, 158, 179, 185–89, 193, 202
Voronezh, 43, 44–45, 68, 109, 110, 127, 162, 183, 185, 202. *See also* Mitrofan Voronezhskii (saint); Tikhon Zadonskii (saint)
Voskresenskii Cathedral (Kashin), 73, 77, 79, 82, 85, 86, 87
Vostorgov, Ioann, 89
VTsIK (All-Union Central Executive Committee), 195, 197

women: and saintly cults, 45–46, 51, 59–60, 66–68, 80; resistance to exhumation, 164–65, 187–89; support for exhumation, 155–58. *See also* cult of the saints; miracles; pilgrimage; relics; saints; shrines
Wood, Elizabeth A., 135
Worobec, Christine D., 56, 61, 68
Wortman, Richard, 75
Wrangel, P. N., 113, 199, 208

Zinoviev, G. E., 175
Zvenigorod, 181–82